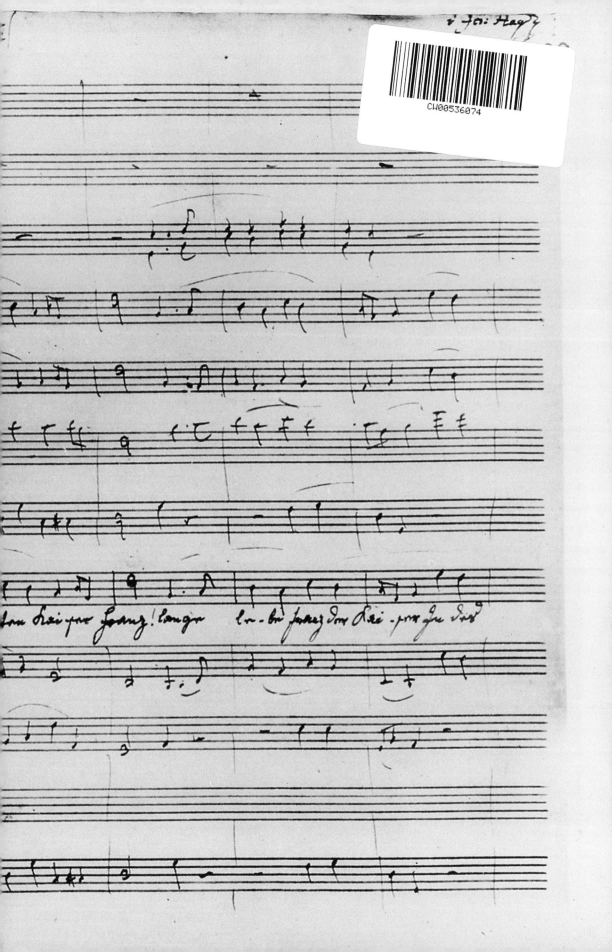

Studies in
Music History
presented to
H. C. Robbins Landon
on his seventieth
birthday

Studies in Music History

presented to

H.C. Robbins Landon

on his seventieth birthday

edited by

Otto Biba &

David Wyn Jones

with 29 illustrations and
27 music examples

Thames and Hudson

Sources of illustrations

Frontispiece portrait © Thames and Hudson Ltd. Other illustrations, all provided by individual contributors to this volume, are reproduced by courtesy of the following: Trustees of the British Library, p. 11; the National Trust for England, p. 13; the Cinema/Television Library and Archives, University of Southern California, Los Angeles, pp. 88, 92, 94–100; Bildarchiv of the Österreichische Nationalbibliothek, Vienna, pp. 169–72; Private Collection, pp. 73–6 (photos A. C. Cooper Ltd), 109.

Music examples set by IAN CHEVERTON

© 1996 Thames and Hudson Ltd, London

First published in Great Britain in 1996
by Thames and Hudson Ltd, London

First published in the United States of America in 1996
by Thames and Hudson Inc., New York

A catalogue record for this book is available from the British Library
Library of Congress Catalog Card Number 95/62054

ISBN 0/500/01696/8

Printed and bound in Slovenia by Mladinska Knjiga

Contents

Editors' Preface

THE YEAR 1996 marks the seventieth birthday of H.C. Robbins Landon. This collection of essays from friends and colleagues is a tribute to a man who has figured prominently in international scholarship for nearly half a century. Much of his limitless energy and enthusiasm has been devoted to his beloved Joseph Haydn and, while Robbie would be the first to acknowledge the work of several distinguished predecessors and contemporaries, his own contribution to the scholarly and popular revival of interest in the composer is unrivalled. His first book, *The Symphonies of Joseph Haydn*, appeared in 1955, and its 862 pages typify the approach that informs his work: fundamental and inquisitive scholarship coupled with unstinting love of the music. As the bibliography at the end of this celebratory volume testifies, many new – often first – editions of large tracts of Haydn's output have been produced by him, from symphonies to piano trios, and English psalms to operas; a volume of the composer's letters and London notebooks was issued in English translation; and, between 1976 and 1980, his most ambitious project came to fruition, five magisterial volumes of biography and commentary, *Haydn. Chronicle and Works*, described by one reviewer as 'One of the great documentary biographies of the century'.

Robbie's missionary work on behalf of Haydn has always been matched by an equivalent interest in the musical environment in which Haydn lived, the music of contemporaries, large and small, Ordoñez and Vanhal as well as Mozart and Beethoven. His pioneering work on several minor composers has stimulated a great deal of scholarly activity throughout the world, while his many publications on Mozart and Beethoven have invariably benefited from his unrivalled knowledge of the period in which they lived.

Yet, to concentrate on Robbie's scholarly achievement alone would be to present an incomplete picture of the man. His desire to share his knowledge with anybody who is willing to be entertained, charmed and challenged is limitless. As a motivator who relishes the cut and thrust of the music business, he has instigated numerous recordings from the earliest days of LP to the modern CD, has stimulated concerts and festivals, advised conductors, performers, writers, producers and publishers, and enlightened the general public through countless programme notes, sleeve notes, broadcast talks and public lectures. He has achieved that rare distinction: a scholar who is also a household name. This marriage of the pioneering researcher working painstakingly alone and the eager communicator yielded its greatest product in the book *1791. Mozart's Last Year*, an international bestseller, translated into no fewer than ten languages.

In March 1789 Haydn wrote a letter to the Viennese publisher Artaria, encouraging him to issue a recently completed work, the Capriccio in C (Hob. XVII:4). In it he remarked that: '. . . In a moment of excellent good humour I have written a quite new Capriccio for the pianoforte, whose tastefulness, singularity and special construction cannot fail to win approbation from connoisseurs and amateurs alike.' Those who have had the privilege of knowing Robbie personally and professionally will recognize in him the same 'excellent good humour', that zest for life that characterized Haydn's own career; and his work fulfils one of the fundamental tenets of eighteenth-century aesthetics, articulated here by the composer, that intellectual endeavour should not preclude accessibility. H.C. Robbins Landon has, indeed, won the approbation of connoisseurs and amateurs. Happy Birthday!

OTTO BIBA
DAVID WYN JONES

Malcolm Boyd

'The music very good indeed': Scarlatti's Tolomeo et Alessandro *recovered*

THE MODERN VISITOR to Rome who climbs the Spanish Steps to admire the view from the top or to visit the church in the Piazza della Trinità de' Monti may scarcely notice the Palazzo Zuccari, an unimposing edifice standing between the Via Sistina and the Via Gregoriana at the point where they both join the piazza. The name 'Zuccari', which is still to be seen engraved above the entrance to the palazzo in the Via Sistina, is that of the painter Federico Zuccari (c. 1540–1609) for whom it was built, but of more importance to the music historian is the fact that it was here that the dowager Queen Maria Casimira of Poland and her court lived from 1701 to 1714. It would be truer to say, as Roberto Pagano has pointed out,[1] that Maria Casimira took up residence on the opposite side of the Via Sistina (known then as the Strada Felice) in premises which were later connected to the Palazzo Zuccari by a bridge built on her instructions. The palazzo itself was used first to house a community of Benedictine nuns she had patronized in Poland and later, from 1708, to accommodate a domestic theatre managed on her behalf by the French-born impresario Count Giacomo d'Alibert.

It was for this theatre, designed possibly by the famous Filippo Juvarra, that Domenico Scarlatti composed at least seven operas between 1710 and 1714, when Maria Casimira left Rome to end her days in the Loire valley (she died at Blois on 29 January 1716). Juvarra designed the sets for most, if not all, of these operas, and the librettos were all the work of Maria Casimira's 'segretario delle lettere italiane e latine', Carlo Sigismondo Capece. They were put on during the period between Christmas and Lent in friendly competition with those of other Roman Maecenases, notably Cardinal Pietro Ottoboni and Prince Ruspoli.

It is evident from reports in the *Avvisi di Roma* now in the Bayerische Staatsbibliothek, Munich, that for the 1711 season both Ruspoli and Ottoboni had planned to put on a heroic opera followed by a pastoral.[2] At Ruspoli's residence, the Palazzo Bonelli, Antonio Caldara's *L'Anagilda, ovvero La fede ne'tradimenti* on 4 January was followed just over a month later, on 9 February, by the same composer's *La costanza in amor vince l'inganno*, a revision of a pastoral opera originally composed for Mantua in 1701. Ottoboni's serious opera in 1711, produced some time before 18 January, was Filippo Amadei's *Teodosio il giovane*; the title and composer of the pastoral that presumably followed it are unknown.[3]

9

Comparisons were inevitably made between the various operatic spectacles on offer. Writing on 17 January 1711, the director of the Académie de France at Rome, Charles-François Poerson, remarked that 'one should see that of Cardinal Ottoboni, hear that of Prince Ruspoli, and forgo that at the Capranica [the public theatre, at which a revival of Mancini and Orefice's *L'Engelberta* could be seen], which is frankly a failure'.[4] But this was two days before Queen Maria Casimira's theatre opened that year with Scarlatti and Capece's *Tolomeo et Alessandro, overo La corona disprezzata*; Ottoboni and Ruspoli were in the audience, along with the singers they employed. The writer of the *Avvisi di Roma* in Munich described the event in the following terms:

> Rome, 24 January 1711
> On Monday evening [19 January] the Queen of Poland had her opera performed for the first time at her residence at the Trinità de' Monti by good singers, male and female; it was generally applauded as superior to all the others.[5]

This opinion was echoed shortly afterwards by Giovan Mario Crescimbeni, chronicler of the Arcadian Academy, who wrote:

> the voices were pleasing, the acting distinguished, the costumes most charming and worked with marvellous design, the music very good indeed and the orchestra outstanding.[6]

Crescimbeni was reviewing a performance put on specially for members of the Arcadian Academy, and there were later revivals in Fermo (1713), Rome (1724) and possibly Jesi (1727). Not to be outdone by Ottoboni and Ruspoli, Maria Casimira followed *Tolomeo et Alessandro* with a pastoral, *L'Orlando*, in the printed libretto of which Domenico Scarlatti is for the first time mentioned as her *maestro di cappella*.

Not a note of *L'Orlando* survives, and until recently contemporary evalutions of *Tolomeo et Alessandro* could be tested only against the printed libretto (see Fig. 1) and a manuscript copy of Act 1 which remains in private hands and is therefore virtually inaccessible.[7] Now, thanks to one of those happy *trouvailles* to which the dedicatee of the present volume is no stranger, we are able to base an assessment of Scarlatti's achievements in this work on a complete full score of the opera.

*   *   *

Belton House is situated a few miles north of Grantham in Lincolnshire. It was built in 1685–6 for Sir John Brownlow, third baronet of Belton, who represented Grantham in Parliament. After his death (apparently by his own hand) in 1697, the house passed, along with the title, to his brother William and then to William's son, another Sir John Brownlow, who lived from 1690 to 1754. This Sir John also pursued a parliamentary career as member for Grantham, and later for Lincolnshire – a career which proved to

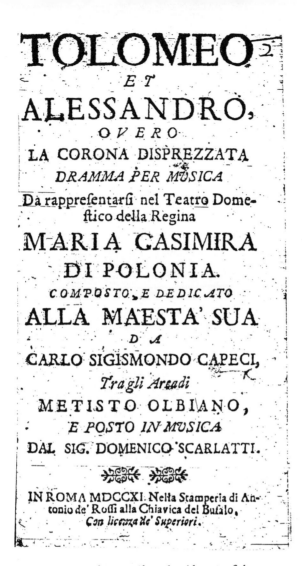

Fig. 1 *Tolomeo et Alessandro*, title page of the
libretto, Rome 1711; British Library, 905.k.8(2).

be, in the words of the Belton House guide book, 'as long as it was undistinguished'.[8]
Sir John was, however, keenly interested in art and literature and assembled an important collection of books and pictures, including paintings by Guido Reni, Van Dyck
and Luca Giordano. When the house and library were acquired by the National Trust
in 1984 it was discovered that he had also owned a manuscript copy of the three acts of
Scarlatti's *Tolomeo et Alessandro*.[9]

Brownlow's interest in music is further attested by the inclusion of his name, as
Lord Tyrconnel (in 1718 he was granted an Irish peerage, becoming Viscount
Tyreonnel and Baron Charleville), among subscribers to the Royal Academy of
Music, the association founded in London in 1719 for the production of Italian opera,

11

with Handel as its leading composer; he also subscribed to the publication of the *Six Cantatas and Six Lessons for the Viola d'Amore* (London, 1724) of Attilio Ariosti, another Academy composer.[10] Brownlow's circle of music-loving friends in London included Frederick, Prince of Wales, the painter Philip Mercier and Handel's acquaintance and admirer Mrs Pendarves (to whom Brownlow proposed marriage after the death of his first wife – and first cousin – Eleanor, in 1730). It is surprising, and a little disappointing, to find that the three volumes of *Tolomeo*, together with a manu-script collection of arias from Alessandro Scarlatti's *Odoardo* and one or two printed items, represent the extent of the music that has survived in Sir John Brownlow's library. Possibly his ownership of the Domenico Scarlatti score was in some way con-nected with his involvement with the Royal Academy of Music, of which he evidently served as a director in 1723.[11] It may, at any rate, be inferred from the bookplates in each of the three volumes that he acquired the copy some time after he had become Viscount Tyrconnel. The manuscript itself is apparently of Italian – probably Roman – origin, and, except for nineteen pages of the aria 'Ditemi voi, dov'è' in Act 2, is written in a single hand throughout (Fig. 2). An unusual feature of the score is that the overture and many (but not all) of the arias have for some reason been numbered consecutively by a later hand, beginning at 227 for the overture and ending at 250 for the last aria in Act 3 (the final *coro* is not numbered).

Capece's libretto is a gloss on the thirty-ninth book of Justinus's epitome of Pompeius Trogus's *Historiae Philippicae*. The background to the action is laid out in the *Argomento* of the printed libretto:

> It is imagined that Ptolemy, banished by his mother Cleopatra, is living in Cyprus disguised as a simple shepherd under the name of Osmin, and that his wife Seleuce, taken from him and sent by Cleopatra to the Syrian tyrant Tryphon, has been shipwrecked and presumed drowned; she has, however, been saved and, knowing Ptolemy to be in Cyprus, has gone there to search for him disguised as a shepherdess called Delia. Meanwhile Cleopatra has sent her other son, Alexander, to Cyprus with a powerful army in order to lay hands on Ptolemy, but Alexander's intention is to spare his brother and restore the crown to him. It is further imagined that Araspe, reigning in Cyprus and living in a delightful coastal villa with his sister Elisa, has fallen in love with 'Delia' (Seleuce) and Elisa with 'Osmin' (Ptolemy), and finally that Dorisbe, daughter of Isauro, Prince of Tyre, at one time loved by Araspe but now abandoned by him, is also living there as a *finta giardiniera* known as Clori.[12]

The scene is thus set for the various intrigues, deceptions and misunderstandings that are the common currency of late Baroque opera plots.

Fig. 2   Extract from the aria 'Pur sento (oh Dio)' in Act 2 of Scarlatti's *Tolomeo et Alessandro* (from the score at Belton House, Lincolnshire, now owned by the National Trust).

Scarlatti's setting begins with one of the finest of all his overtures,[13] a three-movement sinfonia in B flat for oboe and strings in which the opening Presto is a *moto perpetuo* of scurrying semiquavers and sudden dynamic changes that puts one in mind of Mendelssohn. The first act serves mainly to introduce the characters and to define their situations; only at the very end of the act is the action developed beyond this, when Seleuce recognizes her sleeping husband but is immediately disturbed by the jealous Araspe. In his brief comments on this act Ralph Kirkpatrick considered the first two arias, both sung by Ptolemy, to be 'in a fine grand tragic style quite worthy of Juvarra's scenery'.[14] They do indeed paint the tender and resolute aspects of the hero's character superbly well. 'Rendimi, o crudo fato' is one of several arias in which Scarlatti smoothes the rigid corners of the conventional da capo structure so that the music flows

with unbroken continuity;[15] and 'Cielo ingiusto potrai fulminarmi' derives tremendous energy from the unison string phrases, with their dotted rhythms and displaced
accents, that punctuate the vocal line. But no less representative of Scarlatti at his
expressive best is 'È un grave martire', in which Seleuce sympathizes with Dorisbe's
plight while hinting at her own graver sufferings. The vocal writing here [Ex. 1] gives
some idea of the talents of one of Maria Casimira's *cantarine*, Maria Giusti, who sang
the part in the early performances. In another aria characteristic of the composer (and
with parallels in some of his keyboard sonatas) Ptolemy struggles with the impossibility
of taking revenge on his own mother and brother for the presumed death of his wife.

Ex. 1   Aria 'È un grave martire'

Ex. 2   Aria 'Tiranni miei pensieri'

The antitheses in the verse are reinforced in the music by sudden and violent changes of tempo, dynamics and texture [Ex. 2]: there are no fewer than nine switches between *presto e forte* and *adagio e piano* during the course of the aria.

Similar contrasts, with as many oscillations of tempo and dynamics, occur in Dorisbe's Act 2 aria, 'Vorrei vendicarmi . . .' (*allegro e forte*) '. . . ma solo con l'armi che porge l'amor' (*adagio e piano*). The first part of the act is set in the countryside near the 'delightful villa' of Araspe and Elisa; the tranquil breezes and the play of the waves are immediately conjured up in the accompaniment, for two recorders and strings, to Alexander's 'Sempre qui chiara'. In the action that follows Ptolemy and Seleuce reveal their true identities to Elisa and Dorisbe respectively, but chance prevents their recogniz-ing each other until the very end of the act, when they are again immediately separated by the jealous Araspe. They take leave of each other in a poignantly expressive duet, 'Empia man ci divide'. Their parting, they believe, is for ever, and Scarlatti's music, permeated by a simple stepwise descent through the interval of a fifth, certainly per-suades us that it may be so.

Among the other fine numbers in this act perhaps the most strikingly original is Alexander's aria 'Pur sento (oh Dio)', in which long and frequent rests convey his hes-itancy as his conscience struggles between a resolve to spare his brother Ptolemy and his feelings for Ptolemy's lover, Elisa, who has urged him to fratricide (see Fig. 2). What appear to be pause signs over the rests here should more likely be understood as indicat-ing that embellishments and other additions to the music are not to be made.[16]

Events move swiftly in the final act when Araspe and his sister Elisa scheme against Ptolemy and Seleuce (and against each other) to secure their desires. Elisa is ruthless in her pursuit of Ptolemy's love or, failing that, his death. She expresses her feelings in an aria, 'Voglio amore, o pur vendetta', in which Scarlatti again underlines the verbal antitheses, this time not only with changes of tempo and dynamics but also with alternations of metre and instrumentation: a solo flute for expressions of love, oboe and violins for those of vengeance. A dramatic climax, eliciting from Scarlatti the only passages of accompanied recitative in the opera, is reached when Ptolemy know-ingly drinks from a poisoned draught prepared by Dorisbe on Araspe's orders. The key (F minor), the tempo (Adagio), the tritones of the melodic line and the suspensions in the measured accompaniment (recalling Seleuce's 'È un grave martire' in Act 1; see Ex. 2) all serve to heighten the portrayal of Ptolemy's despair at this point [Ex. 3]. Although not virgolated in the printed libretto, a further aria for Ptolemy on the point of death was not set by Scarlatti. Perhaps he felt that 'Stille amare' had said it all, and that it was more convincing to have Ptolemy expire at the end of his *stromentato* recitative where, when the music moves to the dark key of E flat minor, the strings are marked 'smorzino'.

It must have come as no surprise to Scarlatti's audiences that Ptolemy is not, in fact, dead: Dorisbe chose from the garden a plant which would merely send him into a deathlike sleep, from which he now awakes. The dénouements of Baroque opera plots are rarely convincing, and this one is no exception to that. Tyranny must give way to acceptance, enmity to reconciliation, distrust to forgiveness. Ptolemy and Seleuce are

Ex. 3   Aria 'Stille amare'

reunited, Dorisbe wins back a penitent Araspe and (least convincing of all) a compli-
ant Elisa yields finally to a scorned Alexander – and all within the space of one small
page of the libretto. In a final departure from the printed text Scarlatti turned what was
designed as a da capo aria for Seleuce into a dance-like, binary-form ensemble for the
entire cast, pointing a moral from which Queen Maria Casimira's second son no doubt
derived some satisfaction:

> A chi sa meritar le corone
> Il disprezzo ne accresce l'honor.
> [To him who is deserving of crowns,
> the rejecting of them increases honour.]

*   *   *

Both of the librettos that Capece wrote for Scarlatti in 1711 were later adapted for operas that Handel composed in London: *Tolomeo, re di Egitto* in 1728 and *Orlando* in 1733. Reinhard Strohm has suggested that Handel received the 1711 libretto of *Tolomeo* from either Thomas Roseingrave or Filippo Amadei, both of whom were in Rome in 1711 and later went to London.[17] The text of Handel's version, first performed at the King's Theatre on 30 April 1728, was the last of Nicola Haym's many adaptations for Handel to reach the stage before the librettist's death in 1729. Haym satisfied the tastes of London audiences and the requirements of the first Royal Academy of Music by severely pruning all the recitatives and eliminating completely the role of Dorisbe (the substitution of a sleeping draught for the poison in Act 3 is now the work of Elisa). He omitted thirty-two of Capece's forty-five aria texts[18] (as mentioned above, Scarlatti himself also omitted one of them) and substituted fourteen new ones, as well as a final *coro* with a more generalized moral. The result is a much shorter opera in which the action moves more swiftly, but the characters are less fully drawn and their motivation sometimes more obscure. The replacing of Seleuce's aria 'Io vivo o mio bene' in the final scene by a duet for her and Ptolemy results in a more appropriate resolution of their separation, which has been the central thread of the drama, but the desires of the other characters, wicked or otherwise, are left unfulfilled.

A comparison of the purely musical merits of the two operas is facilitated by the thirteen aria texts they have in common. There is nothing in Scarlatti's setting to rival the artless tunefulness of Handel's 'Non lo dirò col labbro' (familiar as a recital item with a substitute text under the title *Silent Worship*), and Handel's ability at turning formal convention to dramatic advantage is well exemplified in Seleuce's F major aria 'Dite, che fa, dov'è' (Act 2; altered from Ptolemy's 'Ditemi voi, dov'è'), in which the expected da capo is interrupted by echoing phrases from Ptolemy, offstage, and finally abandoned. Handel's delicate orchestration here, with muted upper strings and pizzi-cato bass (without harpsichord), captures the pastoral mood that Scarlatti just as effec-tively establishes at the beginning of the act with Alexander's 'Sempre qui chiara e tranquilla' in the same key.

For the rest, Scarlatti has little to fear as a composer in this work from comparison with Handel's *Tolomeo*. One particularly striking feature that such a comparison reveals is how the two composers frequently differ in their response to the same texts. Some idea of this can be gained from the Table overleaf, which lists the key and tempo marking chosen for each of the thirteen arias that the two opera texts have in common: in all but three of these Scarlatti differs radically from Handel in either mode or tempo, and often in both.

One might argue the merits of the unified *Affekt* that Handel embraces in 'Tiranni miei pensieri' and 'Voglio amore o pur vendetta', as against the contrasting of particular phrases in Scarlatti's settings, but it is difficult to avoid the impression that Handel's generally brisker approach reflects a realization that his *Tolomeo* was to bring to an end an operatic venture (the first Royal Academy) that had faltered and failed. Certainly Handel's setting of 'Pur sento (oh Dio)' in Act 2 [Ex. 4] seems almost insouciant beside Scarlatti's strikingly original setting of the same words (see Fig. 2).

Ex. 4   Handel: Aria 'Pur sento (oh Dio)'

A revival of these two operas today would probably reveal Handel's as the more acceptable to a modern audience, especially to a non-Italian audience. But it would also undoubtedly serve to confirm Crescimbeni's judgment that the music of Scarlatti's *Tolomeo et Alessandro* is 'very good indeed'.

TABLE

Comparison between settings by Scarlatti and Handel of arias in C.S. Capece's
Tolomeo et Alessandro[19]

Aria incipit	*Scarlatti: key; tempo marking*	*Handel: key; tempo marking*
Act 1		
Cielo ingiusto, potrai fulminarmi	F major; Allegro	E minor; Allegro
Non lo dirò col labbro	C minor; Allegro	E major; Andante
Tiranni miei pensieri	D major; Presto–Adagio (etc.)	F minor; Larghetta
Respira almeno un poco	G major; Allegro	C minor; Allegro
Torna sol per un momento	G minor; Allegro	E flat major; Larghetta
Act 2		
Il mio core non apprezza	D minor; Allegro	G minor; Allegro
Pur sento (oh Dio)	A minor; Adagio e staccato	B flat major; Andante
Ditemi voi [Dite, che fa], dov'è	C major; Adagio	F major; Andante
Piange pur, ma non sperare	B flat major; Allegro	D minor; Allegro
Act 3		
Se l'interno pur vedono i numi	E flat major; Adagio	D minor; Allegro
Sarò giusto e non tiranno	A minor; Andante	A major; Alla breve
Voglio amore o pur vendetta	C major; Adagio–Presto (etc.)	E minor; Allegro
Stille amore, già vi sento	F minor; Adagio	B flat minor; Larghetto

GEOFFREY CHEW

Haydn's Pastorellas: Genre, Dating and Transmission in the Early Church Works

FOR MORE THAN THIRTY YEARS it has been known that Haydn's early church works include vernacular Christmas pastorellas surviving in eighteenth-century copies. The subject was first raised in two articles by Irmgard Becker-Glauch,[1] who in 1970 published a magisterial overview of the composer's early church works.[2] Various provisional editions of Haydn pastorellas appeared subsequently; for example, in 1975 Otto Biba published the two most reliably authenticated pastorellas (see below). (The pastorellas are discussed also in the chronicle of Haydn's career by H.C. Robbins Landon, who has done much to further our understanding of Haydn's use of pastorellas and of the folk idiom.[3]) In Becker-Glauch's opinion, which has not been contradicted publicly, only two pastorellas are worth considering as genuine Haydn works: 'Herst Nachbä hä sag mä' in D major (Hob. XXIIId:3), and 'Ey wer hat ihm das Ding gedenkt' in G major (Hob. XXIIId:G1).[4] In addition, she accepted two Advent arias as authentic early works, 'Ein' Magd, ein' Dienerin' (Hob. XXIIId:1) and 'Mutter Gottes, mir erlaube' (Hob. XXIIId:2);[5] (these four works are abbreviated below as d:3, d:G1, d:1 and d:2 respectively). And she plausibly regarded another Advent aria ascribed to Haydn, 'Maria Jungfrau rein', as a sacred contrafactum of one of Haydn's early theatrical arias, otherwise lost.[6]

Of the two pastorellas, d:3 is the more reliably attested as Haydn's, through a bass incipit entered in the composer's so-called *Entwurf-Katalog* together with incipits of d:1 and d:2.[7] This *Entwurf-Katalog* entry corresponds, although not exactly, with the bass incipit of one of a pair of pastorellas attributed to Haydn ('Pastorella 2. [. . .] Del Sig: Haydn') in a source from Gröbming in Styria. It is listed in the *Entwurf-Katalog* as an Advent aria, however, and lacks a text incipit there. The second of these two Gröbming pastorellas is d:G1, found ascribed to Haydn ('Auth: Dno Haydn') also in an eighteenth-century source from Weitra, and these two pieces were also linked and ascribed to Haydn in a lost source from the parish church at Währing in Vienna. Other sources, generally regarded as remoter, present the two pieces as contrafacta. The relationship between the sources, generally as currently understood, is given in the 1970 article by Becker-Glauch and summarized with slight additions in the foreword to Biba's edition of 1975.

Since Becker-Glauch's work no one has re-examined the authenticity of Haydn's

minor works for Advent and Christmas; yet these pieces and their sources raise unnoticed issues with implications for dating and authenticity. Moreover, the group of genres
and subgenres to which the works belong is still not well understood; therefore contemporary understandings of genre definition will be examined here, particularly those of
the Esterházy court, before a discussion of Haydn pastorellas and their transmission,
especially through the Hospitallers of St John of God; a hitherto unnoticed anecdote
from Haydn's time in Vienna is also included. Two of the doubtful works will be discussed, one for the first time; however, it is beyond the scope of this essay to discuss all
pastorellas attributed to Haydn in eighteenth- and nineteenth-century manuscripts.

I   The *aria pastorella* (*Pastorell-Arie*) and *pastorella duplex*

The pastorellas d:3 and d:G1 typify so-called *ariae pastorellae* (*Pastorell-Arien*) in the
1760s in the Habsburg lands: simple strophic songs (sometimes da capo arias) without
recitatives for solo voice(s), two violins and bass, with instrumental preludes, interludes
and postludes. In the instrumental sections (sometimes elsewhere) there are usually
quotations or 'allusive clichés' traditionally recognizable as 'pastoral'.[8] These pieces
exemplify one of two forms in which pastorellas had normally been cast since the late
Baroque; the other is a three- or four-movement structure with arias and recitatives.
Throughout the century both types often include obbligato wind instruments capable
of 'pastoral' effects, used as allusive clichés; pastorellas from the 1720s and 1730s made
use of the chalumeau or folk instruments such as bagpipes, hurdy-gurdy (*Drehleier*)
and *tuba pastoritia* (*Hirtenhorn*, *Hirtentrompete*, representing various types of alphorn).[9]
These are not the only allusive clichés in pastorellas – others are mentioned below – but
they are among the most common.

   Most often, however, as in d:3 and d:G1, such instrumental allusive clichés, the
fanfares of the *tuba pastoritia* or the characteristic scale patterns of the bagpipes (such as
'Lydian' sharpened fourths), are not played by these instruments but symbolically imi-
tated in string figuration in the instrumental interludes, either by the violins over drone
basses, or by all parts in unison. In the early eighteenth century, symbolic drone-bass
material of this sort had been given to the violins very extensively in some works, no
doubt in imitation of the famous pastorale from Corelli's Christmas Concerto, at
almost every pause in the vocal texture; the effect is to halt the tonal argument temporar-
ily and unpredictably.[10]

   At the same period, however, it became usual for 'pastoral' allusions over drone
basses to occupy two well-defined positions in pastoral arias (which are almost invariably in major keys): in instrumental interludes, midway through such pieces, immediately after the principal cadences consolidating tonal closure in the dominant; and over

tonic pedals immediately after the principal cadences that close the tonal argument in the home key. This practice became normal in the principal sections of da capo *Pastorell-Arien* in the 1730s; it is attested in d:3 and d:G1 and in other pastorellas and pastoral symphonies of the 1760s;[11] and it is still found in sonata-form pastorellas after 1780.

In consequence, these pastoral allusions came to serve at least three distinct narra-tive, genre-defining roles. The first two are inherited from the *hypotyposis* or 'word-paint-ing' of late-Renaissance madrigals and pastoral music. First, they are semantic units, symbolizing the music-making of the Bethlehem shepherds within a narrative struc-ture (further discussed below). Secondly, they are affective units, like other allusive clichés. The third function is new in the eighteenth century. When they occupy predict-able positions in compositions, underlining and clarifying the structure, such allusions also become syntactical or grammatical units, marking by stylistic contrast the points where tonal goals are reached. (This style contrast may have contributed eventually to the differentiation of first-subject from second-subject style in Classical sonata move-ments.) Their style is characterized by clear two-bar (or sometimes three-bar) phrases, even when the material is otherwise of a *Fortspinnung* type in which phrase-lengths might be expected to be irregular.[12]

The linking of separate movements of pastorellas is normally, and most clearly, seen when there are three or more movements. Such movements may include two or three arias, with or without recitatives, and the last is often a chorus symbolizing the adoration of the shepherds. Such 'cantatas' are attested from the early eighteenth century. But there is also an intermediate category between single aria and 'cantata': a pairing of single-movement *Pastorell-Arien* (even if by different composers). Inventories from the 1720s, and musical sources from not much later, attest the so-called *pastorella duplex* (equivalent terms include '*pastorellae geminae*', etc.), apparently meaning a fascicle with two *Pastorell-Arien*, similar in structure to one another and sometimes – though by no means always – complementary in content.[13] (The practice is attested also for other types of aria: for example, an *offertorium duplex* [*sic*] from Osek [Ossegg], dated 1748, contains two offertories *de tempore* attributed to Caldara, one for the second Sunday after Epiphany and the other for the eighth Sunday after Pentecost: here there is no link of theme or content between the two.[14]) The term seems primarily to refer to the convenient grouping of small manuscripts under a single title page and cover in choir libraries, but in some cases to allow the planning, perhaps by composers, of rudi-mentary cyclic structures. (On the basis of titles, one might speculate, though with extreme caution in view of surviving performance indications, that pairs of pastorellas were sometimes planned to serve as gradual and offertory during the Christmas mid-night mass.)

II Advent and Christmas compositions associated with the Esterházy court before Haydn: terminology and genres

Unsurprisingly, pastorellas were cultivated mainly by parish churches and non-contemplative monastic orders offering pastoral care and elementary education, and it must be asked why the Esterházys were interested in them. J.F. Dack has indeed suggested that the Haydn pastorellas might have been written for an outside commission.[15] Although there is no evidence that they were performed in the Esterházy court repertory, the parish church at Eisenstadt did make use of pastorellas, some by the various Esterházy Kapellmeister. Moreover, the Esterházy interest in the genre may have originated in the influential contribution made by Prince Paul Esterházy to its early development in his *Harmonia caelestis*, a collection of Christmas and other sacred music published in Vienna in 1711 but assembled at least a decade earlier.[16] Paul Esterházy had probably been influenced in turn by the Jesuits, who cultivated pastorellas as an educational tool, and who had educated him.[17] And the collection was remembered at Eisenstadt: a copy now in Budapest formerly belonged to Anton Polzelli (1783–1855), and may have been Haydn's own.[18]

No. 18 of the *Harmonia caelestis*, a pastorella in G major, 'Dormi Jesu dulcissime', quotes as an allusive cliché the melody of a lullaby called 'Eia popeia' ('Heidi pupeidi', etc.) in German, or 'Hajej můj andílku' ('Sleep, my little angel') in Czech.[19] The song was often quoted in later pastorellas and appears in nineteenth-century folk-song collections; it probably originated as an elaborated, dance-like contrafactum of the well-known *Kirchenlied* 'Resonet in laudibus'.[20] Both 'Hajej můj andílku' and 'Resonet in laudibus' were central in the so-called 'Kindelwiegen', the Christmas 'rocking' of the Christ child, attested in both Austria and Bohemia from the fourteenth century and universally well-known in the Baroque,[21] and in pastorellas the melody seems to have symbolized the *Kindelwiegen*. The custom was described in 1691 by Antonio Gavin, an Italian Protestant convert (referring to Italy, though he claims to speak for Germany too), as a ceremonial rocking of the crib in church: attached cords were pulled to and fro by the devout, to the accompaniment of lullabies.[22] Indeed a 'Nà, Nà' lullaby refrain mentioned by Gavin may have been a standard accompaniment to the *Kindelwiegen* and corresponds also to the 'Nä nä nä mi Jesule' of Paul Esterházy's pastorella.

Centrally important in the pastorella narrative, the *Kindelwiegen* is symbolized through quotations of this song with or without texts alluding to 'rocking'; other important allusive clichés comprise the announcement by a night-watchman of midnight, and the angels' song 'Gloria in excelsis Deo'.[23] Together these elements constitute a narrative of the shepherds' awakening in the fields, their call by the angels and their journey to the crib, as a basis for reflection and celebration. They also define the genre. And the symbolic *Kindelwiegen*, or crib-rocking, typically marks the conclusion and culmination of the narrative with the self-oblation of the shepherds, symbolized by pastoral rejoicing.

The terminology used at Eisenstadt for various types of pastorella and Advent aria was not established definitively by Paul Esterházy; another pattern emerges in the 'Catalogus Über die dermalig Brauchbare Chor oder Kirchen Musicalien' assembled by Haydn's predecessor, Gregor Joseph Werner, in 1737–8. This is one of several church inventories from this period in Austria and Moravia which include pastorellas, some dating from twenty or thirty years earlier; Werner lists pieces by himself and by others, dating back to 1720 or earlier.[24] He makes a fairly consistent distinction, not to my knowledge found elsewhere, between the terms 'pastorella', 'Weihnacht(s)lied' and 'Adventslied'. 'Pastorella' means an instrumental composition (or section of a composition, see below) making use of pastoral allusive clichés and the so-called *stylus rusticanus*.[25] 'Weihnachtslied' is used for a vernacular German vocal setting, strophic or comprising several movements, of which some may be settings of dialect texts; in the multi-movement category, separate movements may display different degrees of the *stylus rusticanus*, often to distinguish between material sung by 'shepherds' and material sung by 'angels'. 'Adventslied' refers to a strophic vernacular composition, using neither dialect nor the *stylus rusticanus*; Werner's *Adventslieder* frequently feature the chalumeau, probably to project an 'elevated' pastoral style.[26] The terms 'Weih-nachtslied' and 'Adventslied' are unusual, when titles are almost always given in Latin, and may be informal; the former seems likely to stand for the Latin 'aria pastorella', or the more neutral term 'aria de Nativitate', which appears, however, as a synonym for 'aria pastorella' in other inventories and music manuscripts. (On Werner's use of the term 'cantilena' for this category, see below.) Besides these categories, Werner lists two 'Symphonies en pastoral'; how these are to be distinguished from the instrumental pas-torellas is not clear, but this uncertainty does not affect the present argument.

Two at least of the 'Weihnachtslieder' (the compositions, if not the term) date from before Werner's tenure, and may have helped to define the genre in his mind. These are a chorus, 'Lauffet ihr hürten', and a duet for soprano and bass, 'Last uns gschwind', both lost, by Wenzel Zivilhofer, *Hofkapellmeister* at Eisenstadt between 1714 and 1720. The duet may have been a standard *aria pastorella*, following the pattern described above; the chorus may have been a pastorella of the cantata type or a fragment of one. Or, perhaps, the two together may have been a *pastorella duplex*, intended to be performed in succession, since the narrative sense is continuous: the chorus represents the angels' call to the shepherds, of a type sometimes set for SSA (with or without tenor and bass interruptions from shepherds), and the duet is a response from a young and an old shepherd, expressing their resolve to go to Bethlehem.[27]

Some of the compositions listed by Werner further illustrate the channels of diffusion of the genre: the composers of the nine further 'Weihnachtslieder' and the half-dozen 'pastorellas' in the inventory include a Jesuit, J. Stupan, and the Passau cathedral Kapellmeister, Benedikt Anton Aufschnaiter (1665–1742), also represented in an extensive inventory of pastorellas from the nunnery of Nonnberg in Salzburg[28] and in an inventory from the *Kreuzherren* (*Křížovníci*) in Prague. But in these as well as the Zivilhofer pieces, Werner may well be imposing his own terminology and classification on compositions which came to him under other titles.

Surviving dated pastorellas by Werner begin in 1737, the year of the *Catalogus*, with the 'Weihnacht Lied in der heil. Christnacht zu singen. Vorgestellt mit Engel und Hürten'.[29] This shows Werner's use of the term for the extended 'cantata' pastorella: according to János Hárich's catalogue of Werner's music, it comprises a chorus of angels singing 'Gloria in excelsis Deo', an aria for a shepherd, a second chorus, a second shepherd's aria, an aria for an angel and a third chorus for angels. Among later dated compositions in this inventory, further refinements in terminology are provided by the four-movement *Cantilena in sacratissima Notte di natale del nostro Salvatore Giesu Xto*, 'Anheut ist die Zeit', from 1756: it is set for SATBB (including 'Canto il Angelo' and 'Basso 2 pastori'), two violins and bass, and comprises two arias enclosed by shepherds' choruses; the term 'cantilena in sacratissima notte di natale' is presumably Werner's Italian translation of 'Weihnachtslied'.[30] Another 'Weihnacht Lied', dated 1757, 'Wer da! wer da!', a cantata-type pastorella with a partly dialect text, extends the concept with references to the Seven Years' War (1756–63; Battle of Kolin 1757) and pays a graceful compliment to Prince Paul Anton Esterházy.[31]

Werner's 'Weihnachtslieder' also include simpler strophic solo or duet *arie pastorelle*, which include allusive clichés. The term 'Weihnachtslied' is rendered in Latin as 'cantilena pro Nativitate' in the *Cantilena pro Nativitate Salvatoris Vulgò Der Nachtwachter*, 'Hört ihr Christen und laßt euch sagn'.[32] In this composition, for two basses accompanied by two violins and figured bass, the so-called 'night-watchman's song', quoted at least since the seventeenth century in art music, and common in pastorellas,[33] together with its usual text incipit, 'Hört ihr Christen und laßt euch sagn', is used in the major mode as a *Kopfmotiv* (see Ex. 3 below). Each strophe of this composition concludes with an instrumental ritornello labelled 'pastorella', ten bars long, comprising fanfares over a drone bass, as opposed to the unison passages in the rest of the piece, which are labelled 'in octava'. This use of the term 'pastorella' is attested in works from the previous century. Another work, Werner's *Pastorella alla Hanacha*, is one of a number of eighteenth-century pastorellas alluding to the folk style from the Haná district of Moravia.[34]

Although Werner's use of terminology in his Advent and Christmas pieces does

26

not seem typical, the compositions themselves are representative, and display the full range of stylistic distinctions that originated in multi-movement pastorellas around 1720–30. All of them are in some sense 'pastoral' (that is, they contain references to various types of 'simple' music-making), but the most marked aspects of the *stylus rusti-canus* are reserved for references to the Bethlehem shepherds, and a more elevated (less rustic) style characterizes angels' arias in multi-movement pastorellas and Advent arias. (Such distinctions are relative within the entire repertoire: different composers and different compositions display different degrees of 'rusticity', probably with differing audiences in mind. In any case there are many contrafacta within the repertoire, and in some, such as Haydn's Advent aria 'Maria Jungfrau rein' mentioned above, there was no attempt at remodelling along pastoral lines.) Possibly in order to cater for these finer style distinctions Viennese court composers of the 1720s had introduced into pastorel-las the chalumeau, an instrument capable of symbolizing the pastoral at a less 'realistic' level than the bagpipes, hurdy-gurdy or pastoral trumpet. Such style differences dis-tinguish separate movements within multi-movement pastorellas; they also distinguish Advent arias, in the more elevated style, from *Pastorell-Arien*, with the rustic style, together with the allusive clichés mentioned above, projected within a single movement. And these distinctions are likely to have remained significant to Haydn.

III Haydn's two 'authentic' pastorellas, d:3 and d:GI

It has not hitherto been noticed that one of the manuscript versions of d:GI, that from Weitra (now in the library of the Gesellschaft der Musikfreunde, Vienna), concludes with the 'Hajej můj andílku' melody. This presumably symbolizes the *Kindelwiegen*, since it is presented as a response to the (first-stanza) text 'Eilt, fliegt und wieget ihn' ('Hasten, fly and rock him').[35] [Ex. 1]

No list can be given here of the many quotations of the melody attested between the early seventeenth century and the nineteenth, which include Paul Esterházy's pas-torella and one of W.A. Mozart's juvenilia, the *Galimathias musicum* (K.32). One of the closest parallels to Haydn's quotation occurs, however, in the final movement of a pas-torella ('Mottetta germanica' in the Kremsmünster source) by Michael Haydn (MH 217).[36] [Ex. 2]

In d:GI (Ex. 1, below), Joseph Haydn begins by quoting the incipit of the song literally, with the quotation gradually becoming less distinguishable; nevertheless, it extends at least to b. 28, causing the awkward melodic line at bb. 27–8. The technique recalls Werner's use of allusive clichés in pastorellas, as in the *Cantilena pro Nativitate* 'Hört ihr Christen und laßt euch sagn', where the incipit of the traditional night-watchman's song is quoted at the outset but becomes progressively less literal.[37] [Ex. 3]

Ex. 1   Joseph Haydn, Pastorella d:G1 (Weitra version), bb. 24–28, compared with
traditional melody of 'Hajej můj andílku': canto, violins I/II, organ.

The Weitra version of d:G1 quoted here differs, as is well known, from the other
principal version from Gröbming: much of the detail is shortened in the instrumental
interludes. The passage in the Gröbming version equivalent to bb. 25–9 of the Weitra
version is quoted below. [Ex. 4]

Reworking of pastorellas (sometimes so radical that transmission through
copying seems inconceivable) is well attested and also unpredictable: a piece may be
shortened or lengthened; rhythms and melodic detail may be altered. In this instance,
however, it is the longer (Weitra) version rather than the shorter (Gröbming) that seems
the more authentic, and this emerges from the 'Hajej můj andílku' quotation even more
strongly than from the omission or inclusion of word-painting at bb. 15ff., mentioned
by Becker-Glauch.[38] The Gröbming version lacks the melodic incipit of 'Hajej můj
andílku' but retains its continuation: the awkwardness occurring at bb. 27–8 is

Ex. 2   Michael Haydn, *Mottetta germanica de Nativitate Domini* 'Lauft, ihr Hirten allzugleich', opening of final movement (bb. 198–209): SATB, violins I/II, organ.

Ex. 3   Gregor Joseph Werner, *Cantilena pro Nativitate Salvatoris Vulgò Der Nacht⸗
wachter*, opening, compared with traditional version of night⸗watchman's song:
bass I/II (violins tacent), organ.

thus unmotivated.[39] Moreover, the organ part of the Gröbming source (unlike the other
parts) was originally copied from the fuller version, corresponding exactly to the Weitra
bass part: the extra bars have simply been deleted, while remaining quite legible.
Equally, the original text seems likely to have been transmitted substantially intact in the
Weitra version; the numerous details of word⸗painting correspond to this text. The
possibility still remains, of course, that Weitra incorporates some corruptions of
Haydn's original version; in particular, the first violin part at bb. 4–6 in the Weitra
version has apparently been wrongly assigned to the second violin, and *vice versa*,
perhaps through a copyist's error. [Ex. 5]

In the Weitra version d:GI is not linked with d:3, but they are paired at
Gröbming, and also in a further (lost) manuscript with a common title page, noted in
1970 by Alexander Weinmann, from the Viennese parish church of Währing.[40] This
evidence argues for Haydn's authorship of both pieces, and also suggests that the link
between them may not have been merely one of convenience, indeed that Haydn may
have intended them as a *pastorella duplex* analogous to the two Zivilhofer pastorellas
listed by Werner. (In this case, they correspond with established practice at Eisenstadt

Ex. 4   Joseph Haydn, Pastorella d:G1 (Gröbming version), passage corresponding
to Ex. 1 above: canto, violins I/II, organ.

Ex. 5   Joseph Haydn, Pastorella d:G1 (Weitra version), bb. 4–7: violin I,
violin II, organ.

less in the terminology used to describe them – which may or may not be Haydn's own – than in their internal organization.)

This is backed up also by internal evidence. The status of the pieces as *pastorella duplex* is suggested by their content: d:3 represents a dialogue among the shepherds in the fields, leading up to their resolve to take gifts to the infant; the last stanza is an exhortation to visit the stable; d:GI is a dialogue among the shepherds at the crib, as a meditation on the humility of the Infant. Each stanza of d:GI concludes with an allu-sion to the *Kindelwiegen*, which forms its culmination – and that of the pair of pastorel-las, as it does in some multi-movement pastorellas. The Michael Haydn *Mottetta germanica* mentioned above concludes with a lullaby constructed around this melody, symbolizing the self-offering of the shepherds with which the action concludes; a pas-torella perhaps by Holzbauer or Zechner concludes in comparable fashion, with a reference to the song in its text ('Wir wollen in Andacht und Lieb Voller Treu / Das Kinderl einwiegen, beÿm Haja Popeÿ').[41] There is also a natural tonal progression from d:3 in D major to d:GI in G, reflected in the dominant/tonic relationship between their keys; and the incipit of d:3 in the *Entwurf-Katalog* may perhaps have been intended (as the incipit of the first of a pair) to stand for both compositions. (The putative link between d:3 and d:GI may be reinforced by the title 'Pastorella 2.' in the Gröbming source; but this title may or may not be significant, and d:GI appears first in the sequence, for no apparent good reason.)

Thus the presentation of the works in Biba's edition, with d:3 first, may happily have restored the original ordering, even though this is not attested in surviving sources, and Biba perhaps reordered them to give priority to the better-attested of the two.

IV *Pastorell-Arien* and *Advents-Arien* in Haydn's understanding

A simple identification of d:3 as both the 'Cantilena pro adventu' of the *Entwurf-Katalog* and the D major pastorella of the sources, perhaps as the result of an error by Haydn, is presupposed above, and has been accepted in the literature. Yet this still leaves some aspects of the evidence unsatisfactorily explained. Haydn would hardly have been forgetful enough to have confused pastorellas with Advent arias; as I have argued above, the two genres are distinct both musically and liturgically. The text of d:3 is in dialect and alludes to the fanfares of the pastoral trumpet; the same is true of d:GI, which con-tains further specific allusions to the *Kindelwiegen*. Both these works thus display the *stylus rusticanus*, though there is no other evidence that this was used in Advent arias, however pastoral in tone.

In Werner's pieces, the distinctions of style between pastoral and Advent arias depend largely on the presence or absence of dialect texts, and the avoidance or use of the chalumeau. But these distinctions were outdated by mid-century, when it must have been difficult even to find players of the chalumeau. By this time, within strophic pastoral arias it is primarily the instrumental interludes immediately following important tonal goals within compositions that articulate style distinctions: fanfare or 'folk' motifs over drone basses in the *stylus rusticanus* characterize *Pastorell-Arien*; second-subject figuration not in that style, although sometimes also featuring pastoral motifs, characterizes *Advents-Arien*. This is evidently the practice governing Haydn's pieces. The differences may be illustrated in a comparison of the relevant passages from the pastorella d:3 and from the Advent arias d:1 and d:2, all entered in sequence on p. 2 of the *Entwurf-Katalog*. Space will not permit a full comparison, and I quote the postludes following each principal structural tonic cadence.[42] [Ex. 6a–c].

There is a clear division between the ritornelli in d:1 and d:2 on the one hand and that in d:3 on the other, though all project a 'tranquil' affect and are to some extent pastoral. The postlude in d:1 (Ex. 6a) has a pedal on the dominant, whose effect is not pastoral since it increases tension towards the tonic cadence, rather than releasing it in broken chords over a tonic pedal after the cadence in the manner of the *stylus rusticanus*; it contains no other pastoral allusions. The brief postlude of d:2 (Ex. 6b) contains the only pastoral effect of the aria: a tonic pedal, in which the folk-like arpeggios are attenuated by the abrupt dynamics. By contrast, the postlude of d:3 (Ex. 6c) is markedly 'rustic', with melodies in octaves, Lydian fourths and broken chords over a tonic pedal. Within the range of style represented by these three arias, this piece is analogous to shepherds' choruses in multi-movement pastorellas, and the other two are analogous to angels' arias.

The *Entwurf-Katalog* entries for d:3, d:1 and d:2 are likely to date from around 1768–70.[43] Now, Haydn appears to have composed no pastorellas after the late 1760s; indeed it is only the *Entwurf-Katalog* that provides evidence that Haydn was concerned with pastorellas for Eisenstadt, and this evidence is itself ambiguous. It would in fact seem possible that the *Entwurf-Katalog* entry for d:3 does refer to an Advent aria despite the identification of this work as a pastorella, and despite the evidence presented above that the genres of Advent aria and pastorella were distinct. In this case Haydn may in the late 1760s have taken d:3, written earlier as a pastorella either for Eisenstadt or elsewhere, and turned it into an Advent aria. If so, it would have required a new text, and the replacement or deletion of material in the *stylus rusticanus*: that is, the sections corresponding to Ex. 6c, or in other words most of the instrumental interludes (bb. 5–8, 13–14, 19–20, 29–35). The further problems of fitting this music to a contrafactum text can only be guessed at, but may have been less pressing in d:3 than they would have been in d:G1 with its more carefully integrated pastoral allusions, where (as seen in the Gröbming version) the attenuation of the *stylus rusticanus* gives rise to musical

33

Ex. 6a   Joseph Haydn, Advent aria 'Ein' Magd, ein' Dienerin' d:1, instrumental postlude, bb. 116–130: horns I/II in A, violins I/II, viola/organ.

34

Ex. 6b   Joseph Haydn, Advent aria *a 2* 'Mutter Gottes, mir erlaube' d:2, instrumental postlude, bb. 64–66: violin I, violin II, organ.

Ex. 6c   Joseph Haydn, Pastorella 'Herst Nachbä' d:3, instrumental postlude,
bb. 29–35 (Gröbming version lacking horns and viola): violin I, violin II, organ.

problems. (The difference between the versions of the bass incipit in this piece in its pastorella version and in the *Entwurf-Katalog*, mentioned above, cannot reflect the removal of unsuitable pastoral allusions, but may have something to do with a rearrangement to fit a new text.)

Contemporary documents also supply evidence that Haydn was concerned with the Advent music at this time, in particular with the Rorate (Advent) masses. Werner had signed receipts for the Rorate payments in 1761 and 1762; he was replaced by the organist Johann Novotny in 1763 and 1764, by Haydn from 1765 to 1769, and Franz Novotny in 1770.[44] Just as *Pastorell-Arien* may normally have been intended for the Christmas midnight mass, the Advent arias may have been for these Rorate masses; the *Entwurf-Katalog* entries might then relate to a group of arias for weekly performance during three of the four weeks of Advent, perhaps in the first year (1765) in which Haydn was responsible for the Rorate music, but at any rate between 1765 and 1769. The fourth week, not provided for in this group, might have required special treatment, or Haydn might have made use of existing music by Werner or another composer. In any event, this dating corresponds well with the probable date of the entry in the *Entwurf-Katalog*.[45]

V   The dates and provenance of Haydn's pastorellas

If a date of 1768 or 1769 for d:3, together implied by the *Entwurf-Katalog* entry and the Rorate payments, refers to a reworking by Haydn of an earlier work, it is clear that the questions of the original date of composition of these pastorellas, their original destination and their subsequent transmission, are opened up again; and also that no precise correspondence need be expected between the forms in which the two pastorellas are transmitted and the forms in which Haydn wrote them, nor between the terminology used in surviving sources and Haydn's original terminology for them, whatever this may have been.

H.C. Robbins Landon has suggested that they may originally have been written during Haydn's employment with Count Morzin after 1759.[46] In this event, they would have been intended for Morzin's country estate at Lukavec (south-west of Prague and east of Pilsen, near Příbram); and this might offer a tempting link with the Bohemian transmission of these pieces. However, whether or not pastorellas were customarily performed at the parish church there, and even disregarding the unlikelihood of a noble-man commissioning such pieces at this date, Haydn appears to have resided at Lukavec only during the summer months, and both pastorellas and Advent arias were required during the winter.

In a recent article, drawing on important archival evidence, Otto Biba has enlarged on the possibility (already mentioned in Griesinger's early biography[47]) that Haydn was employed between 1759 and 1761 in the Haugwitz chapel in Vienna, at which time he was in the service of Count Morzin. He argues that 'it is unthinkable that Haydn produced no church works during this time and for this purpose', and suggests a new investigation into the early church works with this possibility in mind.[48] It is clear, in particular, that provision must have been made for the Rorate masses during Advent, for the second mass of Christmas, and for other services during the Christmas season there already in 1759; that Haydn may have been required to compose and that the musical forces used in Haugwitz's chapel must have corresponded broadly with the chamber instrumentation of the pastorellas here discussed. This proposition may offer an attractive hypothesis to explain the origin of these works; once again, however, it may seem improbable that they would have been sought by a patron anxious to be seen to be cultivating the most prestigious and up-to-date church music available in Vienna at the time.

A second possibility is that the pastorellas and Advent arias were intended for an ecclesiastical establishment with which Haydn was associated, to be used as an adjunct to pastoral work. The Piarists at Maria Treu in Vienna, with whom Haydn had connections, particularly through the Haugwitz chapel at which they officiated, or the Hospitallers of St John of God, either in Vienna or elsewhere, might have welcomed them. Of these two possibilities, the Hospitallers seem more likely than the Piarists; there is no evidence that any surviving source is linked with the latter.

Another possibility is that these compositions were meant for an ecclesiastical establishment with which Haydn was associated, to be used as an adjunct to pastoral work. The Piarists at Maria Treu in Vienna, with whom Haydn had connections, particularly through the Haugwitz chapel at which they officiated, or the Hospitallers of St John of God, either in Vienna or elsewhere, might have welcomed them. Of the two the Hospitallers seem more likely than the Piarists; there is no evidence that any surviving source is linked with the latter.

In either case, it may be less likely for Haydn to have supplied them with music after 1761, once he had entered the service of the Esterházys. At Eisenstadt he was not contracted to supply church music; and if they were written in 1761 or later it is surprising that they are not attested at Eisenstadt as are pastorellas by Werner, Michael Haydn, Dittersdorf and others. However, the possibility of their dating from the 1760s does not seem entirely out of the question: a letter of Werner's from October 1765 suggests that Haydn was not averse to supplying music to other places.[49] And in the case of the Hospitallers, at least, the Esterházys themselves maintained an interest in the order; most publicly this was evident in the founding of an Eisenstadt house of the Hospitallers by Prince Paul Anton in 1760,[50] but a network of personal acquaintances linked them with the Esterházys and the imperial house as well as with Haydn (see discussion below).

VI   The geographical distribution of the sources of Haydn's pastorellas

In order to place the answers to these questions on as secure a foundation as possible, it may be helpful to review the geographical distribution of the sources of the pastorellas d:3 and d:G1.

For d:3, five sources are attested, of which two are lost. The Gröbming source is labelled 'A' by Biba in his edition; in another ('C'), from the nearby village of Schladming (now lost), the violins were replaced by flutes in the ritornelli and the vocal line was accompanied by organ alone.[51] Despite the differences in instrumentation, A and C are unlikely to have been independent sources: the two villages are adjacent, and copies of pastorellas, sometimes involving considerable re-arrangement and alteration of the compositions, can be expected to have been diffused locally within a limited area. This leaves unexplained how the work first arrived in the locality. A third source, from Vienna, mentioned but not labelled by Biba, is the lost manuscript from Währing, referred to above.

The remaining two sources for d:3, now in the Muzeum české hudby in Prague, have hitherto been regarded as marginal. One, mentioned (not labelled) by Biba, is a contrafactum, 'Ihr Kinderlein kommet', from the Hospitallers at Kuks; this manuscript is dated December 1837.[52] The other Prague source ('B' in Biba's edition), also a contrafactum, 'Jesu redemptor omnium', is from the *Nachlass* of O. Horník; it is generally said in the literature to be from 'Kráhiv Druž'.[53] Such a name is impossible in Czech, and Horník's inscription on the manuscript in question reads: 'Darem z Král. Dvora n. L. od p. řed. Kafky, 19 4/3 03' ('[Received] as a gift from Králův Dvůr nad Labem, from the director, Mr Kafka, 4/3/1903'). The town of Králův Dvůr nad Labem [Königshof an der Elbe], usually known today as Dvůr Králové, is no more than 5 km from Kuks. Once again, these two sources are unlikely to be independent, and the Dvůr Králové source may well have derived from an eighteenth-century source at Kuks; in this case, one may speculate that the 1837 Kuks source replaced the original eighteenth-century source in a version more consonant with contemporary taste. Whatever their limitations, these may be important sources.

For d:G1, there are or were five sources (four mentioned by Biba), three from the same provenance as three of the sources of d:3: Währing, Gröbming and Kuks. A fourth, regarded by Biba as the principal source of the piece, is from Weitra in the north of Lower Austria, near the Bohemian border; it was sent to Vienna in the early nineteenth century and is part of the Sonnleithner collection of the Gesellschaft der

Musikfreunde, Vienna.[54] The Kuks source is also eighteenth-century, but is fragmentary, comprising only the violone part and title page. It was copied by the same hand as a Kuks copy of Haydn's *Kleine Orgelsolomesse*, and may therefore date from the 1770s or later.[55] The fifth reference, supplied by Landon, is a lost *Pastorella germanica* dated 1764, listed as anonymous in the Göttweig thematic catalogue.[56]

VII   Haydn and the Hospitallers of St John of God

Of these places of provenance, the only one where personal links with Haydn seem likely is Kuks, the authenticity of whose Haydn sources has been recognized since the mid-1960s, when Georg Feder made a provisional report on the holdings of the archive in Prague.[57] The hospital at Kuks (Kukus) was associated with the north-eastern Bohemian castle of the same name, on the estate of Choustníkovo Hradiště adjacent to Dvůr Králové and not far from Trutnov (Trautenau). Here the Sporck family supported the Hospitallers of St John of God (*Barmherzige Brüder* in German, *Milosrdní bratři* in Czech; not, however, 'Brothers of Mercy' in English[58]); the Sporcks also maintained links with Haydn, building up an important collection, now in Prague, of authentic copies of symphonies (for the castle) and church music (for the hospital). Haydn is known to have had personal connections with the Hospitallers: he led the orchestra at their house in Vienna before his employment with the Esterházys, he is known to have played in Vienna for them again in 1768,[59] and he wrote the *Missa brevis Sancti Joannis de Deo* (the *Kleine Orgelsolomesse*) for them, perhaps *c.* 1775.

The Bohemian and to some extent the Austrian Hospitallers of this period are very fully documented in the *Künstler-Lexikon* (1815) of Dlabacz, who has entries for at least fifty-two individuals who were members of, or otherwise connected with, the order.[60] Most of the entries dealing with the Hospitallers refer to the *Annales fratrum Misericordiae provinciae Bohemiae*, but nearly all the information must have come at second hand from a single source, the Hospitaller, bass singer and composer Vinzenz Kneer (1738–1808).[61] (Kneer seems to have sent the information to Dlabacz all at once in 1796, and Dlabacz to have supplemented it later on an unsystematic basis.) Kneer, born at Klosterneuburg, attended the music school at the Augustinians in Vienna until he was taken on by Reutter as an alto chorister at the Stephansdom; he reports that during one Holy Week Joseph and Michael Haydn sang treble, and he himself sang alto, in the Lamentations, before Franz I and Maria Theresa.[62] (This anecdote, hitherto unnoticed as far as I am aware, must date from one of the years between 1745 and 1748 or 1749 at the latest.) He entered the Hospitallers in 1756 at Feldsberg and moved successively to several of the other houses of the order; among other things he was responsible for setting up the hospital at Graz (with which Haydn is already known to have had connections), with the support of Maria Theresa and Joseph II. (The monastic reforms of the second half of the century favoured orders such as the Hospitallers that had a clear social purpose.)

Throughout Dlabacz's entries for these Hospitallers, the same patterns recur: education in music as well as surgery and botany; acquaintanceship with all the most eminent composers; patronage by the imperial family, and also to some extent by the Esterházys (who, like the imperial family, seem to have watched for talent among the members of the order: they employed the 'gamba' (baryton) player Primitiv Niemecz as librarian, and they sent the violinist Alois Holey to Erlau in the unfulfilled hope of having him teach at a university to be set up there). It is not surprising, therefore, that they secured a constant supply of new works from various composers, Haydn among them, with or without the connivance of his patrons. And the brothers of the order frequently moved between its various hospitals, no doubt taking music with them; indeed all the known sources of d:3 and d:G1 could conceivably have been associated with hospitals of the order, though this is no more than speculation.

VIII   Other Kuks pastorellas attributed to Haydn

In view of the probability that Kuks had access to authentic sources of Haydn's music, it seems advisable to reopen the question of the authenticity of the two other pastorellas with the same provenance, even though this has generally been discounted since the work of Becker-Glauch. I shall not attempt to evaluate the quality of these compositions or to guess at their authorship, since we are hardly yet in a position to adjudicate on Haydn's use of the *stylus rusticanus*, but shall merely comment on the correspondence of the manuscripts in matters such as format and handwriting to others in the Kuks collection. The two Advent arias from Kuks are also listed below:

(1) An instrumental *Pastorale à 4tro [. . .] in G Del Sigre Haÿden* (Hob. *deest*) for strings and two horns in G makes extensive use of the *stylus rusticanus*, and the copy evidently corresponds closely in date (1770s or later) with the Kuks manuscript of d:G1;[63] it has the same format as the latter and was copied on the same paper, and like that of d:G1, the manuscript is inscribed 'Sub Regente Chori Fr. Caecilio Wagner' and 'Pro Choro Frum Misericordiae Kukusij'. It is not discussed by Becker-Glauch or Hoboken, perhaps because Haydn bibliography distinguishes so sharply between instrumental and vocal works, and as far as I know it has never been discussed in the Haydn literature. (Admittedly, the ascription to Haydn is non-specific, and Michael Haydn, who wrote a few pastorellas, was clearly as well known as Joseph to the Hospitallers. The piece in question begins with a short binary 3/4 Adagio movement, with several drone basses, and this is followed by a common-time Allegro in G (with a number of allusive clichés,

including the melody of the night-watchman's song in the major), interrupted twice by a 3/4 Andante section quoting the melody of 'Hajej můj andílku' over a drone bass, the first time in D major and the second time in G major [Ex. 7a, 7b]:

Ex. 7   'Pastorale à 4ᵗʳᵒ in G . . . Del Sigʳᵉ Haÿden': horns I/II in G, violins I/II, viola/organ – (a) first movement, incipit; (b) second movement, incipit.

(2) The remaining Kuks pastorella is the *Pastorella à Soprano, Tenore, Violino Primo Violino Secondo con Organo Concto e Violone Del Sigre Giuseppe Hayden*, 'Der Tag, der ist so freudenreich' (Hob. XXIIId:G2), which survives also in a version with two horns in

G from the monastery of St Thomas at Brno.[64] Although the work is attributed specif-
ically to Joseph Haydn in both sources, its authenticity was called into question by
Becker-Glauch. It was not copied by the same hand as the G major *Pastorale* above.
Nevertheless, it was copied on the same kind of paper (local, with the TRAVTENAV
watermark), in the same format, and apparently in the same hand, as a number of the
Haydn symphonies (apparently of the late 1760s), and two of the Haydn offertories, at
Kuks.[65] It is a typical strophic *Pastorell-Arie* of the kind discussed above, with fanfare-
motifs at the end of the initial instrumental ritornello and immediately following the
principal modulations into the dominant and, at the end, back into the tonic; the text is
dialect. [Ex. 8]

Ex. 8   'Pastorella à Soprano, Tenore . . . Del Sig[re] Giuseppe Hayden' d:G2, incipit:
canto, violins I/II, violone/organ.

(3–4) In addition, there are two Advent arias from Kuks, 'Maria Jungfrau rein',
already noted as a probable contrafactum (the hand of the manuscript does not obviously correspond to any other in the collection), and an *Aria pro Adventu a Tenore Solo
Due Violini Organo con Violone Sig. Hayden* in G, 'Was meine matte Brust', in a very
similar musical style and hand, perhaps another contrafactum.[66]

Conclusion

These considerations argue that Haydn's early pastorellas are quite different from his
Advent arias and his other early works, because supplied for a different audience. If d:3

had not appeared, reworked or otherwise, in the *Entwurf-Katalog*, one could hardly have guessed at the authenticity of these pieces: it is difficult to assess their authenticity from internal or stylistic evidence. But, at the beginning of his career, Haydn had friends who needed material of this sort, and we should not be surprised to find these pieces among his earliest compositions. Moreover, the Esterházys themselves may have encouraged him to write them, for Werner had been composing such pieces for years: and some of Werner's pastorellas even postdate 1760. But the tradition, and the *stylus rusticanus* on which it depended, were increasingly out of favour in Austrian centres with pretensions to musical taste in the second half of the century, and were unlikely to survive unaltered at Eisenstadt after Werner's demise. The most natural way of putting pastoral arias to profitable use at Eisenstadt in the late 1760s may have been by transmuting them into the related but distinct form of the Advent aria – a genre which, though not specifically designed to 'ennoble' the pastorella for aristocrats no longer wholly at ease with it, was well able to perform that task when required to do so.

A. PETER BROWN

The Sublime, the Beautiful, and the Ornamental: English Aesthetic Currents and Haydn's London Symphonies

WHEN HAYDN FIRST SET FOOT on English soil on 1 January 1791, he was unprepared for London's lively intellectual and musical environment. While Haydn was to have a profound impact on English music, he in turn would be deeply affected. Though his command of English was at first lacking, the Kapellmeister to the princely Esterházy court was immediately welcomed into England's highest social, intellectual and musical circles.[1] Within a month of his arrival in London Haydn met his most enthusiastic advocate, the critic and historian Dr Charles Burney who, in his recently completed *A General History of Music* (1789), had introduced the composer with hyperbolic flourishes:

> I am now happily arrived at that part of my narrative where it is necessary to speak of HAYDN! the admirable and matchless HAYDN! from whose productions I have received more pleasure late in my life, when tired of most other Music, then I ever received in the most ignorant and rapturous part of my youth, when every thing was new, and the disposition to be pleased undiminished by criticism or satiety.[2]

Burney's enthusiasm had certainly not diminished, for in his 'VERSES on the Arrival in England of the GREAT MUSICIAN HAYDN' he elevated this Austrian above all other composers, to the very peak of Parnassus.[3]

Burney's social and intellectual circle encompassed some of the most sophisticated thinkers in London, including a number of important artists and critics. Among his many friends were such luminaries as the thespian David Garrick, the artist Sir Joshua Reynolds, the aesthetician Edmund Burke, and the lexicographer and critic Samuel Johnson. Burney was also immersed in London's salon life, hobnobbing regularly with the 'Bluestockings' and the 'Streatham Coterie'.[4]

Haydn's primary task was to compose music tailored to the tastes of both the amateurs and the connoisseurs who subscribed to Salomon's concerts and later the Opera Concerts. There can be no doubt that Haydn cultivated a style with special appeal to this audience. According to Charlotte Papendiek:

> Haydn, immediately on his arrival, told Salomon that he should stay the summer in England, and that as he heard there were to be twelve concerts and two benefits

during the season there would be ample time for him to compose his first symphonies after he had had an opportunity of studying the taste of the English. He
was determined that his first production should both amuse and please the
musical public and rivet him in their favour . . .[5]

In addition, Haydn told his biographer Georg August Griesinger that for his second
season he 'was interested in surprising the public with something new and in making a
brilliant début' in order to meet the challenge of his erstwhile pupil Ignaz Pleyel, who
was engaged by the rival Professional Concert series.[6] Thus, Haydn took seriously the
task of speaking to his prospective public in a manner that blended English expectations with his own musical language.

*   *   *

During his first season in London, Haydn must have become aware of several musical
cross-currents. Among the various factions in English music, the most strongly delineated were the advocates of the 'ancient' and of the 'scientific' styles. The Ancients
favoured the Handelian heritage, and nearly everything that came before Handel, to the
exclusion of anything smacking of modernity. Their preferences ran to the English
madrigal school and Henry Purcell, the Italian violin school from Corelli to
Geminiani, and the vocal music of Pergolesi, Jomelli and Hasse.[7] One of their leaders
was Burney's rival music historian, Sir John Hawkins, who concluded his *A General
History of the Science and Practice of Music* with what we would call the Baroque. Indeed,
the fifth volume of Hawkins's *History* included an 'Account . . . of the Academy of
Ancient Music'.[8]

Segregation of the ancient from the modern repertoire was an accepted part of
concert life. In 1796 John Marsh (1752–1828) published anonymously in *The Monthly
Magazine* 'A comparison between the ancient and modern styles of music in which the
merits and demerits of each are respectively pointed out'. He argued that this segregation should cease and that programmes should mix old with new music.[9] This pro-
posal seems to have stimulated a series of partisan letters, beginning with enthusiastic
praise for Dr Arne. The debate came to be known as the 'passionate' controversy.[10]

Johann Christian Bach, Carl Friedrich Abel, Ignaz Pleyel and Joseph Haydn
constituted the core group of 'scientific' or modern composers. Though Burney was
one of the prime advocates of the new style, he did not lack an appreciation for older
music; on commission from King George III he had described events in 1784 in *An
Account of the Musical Performances . . . in Commemoration of Handel* (1785).[11] Still, Burney
did express impatience with the almost cult-like exclusivity of the Handelians.[12]

It would have been impossible for Haydn to remain unaware of this controversy.
In fact, on several occasions he broke through the segregationist barrier, not only by the

45

probably unprecedented performance of his own music at one of the 'ancient' concerts, but by accompanying Madame La Mara in Purcell's song 'From Rosy Bower' at her benefit concert, and by attending the Handel Festivals at Westminster Abbey. The Handel Festivals had a deep and enduring effect on Haydn's concept of the oratorio.[13]

Haydn's audience at the Hanover Square Rooms and later at the King's Theatre overwhelmingly preferred 'scientific' music. Some might wish to note Haydn's use of fugal passages, for example in the finales of Symphonies nos. 95 and 101, as possible concessions to the Ancients. But, given the tastes of his audience, one could also hear the famous slow movement of Symphony no. 93 as a heavy satire: the passages in French overture style with their dotted rhythms, rushing scales and massive sonorities might have been heard as belonging to the Handelian, if not the ancient manner, and the long stretches of triple subdivisions might have brought to mind the older pastoral idiom. These elements set against the modern chamber style of the refrains provide a foil for the bassoon expletive in answer to another ancient reference [Ex. 1]. Could this last juxtaposition be a musical comment upon the ancient *v.* modern debate?

Associated with the ancient style and more specifically the great ghost of Handel himself were such aesthetic descriptions as the 'sublime' and the 'beautiful'. That these, together with a related evaluative vocabulary, came to be associated with Haydn and his music is easily documented, but how Haydn himself may have been introduced to these concepts, one can only speculate.

In 1757 Edmund Burke had published his *Philosophical Inquiry into the Origin of our Ideas on the Sublime and the Beautiful.* Though his ideas are derivative of Longinus and earlier English writings, this much discussed and influential study of aesthetics served as a catalyst for other writings on the sublime, the beautiful and, later, the picturesque.[14] Burney, a friend of Burke's, was certainly familiar with the *Philosophical Inquiry*; according to the auction catalogue of Burney's library, he owned a carefully annotated copy.[15] A later printing of the volume (1792) is listed in the inventory of Haydn's estate.[16] Regardless of when Haydn acquired this treatise, it seems likely that its concepts were brought to his attention early in the 1790s. He simply could not have escaped their import in relation to his own works as well as those of Handel, whose name had become almost synonymous with the sublime in music.[17] Nor could Haydn in his efforts to please his audience have avoided attempts to incorporate or emphasize the rhetoric of the sublime and the beautiful in his own works.

For Burke the sublime and the beautiful were clearly delineated. At the end of the third part of his treatise he writes:

> On closing this general view of beauty, it naturally occurs, that we should compare it with the sublime; and in this comparison there appears a remarkable

Ex. 1   Symphony no. 93/ii, bb. 73–83

contrast. For sublime objects are vast in their dimensions, beautiful ones compar-
atively small; beauty should be smooth, and polished; the great, rugged and negli-
gent; beauty should shun the right line, yet deviate from it insensibly; the great in
many cases loves the right line, and when it deviates, it often makes a strong devia-
tion; beauty should not be obscure; the great ought to be dark and gloomy; beauty
should be light and delicate; the great ought to be solid, and even massive.[18]

As for direct references to music, the closest Burke comes is in the sections on sound.
Concerning the sublime, he writes:

Sounds have a great power in these as in most other passions. I do not mean
words, because words do not affect simply by their sounds, but by means alto-

gether different. Excessive loudness alone is sufficient to overpower the soul, to suspend its action, and to fill it with terror. The noise of vast cataracts, raging storms, thunder, or artillery, awakes a great and aweful sensation in the mind, though we can observe no nicety or artifice in those sorts of music. The shouting of multitudes has a similar effect; and by the sole strength of the sound, so amazes and confounds the imagination, that in this staggering, and hurry of the mind, the best established tempers can scarcely forbear being borne down, and joining in the common cry, and common resolution of the croud.[19]

From Burke's characterization, one can easily imagine how Handel's music, particularly as performed by massed choirs and a large orchestra in Westminster Abbey,

would be defined as sublime.[20] Burke continues by discussing the sudden beginning or cessation of sound and what he describes as a 'low, tremulous, intermitting sound' as producing a sublime effect.

Burke finds beautiful sounds less jarring and, moreover, completely soothing. He offers two reasons:

> The first is; that the beautiful in music will not bear that loudness and strength of sounds, which may be used to raise other passions; nor notes, which are shrill, or harsh, or deep; it agrees best with such as are clear, even, smooth, and weak. The second is; that great variety, and quick transitions from one measure to another, are contrary to the genius of the beautiful in music. Such transitions often excite

mirth, or other sudden and tumultuous passions; but not that sinking, that melting, that languor, which is the characteristical effect of the beautiful, as it regards every sense. The passion excited by beauty is in fact nearer to a species of melancholy, than to jollity and mirth. I do not here mean to confine music to any one species of notes, or tones, neither is it an art in which I can say I have any great skill.[21]

Burke's *Inquiry* is characteristic of its era in that few eighteenth-century treatises look carefully and thoroughly at the sublime and beautiful in their musical manifestations.[22] Not until the appearance of two publications by William Crotch – *Specimens of Various Styles of Music referred to in A Course of Lectures read at Oxford and London* dating from c. 1808 to 1815[23] and the later publication of the lectures themselves as *The Substance of Several Courses of Lectures on Music* (1831) – would music be more closely examined in such a context.[24] The essence of the chapter on 'The Sublime, the Beautiful, and the Ornamental' in the latter publication was probably first written sometime before February 1805, i.e. before the appearance of the *Specimens of Various Styles*.[25] The value of Crotch's lecture is particularly significant, for his explications cite important writings by Sir Joshua Reynolds, Uvedale Price and James Harris, as well as Burke, demonstrating a knowledge of literature since the mid-eighteenth century.[26] One should not be surprised at Crotch's consultation of works on art and landscape; he was himself an artist of some accomplishment and a member of the amateur group known as the Oxford School, self-deprecatingly called by its members 'The Great School'.[27] With the codification of the picturesque by Price in 1796 as a rustic style of landscape, Crotch developed a musical equivalent, the 'ornamental'. He quotes Price himself as having seen the necessity of a new term:

The English word picturesque naturally draws the mind towards pictures; and from that partial and confined view of the subject, what is, in truth, only an illustration of picturesqueness, becomes the foundation of it. The words sublime and beautiful have not the same etymological reference to any one visible art, and therefore are applied to objects of the other senses. Sublime, indeed, in the language from which it is taken, means high; and therefore, perhaps, in strictness, should relate to objects of sight only; yet we no more scruple to call one of Handel's Choruses sublime, than Corelli's Pastorale beautiful. But should any person, simply and without qualifying expressions, call a capricious movement of Dominico Scarlatti, or Haydn, picturesque he would, with great reason, be laughed at; for it is not a term applied to sounds: yet such a movement, from its sudden, unexpected, and abrupt transitions, from a certain playful wildness of character, and an appearance of irregularity, is no less analogous to similar scenery in nature, than the concerto, or the chorus, to what is grand or beautiful to the eye.[28]

Crotch discusses all three concepts in both the *Specimens* and *Lectures* which are selec-tively quoted in the Table overleaf. The three styles, according to Crotch, are 'rarely found in an unmixed state'. He finds mixtures of the sublime and beautiful in church music and in Renaissance madrigals. Mixtures of the sublime and ornamental appear in the introductory Adagios to symphonies and [church?] sonatas, and the example he provides for a mixture of all three styles is from Haydn: the second movement of Symphony no. 82 (*L'ours/The Bear*) from the so-called Paris set.[29]

With all the symphonies that Haydn performed in London at his disposal, Crotch's selection of the second movement of no. 82 seems odd. This Allegretto hardly contains the well etched and deep contrasts among beautiful, sublime and ornamental sections to be found in the dozen London Symphonies. Indeed, these variations on two themes (ABA¹B¹A²) with coda seem to mix only two of the three types: the orna-mental style of the A material with the *minore* of B (b. 33) and C (b. 101), which does not seem to achieve the sublimity promised by Crotch. It might be construed as belong-ing to the second type of the sublime from the *Specimens* where 'the harmony is clear, but the melody and measure dignified and marked'. Alternatively, one might hear the *minore* sections in their context against the more playful materials of the major mode as more 'mock-pathetic' than sublime.

Crotch's example reveals the difficulty he had with Haydn's language. In an exchange of letters between Charles Burney and Crotch that took place in 1805 we find the Oxford professor berated by the author of the *General History*: 'These enlarged and enlightened judges both of old and new Music are unwilling to subscribe to your severe, and even, contemptuous remarks on Haydn'.[30] Crotch's criticisms centred on Haydn's 'whimsicalities', echoing the North German critics of forty years earlier.[31] Burney believed that even after removing this characteristic playfulness 'enough remains of serious, beautiful & sublime, to constitute a truly great man'. He continues with a vigorous defence:

> As to Haydn's comic turn, Shakespear, you know was a writer of Comedies as well as Tragedies, and no one of his admirers is perhaps able to tell you which he loves best. And as there is a comic Music in Burlettas equally good, in its kind, with that of serious Operas, why may not Haydn sometimes be comical, as many of our Poets have been in their Comi-tragedies?
>
> But I am told that you were remarkably severe and sarcastic on the Instrumentation to Haydn's Oratorio of the Creation, and it should seem, without considering that it was a description of Chaos before Order existed, he

had to remind his audience of confusion, floating atoms, and the throes of Nature in labour. . . . If you say in public that you do not approve them, you must give your reasons – If your principal objections are that they do not resemble Handel's Oratorios or Anthems, it will be asked why they should? Surely such an inventive composer as Haydn may be allowed to have a style of his own. His Fugues even have expression, light and shade, and are embellished by ritornels and intersticial symphonies without drawing off the vocal parts from the subject of the Fugue. But are not the answers to all his regular Fugues correctly brought in? If his Fugues resembled those of Handel would it not degrade him into an Imitator, perhaps a plagiary? . . .

It is not only in England that Haydn has been admired, the Germans, of course, are proud of him, but in France and Spain his fame and fortune are still higher than with his votaries here . . .

No man's works could so soon penetrate to such a distance without extraordi⁄ nary merit.[32]

Crotch's reply clearly places him almost entirely in the camp of the Ancients:

There are admirers of Haydn who esteem him 'not only the greatest composer of his age but of all ages.' If his champions are offended that I cannot allow him the same degree of credit for his vocal as for his instrumental productions I am sorry. But surely all Europe is not against me? Will not Italy prefer the vocal melodies of Sacchini, Cimarosa, & Paisiello to those of Haydn? Every one who can sing from Madame Mara to the Chorus Singer will allow that in his Oratorios (to use Madama Mara's own words) 'the voices only accompany the instruments' – Whatever style of Music Haydn adopts, instrumental effects form the chief excellence. – Nor is it in favor of Handel that I content. – I prefer to Haydn's Choral Music that of [—?], Duranti, Purcell, Em'l. Bach, Hasse, Jomelli, Graun, Pergolesi, [—?] & Mozart – & songs of ye whole Italian School from Carissimi to Paisiello. – I am not offended at his inventions for I think his Recitatives & Choral Fugues want novelty. – Where is the vocal flow of melody & transparency of accompaniment which you so happily describe in Italian Songs? – Is not he guilty of the same error in imitating the rising of ye Sun &c for which Handel & others are censured by all good critics?

I am happy to find that Mr Latrobe who is a professed admirer of Haydn thought that my remarks on his Oratorio of ye Creation were, upon ye whole, just. Shakespear is my delight – But I [am] convinced that the Buffoonery in his tragedies was always a fair object of Censure. Some subjects, some passages, some movements strike me as too light for the Sacred Oratorio of ye Creation . . .[33]

TABLE

Crotch on the Sublime, the Beautiful and the Ornamental in music

Preface to *Specimens of Various Styles of Music*, c. 1808–15	The Substance of Several Courses of Lectures on Music (1831)

THE SUBLIME

The Sublime . . . is produced by various and, seemingly, opposite causes: I shall mention and exemplify four. The 1st, and perhaps the most striking, is when a few simple notes are performed in unison or octaves by a variety of instruments or voices, in the manner of the ancients. [*Symphonies to 'Sommi Dei' from Radamisto and to 'Jealousy infernal pest' from Hercules by Handel and Overture to Ifigenie by Gluck.*] II. Another source of the Sublime is when the harmony is clear and simple, but the melody and measure dignified and marked. *Chorus 'Moses and the Children of Israel' from Israel in Egypt and 'How Excellent Thy Name O Lord' from Saul by Handel*] III. When the harmony and modulation are learned and mysterious, when the ear is unable to anticipate the transition from chord to chord, and from key to key, if the melody and measure are grave, the effect will be Sublime. (Of this description are the works of Tye, Tallis, Bird, Farrant, and Gibbons . . .) [*'Who is Like unto Thee' from Israel in Egypt*] IV. The sublime effect of a multitude of voices and instruments, performing species of melody and rhythm at once, yet all conspiring in harmony, must be acknowledged by those who are familiar with choral effects. [*'He Rebuked the Red Sea' from Israel in Egypt*] (*pp. 1–2.*)

The sublime is founded on principles of vastness and incomprehensibility. The word sublime originally signifies high, lofty, elevated; and this style, accordingly, never descends to anything small, delicate, light, pretty, playful, or comic. The grandest style in music is therefore the sacred style – that of the church and oratorio – for it is least inclined to levity, where levity is properly inadmissible, and where the words convey the most awful and striking images (*p. 32*).

In music, the great compass of notes employed in a full orchestra conveys an idea of vastness undefined. A uniform succession of major chords, the most agreeable of all sounds, resembles a blaze of light; while the unintelligible combination of extraneous discords conveys a feeling like that caused by darkness. The clearness of harmony in the madrigal of many voices, or in the full anthem, and the deep science of the organ fugue produce sublimity from seemingly opposite causes; as also a passage performed by many voices or instruments in unisons or octaves, and one in full and florid counterpoint (*pp. 34–35*).

THE BEAUTIFUL

To produce the Beautiful in music all must be soft, smooth, and flowing; the melody must be vocal, the harmony clear and simple, consisting chiefly of concords; the measure or rhythm must be continuous and uninterrupted; and as the minor key has fewer perfect chords than the major, the latter is the most productive of Beauty. [*Minuet from the Overture to Berenice by Handel*] (*p. 2*)

Beauty, in all the arts, is the result of softness, smoothness, delicacy, smallness, gentle undulations, symmetry, and the like. When, therefore, in music the melody is vocal and flowing, the measure symmetrical, the harmony simple and intelligible, and the style of the whole soft, delicate, and sweet, it may with as much propriety be called beautiful, as a small, perfect, Grecian temple, or a landscape of Claude Lorraine (*p. 35*.)

THE ORNAMENTAL

There is a third style of music very different from the Sublime and the Beautiful; its characteristics are playfulness of melody, broken and varied measure, intricacy of harmony and modulation, and a perpetual endeavour to excite surprise in the mind of the auditor. This style . . . is analogous to the Picturesque in Painting; and I shall distinguish it by the term Ornamental, which, however, is not so appropriate as I could wish. [*Sonata for Harpsichord (K. 21) by Domenico Scarlatti*] (*p. 2.*)

The ornamental style is the result of roughness, playful intricacy, and abrupt variations. In painting, splendid draperies, intricate architecture, gold or silver cups and vases, and all such objects are ornamental; aged heads, old hovels, cottages, or mills, ruined temples or castles, rough animals, peasants at a fair, and the like, are picturesque. In music, eccentric and difficult melody; rapid, broken, and varied rhythm; wild and unexpected modulation, indicate this third style (*pp. 35–36*.)

53

Nevertheless, Crotch's *Lectures* present an inconsistency of view, indicating perhaps that Burney's protests against his views had some effect. For Crotch, the choral music of Haydn, Mozart – except for the Requiem – and Beethoven could not equal the sublimity of Handel's.[34] However, Crotch did acknowledge the superiority of Haydn's instrumental music, even though his main stylistic stance was ornamental. Haydn was, in Crotch's own words, 'an instrumental composer' of

> unrivalled powers. . . . Haydn's sinfonias, for number, variety, novelty, brilliancy, and gaiety of style surpass all others. It was this gaiety which was objected to when his compositions first appeared. But it is this alone which renders them more pleasing and amusing than the equally scientific productions of his pupils, Mozart and Beethoven.[35]

But for Crotch the ornamental was the least elevated of the three styles. Therefore, Haydn's predominantly 'ornamental' works could not be considered as worthy as those of Handel. In the larger perspective of Crotch's argument, Haydn represented a general trend in the decline of musical art; unlike the scientific Haydn, Handel's oratorios eschewed the ornamental, containing only music beautiful and sublime, as may be inferred from the musical examples Crotch chose for the *Specimens*. In all three volumes of the *Specimens*, only three examples are from Haydn. In addition to Symphony no. 82 (second movement), the Quartet op. 76 no. 3 (first and second movements) and Symphony no. 74 (all movements) are provided in a keyboard reduction. Furthermore, the examples included by other composers favour the ancient repertoire.

Nevertheless, English critics continued to apply to Haydn's music precisely those adjectives Crotch insisted on reserving for only the worthiest compositions. In describing Haydn's London symphonies the English press regularly invoked a terminology associated with the highest levels of expression in the British literature on aesthetics: 'grandeur' and 'wanton grandeur', 'most striking', 'most powerful effects', 'tremendous', 'astonishing', 'infinite', 'horrid', 'enrapture', 'simple and profound', 'bold and impressive', 'affects every emotion of the soul', and 'an extacy [*sic*] of admiration'.[36] If these are not outright code words for the 'sublime', they go far to suggest sublimity. Burney's own article on Haydn for *Rees's Cyclopaedia*, probably written about the time of his exchange with Crotch, broadens the rhetoric of admiration over that found in *A General History*. In the earlier work only Haydn's slow movements were 'sublime', now Haydn's symphonies *in toto* are so characterized.[37]

*　　*　　*

Of all Haydn's symphonic writing, the slow movements met with special approbation in London, where they were frequently encored. The most specifically sublime of these, according to the London press, was that of Symphony no. 100 (*Military*). The *Morning Chronicle* of 9 April 1794 reported that

> Another new Symphony, by Haydn, was performed for the second time; and the middle movement was again received with absolute shouts of applause. Encore! encore! encore! resounded from every seat: the Ladies themselves could not forbear. It is the advancing to battle; and the march of men, the sounding of the charge, the thundering of the onset, the clash of arms, the groans of the wounded, and what may well be called the hellish roar of war increase to a climax of horrid sublimity! which, if others can conceive, he alone can execute; at least he alone hitherto has effected these wonders.[38]

For this critic the Allegretto is clearly imbued with narrative qualities. The passages referred to are the first episode (b. 57), with its introduction of the percussion and turn to the minor, and the coda (b. 153), with its trumpet-call and harmonically deceptive *fortissimo* (A flat major introduced by a solo timpani crescendo).

The ornamental style of the refrains here enhances the sublimity of the episodes and coda. For even though the refrains use march material, they hardly adumbrate or even hint at the dramatic turn of events. Thus, contrast of affect becomes a potent tool in Haydn's forms, even in those using homogeneous or undifferentiated themes.

A notice in the *Morning Chronicle* of 5 May 1794 again recognized the sublime nature of this movement, but objected to the use of the percussion in the finale.

> We cannot help remarking, that the cymbals introduced in the military movement, though they there produce a fine effect, are in themselves discordant, grating, and offensive, and ought not to have been introduced, either in the last movement of that Overture, or in the Finale at the close of the Concert. The reason of the great effect they produce in the military movement is that they mark and tell the story: they inform us that the army is marching to battle, and, calling up all the ideas of the terror of such a scene, give it reality. Discordant sounds are then sublime; for what can be more horribly discordant to the heart than thousands of men meeting to murder each other.[39]

This comment shows the critic's sensitivity to context: in the march of the second movement, the 'military' instruments were consonant with its character; for the jig of the finale, they were clearly inappropriate.

Would one also wish to conclude that the famous 'surprise' of Symphony no. 94 was a sublime moment? After the first performance, the 'New Overture' was described as 'simple, profound, and sublime' by the *Diary; or Woodfall's Register* of 24 March 1792,[40] while the *Oracle* of the same date wrote: 'the surprise might not be unaptly likened to the situation of a beautiful Shepherdess who, lulled to slumber by the murmur of a distant Waterfall, starts alarmed by the unexpected firing of a fowling‑piece'.[41] Thus, one observer heard the movement as a serene pastoral interrupted by a moment of sublimity as defined by Burke: 'a sudden beginning, or sudden cessation of sound of any considerable force'.[42]

Other slow movements from the final London series also aspire to the sublime. In the Andante of no. 101 (*Clock*) Haydn articulates the beginning of the episode in a

Ex. 2   Symphony no. 104/ii, bb. 38–59

manner not unlike that in Crotch's example from Symphony no. 82. But in the later movement, Haydn's contrasts run deeper. It is thus more convincingly sublime. If Haydn did tailor his symphonies for the London audience, the venue for which this one was intended – the Hanover Square Rooms – perhaps demanded such a deep contrast.[43] For the slow movement of the *Drum Roll* Symphony (no. 103), the trumpet and timpani fanfares for the variation of the *minore* theme (b. 109) recall something of the similar passage in Symphony no. 100, though without duplicating the scoring with 'dissonant' percussion. In the slow movement of no. 104 (*London*) the episode responds to a quiet woodwind statement with a sudden tutti *fortissimo* development-like passage that stops *in medias res* more suddenly than it began, providing a suitably sublime gesture [Ex. 2]. This is just one remarkable moment of several that occur in this movement

involving both effect and structure, digressions and expansions that stretch its essen-
tially simple ternary shape.[44]

However, Haydn's main focus in these second movements is on the beautiful and
ornamental styles. This could also be said of Symphonies nos. 97, 98, 99 and 102, as
well as some of the slow pieces already discussed for their sublime moments and sections. By way of example, the Adagio of no. 98 begins with an idealization of the
musically beautiful: its cantabile step-wise melody and its simple and direct harmonies
project – despite the rests within the consequent portion of the phrase – a smooth and
flowing line. The final two-bar phrase is more playfully ornamental with its broken and
more intricate surface activities. [Ex. 3]. While the material in b. 15 derives from the
consequent phrase of the main theme (b. 5), it is initially given greater continuity,
which lasts through to b. 23, only to be broken with the development section (b. 26) as
the mode turns to the minor, the dynamics move first to *forte* and then to *fortissimo*, and
the tonal materials are more coloured. None of this, however, qualifies as a sublime
gesture, for the simple reason that it is not delivered with surprise.

In the slow movements of Symphonies nos. 95 and 96 Haydn remains in a more
neutral realm. According to Crotch's guidelines, the thematic materials of these variation movements are neither beautiful nor ornamental. But neither do they achieve sub-

Ex. 3   Symphony no. 98/ii, bb. 1–10

limity; Haydn's reliance on understatement ensures that not even during the single contrapuntal variation in each movement will the listener be overwhelmed.

In both its genesis and end result, the Adagio of Symphony no. 102 is the most monolithically beautiful of all the London slow movements. Its source is the Adagio cantabile of the piano trio (Hob.XV:26) in which the keyboard dominates the texture, leaving the violin and cello to serve mostly as accompaniment. The fact that the keyboard part was intended for a specific woman player, Rebecca Schroeter – the composer's reputed lover – makes its style seem all the more appropriate, since the concept of beauty held decidedly feminine associations. One may question if the melody itself is beautiful in the same sense as that of Symphony no. 98/2; but in no. 102/2 we have a different sort of cantabile, an elaborate vocalise. In the piano trio context, it follows an extraordinary first movement (Allegro) in the minor mode, whose abject melancholy is swept away by this Adagio cantabile in the tonic major.[45] In the Symphony, the Adagio in F major follows a bright Vivace in B flat, thereby considerably altering its contextual affect. As for the orchestral version, it underlines the only potentially sublime moment (bb 54–6), as a dominant sonority is resolved deceptively with an unexpected *fortissimo*. [Ex. 4].

One might expect the minuet, as a generic type, to be ornamental, and the trio (if it changes style), to belong to the realm of the beautiful. And indeed this is often true of Haydn, whose trios tended to be more soloistic and/or more cantabile than the minuet proper. Haydn was conscious of the problems posed for a composer by a genre so highly stereotyped and ubiquitous.[46] Perhaps one of the most original minuets of the London symphonies is that of no. 93. Not only do the repeats in the trio break from the binary form, but the trio's aesthetic stance completely thwarts all expectations. Haydn juxta-

Ex. 4   Symphony no. 102/ii, bb. 53–56

poses *forte* wind fanfares with a *piano* cantabile passage for strings; the sublime is here effected by the unexpected suddenness of the loud fanfare, a call to battle, replayed six times before the end of the trio.

Like the minuet, the finale of the late eighteenth-century symphony also made use of a predominant type: a dance movement of some sort in 2/4 or 6/8 time. Such use of the country dance or gigue would seem to favour the ornamental style. Yet, in most of the finales in the London symphonies one can still find passages that evoke the sublime. In the transition to the refrain (bb. 169–70) of Symphony no. 93, the impact of the unexpected tutti *fortissimo* can be almost as startling as that of the famous surprise in no. 94. In the finale of Symphony no 94. the thundering change in the timpani's dynamic followed by the tutti refrain in E flat major provides a dramatic turn from the country dance to the terror of the sublime. Both this passage and the surprise in its Andante reflect the work's German nickname: *mit dem Paukenschlag*. The coda in the finale of Symphony no. 96, as it suddenly turns to the *Sturm und Drang* style (b. 210) just before the final fanfares and cadences, has much the same effect. In the finale of Symphony no. 95 the two fugato episodes, bordering on the *stile antico*, approach Crotch's fourth cate-gory of the sublime as described in the *Specimens* despite the absence of a chorus.

With the second series of London symphonies, the finales take on a stronger contrapuntal stance, with long stretches of learned writing in Symphonies nos. 99, 101, 103 and 104, while nos. 100 and 102 are more like those of the first set. In nos. 101, 103 and 104 *alla breve* replaces 2/4, establishing a loftier tone and a heavier articulation of the pulse. On the other hand, the fugal texture in no. 99/4 seems to enhance the playful aspect of this rollicking movement. At the same time one is tempted to suggest that the highly contrapuntal development of the second episode (bb. 128–85) is paradoxically both sublime in its treatment and ornamental in its content, combining a playful theme with counterpoint and modulation, respectively Crotch's third and fourth categories of the sublime.

A similar combination is to be found in the last movement of Symphony no. 103 (*Drum Roll*). Its sudden change from *forte* to *fortissimo* with a transfer to the submediant minor chord at the end of the opening and closing refrains (b. 101; b. 310) reaches toward, if it does not attain, sublimity. As in no. 103 Haydn grasps at sublimity in the final refrain to no. 101 (b. 189). Commencing with a *pianissimo* double fugue for strings, which recalls the hushed fugal finales of the string quartets from op. 20, it is interrupted by a tutti *fortissimo* statement of the subject. Never satisfied to duplicate a gesture, Haydn pursues a different form of the sublime in no. 104, which conforms to Crotch's third category, wherein 'one cannot anticipate the transitions from chord to chord'. Here Haydn takes the end of the second subject (b. 84) with its decided slowing of activity and, at the end of the development section (b. 167), gives it an astonishing altered harmonization. This must qualify as one of the most understated sublime moments in the entire eighteenth-century symphonie repertoire.

That Haydn creates sublime or near sublime moments in these finales represents a significant shift in late eighteenth-century practice; these last movements begin to approximate the power and interest of the opening piece. Granted, there were instances of this in Haydn's earlier output, such as the finale to Symphony no. 88 where, in a breathtaking passage (bb. 109–22), the main theme is treated as an extended canon. But Symphony no. 88 does not take advantage of its full instrumentation with trumpets and drums, and thus it fails to match the 'grand' character of the London symphonies.[47] Haydn performed only three pre-existing symphonies at the London concerts, nos. 90,

91 and 92, and except for no. 91/4 they have potent finales on a scale probably not previously heard in the English capital. In the London works Haydn increases the use of
dramatic, if not always sublime, gestures. Even so, he never produced a finale as climac-
tic as those found in Mozart's *Prague* Symphony (K.504), K.550 in G minor, and especially K. 551 in C major, dubbed by Salomon the *Jupiter*.[48]

Part of this shift in Haydn's symphonies of the 1790s may have been a result of
London concert-room practice. Were these symphonies always heard in their entirety as
four-movement units or were the first three movements performed with the finale sometimes saved for the end of the concert's first 'act', or was the finale perhaps repeated at the
act's end? The report in the *Morning Chronicle* of 5 May 1794, though commenting on
this aspect, remains ambiguous (see above, p. 55). While these questions cannot at
present be answered with certainty, they do bear on the character of the finale and its
relationship to the cycle as a whole. As a *finis coronat opus* the finale would need to equal
or exceed the aesthetic interest of the previous movements, but as a separate 'final' or
'full piece', this point would be less relevant to what Friedrich Blume called the 'finale
problem' (referring to the nineteenth century).[49] Nevertheless, in Haydn's London
symphonies the finales do not usually outstrip the first movements in the pursuit of the
sublime. The centre of weight is consistently found at the beginning rather than at the
conclusion of each work.

In this sense it is perhaps no accident that all but one of the Haydn symphonies
performed in or composed for London begin with a slow introduction. The exception,
no. 95, is also the only English symphony by Haydn in the minor mode. Though an
exception in London, it fits precisely in Haydn's œuvre; not one of his symphonies in
minor keys begins with a slow introduction. If the minor mode had a special expressive
niche in opposition to the major mode during the second half of the eighteenth century,
the lack of an introduction in Symphony no. 95 is explicable by the fact that a serious
'dark' patch appears in every slow introduction among the London works. By having
the main body of the movement in the minor mode a serious *exordium* to the Allegro is
no longer necessary.

The introduction often begins with a declamatory opening statement, followed
by a 'darker' area and a closing which leads to the main body of the movement.
Symphonies nos. 93, 96, 99, 102 and 104 use this plan, nos. 94 and 100 replace the first
section with a quiet but brightly coloured beginning, no. 98 alters and rearranges these
functions and nos. 101 and 103 are consistently of a dark and mysterious character.
While nos. 101 and 103 are clearly sublime in their effect throughout, others also
contain material that can be so considered. The introduction to Symphony no. 97 is the
only one that neither reaches for nor achieves sublimity.[50]

In Symphony no. 98 Haydn strips his introduction down to the barest of essentials, unison (octave) passages chiefly in the minor mode punctuated by annunciatory flourishes concluding with dotted rhythms; this certainly approaches Crotch's first category of the sublime. If no. 98 is tight in its presentation, no. 104 is more prolix; it combines three annunciatory unisons with quiet responses cloaked in mysterious harmonies, thereby juxtaposing two of Crotch's sublime types. However, it was Symphony no. 103, with its juxtaposition of sublime introduction and mostly ornamental main body, that engendered a narrative from the French critic and theorist Jérôme-Joseph de Momigny (1762–1842). Momigny supplied for this first movement both a musical and a 'picturesque'/poetic explication.[51]

For Momigny, the opening timpani roll represents a clap of thunder, which had frightened the peasant populace into the church to pray. First the men pray in chant style (b. 2), then the women (b. 14) with a sobbing accompaniment.[52] One can well imagine that the final bars with their *sforzandi* represent spasms of terror. The Allegro con spirito (6/8) begins with the ridicule of the devout by those less inclined to religious belief, and the shepherds and shepherdesses commence a country dance at the second subject (b. 80), with everyone joining in at the codetta (b. 87). After the double bar (b. 94) an argument commences, with accusations of unwarranted fear passing among the neighbours. Those who prayed are then mocked with a diminution of the material of the introduction (b. 112) and the country dance returns (b. 143). The recapitulation brings back the first subject (b. 159), the second subject (b. 179), and then builds to 'a moment of most violent crisis', its sublime climax [Ex. 5]. In its Adagio tempo, the introduction returns (b. 202) as the worshippers return to prayer before a terse, *a tempo* coda of the dance music; the clouds have dissipated and with them the terror experienced by the country folk.

Momigny's discussion seems uncanny in relation to Edmund Burke's treatise, which profferred the idea that 'Whatever is fitted in any sort to excite the ideas of pain, that is to say, whatever is in any sort terrible, or is conversant about terrible objects, or operates in a manner analogous to terror, is a source of the *sublime*; that is, it is productive of the strongest emotion which the mind is capable of feeling'.[53] Whether or not Momigny's account was influenced by Burke's concept of the sublime, the music of Haydn stimulated in the French theorist and critic the same emotions that the British aesthetician thought necessary for a sublime experience. In this example Haydn again combines elements of the ornamental and the sublime as defined by Crotch's criteria. But perhaps the main point in a piece of this sort is how the ornamental style becomes a foil for the sublime, thereby rendering the sublime gestures as enhanced climaxes.

Unlike the first movement of that of Symphony no. 103, Symphony no. 104 seems to play more on the style of the beautiful, which becomes transformed into a heroic/sublime climax rather than one that elicits terror. After the elevated introduc-

Ex. 5   Symphony no. 103/i, bb. 185–194

tion, Haydn's exposition incorporates every characteristic outlined in Crotch's *Specimens* as belonging to the beautiful. However, not until the second part of the move- ment (i.e. development and recapitulation) does Haydn reveal the crucial thematic element which will dominate: the third and fourth bars of the first subject (henceforth figure X). After a strong development, the opening period is restated for the recapitula- tion. Figure X then continues its development and builds to a climax (b. 228), receives further development, and moves to a second climax (b. 277), just before the final fan- fares and cadences. Here is Haydn at his calculating best: the concealment of figure X in the exposition and its revelation in the development, together with the subsequent

double peroration in the recapitulation can only be considered attainments of sublimity. Thus, the opening movements of Symphonies nos. 103 and 104 share a similar
structural strategy, even though their means and character are totally different.

One might argue that in these last two symphonies Haydn composes his most
effective first movements. They certainly caught the fancy of the audience in eighteenth-
century London. For this observer, however, the most sublime moment in all of these
works is to be found in a symphony which Robbins Landon believes to have been
among the least well received, no. 96, mistakenly named the *Miracle*.[54] After an
appropriately solemn introduction, the Allegro assai is saturated with ornamental

material. Its playfulness is the result of Haydn's careful manipulation of a simple rhyth‑
mic figure of three quarters, sometimes occurring as upbeats in a 3/4 bar and at other
times positioned on the downbeat. By keeping this figure at the forefront of attention
Haydn leaves no room for contrasting ideas. In the exposition, the most potent variant
occurs at the end of the first subject in the winds (b. 43), but this is offset by another
version of the rhythm in the strings. At the equivalent point in the recapitulation (b.
189), as the entire orchestra proclaims the fanfare rhythm on the dominant, which then
resolves unexpectedly to the tonic minor chord just before the final cadence. [Ex. 6].
This sublime moment is enhanced by the open‑ended phrases and grand pauses that
remain unresolved until this climax. It represents a turn in the action of the drama from

Ex. 6   Symphony no. 96/i, bb. 190–203

an almost comic to a tragic stance, a musical peripeteia that is the most thrilling gesture
in all of the London works.

In the first movements of Symphonies nos. 96, 103 and 104, the sublime passages,
especially in nos. 96 and no. 104, result from a long-term process. Except for Mozart,
Haydn and Beethoven, this concept seems foreign to late eighteenth-century musical
rhetoric, but it is one that became almost a requirement of symphonic music during the
nineteenth century. Today's musical *Kenner* and *Liebhaber* may find such notions as
'sublime' and 'climax' oxymorons when applied to music of the so-called 'Classical'
style. But with the recent revelations of historically informed performances using period
instruments in rooms of a size similar to those in which these works were first heard, it

has been possible to achieve expressive heights previously thought impossible or inappropriate. Even those whose sensitivities have been dulled by the overwrought expression and overpowering sonorities of Bruckner, Mahler and Richard Strauss find their reactions to late eighteenth-century orchestral music revitalized when the works are heard in circumstances and surroundings appropriate to their historical scale.

*   *   *

British critics at the turn of the nineteenth century and listeners of today agree on one example of sublimity in Haydn: the 'Representation of Chaos' in *The Creation* followed by 'And there was LIGHT', a dramatic moment with a doubly sublime background in that the words alone, considered sublime by Longinus, were subsequently rendered more powerful by Haydn's setting. Haydn accomplished his own sublimity by marshalling every available contrast, including changes of mode, texture, orchestra-

tion, dynamics and range, as well as the juxtaposition of chromaticism with tonal purity.[55] Even commentators such as Crotch, who did not appreciate *The Creation* as a whole, could not avoid expressing admiration for this sublime musical gesture. He called it 'awful', in the traditional sense of the word, but still found it wanting in dignity.[56] Such climaxes in both the London Symphonies, as well as *The Creation* and *The Seasons*, became models for Beethoven, who could not cast them aside as he sought repeatedly in his own works to recreate the gesture of darkness supplanted by light.[57] Such passages owe their origins to the concepts of the ornamental, the beautiful and the sublime in the writings of Burke, his antagonists and his proponents. Though the trans- formation of Haydn's symphonic style during the 1780s and 1790s is certainly a complex phenomenon, English aesthetic currents which formed the expectations of the London audience were significant contributors to the intensification of Haydn's musical rhetoric.[58]

ALBI ROSENTHAL

The Contract between Joseph Haydn and Frederick Augustus Hyde (1796)

IN HIS FIVE-VOLUME BIOGRAPHICAL STUDY, *Haydn. Chronicle and Works*, H.C. Robbins Landon noted:[1]

> By an extraordinary coincidence, the contract concluded in August 1796 between Haydn and Frederick Augustus Hyde in London turned up just before [the text of] this volume was delivered to the printers. The contract was sold at Sotheby's on 8 February 1976 and was purchased by Mr Richard Macnutt of Tunbridge Wells for some £2,800.[2]

A few years later the same document turned up at auction again, this time in New York, and is now in a private collection in England. This is one of the very few surviving contracts from the eighteenth century between a composer and his publisher, and the only one linking Haydn with an English publisher. The full text of the document, reproduced in Pls. 1–4, appears in print here for the first time. The summary description on the outer page of the contract reads:

Dated   1796

Mr Frederick Augustus Hyde
with
Doctor Haydn

Articles of Agreement

Medley
St Margaret Street Westminster

The text, together with the accompanying signatures and seals of the parties to the contract and their witnesses, occupies three ms. pages (each 360 × 248 mm). The content is presented line for line as in the original document (see pp. 77–9).

Pages 73–6: Pls. 1–4   Text and detail of outer page of Haydn's contract with Frederick Augustus Hyde.

Articles of Agreement

Indented had made concluded and fully agreed upon this 30th ———— day of July ———— in the year of our Lord One thousand seven Hundred and ninety six Between Frederick Augustus Hyde of the Haymarket in the City of Westminster Musick seller of the one Part and Joseph Haydn of Vienna Doctor of Musick of the other Part.—

The said Joseph Haydn doth hereby Covenant Promise and agree to and with the said Frederick Augustus Hyde in manner following (that is to say) that he the said Joseph Haydn shall and will Yearly and every Year for and during the time and term of Five Years if he the said Joseph Haydn shall so long live and continue in Health so as to be capable of Writing and Composing Musick Write and Compose new and Original Musick for the said Frederick Augustus Hyde as he the said Frederick Augustus Hyde shall request the same to be delivered at the several prices and according to the Rates hereinafter Mentioned And the said Joseph Haydn doth further Covenant Promise Grant and agree to and with the said Frederick Augustus Hyde that from and after such new and Original Musick shall be so Written for and delivered to the said Frederick Augustus Hyde the same shall become his absolute Property and no Copy thereof shall be delivered or sold by him the said Joseph Haydn to any other Person or Persons under any pretence or upon any Account whatsoever And the said Frederick Augustus Hyde Doth hereby Covenant Promise and agree to and with the said Joseph Haydn that he the said Frederick Augustus Hyde shall and will Yearly and every Year during the said Term of Five Years if he shall so long live purchase of the said Joseph Haydn new and Original Musick so to be composed and written as aforesaid to the Amount or Value of One Hundred and Fifty pounds and shall and will well and faithfully pay the said sum of One Hundred and fifty pounds as the same shall become due to or to the order of the said Joseph Haydn either at Vienna or elsewhere on the Delivery of such new and Original Compositions as aforesaid And the said Parties do hereby further mutually agree to and with each other that in Case he the said Joseph Haydn should write and compose Musick to a greater Value than the ————

said Sum of One Hundred and Fifty pounds in any one Year during the Term aforesaid then and in such Case He the said Frederick Augustus Hyde shall be at Liberty to purchase the same if he shall think proper at the usual prices specified in this Agreement And in all Cases he the said Frederick Augustus Hyde shall have the refusal thereof before the said Joseph Haydn shall offer the same to sale to any other Musick Seller whatsoever And it is further agreed by the said parties that in Case the said Joseph Haydn shall come to England at any time within the said time or term of Five Years and during the time of his residence in London the said Frederick Augustus Hyde shall request the said Joseph Haydn to compose either Quartetts or Simphonies and he shall be in health and capable of so doing He the said Frederick Augustus Hyde shall and will permit the said Joseph Haydn to produce such Quartetts and Simphonies in Public during the season for his Concerts before such Quartetts and Simphonies are printed And the said parties for the more effectually performing this agreement do hereby bind himself unto the other in the sum of Three Hundred pounds of Lawfull Money of Great Britain Provided Always Nevertheless it is hereby further mutually agreed by and between the said parties to these presents that if the said Frederick Augustus Hyde shall be minded or desirous to dissolve make void or disannul this agreement at the end or acepiration of the first three Years of the said Term of Five Years it shall and may be Lawful for the said Frederick Augustus Hyde so to do on giving to the said Joseph Haydn three Months previous Notice in writing of such his intention In Witness whereof the said parties to these presents have hereunto interchangeably set their hands and seals the day and Year first above Written.—

Sealed and Delivered
in the presence off

R: Schroeter
Edw.ᵈ _____ St. Margaret St. Westm.ᵈ

Fredk Augustus Hyde

Joseph Haydn, Doctor of Music.

Three Sonatas for the Piano Forte or Harpsicord with an   } £75
accompaniment for a Violin and Violoncello . . . .

Three Sonatas for the Piano Forte without accompaniment .   60

Three Quartetts for two Violins Tenn and Violoncello   75

Three Quartetts for different instruments . . . . . £ 75
Three Grand Sinfonies 100
Three Trios for the Flute 45
Three Quintetts or Sextetts 80
Six English Songs with accompt. for Piano Forte . . . 75
Six Italian Songs in the same manner 60
Six Italian Duetts 75
Six Glees 40
Six Catches 50
One Concert for the Piano forte with all Instruments . . 36
One Concertant Sinfonie 30
One Grand Italian Aria 20
One Violin Solo 15

Witness
R. Schroeter
Edwd. Radley

Fredk. Augustus Hyde

Praesens Instrumentum a Domino Josepho Haydn propria
manu subscriptum, et proprio Sigillo munitum fuisse, attestor. Viennae Die 10ma Augusti 1796.

Antonius Riedl Authoritate
Caesarea Notarius Publicus
juratus, et Advocatus in Cambialibus,
in fidem praemissorum legitime
requisitus.

Dated   1796

Mr. Frederick Augustus Hyde

with

Doctor Haydn . . . . . .

Articles of Agreement

Medley
St. Margaret Street Westminster

Articles of Agreement
Indented had made concluded and fully agreed
upon this 30th———day of July³———in the
year of our Lord One thousand seven Hundred
and Ninety six Between Frederick Augustus
Hyde of the Haymarket in the City of Westminster
Musick seller of the one part and Joseph
Haydn of Vienna Doctor of Musick of the
other part.——

The said Joseph Haydn doth hereby covenant promise and agree
to and with the said Frederick Augustus Hyde in manner
following / that is to say / that he the said Joseph Haydn shall and
will yearly and every year for and during the time and term
of Five years if he the said Joseph Haydn shall so long live
and continue in Health so as to be capable of Writing and Composing
Musick Write and Compose new and Original Musick for the said
Frederick Augustus Hyde as he the said Frederick Augustus Hyde
shall request the same to be delivered at the several prices and
according to the Rates hereinafter Mentioned And the said Joseph
Haydn doth further Covenant Promise Grant and Agree to and
with the said Frederick Augustus Hyde that from and after such
new and Original Musick shall be written for and delivered to
the said Frederick Augustus Hyde the same shall become his
absolute Property and no copy thereof shall be delivered or sold
by him the said Joseph Haydn to any other Person or Persons
under any pretence or upon any account whatsoever And the
said Frederick Augustus Hyde Doth hereby Covenant Promise
and agree to and with the said Joseph Haydn that he the said
Frederick Augustus Hyde shall and will yearly and every year
during the said Term of Five years if he shall so long live purchase
of the said Joseph Haydn new and Original Musick so to be composed
and written as aforesaid to the amount or value of One Hundred and
Fifty pounds and shall and will well and faithfully pay the said
sum of One Hundred and fifty pounds as the same shall become
due to or to the order of the said Joseph Haydn either of Vienna or
elsewhere on the Delivery of such new and Original Compositions as
aforesaid And the said parties do hereby further mutually agree
to and with each other that in case he the said Joseph Haydn
should write and compose Musick to a greater Value than the

[p. 2]

said sum of One Hundred and Fifty pounds in any one year during
the Term aforesaid then and in such case He the said Frederick
Augustus Hyde shall be at Liberty to purchase the same if he shall
think proper at the usual prices specified in the Agreement And in
all cases he the said Frederick Augustus Hyde shall have the refusal
thereof before the said Joseph Haydn shall offer the same to
sale to any other Musick Seller whatsoever And it is further agreed by
the said parties that in case the said Joseph Haydn shall come
to England at any time within the said time or term of Five Years
and during the time of his residence in London the said Frederick
Augustus Hyde shall request the said Joseph Haydn to compose
either Quartetts or Simphonies and he shall be in health and
capable of so doing He the said Frederick Augustus Hyde shall and
will permit the said Joseph Haydn to produce such Quartetts and Simphonies
in Public during the season for the Concerts before such Quartetts and
Simphonies are printed And the said parties for the more effectually
performing this Agreement do hereby bind himself unto the other
in the sum of Three Hundred pounds of lawful Money of Great
Britain PROVIDED ALWAYS Nevertheless it is hereby further
mutually agreed by and between the said parties to these presents
that if the said Frederick Augustus Hyde shall be minded or desirous
to dissolve make void or disannul this Agreement at the end or expiration
of the first three years of the said Term of Five years it shall and may
be Lawful for the said Frederick Augustus Hyde so to do on giving
to the said Joseph Haydn three Months previous Notice in Writing of
such his intention IN WITNESS whereof the said parties to these presents
have hereunto interchangeably set their hands and seals the day and year first above
written. —

Sealed and Delivered   [signed] Fredk Augustus Hyde   (seal EM)
in the presence of   (seal JH) [signed] Joseph Haydn Doctor of Music

[signed:] R. Schroeter
[signed:] Edwd Medley St. Margaret St. Westm^r

Three Sonatas for the Piano Forte or Harpsicord [*sic*] with an
accompaniment for a Violin and Violoncello £75
Three Sonatas for the Piano Forte without accompaniment...60
Three Quartettos for two Violins Tenor and Violoncello...75

[p. 3]

Three Quartettos for different instruments 75

Three Grand Sinfonies 100

Three Trios for the Flute 45

Three Quintetts or Sextetts 80

Six English Songs with accompts. for Piano Forte 75

Six Italian songs in the same manner 60

Six Italian Duetts 75

Six Glees 40

Six Catches 50

One Concert for the Piano forte with all Instruments 36

One Concertant Sinfonie 30

One Grand Italian Aria 20

One Violin Solo 15

Witness   [signed:] Fredk Augustus Hyde
[signed:] R. Schroeter
      Edwd. Medley

Praesens Instrumentum a Domino Josepho Haÿdn propria
manu subscriptum, et proprio Sigillo munitum fuisse attestor.
Viennae Die 10ma Augusti 1796.

      (Notarial Seal   Antonius Riedl impria Authoritate
      of A. Riedl)   Cæsarea Notarius Publicus
                      juratus, et Avocatus in Cambialibus,
                      in fidem præmissorum legitime
                      requisitus.

Thus, the contract was written in London in July 1796 and signed there by Hyde in the presence of Rebecca Schroeter and Edward Medley. Shortly afterwards, on 10 August, the document was signed and sealed by Haydn in Vienna, and attested by the notary public Anton Riedl.

    Frederick Augustus Hyde is a rather shadowy figure among English music publishers of the period. His name is not listed separately in any of the standard works on music publishing in Great Britain and is mentioned, if at all, only in his capacity of partner in firms such as Longman & Broderip (which went bankrupt in 1798) and subsequently in the new partnership with John Longman, Frederick William Collard, Josiah Banger and David Davis. According to Humphries & Smith,[4] there was also a firm named Lewis Houston & Hyde, Music Sellers and Publishers, 45 Holborn, from

1795 to 1797, who succeeded John Bland and advertised the business for sale ('ca. 12000 plates') in March 1797. The new firm of Longman, Clementi & Co. was in business at the former premises of Longman & Broderip in Cheapside until June 1800. Longman then left to establish his own firm, and the new partnership began publish￿ ing under the imprint Clementi, Banger, Hyde, Collard and Davis (sometimes, more briefly, Clementi & Co.). *The British Library Catalogue of Printed Music* lists[5] under HYDE, Frederick Augustus: 'A Miscellaneous Collection of Songs, Ballads, Canzonets. . . . compiled by Fred^k. Aug^s. Hyde. 2 vol. Printed for F. Hyde, F.W. Collard, & D. Davis, by Longman & Broderip, London, [1798].' A reissue in 1800 was published by Clementi & Co.; Hoboken has a note 'Hyde. 1810+ führt Clementi & Co.'s "A Miscellaneous Collection of Songs" ab 1810 allein weiter'.[6]

The present contract appears to be the only known document in which Hyde functions as sole and independent 'Music Seller'. H.C. Robbins Landon has suggested that the contract may be 'the written result of a verbal agreement made about 1794',[7] which may indicate that Frederick Augustus Hyde acted briefly as an independent music seller from that date onward (until *c.* 1797). It was certainly a very remarkable achievement for him to secure a contract with the celebrated Dr Haydn and to have it offi￿ cially signed, sealed and delivered in Vienna on 10 August 1796. It may well be that Hyde was initially hoping to publish as many of the 55 works proposed in the agreement as Haydn might be able to supply in the five ensuing years. However, he must have real￿ ized soon after it came into force that he could survive only as an associate of or partner in more powerful firms, under whose imprints, with or without a mention of his name, some of the works specified in the contract were eventually printed, e.g. the 'Three Sonatas for the Piano Forte or Harpsichord with an accompaniment for a Violin & Violoncello' (op. 75) which Longman & Broderip published in 1797, and the 'Three Quartetts' (op. 76, nos. 1–3) which were issued by Longman, Clementi & Co. in 1799.

One or two further references to the ubiquitous, but elusive Hyde can be quoted: he figures in the list of Subscribers to the first edition of *The Creation* ('Mr. Hyde') – as does Rebecca Schroeter, who witnessed Hyde's signature on the document – and a letter was addressed by Haydn to 'Mr Hyde and Clementi, No. 26 Cheapside, London', on 28 April 1801,[8] saying that *The Seasons*, newly performed in Vienna, had been received with the same approbation as *The Creation*. He also writes that he intends to compose '3 good pianoforte sonatas [i.e. Piano Trios] by the end of the summer', but these were never written.

According to H.C. Robbins Landon, 'the contract is perhaps not, strictly speak￿ ing, an agreement for these 55 works, but rather a price table to be used against whatever Haydn could and would deliver.'[9] This view seems to be confirmed by the fact that Haydn, in 1796 or shortly afterwards, sent the E flat Trio, no. 42 (Hob. XV:30), not only to Leipzig, but also to Corri & Dussek in London, and presumably he sold the work to Artaria as well, for textually the Leipzig and Vienna prints, while similar, are independent. Each must have had an ms. copy of the autograph by Johann Elssler similar to the one now in the Esterházy Archives in Budapest.[10]

Whereas the name of Hyde is relatively little known, that of Rebecca Schroeter is a familiar one to devotees of Haydn. The widow of the pianist and composer Johann Samuel Schroeter (1752–88), she maintained a close friendship with Haydn during his visits to London, as evidenced by the loving letters from her which the composer copied into his London notebooks. Haydn was to remark to his biographer Georg August Griesinger that he might have married Mrs Schroeter had he been free to do so. H.C. Robbins Landon comments on her being a witness to the contract: 'It is touching that Haydn's friend Rebecca Schroeter was still [i.e. a year after his return to Vienna] acting as a go-between for him in England.'[11]

The most revealing document about the contract is a letter, written from Vienna by Haydn's biographer Georg August Griesinger to Christoph Gottlob Härtel in Leipzig. Dated 12 June 1799, it contains the following passage: 'His [i.e. Haydn's] publisher in England is Mr. Bay, a rather unimportant man, as Haydn said, but associated with Clementi and Broderip. His agreement is for five years, of which three are now finished, and Bay has agreed to take everything he composes, and the price of every psalm, sonata, &c. has been established beforehand. But because of the great amount of work on his shoulders, he has only delivered some quartets in these three years, and these were sent to England quite recently. Bay is pushing him especially hard for piano sonatas, but up to now he hasn't been able to fulful his wish . . .'[12]

There can be no doubt that Griesinger, quoting Haydn, is referring to the present contract. In the welter of names of associates and partners of the London publishing houses, with their constant changes of names and personnel referred to above, it is not surprising that, when Haydn called an otherwise unidentifiable 'Mr. Bay' his 'publisher in England', he actually meant 'Mr. Hyde'.

Griesinger's letter also indicates that in spite of some negotiations with other firms, Haydn still regarded himself as tied, if only loosely, to the contract with Hyde. During 1796 and in succeeding years Haydn was fully occupied composing masses, *The Creation* (both of these categories not called for in Hyde's contract) and other works. As Griesinger wrote to Härtel, Haydn could not supply more of the intended compositions on account of 'the great amount of work on his shoulders'.

The contract remains a great testimony to Haydn's astonishing productivity and to his confidence in its future during the prolific London periods (he had finally left London on 15 August 1795). In the end, its promise was to remain unfulfilled, but:

UT DESINT VIRES, TAMEN EST LAUDANDA VOLUNTAS.[13]

CHRISTOPHER HOGWOOD

In praise of arrangements: the 'Symphony Quintetto'

FOR THE THIRD of his regular Thursday lectures given at the Royal Institution in London in 1828, Samuel Wesley chose the subject of 'Chamber Musick':

> That Species of musical Composition which I conceive to be best fitted for the Chamber or private Concert Room ought to consist of vocal Solos, Songs[,] Duets, Trios, & Quartettos, (the Words not being exclusively confined to any one Language –) and Instrumental Solos, Duets, Trios, & Quartettos, & Quintettos.
>
> Notwithstanding that this appears to me the most rational Distribution of Chamber Music, I have not forgotten that certain invaluable Works originally constructed for a full Band have been very ingeniously contracted for the convenient Accommodation of small musical Parties: – and among them let me instance twelve delectable Symphonies of Haydn, which have been reduced from the Score with extraordinary Ingenuity and accurate Judgement, by the late accomplished and energetic Master of his Art, John Peter Salomon, and nicely adapted for two Violins, Tenor, Base, Flute, & a supporting accompaniment on the Piano Forte.[1]

It must have seemed a little strange to his audience, as it does to us today, that Wesley's first mention of a specific item of chamber music should be an arrangement – where were the Mozart quartets, the Beethoven trios, even the Weber or the Onslow? But Wesley seems to have had a particular affection for these pieces and their arranger. He returned to them several times in his *Reminiscences* of 1836 ('. . . twelve inimitable Symphonies for a grand Orchestra which were afterwards ably and successfully adapted for four stringed Instruments [*sic*] with a Piano Forte Accompaniment' and elsewhere 'twelve Symphonies, all of which may be justly enumerated among the most valuable of his Productions, and are replete with the most erudite & interesting succession of varieties. These have been reduced from Score with extraordinary . . .'), and he declared that Salomon 'may justly [be] ranked among the most acute, dispassionate, and liberal Criticks that we find in the Annals of English musical Literature'.[2] But at the time of Wesley's lecture Haydn had been dead nearly twenty years, Salomon himself had died in 1815, and the symphony arrangements had been available in print for more than a quarter of a century; true, the London symphonies were born immortal, but these must be exceptional and long-lived adaptations to warrant this puff, and, one suspects, worth at least a moment's study.

Today, the words 'arranged by . . .' are anathema to scholars and a deterrent to many performers. But in the fast-expanding world of commercial music-making at the turn of the eighteenth century, arrangement was for composers a way of life and for publishers a sure way of prospering; many of their better-wrought products could easily be taken into the repertoire of today's performers.

Normally adaptations would be from larger to smaller forces; in particular the 'top and bottom' style of the galant and Italianate composers could readily be translated from largest to smallest forces, and 'The Celebrated Overture . . . adapted for the Pianoforte or Harpsichord' was a common title in the catalogues of Bland, Preston, Longman & Broderip, Birchall and Monzani & Cimador, to mention only a selection of London publishers. Thin though the textures of such pieces may seem, these adaptations could be an effective replacement for, say, a Scarlatti group in a modern harpsichordist's programme. Similarly, the collections of 'Leichter Clavierstücke' adapted from symphonic slow movements that feature in the lists of Breitkopf & Härtel, Artaria, Hoffmeister and Simrock justify the German enthusiasm for expressive clavichord repertoire, and could well be revived today.[3]

Arrangements made by the original composer are more acceptable – Mozart's quintet version of the C minor Serenade (K.388), for example, or Beethoven's strikingly rethought version of his Second Symphony as a piano trio – but the door should also be open to Gelinek's excellent version of the Clarinet Quintet (K.581) for piano quartet,[4] the wind-ensemble transcription of Beethoven's Seventh Symphony, C.F.G. Schwencke's adaptation of Mozart's B flat Serenade (K.361) for oboe, fortepiano and strings, and the anonymous transcription of Haydn's Sinfonia Concertante for string sextet (all arrangements, incidentally, providing challenging textual comparisons with their originals). An even more general plea should be made in passing for the resurrection of original, playable and stylish keyboard scores of eighteenth-century opera and oratorio, rather than the usual modern short-score of Richard Strauss-like density, with a texture quite unsuited to the appropriate vocal style, and frequently quite unplayable.

Some present-day antipathy to arrangements springs from their association with 'extracts'; not every movement of a symphony was suitable for transcription, nor even every item in a sequence of variations. Haydn was both scrupulous and practical on this point; in his own exemplary keyboard arrangement of the variations on 'Gott erhalte Franz den Kaiser' he retained all four variations but adapted the part-writing to suit the keyboard.[5] Earlier, however, in a letter to Artaria (8 April 1783)[6] he had criticized a keyboard arrangement of the *Laudon* Symphony (no. 69) and removed a whole movement: 'I send you herewith the Symphony, Sir, which was so full of mistakes the fellow who made it should have his paw chopped off. The last or 4th movement is not practicable for the keyboard, and I don't think it is necessary to include it in the print.'

The keyboard version of Symphony no. 96, once thought to be autograph,[7] omits the slow movement; the final Presto is also cut from the ingenious keyboard version of the variation movement from Symphony no. 31 (*Hornsignal*) published anonymously as 'Andantino con VII variazioni' in Rellstab's *Clavier-Magazin* (1787).

An arrangement of the 'al roverso' minuet and trio from Symphony no. 47, presumably made by Haydn himself, although it is missing from the autograph, was included ten years earlier as the second movement of the Sonata in A major (Hob. XVI:26), and in 1791 the composer sent a keyboard arrangement of the slow movement of Symphony no. 95 from London as a present to Maria Anna von Genzinger.[8] However, when the score appears to have been lost in the post, he tells her that she can make the arrangements of the two (whole?) symphonies nos. 95 and 96 herself, if she feels so inclined.[9] From these letters, and from his correspondence with Artaria over the proofs of the keyboard version of the *Seven Last Words*, we see that while Haydn was concerned over the idiomatic nicety of an arrangement, he was perfectly prepared to farm it out to a musician he could trust (as Mozart did, for example, with Kuchař for his operatic piano scores) and happy to see the result in print.

In the case of Haydn's symphonies, while single movements of the earlier works were clearly eligible for transcription to a variety of media, the cyclic nature of the later works was respected with publication *in toto*. Bland, introducing his series of four 'Grande Orchestre Sinfonie as Performed at the Nobility's Concerts; Adapted for the Organ, Harpsichord, or Piano Forte . . . by Mr. Tindal' (*c.* 1790), was anxious that the public realize this was 'Not a Mutilated Copy but the Intire [*sic*] Symphony'. His series took in nos. 47, 85, 73 and 69 – the last including the final movement, which Haydn himself had thought not practicable for keyboard, but which William Tindal managed with some dexterity.

But there was a limit to the technical demands that the amateur market could accommodate, and Bland had his eye on larger chamber groups with his series of twelve symphonies (issued from 1782 onwards) in parts for full orchestra,[10] but with the additional rubric on each title page that 'This Sinfonie may be played as a Quintett'. It is not clear exactly how this system coped with wind solos, nor in fact what parts the quintet should play, since both cello and double bass used the same Basso part. Later issues were modified to read 'as a Quartett', but this still left the problem of wind solos, which occur in most works in the set. Commercial instinct seems here to have run ahead of musical common sense.

Salomon signed an agreement with Haydn for the rights on the first six London symphonies on 13 August 1795, just before the composer left England for the last time; from Vienna on 27 February 1796 Haydn sent the contract for the second set of six (one wonders why this delay?), and Salomon was now free to exploit his property. This consisted of his personal set of parts, plus newly copied scores made from Haydn's origi-nals (save for Symphonies nos. 95 and 96, for which Salomon had the autographs). These scores, which passed after Salomon's death to William Ayrton and from him to the Royal Philharmonic Society, were first noted by Alec Hyatt King in 1981, and described by Arthur Searle.[11] The initial publication (and possibly pirating) of the orchestral parts by André, Artaria, Simrock, Imbault and others has been covered by Landon and colleagues. Salomon's decision to delegate the publication of orchestral material but to make and self-publish two different arrangements of the whole set has received less attention. Clearly his aim was the widest dissemination of these remark-able works; keyboard transcriptions came first, 'Adapted for the Piano Forte, with an Accompaniment for a Violin & Violoncello, (ad libitum)', which are described as for piano trio, although the entire musical content is contained in the keyboard part (as it is, for instance, in the later Clementi and Hummel arrangements). These were published in three batches, and entered at Stationers' Hall: nos. 1–4 (25 June 1796), nos. 5–6 (1 July 1796) and nos. 7–12, after an unexplained gap, on 2 October 1797 (not 30 September as usually given).[12]

Inevitably, much detail had to be omitted in this transcription (the missing horn calls at the end of the *London* Symphony's slow movement are only one of many star-tling gaps), and some moments call for heroic pianism. Although of great interest tex-tually, these trios cannot give a very fair representation of the whole symphonic texture.[13] Salomon solved this problem 'with extraordinary Ingenuity' by an alternative arrangement 'for five Instruments, vizt. Two Violins, a German Flute, a Tenor, and a Violoncello: with an Accompaniment for the Piano Forte ad libitum. . . . Pr. 15s . . . NB A separate Bass Part pr. 2s 6d.' Publication was announced in *The Times* on 19 June 1798, but despite the claim on the title page, no entry for these works has yet been traced in the Stationers' Hall records.[14]

There was little precedent for this chamber combination, although its very longevity defends Salomon's 'accurate Judgement'. The Kraus flute quintets of 1783 appeared in print only in 1799, and Boccherini's two sets from the early 1770s (G.419–24, G.425–30) spoke a very different language. The unique but problematic sextet by Stephen Storace is the model nearest to hand, though here the keyboard, far from being *ad libitum*, is hyperactive.[15]

As a vehicle for orchestral transcription the combination proved immediately successful, and Salomon negotiated almost simultaneous publication in Bonn with Simrock, who had already issued the trio arrangements. A first announcement, 'Neue Musikalien . . . bey Günther und Böhme in Hamburg . . . Haydn. 3 Quintetti arr. des gr. Sinfonies à une Flûte, 2 Violons, Alto et Violoncelle avec acc. de Pianoforte ad lib.', is found in the Intelligenz-Blatt of the *Allgemeine musikalische Zeitung* for March 1799.[16]

Later issues appeared in England from Robert Birchall (with whom Salomon published the orchestral material after Haydn's death), the rights eventually passing to Birchall's son-in-law Richard Mills (Mills and Lonsdale, *c.* 1830). It has always been assumed that these editions were identical, and they have been used thus for reference (and recording);[17] in fact each later issue was altered and adapted. The Simrock readings have yet to be collated with the various English texts, as has the later expanded collection by Gambaro in Paris (see Appendix for a listing of 'quintetto' publications).

Fortunately, Salomon's autograph score used for the first engraving not only clarifies his intentions, but in it (as a composing copy) we can trace his procedures and experiments, and garner evidence both of the changes that overtook the London versions of these pieces, and of that collaboration between author and performer which was so much part of eighteenth-century musical practice. 'Every performer is co-author of the work he performs'[18] and here the modern performer can find a 'catalyst' text to place alongside the *Urtext*. It may be observed that all 'historically informed' performance groups today alter, adapt or add to the markings that are provided in an *Urtext* (though some ensembles are more reluctant to admit it than others). Pencils, bowings, bar numbers (and conductors!) are as integral to rehearsal now as they were absent from concert-preparation in Haydn's time. This being so, it is useful for the modern performer to have access to a 'catalyst' set of alternatives from a source that is both technically accomplished and as close to the composer as one can reasonably hope to find. Mostly we consult normal secondary material, in which a copyist – in Haydn's case the trusted Johann Elssler – is simply and obediently aiming to reproduce, or clarify, what the composer notated; with Salomon we have the contribution of a performing musician who worked alongside Haydn from the conception of many of these symphonies and saw them through first (and consequent) performances and eventually into print in a variety of forms. What was discussed privately, or tried experimentally in rehearsal we may never know, although the gradual emergence of more of the London performance material is helping to illuminate this tantalising area, and giving increased credibility to the ideas found in the 'quintettos'.[19]

Salomon's score is now held in the Cinema-Television Library and Archives of Performing Arts, University of Southern California.[20] The volume is labelled on the spine: 'Haydn's / XII Symphonies / as Quintetts / in score', and the title page, handwritten in a printed nineteenth-century cartouche, reads:

XII GRAND SYMPHONIES, By HAYDN,
arranged as Quintets, by J.P. SALOMON.
(The original Score in Mr. Salomon's hand-writing.)

The description and the binding are probably the responsibility of William Ayrton,[21] who presumably inherited this score with all Salomon's music that was left to him in 1815.[22] There is no mention of the volume in the sale of Ayrton's musical effects on 3 July 1858 (Puttick & Simpson sale catalogue, British Library P.R. 2.D.15 (7)); the bookplate of the collector Edward Wrey Whinfield (died 1904) provides the only clue to its whereabouts until it was bought by the film-score composer Alfred Newman in the 1950s.

The manuscript, originally two volumes, now bound in one and containing symphonies numbered I–VI and VII–XII, is written on English paper 9½ × 11¾ inches, watermarked with a crown over fleur-de-lys in shield and 'GR 1794'.[23] The date – if it can be taken as an indication of the year of composition – is surprisingly early; Salomon had no contract yet with Haydn, and yet the hasty script, particularly in the later symphonies, is obviously written under pressure. Possibly the quintettos were to be performed in MS. before publication, maybe even before Haydn's departure?

The twelve symphonies are arranged in the traditional order as follows:

Vol. 1			Vol. 2		
Symphony	Page	Modern numbering	Symphony	Page	Modern numbering
1	1	97	7	1	104 (*London/Salomon*)
2	35	93	8	34	103 (*Drum Roll*)
3	64	94 (*Surprise*)[24]	9	67	102
4	96	98	10	99	99
5	130	95	11	128	101 (*Clock*)
6	152	96 (*Miracle*)	12	164	100 (*Military*)

The score is laid out for Flauto, Viol. 1mo, Viol. 2do, Viola and Violoncello (replacing 'Basso' which has been deleted at the start of Symphony no. 1). There is no indication of an independent double-bass line in the arrangement; the separate part advertised by the publishers was probably an individual cello part to avoid the inconvenience of playing from the left hand of the pianoforte part. (The Simrock edition, which must have been made from material supplied by Salomon, does have a specific part marked for 'Violoncello e Basso', the two instruments carefully distinguished, but for the most part related to the full orchestral version.) There is no written-out keyboard part in the score; the bass line is figured at first, fully in Symphony no. 1, sparsely in no. 2 (bb.112–15), after which Salomon (if it is his hand) gives up. [Fig. 1]

The first questions concern Salomon's sources and working methods. Since this is a working score, not only the deletions and experiments, but also the sureness of hand help us to reconstruct his procedures. From his corrections and second thoughts it is clear that he was copying from a score, specifically, it has been assumed, from the 'Royal

Fig. 1   Symphony no. 97: the opening of the first movement in Salomon's quintet arrangement with figured bass (Vol. 1, p. 1).

Philharmonic Society' scores (now BL Add. 64931–64942). We can now demonstrate that the alterations made to these scores, discussed by Arthur Searle,[25] are largely
in Salomon's hand, since pencilled annotations in the same hand in BL Add. 64937
f.22r show a working-out of a passage in his own quintetto arrangement (no.
104/i/bb.247–50). Here note-heads, rests and clefs correspond to Salomon's hand, and
the pencil version of this problematic passage has finally been incorporated on a paste-
over in Salomon's score (Vol. 2, p. 10).

However, not all the corrected readings in the London full-scores are reproduced
in the quintetto version. In fact Salomon's readings, though rarely unique, are never
concordant with one single source (neither the London scores, nor the parts which
relate to the London performances under Haydn, now in Donaueschingen, or the versions later published by Birchall from Salomon's material). These differences remain to
be studied in detail, but the quintetto version would seem to 'freeze' those changes that
Salomon made up to the date of arrangement; later corrections could have been made
up to his death in 1815, although the changes made by Haydn after his return to Vienna
did not find their way back to London. The accuracy of the first version of the printed
parts leaves much to be desired; although it can be shown that the engraver (perhaps
more than one) was working from Salomon's manuscript (see below), there are many
arbitrary changes, misplacings, omissions and, more interestingly, additions. The distinction between dots and daggers is preserved, though not in accordance with the
Salomon's markings, and a number of new dynamic marks appear. Clearly there was
some supplementary stage (either a cursory proof-reading or a comparison with a
marked set of working parts), but the variants that are present are too careless to allow
the printed parts to be treated as a reliable source. Sample evidence can be arranged in
the following categories:

Correlations with London scores (= LON) and Birchall parts:
no. 94/i/b.167: Violin 2 as autograph, not as altered in LON and Birchall's plates;
no. 96/iv/b.70 as autograph, not LON/Birchall (or other sources);
no. 99/ii/b.21: Violin 2 (= oboe) in LON, London/Birchall version, not autograph;
no. 99/iv/b.41: Flute has B flat as in LON alteration and Birchall, rather than G as in
   the autograph;
no. 101/i/b.168: Violin 2 has G, not F sharp as altered in LON and as the London
   (Donaueschingen) and Birchall parts;
no. 101/i/bb.207–8: Violin 2 and Viola changes confirm the alteration made by
   Salomon in the London scores, making bb.207–8 a repeat of bb.203–4. Here,
   however, LON is first altered and then changed back to the first version (? in
   another hand);

no. 101/i/bb.321–2: does not include the wind parts added later to LON;

no. 101/ii/b.115: Salomon takes LON/Birchall Oboe 2 part, but then deletes it;

no. 104/i/b.270: Vc (=horn) as Birchall, not autograph; =LON alteration.

Changes not transmitted from Vienna:

no. 97/iv marked 'Spiritoso', not Haydn's later 'Presto assai';

no. 102/iii/bb.31–4: Salomon has the London version, without the later Viennese wind parts;

no. 96/iv: 'Vivace' not 'Vivace assai'.

Engraving errors deriving from the Salomon MS.:

no. 94/iv/b.79: the engraver's confusion shows that he was working from the score;

no. 104/i/b.109: Violin 2, note 4 corrected from A to G sharp but not well enough for the engraver, who reads A (as in Trio version, and Birchall). LON gives G sharp.

Additions and alterations in the printed parts:

no. 94/i, bb.143–7 of the cello part are empty in Salomon's score. The printed part is not identical to the orchestral version;

no. 94/ii/b.153: the Viola part has an added 'caland[o]';

no. 104/ii/b.45 has a revised Viola part.

In the first movement of the *Clock* symphony, two passages that underwent revision by Haydn give an indication of the complex relationship of the trio and quintet arrangements vis-à-vis the orchestral versions; for bb.130–3, Salomon's quintet manuscript, his printed parts and the Simrock edition all follow the autograph reading (though Salomon offers different articulation). [Ex. 1]

Haydn autograph

Salomon

(*)

(*) The MS is unclear: C and D are given. The printed parts give C, but omit the slurs in the third bar.

On the other hand, both Salomon's trio arrangement and the quintets as later issued by Birchall and Mills & Lonsdale follow the notes of the Birchall (Salomon) orchestral version, but again with varied articulation. [Ex. 2]

A similar passage was altered towards the end of the same movement (bb.315ff.); here, however, all the Salomon arrangements and Simrock follow the autograph, and only Mills & Lonsdale follows Birchall's orchestral parts. [Ex. 3]

A *pons asinorum* is the Trio – called 'Alternativo' by Salomon[26] – of the same symphony, where Haydn's intention was clearly to have an unchanging D major harmony accompanying the flute for twelve bars. In Salomon's score the harmony changes for bb.6 and 7, but the whole passage was then crossed out. [Fig. 2] There is no corrected version, nor any sign of a paste-over (as found elsewhere with major corrections), yet in the printed parts the 'correct' Haydn text is given. However, in Simrock, and in Birchall's later set, it is again altered (and in Mills & Lonsdale the string parts are rewritten to include Violin 1 *and* the altered harmony). To compound the problem, the piano part issued with Salomon's first print has the altered harmony, thus contradicting the published string parts. Presumably that part must have been made from the score, and possibly not by Salomon; one senses here a difference of opinion between Salomon and Haydn.

In many of his working methods Salomon was at his most ingenious when presented with an awkward demand by Haydn. The changing of orchestral texture was very important to him; the bassoon doubling of a violin line (taken by the viola in no. 104/iii, for example), or the subtle way that Salomon distinguished between the solo quartet opening of no. 93/ii and the tutti repeat of the same material (bb.9ff.), where he

Fig. 2   Symphony no. 101/iii: Salomon's deletion in the Trio ('Alternativo') of the quintet version (Vol. 2, p. 152).

thickens the textures with viola doubling (=bassoon) and Violin 2 double-stops and cello octaves. [Ex. 4]

The variety of perspective when the winds take over the argument is represented for Salomon by the absence of Violin 1, a sense of power in reserve for the re-entry of the tutti (no. 100/i/bb.200–9 for the reappearance of the tutti at b.210), even when this entails Violin 2 taking over both violin parts in double-stopping. He cannot resist making a censorius note when he discovers bad grammar (in the finale of no. 94, for instance he marks bars 14 and 15 with a cross and notes '2 fifths' in the margin), though, just occasionally, there is a sense of triumph when he chooses a line for Violin 1 differing from the original and in the process by-passes a problem that Haydn had to

Ex. 4

contend with; in no. 100/ii/b.110, for instance, he followed the Clarinet 1 part and in so doing created a more fluent Viola line, side-stepping the consecutive octaves that faced Haydn. [Ex. 5]

Fig. 3 Symphony no. 99/i: Salomon's treatment of Haydn's accent > as an extended diminuendo at the beginning of the development section. Note also the flute cue in Violin 1 (Vol. 2, p. 103).

As we have seen, although Salomon altered very few notes in his transcription, in matters of phrasing, bowing and dynamics his treatment appears cavalier. It is not hard to distinguish those changes that are made for purely practical reasons: a new rhythm in no. 101/i/b.75 to assist the double-stop, or the slur added to no.101/iii/bb.130ff. to help the effect of the decrescendo. Salomon also had personal preferences; he favoured repeated notes under one bow, for which he used the notation of a wavy line, accented up-beats and syncopations, scale passages slurred to their final note, and 'sf' rather than Haydn's 'fz'.[27] Where Haydn had first introduced the new accent sign (>) at the beginning of the development section of no. 99/i, Salomon very firmly interpreted it as an extended diminuendo. [Fig. 3]

Many other changes seem whimsical, yet offer an interesting alternative for the performer; nowhere do these arrangements support the conventional claim that in the eighteenth century amateur string-playing was incompetent (a view usually advanced to excuse the piano trios). In particular Salomon is never afraid to expand the viola's role well beyond its symphonic status to accommodate missing instrumental parts.

None of Salomon's alternatives lies outside the purlieu of normal late eighteenth-century style; none would have shocked Haydn — several in fact tally with the sort of changes the composer himself made in his string quartets[28] — though some may be thought more apt for one-to-a-part chamber music. He abandons, for instance, the 'al ponticello' effect for the violins in no. 97/ii/b.84 when the dynamic is *forte*, but gives 'Sul Ponticello' in bb.92 and 98 in *piano* (original = 'vicino al ponticello'); he reverts to 'Naturale' in bb.100–10, while Haydn carries the marking right through to b.127, clearly suggesting that at close quarters Salomon felt there could be too much of a good effect. The changed bowing is very much Salomon's own, however. [Fig. 4]

Other devices increase the dynamic variety and contrast of the smaller group; *forte* semiquaver passages will sound more active when not slurred in groups of four, while a *piano* effect can be enhanced by the addition of a slur (no. 96/ii/b.34). Added dynamics

Fig. 4   Symphony no. 97/ii/bb.89–103: an example of Salomon's 'sul ponticello' markings in the Violin parts (Vol. 1, pp. 16–17).

help to distinguish horns from woodwinds (no. 101/ii/bb.121–3, or no. 99/iii/bb.69ff.), and the horn parts are even marked '*f*' when the overall dynamic is '*p*' (no. 97/iv), suggesting an assertive eighteenth-century style of playing. On the other hand, Salomon uses '*mf*', a rare marking for Haydn (no. 99/iii/b.41, no. 104/ii/b.149) and the joke of no. 104/iii/b.44 is '*piano*'.

In several cases Salomon's solutions supplement a Haydn effect, and suggest an interpretation that might have been given verbally at rehearsal by the composer: the crescendo from b.343 to b.356 in no. 98/i, the *fortissimo* in no. 104/i/b.172, and the crescendo and diminuendo in the bridge passage (bb.95–104) before the da capo Minuetto in no. 104 (often a stagnant moment in orchestral performances).

Other additions suggest players' contributions in rehearsal; little trills added to flute and 'oboe 1' in no. 104/iv/b.286, and the omission of the tie in no. 94/ii/bb.96 and 104 for flute and 'oboe' are imitable whims that could, out of curiosity, be tried in the full orchestral version. Note also Salomon's struggles to reduce the following *fortissimo* tutti (no. 94/ii/b.107) to quintetto proportions. [Fig. 5]

Salomon's markings of his 'own' solos are few: no. 95/i/b.139 (originally unmarked) is given staccato dots, and the solo in no. 96/ii/b.75 is resolutely without a trill on the first tied note in his MS. (as in Haydn), although it is added in all the printed parts. The solo in no. 103/ii is almost unphrased (just a few differences marked in bb.85–6) and the 'Salomon Solo ma piano' octave doubling in the Trio of no. 97 is here entrusted to the flute (a nice touch of democracy for the knowing chamber player).

The flute's role in these arrangements is ambiguous. On the one hand, Salomon gave it an amalgam of woodwind solo lines, and in fact recomposed many sections to add interest and mobility. On the other hand, increasingly in volume 2 he cued flute solos into the Violin 1 part, often creating unnecessary complications for the remaining players while the leader remains silent (see for instance Fig. 2). For structural reasons this could be to hold power in reserve to signal the return of a tutti (e.g. no. 100/i/bb.200–9 before the tutti at b.210), although this is more the aesthetic of the full orchestra than a procedure of classical chamber music. In practical terms the cues may indicate nothing more than the fact that the Violin I was the nearest thing to a full score for leading. However, Salomon was catering to a commercial market where the 'ad lib' marking was king; one of the more compromising title pages of this period managed to describe the flute as both obbligato and *ad libitum*, with the disingenuous statement 'N.B. The Flute part being very beautiful & yet not absolutely necessary accounts for the APPARENT Contradiction in the terms OBLIGATO and AD LIBITUM'.[29]

Fig. 5   Symphony no. 94/ii/bb.103–114: Salomon's handling of Haydn's *fortissimo* tutti in the quintet version (Vol. 1, p. 80).

Fig. 6   Symphony no. 94/iii/bb.27–35: Salomon's cancelled earlier versions of the Flute part
(Vol. 1, p. 83).

Salomon's efforts to make the flute part of musical value, even in tutti passages, can be traced in his MS.; for the third movement of no. 94 he sketched two new versions of a flute 'in fill' before reverting to the less exposed original. [Fig. 6] With commend-able sympathy for the non-professional market he gave the low C sharp of the original flute part (no. 104/iv/b.278) to the violin, since this note was not available on many flutes of the period.

In several of Salomon's deleted passages we can see his formulas for dealing with Haydn's wind-writing; while isolated three-part writing is no problem (flute, plus two violins, or violin and viola), his ingenuity was tested by the need to retain question and answer and reproduce antiphony that passed throughout the sections of the full orches-tra. It took several attempts for him to capture the three-way conversations in no. 99/iv/bb.211ff. between the horns, the winds (flute plus bassoons/oboes), and the clar-inets plus strings. [Fig. 7]

In no. 102/i/bb.222ff. Salomon corrected his layout by giving a phrase to Violin 2 that had been Violin 1, in order to allocate Oboe 1 to Violin 1, and preserve the Flute part unchanged. [Fig. 8] Even the flute's original contribution to the main theme is retrenched here (one finds it tried and then deleted at the first appearance in bb.24–5) so that the distinction of bars with and without oboe could be retained.

Special effects get special attention. The 'Great Bassoon Joke' (no. 93/ii) is given to all the strings playing octaves, *fortissimo*, and the trumpet calls of the *Military* sym-phony go to two strings (it is arguable that Haydn had actually anticipated two trum-pets in the orchestral version). The opening of the *Drum Roll* presents interesting new evidence for the puzzling timpani 'Intrada'; in the trio adaptation, Salomon retained

Fig. 7   Symphony no. 99/iv/bb.210–219: Salomon's cancelled passage in the quintet version
(Vol. 2, pp. 125–6).

Fig. 8   Symphony no. 102/i/bb.233–226: Salomon's reallocation of parts for Flute and Violins 1
and 2 (Vol. 2, p. 76).

Fig. 9   Symphony no. 103/i: the opening of the work in quintet reduction, showing Salomon's
rewriting of the original drum roll (Vol. 2, p. 34).

the original notation, and asked for a keyboard 'Tremolo all'imitazione dei timpani'. In
the quintet MS. he substituted *tremolando* strings, marked *fortissimo*, but with *four* crotch-
ets in place of the dotted minim, cadencing in an extra bar, with a two-beat silence
before the movement recommences. In the print the string *tremolo* is omitted, and most
parts are marked *ff*, with a 'hair-pin' effect < > (this seems to have been a later addition
in the MS.). While these dynamics can be used to support both the view of Landon
and the opposite opinion of Rosen,[30] the notated pause sheds useful new light on
Haydn's performance practice. [Fig. 9]

   Salomon needed his greatest 'Ingenuity and accurate Judgement' to create variety
or to maintain equality where Haydn's orchestral picture was painted in other tints and
shades. He created antiphony where there was none before (no. 101/ii/bb.142–3); in
the slow movement of no. 95 the cello retains its solo, but in the Trio (which it presages)
the cello solo goes to the first violin, coloured at moments by viola and flute, where
Haydn used no doubling (is this tactical chamber music reallocation?). In particular,
throughout the set Salomon avoided repetition, either of colour or articulation, even in
identical passages: in no. 96/iii/b.81 the flute phrasing is altered to differ from b.83; in
the Minuetto of no. 102, bb.39–49, where Haydn specified consistent slurred pairs of
quavers, Salomon followed him for the first four bars, but when the same material
returns he used six, then 4+2 before returning to 2+2+2 in the final bars. [Ex. 6]

Ex. 6

The ad lib part for the Pianoforte, if it is by Salomon, is his least adventurous contribution (though it could well demonstrate the straightforward continuo style that Haydn favoured). The occasional arpeggiated chord (no. 101/i/b.22 for instance) is almost the only concession to pianism, except for the inclusion of the famous 'Cembalo Solo' that ends no. 98/iv, complete with the top Gs for the extended range of the English pianos 'with additional keys' (but without the left-hand chords printed in Birchall's Trio version 'which Dr Haydn used to play'). However, Salomon also devised an alternative part in semiquavers for Violin 2 at this point, which would probably have been simplified or omitted when the piano solo was played.

*　　*　　*

Both the concept and the combination of the 'Symphony Quintetto' met with approval, and led to much competition. Birchall put out a second set of arrangements, also attributed to Salomon, c.1820;[31] Gambaro and Simrock extended their lists (not always with the same works), but in England the best follow-up was the earliest, by Charles Hague, Professor of Music at Cambridge, published by Preston (c.1807) with the heading 'These 12 Symphonies form a sequal to those arranged by Saloman' [sic]. He chose Symphonies nos. 66, 69, 74, 44, 63, 75, 70, 41, 71, 47, 77 and 53, and dealt with them by much the same techniques as Salomon, and with the same string-player's freedom in rewriting the articulation. His keyboard part – 'an adaption or Thorough Bass for the Piano Forte' – is more substantial and 'full' than Salomon's, often including right-hand passage-work without the left hand, and generally behaving less like continuo, and more as a substitute for the 'Corni' and 'Oboe' parts that are identified in it. In the 'reversed' Minuetto of no. 47 all the players (except the keyboard) are told at the end of the first half 'NB For the 2d. Part read backwards'. There are very occasional flute cues in the violin part (not sufficient to exempt it from the group) and the cello part sometimes separates into Violoncello and Double Bass.

A few years later there appeared 'A New Selection of Haydn's Grand Sinfonias' arranged both for trio and quintet by F. W. Crouch (but including one by Michael Haydn and one thought to be by Gyrowetz); by 1815 Lavenu & Co. were offering two arrangements by Masi of 'Haydn's celebrated old Symphonies', and taste in new quintets had moved on to Weber, the Rombergs and a peculiarly English cult of the 'Concerto da Camera' written for this combination, but with concertante keyboard (Wölfl, Cramer, Corri, Griffin and Latour all deserve investigation for this phenomenon). Sadly, the strongest deterrent to the revival of this repertoire is our lack of appetite; our houses no longer need *Hausmusik*. Yet there must be many musicians now who could honestly say, like the Rev. Thomas Twining asking to come to a 'snug quartett party' with Haydn: 'I know not how it is, but I really receive more musical pleasure from such private *cameranious* fiddlings, & singings, & keyed instrument playings, than from all the *apprêt* of public & crowded performances'.[32]

For such musicians this repertoire is a gold mine. If a Festschrift could come to life and make music for its recipient it could do worse than plan a celebratory chamber concert on the lines suggested by Wesley to conclude his lecture on chamber music, with provision made for two 'Symphony Quintettos'.[33] He wrote:

> My guess is that something like the following Order would be proper for the Formation of a private Concert:
>
> ### 1st Part
> 1 An arranged Symphony, or Quartetto. 2dly A sacred Song. 3d a Piano Forte Sonata. 4thly a Vocal Duet or Trio. 5thly a Concerto or Solo on the Violin, Violoncello or Flute.
>
> ### 2d Part
> 1 A Glee for 4 or more Voices. 2dly a Quartetto or Quintetto. 3d A secular Song – Italian or English Bravura – 4thly an Organ Piece, or a Sonata on the Harp, if there be no Organ – 5thly A pathetic Ballad. 6thly A spirited Glee, or Chorus if there be Voices enow.

APPENDIX

HAYDN SYMPHONIES IN QUINTETTO ARRANGEMENTS

SALOMON [1798]
No. [1–12] of Haydn's Grand Symphonies. Composed for Mr Salomon's Concerts, and arranged for five Instruments, vizt. Two Violins, a German Flute, a Tenor, and a Violoncello: with an Accompaniment for the Piano Forte ad libitum. By J.P. Salomon. Entd. at Stat. Hall. – Pr. 15s London. Printed for the Proprietor Mr Salomon, and to be had of him at the Hanover Square Rooms.
NB A separate Bass Part pr. 2s 6d.

Issued in four sets:

nos. 97, 93, 94; 98, 95, 96; 104, 103, 102; 99, 101, 100

SIMROCK [c. 1801]
Trois Grandes Simphonies [nos. 1–3, 4–6, 7–9, 10–12] composes par J. Haydn, arrangés [sic] pour Deux Violons, Deux Violas, Violoncelle, Contrebasse, Flute et Deux Cors (La Flute, les Cors, et Contre Basse obligato ou ad libitum.) ou Deux Violons, Viola, Violoncelle et Flute. Par Mr. Salomon. NB La Contradiction apparente dans les mots Obligato et Ad libitum vient de ce que les parties de Flute, Cors et Contrebasse, quoique fort belle ne sont pourtant pas absolument nécessaire . . . Bonn chez N. Simrock [Plate numbers 125, 163]

Issued in four sets:
nos. 97, 93, 94; 98, 95, 96; 104, 103, 102; 99, 101, 100

PRESTON (arr. Hague) [c. 1807]
Dr Haydn's 12 Symphonies Arranged as Quintettos for a Flute, two Violins, Tenor, and Violoncello with an adaption or Thorough Bass for the Piano Forte. by Dr Hague Professor of Music in the University of Cambridge. London

[at the head of the title page]:
'These 12 Symphonies form a sequel to those arranged by Saloman' [sic]

Nos. 66, 69, 74, 44, 63, 75, 70, 41, 71, 47, 77, 53

WELSH AND HAWES (arr. Crouch) [c. 1810]
A New Selection of Haydn's Grand Sinfonias Arranged as Quintetts for Two Violins, Viola, Flute & Violoncello with a Separate Accompaniment for the Piano Forte by F.W. Crouch. London Welsh and Hawes . . . at the Royal Harmonic Institution (n.d. but water-marked 1810).
[Frederick William Crouch, c.1783–1844, was the author of a *Complete Treatise on the Violoncello* (1826), and father of the composer of 'Kathleen Mavourneen'].

Nos. 56, 76, 81, 67, 78, 79, Hob. I: G3, 43, 57, 55, Hob. I:B2, 61

LAVENU & CO. London (arr. Masi) [c. 1815]
No. [1–2] of Haydn's celebrated old Symphonies, arranged as Quintetts, for two violins, tenor, vio-loncello & flute, with a part for the Piano Forte or Extra Bass, ad lib. by G. Masi.

Nos. 87, Hob. I:G3

BIRCHALL first set [c. 1820, no watermark]
[title as Salomon 1798]

A reissue (with alterations) of Salomon 1798, issued in four sets:
nos. 97, 93, 94; 98, 95, 96; 104, 103, 102; 99, 101, 100

BIRCHALL second set [c. 1820, no watermark]
[title as Salomon 1798, but 'Sets 5–8']

Issued in four sets:
nos. 85, 83, 90; 92, 51, 91; 48, 64, 88; 82, 80, 73 [copies in Liverpool Public Library].
[Nos. 85, 51 and 91 are probably not arranged by Salomon, and the other numbers are dubious.]

ROBERT COCKS & CO. [after 1823]
Later reissue of Preston c. 1807

SIMROCK [1798–c. 1802]
Quinze Quintuors pour la Flûte, 2 Violons, Alto & Violoncelle Nos. 1 à 6 avec accompagn: de Piano Forte ad libitum arrangés des grandes Simphonies composées pour les Concerts de Mr. Salomon à Londres par Joseph Haydn . . . Chez N. Simrock à Berlin. [Plate numbers 84, 85, 125, 165, 1249]

Nos. 97, 93, 94; 98, 95, 96; 104, 103, 102; 99, 101, 100; 85, 83 [listed as D minor], 90

GAMBARO [c. 1820]
Vingt-quatre Simphonies d'Haydn arrangées en Quintette pour deux violons, flûte, alto & basse avec piano-forte ad libitum par J.P. Salomon . . . Paris

Nos. 93–104, 85, 90, 92, 91, 82, 73, 83, 44, 86, Hob. I:G3, 75, 53 [The last five symphonies do not occur in the Birchall or Simrock editions; no. 44 was arranged by Hague, so it is unlikely to have been chosen by Salomon.]

DAVID WYN JONES

From Artaria to Longman & Broderip:
Mozart's music on sale in London

THE FIRST ENGLISH NEWSPAPER to carry a report of Mozart's death was *The World*. On 21 December 1791, just over a fortnight after the death of the composer, it announced: 'WOLFGANG MOZART, the celebrated German Composer, died at Vienna on the night of 5th inst. – By his death the Musical World will sustain an irreparable loss.'[1] His close friend Joseph Haydn was in London at the time preparing for his second season of participation in 'Mr Salomon's Concert' series held in the Hanover Square Rooms. Some time in January, he wrote a letter to Michael Puchberg, the banker in Vienna who had been lending Mozart money at intervals over a period of several years:

> For some time I was beside myself about his death, and I could not believe that Providence would so soon claim the life of such an indispensable man. I only regret that before his death he could not convince the English, who walk in darkness in this respect, of his greatness – a subject about which I have been sermonizing to them every single day . . . You will be good enough, my kind friend, to send me a catalogue of those pieces which are not yet known here, and I shall make every possible effort to promote such works for the widow's benefit . . .[2]

It is not known whether Puchberg ever prepared such a list for Haydn and certainly there was never anything like a Mozart memorial concert in London's active musical calendar in 1792. That Haydn continued to advocate Mozart's music in London is suggested by a passage in Charles Burney's article on the composer in Rees's *Cyclopaedia*, published over a quarter of a century later:

> After his decease, when Haydn was asked in our hearing by Broderip, in his music-shop, whether Mozart had left any MS. compositions behind him that were worth purchasing, as his widow had offered his unedited papers at a high price to the principal publishers of music through-out Europe; Haydn eagerly said: 'purchase them by all means. He was truly a great musician. I have been often flattered by my friends with having some genius; but he was much my superior.'
> Though this declaration had more of modesty than truth in it, yet if Mozart's

genius had been granted as many years to expand as that of Haydn's, the assertion might perhaps have been realized in many particulars.[3]

The clear impression gained from these two reports is that Mozart's music was little known in London at the time of his death, and certainly unappreciated. Three years earlier, in 1788, Charles Burney had completed the fourth and final volume of his monumental *A General History of Music from the Earliest Ages to the Present Period*, and its coverage of Haydn and Mozart points out in a particularly dramatic way the relative status of the two composers in London at that time. Burney introduces his coverage of Haydn with a burst of purple prose.

> I am now happily arrived at that part of my narrative where it is necessary to speak of HAYDN! the admirable and matchless HAYDN! from whose productions I have received more pleasure late in my life, when tired of most other Music, than I ever received in the most ignorant and rapturous part of my youth . . .

There follows an account of the composer's life, a survey of his principal output — including quartets, symphonies, baryton music, the Stabat Mater, *Il ritorno di Tobia* and *The Seven Last Words* — and, finally, a discussion of that aspect of Haydn's musical personality that intrigued Burney and other commentators, the mixing of the comic and the serious in the same movement or work. In total the coverage runs to five full paragraphs.[4] Six lines later, Burney turns to Mozart:

> Mozart, who astonished all Europe by his premature talents during infancy, is now no less the wonder of the musical world for his fertility and knowledge, as a composer.[5]

That is it! No biography, no mention of a single work or an evaluation of the composer's style. In fact Mozart is allotted the same amount of space as given in proximate paragraphs to Johann Gottlieb Naumann, Carl Stamitz and Jacob Herschel. The lavish coverage given to Haydn appropriately reflects his popularity in London in the 1780s, when public concert life included regular performances of his music, a good deal of which was available in printed form, and newspapers and journals readily featured his name, both in serious appraisal and in flimsy anecdote.[6] Burney's general remarks on Mozart, on the other hand, suggest that he knew very little about the composer and his music.

In recent years several scholars have provided clear documentary evidence of Mozart's reputation in London in the last decade of the composer's life and, while it never began to equal that of Haydn, it was not insubstantial. Some compositions were published in London, his music did feature occasionally in concert life and his name was certainly known to devotees of Italian opera; he was, in fact, invited to London to be the house composer at the Pantheon opera in the 1790–91 season.[7] However, one aspect of London's active musical life remains undervalued in this respect: that is the extent to which music publications from Vienna, specifically those by Mozart's princi-pal publisher Artaria, were available in London.

The 'Broderip' music-shop which Haydn and Burney visited together was the most important in London. It was run by the publishing firm of Longman & Broderip, which since the early 1780s had been the most enterprising in the capital. As well as publishing and selling music, it manufactured and imported instruments, hired out music and instruments, had a network of dealers throughout the provinces and, from 1786, even an agent in Calcutta to cater for the English community on the Indian subcontinent. The music historian Thomas Busby was to summarize the firm's central place in English musical life, which

> ... has been much indebted to the spirit of enterprise in certain publishers. The musical genius of this country was much promoted by the liberal spirit of the house of Longman and Broderip, which flourished between the years 1780 and 1800, and still continues under the firm of Clementi, Collard, and Co. Those tradesmen, by bringing a respectable capital and extensive credit to bear on the interests of music, not only improved every kind of musical instrument, and created a commerce in them with every part of the world, but gave prices for copy-rights, far surpassing any thing that had been anticipated by the 'previous generation' ... nor was the benefit to the musical profession, derived from these gentlemen, confined merely to the purse; but they conferred a nearly equal service by keeping an open table at which professors and amateurs, from every part of the world, had the opportunity of meeting, and of eliciting from each other informa-tion of mutual and considerable advantage.[8]

Importing music publications from the Continent was a well-established prac-tice in eighteenth-century London, starting with Walsh in the first half of the century, and followed in the 1760s and 1770s by Robert Bremner, who regularly imported music from Amsterdam and Paris. It became a notable feature of Longman & Broderip's business practice; on at least two occasions the firm issued special catalogues devoted to these imports. The first appeared in February 1786, *A Complete Register of all the New Musical Publications imported from different parts of Europe by Longman and Broderip*.[9] It contains five items by Mozart: 'Concertos Nos. 1, 2 and 3' for the harpsichord or pianoforte, which can be identified as the three concertos, K.413–415, published by Artaria in 1785; keyboard sonatas identified as op. 1 which is probably a reference to the publication by Sieber (Paris) of six sonatas for piano and violin (K.301–306) in 1778; and two books of sonatas labelled op. 2, probably referring to the six sonatas with violin (K.376, 296, 377–380) published in Vienna by Artaria. In July 1788 Longman & Broderip advertised the availability of 'A complete Register of New Music published in England, and imported from different parts of Europe, within the last eight months',[10] but no copy of this catalogue has yet been traced.

In the same way that the firm of Longman & Broderip regularly advertised its own publications in the London newspapers of the time, principally *The Morning Chronicle*, *The Public Advertiser*, *The Times* and *The World*, advertisements for foreign publications available from the shop are found too, and they provide a much fuller and more detailed picture of this aspect of the firm's activities than that afforded by extant catalogues. Although the firm of Artaria had been established in Vienna in 1778 and Longman & Broderip was claiming 'a Correspondence with all the Publishers of Music in Europe' as early as 1781, the first newspaper advertisement for an imported music publication from Vienna occurred in January 1784, when *The Public Advertiser* offered 'The last set of Haydn's Symphonies for Concerts Op. 35, just imported from Vienna', that is the Artaria publication of the overtures to *L'isola disabitata*, *L'incontro improvviso*, *Lo speziale*, *La vera costanza*, *L'infedeltà delusa* and *Il ritorno di Tobia*.[11] Haydn's music, especially his symphonies, was beginning to enjoy success in London. This was largely prompted by the enterprise of another publisher, William Forster, who had established direct contact with the composer in 1781, leading to the publication of fifteen symphonies and other works in the next few years.[12] To capitalize on this burgeoning market and to counter Forster's coup, Longman & Broderip did the next best thing, establishing a business relationship with the composer's principal publisher in Vienna, Artaria; in effect the firm became Artaria's agent in London. While obtaining music by the popular Haydn must have been the initial incentive for setting up the business relationship with Artaria, Longman & Broderip subsequently moved on to importing music by other composers whose works featured in Artaria's catalogue: Luigi Boccherini, Leopold Koželuch, Franz Anton Rosetti, Johann Baptist Vanhal and, naturally, Mozart. All these publications contributed vitally to the increasingly cosmopolitan nature of the music repertoire in London and Britain generally towards the end of the century.

The first advertisement for an import of an Artaria edition of a work by Mozart occurred in *The Daily Universal Register* on 24 September 1785: 'NEW MUSIC. Just imported from Vienna, and to be had at the Print Warehouse, No. 28, the Top of the Haymarket'. The name Longman & Broderip does not feature in the advertisement, but the address is that of the publisher.[13] Works by Haydn, Fiala and Koželuch are offered, together with three keyboard concertos by 'Morat', Op. 1, 2 and 3; these are

Fig. 1   Title page of two sonatas for piano duet (K.381, 358) published by Artaria & Co. as
Mozart's 'op. 3', showing gummed import label.

K.414, K.413 and K.415 respectively, the works that were to be included in the publisher's *Complete Register of all the New Musical Publications imported from different parts of
Europe* of the following year. For the next few years publications by Artaria of Mozart's
music were regularly imported by Longman & Broderip and advertised for sale in the
daily press. As was the case with all of the firm's imports of music from foreign
publishers, a small gummed label was attached to the title page: 'Imported and Sold by
Longman & Broderip. No. 26 Cheapside & No. 13 Hay Market London Who have a
regular Correspondence with all the most eminent Professors and Publishers of Music
in every part of Europe.' Some of the exemplars of Artaria's publications of music by
Mozart and, indeed, other composers still carry these labels (Fig. 1). In a few cases, presumably where Longman & Broderip thought that there was the prospect of greater
financial gain, the imported edition was used as the basis of a new edition; copyright for
these new editions was then claimed in the usual way by entering them in the ledgers of
Stationers' Hall.

The Appendix lists all the Artaria publications of music by Mozart made available in London between 1785 and 1791 (and beyond). Details of all the music by Mozart published by Artaria during the composer's lifetime are given, publications that were, in theory, available to Longman & Broderip; under each item its availability in London is noted, either in the original form or as the basis of a new edition, together with the date.

During this period thirty-four works were made available in London, covering a variety of genres: sonatas and variations for piano, violin sonatas, sonatas for piano duet, piano trios, a piano quartet, string quartets, concertos and symphonies. Clearly, the business connection between Artaria and Longman & Broderip provided the single most important source for Mozart's music in London at the time. Until the end of 1787 the music imported by Longman & Broderip had been available in Vienna for about a year, in the case of the op. 2 violin sonatas considerably longer. In 1788–89 the gap between publication in Vienna and availability in London narrowed to a few months; for instance, the *Kegelstatt* trio (K.498) was published in Vienna in September 1788 and could be purchased in London by the end of November.

Not everything by Mozart published by Artaria was made available in London, suggesting that Longman & Broderip was able to select individual items as the firm wished. Obviously, there was no market in London for the Masonic cantata with a German text, *Die Maurerfreude* (K.471), which, in any case, was sold by Artaria on behalf of the Freemasons rather than being an original publication. It might be thought that the four songs published by Artaria in 1789 could have been imported, an English text substituted, and new editions prepared. But London music publishers issued liberal quantities of songs every year, from Pleasure Garden songs, through arrangements of folksongs and popular movements from contemporary instrumental works, to Favourite Songs from operas; consequently, there would have been little demand for similar works from Vienna. From January 1789 most of Artaria's publications of works by Mozart consisted of dance music, following the composer's appointment as *Kammermusicus* by Emperor Joseph II at the end of the previous year. There was no market in London for Viennese dance music and as a result none was imported by Longman & Broderip.

Many of the works by Mozart imported by Longman & Broderip were played in public concerts in London, including the *Kegelstatt* trio and several performances of the piano concertos and of the *Haffner* symphony (K.385) and the B flat major symphony (K.319).[14] This constituted a promising beginning to a popularity that might have come to equal that of Haydn; but, ironically, the very works that Longman & Broderip needed to extend this popularity were not available from Artaria. From 1785 onwards Mozart continued to compose symphonies and, especially, concertos, but after this date only one concerto was published by Artaria and no symphonies.[15] It is an intriguing thought that, had Artaria published the *Prague*, the *Jupiter* and the G minor symphonies, the A major piano concerto (K.488), the C minor piano concerto (K.491) and many other major compositions, they would almost certainly have been imported into London by Longman & Broderip. Perhaps Haydn would not then have had cause to lament English ignorance of Mozart's genius.

Nevertheless, for any discerning musician the corpus of Mozart works provided by Longman & Broderip constituted a good basis for exploring and evaluating the composer's output, a corpus of works easily supplemented by the handful of Mozart works available in London from other publishers, including three piano sonatas (K.309–311), the rondo for piano (K.494) and the variations for piano duet (K.501).[16] All this makes Burney's nugatory few lines on the composer in *A General History of Music* seem rather odd. The explanation is probably a simple one. According to Roger Lonsdale,[17] Burney was writing the fourth part of his history in 1786–7 at the very beginning of the influx of Artaria publications and – a direct consequence – a notable increase in performances of the composer's music in London; the fact that there is no specific mention of a concerto, a symphony or a quartet by Mozart to be found in *A General History* suggests that this portion of the volume may have been drafted in 1786 rather than 1787.

What about Haydn's remarks in 1792, his 'sermonizing to them every day'? From the end of 1788 the number of Artaria publications of Mozart's music reaching London declines suddenly; the available evidence suggests that nothing was imported in 1790 and 1791.[18] This picture is mirrored in the number of public performances of Mozart's music that took place in London. For instance, London's subscription concerts in 1788 included five performances, in 1789 and 1790 none, and in 1791 two performances (both in Salomon's concerts).[19] Haydn's remarks must be seen against this general decline. Haydn would have known of Longman & Broderip's relationship with Artaria, and he would have appreciated the part the firm played in promoting his own popularity right up to the time of his arrival in London in 1791. Mozart, on the other hand, had a considerably less secure international reputation and, in London, it was significantly dependent on the business relationship between Longman & Broderip and Artaria. When Artaria was no longer able to offer the kind of music that Longman & Broderip wanted, and that the London public had demonstrated that it appreciated, Mozart moved inevitably to the periphery of musical life there.

APPENDIX

MOZART'S WORKS PUBLISHED OR IMPORTED BY LONGMAN & BRODERIP
IN 1785–91 (AND BEYOND)

Details of Artaria's publications are taken from A. Weinmann, *Vollständiges Verlagverzeichnis Artaria & Comp. Beiträge zur Geschichte des Alt-Wiener Musikverlages 2/2* (Vienna, 1952); Artaria's inconsistent use of arabic and roman numerals for opus numbers is retained. Works listed are identi-fied by their numbers in *Répertoire International des Sources Musicales (RISM)*, Series A/I, *Einzel-drucke vor 1800*, vi (Kassel, 1976).

Eisen = C. Eisen, *New Mozart Documents. A supplement to O.E. Deutsch's Documentary Biography* (London 1991).

Haberkamp = G. Haberkamp, *Die Erstdrucke der Werke von Wolfgang Amadeus Mozart* (Tutzing 1986), Textband.

Library sigla
Cu = Cambridge University Library.
Lbl = British Library, London.
Mbs = Bayerische Staatsbibliothek, Munich.
Mp = Manchester Public Library.
Orosenthal = private collection of Albi Rosenthal, Oxford.
Wn-h = Hoboken collection, Österreichische Nationalbibliothek, Vienna.

K.376, 296, 377–380
Artaria: six violin sonatas, op. II (RISM M6492), published in December 1781.
Longman & Broderip: imported, advertised in the *The Public Advertiser*, 11 January 1786. Exemplar of Artaria print in Orosenthal has import label (Haberkamp, pp. 173–4).

K.381, 358
Artaria: two sonatas for piano duet, op. 3 (RISM M6678), published in May 1781.
Longman & Broderip: imported, some time in 1786? (See Fig. 1, p. 109).

K.454
Artaria: violin sonata, op. 5 (RISM M6532), pub-lished by Torricella in July 1784, taken over by Artaria in 1786.
Longman & Broderip: no record.

K.330–332
Artaria: three piano sonatas, op. VI (RISM M6780), published in August 1784.
Longman & Broderip: no record.

K.333, 284
Artaria: two piano sonatas, op. 7 (RISM M6803), published in August 1784.
Longman & Broderip: new edition (RISM M6801), entered at Stationers' Hall on 25

September 1786, advertised in *The Daily Universal Register*, 17 October 1786 (advertisement quoted in Eisen, p. 142).

K.414
Artaria: piano concerto in A, op. IV, Liv. 1 (RISM M5798), published in March 1785.
Longman & Broderip: imported, advertised in *The Daily Universal Register*, 24 September 1785 (advertisement quoted in Eisen, p. 140).

K.413
Artaria: piano concerto in F, op. IV, Liv. 2 (RISM M5793), published in ?March 1785.
Longman & Broderip: imported, advertised in *The Daily Universal Register*, 24 September 1785 (advertisement quoted in Eisen, p. 140).

K.415
Artaria: piano concerto in C, op. IV, Liv. 3 (RISM M5805), published in ?March 1785.
Longman & Broderip: imported, advertised in *The Daily Universal Register*, 24 September 1785 (advertisement quoted in Eisen, p. 140).

K.385 (*Haffner*), 319
Artaria: symphony in D and symphony in B flat, op. VII [*sic*] (RISM M5516, M5512), published some time in 1785.
Longman & Broderip: imported, advertised in *The*

World, 21 December 1787. Exemplar of Artaria print in Mbs has the import label (Haberkamp, p. 133, p. 181).[20] Later advertisements in *The Times* quoted in Eisen, p. 145.

K.387, 421, 458 (*Hunt*), 428, 464, 465 (*Dissonance*)
Artaria: six quartets, op. X (RISM M6110), published in August 1785.
Longman & Broderip: imported, advertised in *The World*, 21 December 1787. One exemplar of the Artaria print in Mp (BR640.1 Mx646) has the import label.[21] Later advertisement in *The Times* quoted in Eisen, p. 145.

K.471
Artaria: cantata, *Die Maurerfreude* (RISM M4158), published in August 1785.
Longman & Broderip: no record.

K.475, 457
Artaria: fantasia and sonata in C minor for piano, op. XI (RISM M6810), published in December 1785.
Longman & Broderip: new edition (RISM M6825), entered at Stationers' Hall, 6 December 1786, advertised in *The World*, 2 January 1787.

K.264, 353, 455, 398, 352, 360, 359
Artaria: variations for piano on 'Lison dormait' (RISM M6958), published in April 1786; variations for piano on 'La belle françoise' (RISM M7012), published in August 1786; variations for piano on 'Unser dummer Pöbel meint' (RISM M7055), published in August 1786; variations for piano on 'Salve tu, domine' (RISM M7042), published in August 1786; variations for piano on 'Dieu d'amour' (RISM M6994), published in August 1786; variations for piano and violin on 'Hélas! j'ai perdu mon amant' (RISM M6571), published in August 1786; variations for piano and violin on 'La bergère Célimène' (RISM M6561), published in August 1786.
Longman & Broderip: new edition of all seven sets (RISM M6978), entered at Stationers' Hall, 15 October 1787, advertised in *The World*, 3 December 1787.

K.493
Artaria: piano quartet in E flat, op. 13 (RISM M6325), published in July 1787.
Longman & Broderip: imported, advertised in *The Times*, 1 December 1787. Exemplar of Artaria print in Lbl (e. 490. cc [3]) has remains of what could well have been an import label.

K.497
Artaria: sonata in F major for piano duet, op. 12 (RISM M6690), published in December 1787.
Longman & Broderip: imported, advertised in *The Times*, 17 March 1788. Exemplar of Artaria print in Orosenthal has import label (Haberkamp, p. 266).

K.382 (Anh.209)
Artaria: rondeau varié in D for piano (RISM M5857), published some time in 1787.
Longman & Broderip: no record.

K.265
Artaria: variations for piano on 'Ah vous dirai-je Maman' (RISM M6980), published some time in 1787.
Longman & Broderip: no record.

K.498 (*Kegelstatt* trio)
Artaria: trio in E flat for piano, clarinet and viola, op. 14 (RISM M6365), published in September 1788.
Longman & Broderip: new edition (RISM M6376), entered at Stationers' Hall, 3 December 1788, advertised in *The Times*, 28 November 1788.

K.527
Artaria: overture: *Don Giovanni*, arr. for piano (RISM M4539), published some time in 1788.
Longman & Broderip: no record.

K.502, 542, 548
Artaria: three piano trios, op. 15 (RISM M6391), published in November 1788.
Longman & Broderip: new edition (RISM M6384, M6396), entered at Stationers' Hall, 8 April 1789, advertised in *The World*, 21 April 1789.

K.462 no. 3, 534, 535, 535a
Artaria: four contredanses arr. for piano (RISM M5667), published in January 1789.
Longman & Broderip: no record.

K.536, 567
Artaria: twelve German dances (RISM M5671), published in early 1789.
Longman & Broderip: no record.

K.536, 567
Artaria: twelve German dances arr. for piano (RISM M5670), published in March 1789.
Longman & Broderip: no record.

K.568
Artaria: twelve minuets (RISM M5682), published in early 1789.
Longman & Broderip: no record.

K.568
Artaria: twelve minuets arr. for piano (RISM M5684), published in March 1789.
Longman & Broderip: no record.

K.523, 524
Artaria: 'Abendempfindung Laura', 'An Chloe' (RISM M5382), published in March 1789.
Longman & Broderip: no record.

K.476, 519
Artaria: 'Das Veilchen', 'Das Lied der Trennung' (RISM M5360), published in September 1789.
Longman & Broderip: no record.

K.515
Artaria: string quintet in C (RISM M5973), published in September 1789.
Longman & Broderip: imported, after 1791. Exemplar of Artaria print in Lbl (Hirsch IV, 122) has import label (Haberkamp, p. 282).

K.509
Artaria: six German dances arr. for piano (RISM M5668), published in early 1790.
Longman & Broderip: no record.

K.516
Artaria: string quintet in G minor (RISM M5989), published in August 1790.
Longman & Broderip: imported, after 1791. Exemplars of Artaria print in Wn-h and Lbl (RM 17. b. 3) have import label; former is a second impression (July 1792), latter a third impression (May 1793) (Haberkamp, p. 284).

K.564
Artaria: piano trio in G, op. 16 (RISM 6398), published in October 1790.
Longman & Broderip: no record.

K.613
Artaria: variations for piano on 'Ein Weib ist das

herrlichste Ding' (RISM M7096), published in June 1791.
Longman & Broderip: no record.

K.599, 601, 604
Artaria: twelve minuets arr. for piano (RISM M5697), published in August 1791.
Longman & Broderip: no record.

K.600, 602, 605
Artaria: thirteen German dances arr. for piano (RISM M5701), published in August 1791.
Longman & Broderip: no record.

K595
Artaria: piano concerto in B flat, op. 17 (RISM M5846), published in August 1791.
Longman & Broderip: imported, after 1791. Exemplar of Artaria print in Orosenthal has import label.

K.585
Artaria: twelve minuets arr. for piano (RISM M5689), published in August 1791.
Longman & Broderip: no record.

K.586
Artaria: twelve German dances arr. for piano (RISM M5693), published in August 1791.
Longman & Broderip: no record.

K.616 (Anh.145a)
Artaria: rondo for piano (RISM M7180–81), published in August 1791.
Longman & Broderip: no record.

K.575, 589, 590 (*Prussian*)
Artaria: three quartets, op. 18 (RISM M6169), published in December 1791.
Longman & Broderip: imported after 1791. Exemplar of Artaria print in Lbl (RM 11 g. 17 [15]) has import label.

K.599, 601, 604
Artaria: twelve minuets arr. for string trio (RISM M5696), published in December 1791.
Longman & Broderip: no record.

K.600, 602, 605
Artaria: thirteen German dances arr. for string trio (RISM M5700), published in December 1791.
Longman & Broderip: no record.

WALTHER BRAUNEIS

Die Wiener Freimaurer unter Kaiser Leopold II.: Mozarts Zauberflöte als emblematische Standortbestimmung

AM 30. SEPTEMBER 1791 wurde am Anschlagzettel des Wiedner Theaters im Starhembergschen Freihaus zum erstenmal eine Aufführung von Mozarts *Zauberflöte* angekündigt. Zu Beginn des zweiten Aufzuges fand sich das Publikum inmitten einer von Sarastro einberufenen Versammlung seiner Priesterschaft, die er selbst einleitend als 'eine der wichtigsten unserer Zeit' bezeichnete, um dann mit eindringlichen Worten auf die Verfemungen seiner von der Königin der Nacht personifizierten Feinde zu sprechen zu kommen: 'Mag immer das Vorurtheil seinen Tadel über uns Eingeweihte auslassen! – Weisheit und Vernunft zerstückt es gleich dem Spinnengewebe'. Wer mit den 'Eingeweihten' gemeint war, wußten die im Zuschauerraum anwesenden Freimaurer. Sie waren insgesamt durch die eskalierenden Ereignisse in Frankreich ins Gerede gekommen, was deutlich im Kreise von Sarastros Gegenspielerin ausgesprochen wurde: 'Man zischelt viel sich in die Ohren / Von dieser Priester falschem Sinn.' Verstanden wurde auch der versteckte Hinweis auf die päpstliche Bulle 'In eminenti', durch die der Bannstrahl der Exkommunikation auf sie gelenkt worden war: 'Man sagt, wer ihrem Bunde schwört, / Der ist verwünscht mit Haut und Haar.' Trotz allem aber gibt sich Sarastro zuversichtlich: 'Jedoch, das böse Vorurtheil soll schwinden; und es wird schwinden, sobald Tamino selbst die Größe unserer schweren Kunst besitzen wird.' Treffender hätte man kaum die Situation der Freimaurerei in den habsburgischen Ländern eineinhalb Jahre nach dem Regierungsantritt von Kaiser Leopold II. charakterisieren können.

Dem neuen Kaiser war der Ruf vorausgeeilt, in vielen Bereichen weitaus weniger restriktiv vorgehen zu wollen, als sein verstorbener Bruder. Im Rückblick hatte die josephinische Epoche, die H.C. Robbins Landon mit den 'Goldenen Jahren' in Mozarts Leben gleichzusetzen wußte, das Freimaurertum in den habsburgischen Ländern in mehrfacher Hinsicht gewandelt.[1] Ausgelöst wurden diese Veränderungen vor allem durch das kaiserliche Patent vom 26. März 1781, das die österreichischen Freimaurer glauben ließ, sie müßten sich von allen auswärtigen Abhängigkeiten befreien. Im wesentlichen betraf es diejenigen von der Großen

Landesloge von Deutschland in Berlin und die vom Braunschweiger Ordensdirektorium. Erstere benutzte das von der Großloge von England anerkannte 'Zinnendorfsche System', während Braunschweig das Zentrum der sich von dem facettenreichen französischen Écossisme (Schottisches System) herleitenden 'Strikten Observanz' war. Beide Hochgradsysteme verstanden sich als christliche Ritterorden, wobei vor allem die Strikte Observanz sich als Nachfolgerin des 1314 erloschenen Templer-Ritterordens legitimierte. Erst der Wilhelmsbader Konvent von 1782 führte mit dem 'Rektifizierten Ritus' zu einer Neuausrichtung ohne vordergründigen Bezug zur Templertradition. In den Schlußakten werden 'Wohltätigkeit', 'Bruderliebe', 'Freiheit' und 'völlige Gleichheit' erklärtes Ziel einer erneuerten Freimaurerei, die sich als Sprecherin für eine 'unterdrückte . . . leidende Menschheit' versteht. Dieses modifizierte Hochgradsystem gewann neben dem in Wien führenden Zinnendorfschen System, das fast alle Wiener Logen benutzten, auch in der kaiserlichen Residenzstadt einigen Einfluß. Umgekehrt proportional verhielten sich die Abhängigkeiten in Prag, das zum Zentrum des Schottischen Hochgradsystems geworden war.

Während die Anhänger der Strikten Observanz in den habsburgischen Ländern bereits am 28. August 1782 eine eigenständige Ordensprovinz (VII. Provinz) gebildet hatten, trennten sich die Anhänger des Zinnendorfschen Systems erst nach langwierigen Verhandlungen von Berlin. Am 24. April 1784 konnte dann eine nationalstaatliche 'Große Landesloge' für Österreich in Wien installiert werden, der in den habsburgischen Ländern sieben Provinziallogen unterstehen sollten. Der 'Provinzialloge von Österreich' waren vier Bezirkslogen untergeordnet, in die Vertreter der acht Wiener Logen sowie von Logen in den Provinzstädten zu entsenden waren. Diese nach Johannes dem Täufer als Patron der alten Steinmetzbruderschaften benannten Johannis-Logen waren an der Leitfarbe 'Blau' erkennbar. In völliger Vereinheitlichung gelangte nun in den von ihnen bearbeiteten Symbolischen Graden (Lehrling, Geselle, Meister) das Ritual des Zinnendorfschen Systems zur Anwendung, da 'es in höheren Wissenschaften gleichgültig sey in den drey Graden der Maurerey diesem oder jenem Ritual zu folgen, wenn es nur ein masonisches Rituel sey.'[2]

Das eigentliche Augenmerk vieler Freimaurer galt ausschließlich diesen mit 'höheren Wissenschaften' umschriebenen Hochgraden, die auf den drei Symbolischen Graden aufbauten. Das System der Strikten Observanz hatte als ersten Hochgrad den Schottischen Meistergrad eingeführt, der mit der Anwartschaft auf die Ritterschaft des hl. Andreas verbunden war. Dieser Grad galt als Vorstufe zum Inneren Orden, der seit 1785 nur unter den im Wilhelmsbader Konvent getroffenen Einschränkungen, also ohne Bezug zur Templertradition, fortgesetzt werden durfte. Der Innere Orden bestand aus dem Novizengrad und dem ursprünglich 'Chevalier Rose-Croix' (Ritter vom rosenfarbenen [roten Templer] Kreuz)[3] genannten Grad des 'Ritters der Wohltätigkeit'. Für Brüder, 'die sich der chymischen Arbeit im Inneren Orden widmen wollten', sah der Ordensplan eigene Einführungen vor. In sogenannten 'Praktischen Logen', wie der in Wien um 1774 genannten Loge 'Zum vierfachen Bunde', wurden die 'Laboranten' in die Kunst der Alchemie und der Herstellung von Lebenselixieren eingeweiht. Seit etwa 1780 besaß auch die Loge 'Zur gekrönten Hoffnung' ein Reglement für die alchemistischen Arbeiten ihrer Mitglieder.

Hingegen beinhaltete das als 'englisch' bezeichnete Zinnendorfsche System im Hochgradbereich zwei schottische Andreasgrade sowie ein vierstufiges Ordenskapitel. Die Kapitelgrade umfaßten zwei Rittergrade, an die sich die Grade des 'Vertrauten der Johannisloge' und des 'Vertrauten des heiligen Andreas' anschlossen. Auch in diesem System spielten in den Hochgraden die Tempelritter eine große Rolle. Allerdings verstand sich der Orden nicht als deren direkte Nachfolgeorganisation, sondern als Sachwalter ihres geistigen Erbes unter der Kreuzesfahne. Im Mittelpunkt der Lehre stand das Verhältnis zu Christus als unsichtbarem Obermeister des Ordens. In beiden Hochgradsystemen wurde dem Ritterbruder ein lateinischer 'nom de guerre' verliehen.

Kennzeichnend für die Hochgrade war die absolute Geheimhaltung, von der sie auch gegenüber staatlichen Stellen nicht abzugehen bereit waren: 'Da sich insbesondere nach den Grundsätzen des Zinnendorfschen Systems die maurerische Publizität nur auf die drey untern Grade erstreckt, so glaubt die Loge nicht schuldig zu seyn, sich zu erklären, ob und was für ein inneres System sie habe . . .'[4] Diese Verweigerung gründete sich auf der Tatsache, daß man sich von Berlin nur insoweit losgesagt hatte, als 'von denen drey untern Graden die Rede ist'.[5] Die Abhängigkeit bei den Hochgraden blieb davon unberührt. Ähnlich verhielt es sich mit dem Schottischen Hochgradsystem des Rektifizierten Ritus und seiner Abhängigkeit von dem Direktorialkapitel in Prag, dem versichert worden war, 'dass die Provincialloge und künftig zu errichtende Nationalloge von den höheren Graden keine Notiz nehmen wolle'.[6] Auch hier war man bestrebt, die Rittergrade[7] möglichst geheim zu halten, und hat die Mitglieder zu wiederholten Malen auf ihre Verschwiegenheitspflicht hingewiesen. Damit ist weitgehend das fast völlige Fehlen von historischen Hinweisen auf die Bearbeitung von Hochgraden erklärt. Nur gelegentlich erfährt man daher, mehr zufällig, einiges über die Existenz von Hochgradlogen in Wien: So 1782 von einem Schottischen Kapitel 'Zur Unschuld', das vermutlich von dem Negotianten Joseph von Sauvaigne begründet worden war.

Hochgrade existierten im josephinischen Wien aber auch in zwei weiteren,

mehr oder weniger einflußreichen para‑maurerischen Geheimgesellschaften, die sich
aus dem Niedergang der Templertradition während des Wilhelmsbader Konvents
einen beträchtlichen Mitgliederzuwachs erhofft hatten. Bereits 1771 ist der 'Orden
vom Goldenen Rosenkreuz'[8] in Wien nachweisbar, während sich der spätere 'Orden
der Ritter und Brüder St. Johann des Evangelisten aus Asien in Europa' (kurz:
'Asiatische Brüder')[9] erst allmählich aus einem 1780 begründeten Vorläufer
entwickelt hatte. Sowohl Rosenkreuzer als auch Asiatische Brüder – letztere nahmen
als einzige Vereinigung auch die durch das josephinische Toleranzedikt in der
Glaubensausübung gleichgestellten Juden auf – arbeiteten nach einem christlichen
Lehrgebäude, wenngleich stark alchemistisch orientiert und einerseits von
pansophischem und andererseits von gnostisch‑kabbalistischem Gedankengut
durchsetzt. Zur besseren Geheimhaltung erhielten die Mitglieder der Rosenkreuzer
einen aus dem Anagramm ihres Namens gebildeten Ordensnamen, während für die
neuaufgenommenen Asiatischen Brüder hebräische Decknamen ausgewählt
wurden. Diese religiösen und magischen 'Schwärmer' betrachteten die in den
Symbolischen Graden arbeitenden Freimaurerlogen als Pflanzschulen und suchten
sie mit ihren Mitgliedern zu unterwandern.

Wie stark der Hang zu Mystizismus, Wunderglauben und Geheimniskrämerei
die zwar 'aufgeklärte', aber der Aufklärung bereits wieder überdrüssige Gesellschaft
prägte und den verschiedensten esoterischen Strömungen mit ihren theosophischen,
aber auch alchemistischen oder okkulten Weisheitslehren und Praktiken größten
Zustrom brachte, schildert Henriette Louise Baronin Oberkirch in ihren berühmten
Memoiren: 'Das Ende des 18. Jahrhunderts ist gekennzeichnet durch einen geradezu
unbegreiflichen Charakter der Vorliebe für das Wunderbare . . . Sicherlich waren
niemals die Rosenkreuzer, die Geheimmeister, die Propheten und jene, die sich ihnen
anschlossen, so zahlreich und selbst bei den ernsteren Menschen beachtet. Die
Gespräche drehten sich fast nur noch um Alchemie, Mesmerismus und
Geistererscheinungen.' Auch August Friedrich Goué bestätigt dies in seiner Schrift
'Über das Ganze der Maurerey': 'Hier in Wien findest du Logen von der strikten,
der laten [d.h. leichteren, rektifizierten] und der berlinischen Observanz, praktische,
chemische, magische . . . Du mußt wissen, daß in Wien darauf gesehen wird, ob
man von Chemie zu reden weiß. Jeder Mensch von gutem Tone hat sein
Laboratorium und seine alchemistische Bibliothek.' Auch Leopold Alois
Hoffmann weiß 1786 in einem der 'Briefe eines Biedermannes an einen Biedermann
ueber die Freymaeurer in Wien' zu berichten, 'daß es in jeder Loge Goldmacher,
Geisterbeschwörer und sogar Schatzgräber giebt . . . Es giebt aber nicht blos
Thoren, sondern auch Betrüger unter ihnen, die ich fast wirkliche Goldmacher
nennen möchte, weil sie sich auf Kosten der Leichtgläubigen zu bereichern wissen.'

Einen den die Alchemie beinahe an den Bettelstab gebracht hatte, war der Literat Johann Baptist Alxinger, von dem der dänische Protestant und Theologe Friedrich Münter zu berichten wußte, er hätte 30.000 Gulden schon mit 'Rosenkreuzerei' durch den Ofen gejagt.

Eine weitere Geheimgesellschaft – der 'Orden der Illuminaten'[10] – verfolgte ganz andere Ziele und stand zu Rosenkreuzern und Asiatischen Brüdern in offenem Gegensatz. Das Illuminatentum war 1776 von dem Ingolstädter Kirchenrechts- und Philosophieprofessor Adam Weishaupt begründet worden und hatte 1782 durch Freiherrn Adolf von Knigge seine endgültige Form erhalten. Antiklerikal, insbesondere antijesuitisch eingestellt, wandten sich die Illuminaten an eine etablierte und gebildete Schicht von Hofbeamten, Professoren und Weltgeistlichen. Im Gegensatz zu den anderen Gruppierungen, die letztlich esoterisch-ritualisierte Gemeinschaften ohne besondere ideologische Ausrichtung bildeten, war der Illuminatismus ein rational-aufgeklärtes System mit ideologisch-politischer Zielsetzung. Langfristig sollten Staatsämter und kirchliche Positionen mit Illuminaten durchdrungen werden, um dem Ideengut der Aufklärung vor allem im öffentlichen Leben Gehör zu verschaffen. Insgesamt war man bestrebt, Kritik am Bestehenden zu üben, Interessen an wirtschaftlichen und sozialen Fragen zu fördern und Einfluß auf die Staatsführung zu gewinnen.

In Wien lag die Führung der Illuminaten in Händen des Rechtswissenschaftlers Joseph von Sonnenfels, der im Orden die Position eines 'Provinzial von Österreich' bekleidete, und des Mineralogen und Montanisten Ignaz von Born. Die Johannis-Loge 'Zur wahren Eintracht' und die im Aufbau befindliche, ebenfalls 'blaue' Loge 'Zur Wohltätigkeit' wurden zu Pflanzschulen ihres aus drei Klassen bestehenden Ordenssystems, in dem sich bedeutende Vertreter aus Politik, Wissenschaft und Kunst zusammengefunden hatten. In 'Minervalkirchen', wie die Versammlungen der unteren Ordensklasse benannt wurden, sollte mit 'Übungslogen' für die Verbreitung von Gedankengut der Aufklärung gesorgt werden. Als Erkennungszeichen diente die Eule der Minerva mit dem Wahlspruch 'P[er] M[e] C[oeci] V[ident]'. Bestens informiert in dieser Beziehung zeigte sich der Schriftsteller und Forschungsreisende Georg Forster in einem Brief vom 14. August 1784:[11] 'Die Loge zur wahren Eintracht ist diejenige, welche am allermeisten zur Aufklärung wirkt . . . Born ist M[eister] v[om] St[uhl] darin . . . Von aller Schwärmerei sind die Br[üder] ganz frei. – Gemmingen ist M[eister] v[om] St[uhl] von der Loge zur Wohlthätigkeit, die nämliche Grund-sätze hat.'

Mit Johann Baptist Graf Dietrichstein stand allerdings seit 1784 ein solcher Schwärmer als Landes-Großmeister an der Spitze des habsburgischen

Logenwesens. Der kaiserliche Intimus und einflußreiche Oberst-Stallmeister war langjähriger Rosenkreuzer und überdies 'Ober-Haupt-Direktor' der Wiener Rosenkreuzerzirkel. Maßgebliche Positionen konnte er in den neu konstituierten Exekutivorganen mit den Rosenkreuzern Johann Martin Loibel, Max von Linden und Bernhard Samuel von Matolay oder dem Asiatischen Bruder und Hofmedicus Johann Ost besetzen. Aber auch einstige Anhänger der Strikten Observanz, wie etwa Konrad Heinrich von Pufendorf, finden sich in der Liste der Dignitäre. Dietrichsteins Einfluß zeigt sich wohl am deutlichsten in der ausschließlich von rosenkreuzerischem Gedankengut geprägten Emblematik der Siegel der Großen Landesloge und der Provinzialloge von Österreich.[12] Wenn Georg Forster in seiner Korrespondenz weiters berichtet, Dietrichstein könne nichts für die Sache der Rosenkreuzer bewirken, denn es wirke die gesamte Freimaurerei auf Aufklärung, lag dieser Nachricht wohl einiger Zweckoptimismus zugrunde.

Immerhin war es Born gelungen, sich als Großsekretär in die Große Landesloge hineinwählen zu lassen und, unterstützt von Otto von Gemmingen als Provinzial-Großsekretär, auch als Erster Provinzial-Großaufseher in der Provinzialloge von Österreich präsent zu sein, sowie die Großmeisterschaft in der Bezirksloge 'Zur wohltätigen Eintracht' mit dem Illuminaten Joseph von Sonnenfels zu besetzen. Die überwiegende Zahl der Freimaurer in den habsburgischen Ländern aber stand den Intentionen Borns mit ihrer intellektuellen und antiklerikalen Ausrichtung mehr als reserviert gegenüber. Zudem war am 22. Juni 1784 in Bayern durch kurfürstlichen Erlaß der Orden der Illuminaten verboten worden. Und im April des folgenden Jahres verkündete die Ordensleitung offiziell die Selbstauflösung für die deutsche Ordensprovinz.

Borns Illuminatentum war vielen Mitgliedern seiner Loge 'Zur wahren Eintracht' und der Tochterloge 'Zur Wohltätigkeit' verborgen geblieben. Nach außen hin vollzog er dort ein christlich orientiertes, ritterliches Ritual, wie wir aus dem Lobspruch zu seiner Geburtstagsfeier am 26. Dezember 1784 aus Alois Blumauers Mund erfahren:[13] 'Er, der die meisten hier in unserm Kreis / Zu Rittern schlug . . .'. Als Illuminat dagegen sah Born in religiösen und magischen Schwärmern sein erklärtes Feindbild. Damit wußte er sich in stillschweigendem Einverständnis mit Joseph II., der sich in seinen Verordnungen wiederholt gegen Bigotterie und Mystizismus gewandt hatte.

Borns Einstellung zur Kirche seiner Zeit spiegelt sich am deutlichsten in der 1783 in Augsburg unter dem Titel 'Joannis Physiophili specimen monachologiae methodo Linnaeana . . .' erschienenen Spottschrift auf die Mönchsorden, die durchaus als publizistische Flankendeckung der josephinischen Klosteraufhebungen verstanden werden kann. Die deutsche Übersetzung dieses bösartigen Pasquills erschien 'In Oesterreich' gleichzeitig als 'Neueste Naturgeschichte des Mönchthums, ... von Ignaz Lojola Kuttenpeitscher' und erfuhr noch zu Borns Lebzeiten Übersetzungen ins Französische, Italienische und Englische. Antiklerikal eingestellt war auch die von ihm geleitete Loge 'Zur wahren Eintracht', über die der protestantische Theologe Friedrich Münter seinem Tagebuch anvertraute:[14] 'Die Bornische Loge heißt unter den Andern die Deistenloge, weil da am freysten wider die Pfaffen losgezogen wird.' Auch das Provinziallogengesetz von 1784 trägt in dieser Frage deutlich die Handschrift Borns.[15] Erstmals wird nämlich darin das sonst übliche öffentliche Bekenntnis zur christlichen Religion als eine der unverletzlichen Pflichten eines Freimaurers nicht mehr ausdrücklich erwähnt. Und als im selben Jahr in Prag das von dem Ex-Jesuiten Ignaz Cornova verfaßte *Bethbuch für Freymaurer* erschien, war in dem von den Illuminaten patronierten *Journal für Freymaurer* zu lesen:[16] 'Der Verfasser dieses Gebetbuches glaubt die Sprache der Empfindung zu sprechen, wenn er Schwulst und Nonsens spricht, und begeistert zu seyn, wenn er schwärmt.'

Eine Ausgliederung der Schwärmer aus den Logen schien den Intentionen des Kaisers entgegenzukommen. Sie war durch eine drastische Verminderung der Zahl der Logen in Form einer Verschmelzung zu einigen wenigen 'Sammellogen' realisierbar, die allerdings nur durch eine von allerhöchster Stelle angeordnete Logenreform veranlaßt werden konnte. Die notwendigerweise damit verbundene Reduzierung der Mitglieder glaubte man durch die Prozedur einer Wiederwahl, der sich jeder Freimaurer unterziehen mußte, bewerkstelligen zu können. Dadurch sollte es möglich sein, den Illuminaten eine Vorrangstellung zu verschaffen. Nach den Vorstellungen von Graf Dietrichstein,[17] der sich, von den Rosenkreuzern enttäuscht, im letzten Augenblick der Gruppe um Sonnenfels und Born angeschlossen hatte, sollte in jeder Landeshauptstadt nur eine Loge zugelassen, bei Bedarf allerdings auch eine zweite oder dritte gestattet sein. Nach dem kaiserlichen Handbillet vom 11. Dezember 1785 erlangten die gegen 'Gauckeleyen' und 'Geldschneiderey ... der sogenannten Freymäurer Gesellschaften' gerichteten Vorschläge in dem sechs Tage später in der *Wiener Zeitung* verlautbarten Freimaurerpatent Gesetzeskraft.

Derartige Sammellogen begannen sich zu Anfang des Jahres 1786 in allen Teilen der habsburgischen Länder zu konstituieren. In Wien waren ursprünglich drei Sammellogen geplant, wovon nur zwei zustande kamen. In der Sammelloge 'Zur Wahrheit' vereinigten sich Mitglieder aus den Logen 'Zur wahren Eintracht', 'Zu den drei Adlern' und 'Zum Palmbaum', während in der Sammelloge 'Zur neugekrönten Hoffnung' sich Brüder aus den Logen 'Zur gekrönten Hoffnung', 'Zur Wohltätigkeit' und 'Zu den drei Feuern' zusammenfanden. Zahlreiche Mitglieder aus den Logen 'Zur Beständigkeit' und 'Zum heiligen Joseph', die sich selbst aufgelöst hatten, waren in die eine oder andere der beiden neu errichteten Sammellogen übergetreten.[18] Bemerkenswert an dieser Umstrukturierung ist die Tatsache, daß sich die beiden von Illuminaten unterwanderten Logen 'Zur wahren Eintracht' und 'Zur Wohltätigkeit' nicht in einer Sammelloge vereinigt hatten, sondern durch eine Separierung hofften, nicht nur eine breitere Basis bilden, sondern sich auch allfälligen Nachforschungen leichter entziehen zu können. Aber die Tage der österreichischen Illuminaten waren längst gezählt. Schon im Sommer 1786 hatte Gottlieb Leon, Offizial an der Wiener Hofbibliothek, in einem Brief zu berichten gewußt:[19] 'Vom Illuminatenwesen ist bei uns lange schon weder Rede noch Frage mehr. Der Orden hat bei uns völlig aufgehört . . . Sein Leben und Weben . . . hat hier nicht länger als 1¼ Jahr gedauert.' Als Born den anhaltenden inneren Widerstand unter den Wiener Freimaurern gegen die Logenreform und damit das Scheitern seiner Idee einer aufgeklärten Bildungsgesellschaft erkannte, zog er sich im Herbst 1786 aus allen Funktionen zurück. Kaum ein Jahr später, am 8. Juni 1787, sistierte die Sammelloge 'Zur Wahrheit' ihre Arbeiten auf unbestimmte Zeit. Das Ende des Ordens der Illuminaten war aber auch an dem zu Johannis 1786 verlautbarten 'Logengesetz für die Provinz Österreich' ablesbar, in dem der Passus über das öffentliche Bekenntnis zur christlichen Religion wieder eingeführt worden war.[20]

Durch die Logenreform war aber auch unter Rosenkreuzern und Asiatischen Brüdern einige Verunsicherung entstanden. Die Rosenkreuzer hatten nach dem Austritt von Graf Dietrichstein 1786 mit Joseph Mesmer, Rektor der Bürgerschule bei St. Stephan, als neuen 'Ober-Haupt-Direktor' verlorenes Terrain wiederzugewinnen versucht, doch wurde bereits ein Jahr später durch die von der Ordensleitung angeordnete Stillegung ('Silanum') jede weitere Tätigkeit unterbunden. Den Asiatischen Brüdern war es dagegen 1787 gelungen, die Administrations-Kapitel in Österreich, Böhmen, Tirol und Triest neu zu konstituieren.[21] Unter ihren Wiener Mitgliedern finden sich interessanterweise der Mozart-Schwager Joseph Lange (Ordensname: 'Hevila') und der Bruder von Mozarts Schwiegervater Franz Anton Weber ('Seir') sowie der Hofopernkapellmeister Paul Wranitzky ('Korah'). Von den wenigen jüdischen Mitgliedern ist der Banquier Nathan Adam Arnsteiner ('Johannes Ben Achduth') zu erwähnen, der zu den Subskribenten von Mozarts Konzerten zählte.

Das Freimaurerpatent hatte ganz offensichtlich viele Freimaurer – nicht nur in Wien – verbittert und in der Folge veranlaßt, Deckung zu suchen. Aber noch viel schwerwiegender war die Tatsache, daß durch die Logenreform das hierarchische Gefüge des habsburgischen Logenwesens funktionslos geworden war. Zwar sind anfangs vereinzelt noch Aktivitäten der Exekutivorgane nachweisbar, eine

Nachbesetzung nach Ablauf der dreijährigen Funktionsperiode ist allerdings 1787 nicht mehr erfolgt. Die nationalstaatliche Große Landesloge für die habsburgischen Länder und die ihr untergeordneten Provinzial- und Bezirkslogen hatten zu bestehen aufgehört.

Damit stellte sich aber für die Sammelloge 'Zur neugekrönten Hoffnung', die nun als einzige Loge in Wien noch aktiv war, die Frage nach einer neuen Patronanz, wobei der Wunsch nach Bearbeitung von Hochgraden moniert wurde. Ein Wiederanschluß an Berlin war nach den geltenden Gesetzen nicht möglich. Die Wiener Freimaurer als stärkste Fraktion in der einstigen Provinzialloge von Österreich lösten die Frage für sich mit einer Annäherung an Prag durch Reaktivierung der alten Ordensprovinz.[22] Nach außen hin verdeutlichte sich diese Neuorientierung in der Namensänderung der Loge 'Zur neugekrönten Hoffnung', die sich ab Johannis 1788 wieder ihres alten Namens 'Zur gekrönten Hoffnung' bediente. Darüber hinaus wurde in den jährlichen Mitgliederlisten als Titelvignette ein aus freimaurerischen Symbolen gebildetes Emblem verwendet, das erstmals in den gedruckten Berichten über den Wilhelmsbader Konvent und das Schottische Hochgradsystem des Rektifizierten Ritus zu finden ist. Dieses Emblem schmückt auch die Titelseite der 1785 in deutscher Sprache veröffentlichten 'Freymaurerregeln nach dem Französischen des Conventschlusses zu Wilhelmsbad'.

Gleichzeitig wurde innerhalb der Provinzialloge nun die Einrichtung einer Schottischen Loge zur Bearbeitung des IV. Grades (Schottischer Meister und Ritter des hl. Andreas) zugestanden.[23] Diese Schottische Loge war als Aufsichtsbehörde über alle Symbolischen Logen gedacht. Sie reglementierte deren Arbeit und bestimmte gleichzeitig die Logenpolitik in der Provinzialloge. Damit hatte sich im Hochgradbereich die seit langem bestehende Rivalität zugunsten des Schottischen Hochgradsystems des Rektifizierten Ritus entschieden. Einer der ersten der mit 'Einstimmung der Directorii' nach dem Rektifizierten Ritus zum 'Schott[ischen] Meister u[nd] Ritter des heil[igen] Andreas', der ersten (übergeordneten) Erkenntnisstufe in diesem System, aufgenommen wurde, war der Grenadier-Hauptmann Joseph von Schlieben.[24] Schlieben sollte sich wenig später gegenüber Leopold II. für eine nationalstaatliche Große Landesloge mit dem Kaiser als Großmeister einsetzen.

Im Schottischen Meistergrad werden die drei freimaurerischen Ideale (Weisheit, Stärke und Schönheit) um eine vierte Dimension, die des christlichen Glaubens, erweitert. Dem Aufzunehmenden werden die Aufgaben und Pflichten eines künftigen Schottischen Meisters aus dieser Perspektive erläutert, wie es aus einem, in den Vertraulichen Akten des Österreichischen Staatsarchivs bewahrten handschriftlichen Ritual nachvollziehbar ist:[25] 'Ein Bruder der drey untern Stuffen, worinnen Sie bisher Meister gewesen, hat die Verehrung der Gottheit unter dem Namen eines größten und allerweisesten Baumeisters zu seinem Gegenstand; allein ein schottischer Meister hat den allmächtigen Gott viel tiefer und empfindender zu verehren . . .'. Gegenüber den Ritualen der Symbolischen Grade kommt hier der 'Geheimen Offenbarung' des Evangelisten Johannes wegen ihres esoterischen Inhalts besondere Bedeutung zu.

In dem von Hiram errichteten Salomonischen Tempel sieht der Freimaurer die höchste Stufe der Vollendung. Der legendäre Baumeister hatte sein Leben geopfert, um das Erkennungswort der Meister nicht preisgeben zu müssen. Gleichwohl wird das im Angesicht des Hingemordeten ausgesprochene 'Mac benac' im Symbolischen Meistergrad aus Sicherheitsgründen zum neugewählten Meisterwort. Dagegen gilt dem von Hiram mit ins Grab genommenen, also 'verlorenen' Meisterwort die Legende des Schottischen Meistergrades. In einem unterirdischen Gewölbe hatte es, in Stein gemeißelt, die Zerstörung des Salomonischen Tempels überdauert. In 'Jehova' eröffnete sich ihm als Schottischem Meister das alte Meisterwort. Der nach höheren Erkenntnissen strebende Freimaurer war aufgerufen, symbolisch an dem durch den judäischen Statthalter Zerubbabel zu Zeiten des Hohepriesters Josua ins Werk gesetzten Wiederaufbau mitzuwirken. Die geborstene Säule mit der Devise 'Adhuc stat' war das emblematische Leitbild, in dem sich die Hoffnung auf die Erneuerung des Salomonischen Tempels durch eine christliche Ritterschaft manifestierte. Eine geborstene Säule wird später auch die mutmaßliche Grabstätte Mozarts bezeichnen.

In Wien arbeitete die Schottische Loge als Schottisches Kapitel unter dem Namen 'Zur Verschwiegenheit'; seit 1788 wurden von ihr auch die Funktionen einer Provinzialloge von Österreich wahrgenommen.[26] Als Provinzial-Großmeister wirkte anfangs ein Protestant: Freiherr Maximilian von Calisch, kaiserlicher Rat und Assessor des Consistoriums der Augsburger Confession. Es war beschlossene Sache, 'daß die Versammlungen der Provinzialloge äußerlich nur das engere Verband der Brüder, im in[n]eren aber die Arbeiten der schottischen Grade zum Gegenstand haben sollten'. Der hierarchische Aufbau wird an anderer Stelle klar definiert:[27] 'Sämtliche Schottische Logen haben ihren Vereinigungspunkt in einer großen Schottischen Loge'. Diese als Direktorium fungierende Altschottische Ordensloge hatte ihren Sitz in Prag, trug den Namen 'Casimir zu neun Sternen' und stand unter der Leitung des Altschottischen Obermeisters Kaspar Hermann Graf Kinigl.[28] Ihm wird sich 1792 auch die mit Billigung von Kaiser Leopold II. in Pesth gegründete Loge 'Zu den sieben Sternen' unterstellen.[29]

Bewegung in die Wiener Freimaurerszene kam erst wieder nach dem Tode von Kaiser Joseph II. Und dies trotz der Ereignisse in Frankreich. Vermutlich lag die

Ursache in einem heute nicht mehr eindeutig verifizierbaren Gerücht, nach dem der neue Kaiser noch in Florenz den Grad des 'Souverain Prince Rose Croix' erreicht haben sollte.[30] So fanden sich die versprengten Mitglieder der Loge 'Zum heiligen Joseph' wieder zusammen und wählten am 12. Juli 1790 ihre Dignitäre.[31] Eine Woche später wurde das 'Fest des hohen Ordens' begangen. Stolz konnten sie dann von sich behaupten, sie hätten am 9. August 1790 den 'bisher unterbrochenen Bau wieder . . . eröffnet'.

Während die Asiatischen Brüder nach dem Tod ihres Begründers Hans Heinrich von Ecker und Eckhoffen im Jahr 1790 von der Bildfläche verschwanden, begannen sich die Rosenkreuzer neu zu formieren. Vielleicht ist in Mozarts *Così fan tutte* mit der Magnetsteinkur der als Doktor verkleideten Despina das Wiederaufflackern dieser nach dem Stein der Weisen strebenden Geheimgesellschaft unter Joseph Mesmer, dem Vetter des berühmten Magnetiseurs Franz Anton Mesmer,[32] persifliert. In Auslegung des Freimaurerpatents, das für Wien drei Logen möglich machte, versuchte Mesmer über Strohmänner eine Loge zu etablieren, die sich zu einer Pflanzschule für neue, als Rosenkreuzerzirkel benannte Hochgradlogen entwickeln sollte. Sie wurde am 20. Juni 1790 unter dem Namen 'Zur Liebe und Wahrheit' mit ausdrücklicher Genehmigung Leopolds II. zugelassen und konnte schon am 24. Februar 1791 ihr Konstitutionsfest begehen.[33] Jegliche Unterwanderung, namentlich durch Illuminaten und Deutsche Unionisten,[34] wollten die Mitglieder von Anfang an unterbinden. Dagegen konnten die 'Ober-Haupt-Direktion' und die ihr untergeordneten Rosenkreuzerzirkel formal erst am 19. Februar 1792 wiedererrichtet werden. Als 'Die Stillen im Lande' sollte dann das Direktorium nach der am 7. April 1792 verkündeten endgültigen Auflösung des Ordens noch einige Zeit im Geheimen weiterbestehen.

Auch das Illuminatentum war weitab im thüringischen Gotha, dem Sitz von Herzog Ernst II. von Sachsen-Gotha und Altenburg, unter dem Verleger Johann Joachim Christoph Bode wieder aufgeflammt, freilich mit geringem Zulauf.[35] Der im September 1790 erlassene 'Gothaer Circularbrief' zeigt eine realistische Einschätzung der auf gesellschaftliche Veränderungen in Europa hinzielenden Ereignisse: 'Freiheit und Gleichheit . . . sind nun in dem Sinne aufgefaßt, welche eben über Frankreich die Gräuel der Anarchie verbreitete.' Das Erbe der Illuminaten aber hatte die 'Deutsche Union' angetreten, die 1786 von dem protestantischen Ex-Theologen Karl Friedrich Bahrdt begründet worden war. Die Unionisten sahen ihr Hauptziel in der 'Dethronisierung' oder 'Entthronung des . . . Despotismus'. Im 'Geheimsten Operationsplan' von 1788 werden 'große bevorstehende Revolutionen' angekündigt, die dazu bestimmt seien, 'der Menschheit eine neue Gestalt zu geben'. Das Endziel sei 'Freiheit . . . brüderliche Eintracht . . .

und zuletzt vielleicht – – –'. Die im Druck ausgesparte Stelle könnte im Sinne Bahrdts mit den Worten ergänzt werden: 'Volle Gleichheit unter Menschen'. Die Unionisten wirkten im Untergrund, wo sie 'im stillen' über Bücherläden und Lesegesellschaften in den Städten ein weitverzweigtes Netz konspirativer Adressen aufgebaut hatten. In Wien besaß diese Organisation in dem Buchhändler Georg Philipp Wucherer ihren geschäftigsten Exponenten, dem es als 'Haupt-Diözesan der k.k. Staaten' innerhalb von nur zwei Jahren gelungen war, hundertelf Mitglieder zu werben. Zwar wurde Wucherer nach einer Polizeiaktion 1789 aus den habsburgischen Ländern ausgewiesen, doch das Mißtrauen gegen *die* Freimaurer blieb bestehen.

Die tieferen Wurzeln dieser staatsverneinenden und antiklerikalen Einstellung einiger weniger konspirativer Gruppierungen können in der 1738 mit Wissen des französischen Königs Ludwig XV. von Papst Clemens XII. erlassenen, die Freimaurer diskriminierenden Bulle 'In eminenti' vermutet werden. Ein Teil der in Frankreich nach Schottischem Ritus arbeitenden und sich als Hüter der Templer-tradition verstehenden Freimaurer sahen darin sozusagen eine zweite Aufhebung des Templer-Ritterordens. Als Reaktion entstand um 1743 der sogenannte 'Rächergrad', in dem als Vergeltung für die Hinrichtung des letzten Templer-Großmeisters Jacques de Molay dem geistlichen Despotismus und dem weltlichen Absolutismus symbolisch Rache geschworen wurde. Erkennbar waren die Mitglieder dieses Grades an einem Dolch-Attribut, das als Logenabzeichen (Bijou) getragen wurde oder mit dem der Schurz geziert war. Das hebräische 'Nicum' (Rache) wurde zu ihrem Losungswort. Dieser extrem antimonarchistischen und antiklerikalen Richtung innerhalb der Hochgrade hatten schon 1782 die Mitglieder des Rektifizierten Ritus beim Wilhelmsbader Konvent eine deutliche Absage erteilt:[36] 'Besuchende Brüder aus anderen Oboedienzen dürfen die Loge mit Schurz, Band und Bijou betreten – niemals aber mit dem Dolche am schwarzen Band und den Insignien des Grades der "Auserwählten Meister" noch mit dem Zeichen anderer Grade, welche darauf Bezug nehmen, und die in unseren Logen verboten sind.'

Wenig später hatten die von den Zeitzeugen nur schwer begreifbaren Ereignisse der Französischen Revolution im Anschluß an 1789, welche die unantastbar scheinenden Vorrechte von Adel, Klerus und Königtum von Gottes Gnaden in nie dagewesener Form in Frage stellten, nach einer Erklärung verlangt und sie in den zahlreichen geheimen Gesellschaften zu finden geglaubt. Da sie aber unter strengstem Stillschweigen agierten und mit ihrer Vielzahl an verschiedenartigsten Systemen schwer zu differenzieren waren, verstand man 'dann allzeit die Freymaurerey primo loco darunter'[37] und brandmarkte deren Mitglieder unverhohlen als Drahtzieher der wenig später völlig außer Kontrolle geratenden

Ereignisse. Auch die französische Königin Marie Antoinette konnte ihren Bruder Leopold nur ganz allgemein vor dem Freimaurertum warnen:[38] '. . . prenez bien garde là‚bas à toute association de franc‚maçons. On doit déjà vous avoir averti; c'est par cette voie que tous les monstres d'ici comptent d'arriver dans tous les pays au même but. Oh! Dieu garde ma patrie et vous de pareils malheurs!'

* * *

Es war demnach vor diesem Entwicklungshorizont Anfang der neunziger Jahre für die Freimaurerei in Österreich ein Gebot der Stunde, gegenüber dem neuen Kaiser in aller Öffentlichkeit eine Ergebenheitsadresse abzugeben und sich deutlich gegenüber allen konspirativen para‚maurerischen Geheimgesellschaften abzugrenzen. Eine der Möglichkeiten für eine solche Loyalitätserklärung bot sich dazu auf dem Theater. Wer die Idee zu einer derartigen theatralischen Aufarbeitung in Form einer großen Oper ins Spiel gebracht hatte und dafür Mozart gewinnen konnte, muß vorerst offen bleiben. Mozart war erst nach Gründung der nationalstaatlichen Großen Landesloge dem Bund beigetreten und am 14. Dezember 1784 in die Wiener Loge 'Zur Wohltätigkeit' aufgenommen worden.[39] Die Aufnahmerede hatte der Schriftsteller Friedrich Hegrad verfaßt und vermutlich als substituierter Redner auch selbst vorgetragen.[40] Bereits am 7. Januar 1785 wurde Mozart mit den gewöhnlichen Zeremonien zum Gesellen befördert. Der Zeitpunkt der Meistererhebung ist bisher nicht bekannt, kann aber mit Mozarts Anwesenheit bei der Meisterloge am 22. April 1785 eingegrenzt werden. Fast gleichzeitig wird auch Mozarts Vater in die Loge 'Zur Wohltätigkeit' aufgenommen und durchläuft in kürzester Frist die drei Symbolischen Grade.

Fraglos hängt Mozarts Beitritt mit der mehrfach an ihm zu beobachtenden äußersten Sensibilität zusammen, mit der er als Zeitzeuge der josephinischen Epoche auf alle Verwandlungen der gesellschaftlichen Leitbilder reagierte. Solche Umwälzungen waren von diesem Männerbund zu erwarten, der von England seinen Ausgang genommen hatte und als Nachweis uralter Herkunft und beeindruckender geistiger Tradition sich auf das Symbol des Salomonischen Tempelbaus und auf die mittelalterlichen Bauhütten‚Bruderschaften stützte. Humanität und Toleranz waren die neuen Leitbilder, durch die die alten feudalistischen Strukturen verändert werden sollten. Weder weltanschauliche Gründe noch politische Überzeugung oder soziale Herkunft bildeten ein Hemmnis für die Aufnahme. Dadurch erschloß sich den Logen ein hohes geistiges Potential, wodurch die Freimaurerei in den Jahrzehnten vor der Französischen Revolution zum Umschlagplatz neuer Ideen und damit zu einem Sammelbecken der Auf‚klärungsphilosophie zu werden versprach.

Ob Mozart auch die geheimen Ziele seiner von Illuminaten unterwanderten Loge bewußt waren und seinen Vorstellungen entsprachen, muß dahingestellt bleiben, doch hat er sich noch vor Erlaß des josephinischen Freimaurerpatents mit mehreren Kompositionen an der musikalischen Erneuerung des Logenlebens beteiligt. Neben drei rituellen Kompositionen, wovon allerdings zwei vorerst als verloren gelten müssen und nur die 'Gesellenreise' (KV 468) erhalten geblieben ist, finden sich bereits zwei Hauptwerke seines masonischen Musikschaffens: Die Kantate 'Die Maurerfreude' (KV 471) als musikalische Huldigung für den Illuminaten Ignaz von Born und die 'Maurerische Trauermusik' (KV 477) zu den Totenfeiern für den Anhänger des Zinnendorfschen Systems Franz Graf Esterházy und den Vertreter der Strikten Observanz Herzog Georg August von Mecklenburg-Strelitz. Mit einiger Vorsicht kann dieser ersten Schaffensperiode ein bisher in diesem Zusammenhang noch nie genanntes Werk zugeschrieben werden: Es handelt sich um die 1785 erfolgte Vertonung des von Alois Blumauer stammenden Gedichtes 'An die Freiheit' (KV 506), das mit Melodie und Text im darauffolgenden Jahr in dem von ihm gemeinsam mit Joseph Franz Ratschky herausgegebenen *Wiener Musenalmanach* veröffentlicht wurde.[41] Alle an Entstehung und Veröffentlichung dieses Liedes Beteiligten waren Mitglieder einer der beiden Wiener Illuminatenlogen. Besungen wird der wahrhaft freie Mann, dem es gelingt, sich aus allen Abhängigkeiten von Familie, Staat und Geld zu lösen. In inhaltlicher Übereinstimmung meint nur wenig später Ratschky auch im *Journal für Freymaurer*, es wäre 'das wichtigste und größte Geheimnis des Freimaurers ... ein freyer Mann zu werden, ein Mann, der die Kunst besitzt, seine Neigungen zu überwinden, seine Begierden zu mäßigen und seinen Willen den Gesetzen der Vernunft zu unterwerfen'.[42]

Nach dem Freimaurerpatent gehörte Mozart bis zu seinem Tode der Sammelloge 'Zur (neu)gekrönten Hoffnung' an,[43] für deren feierliche Eröffnung am 14. Januar 1786 von ihm zwei Logengesänge (KV 483, 484) beigesteuert wurden. Bezeichnenderweise hat er sich erst mehr als fünf Jahre später mit der Kantate 'Die ihr des unermeßlichen Weltalls Schöpfer ehrt' (KV 619), der *Zauberflöte* (KV 620) und der am 17. November 1791 erstmals aufgeführten 'Kleinen Freimaurerkantate' (KV 623) musikalisch wieder zur Wort gemeldet.[44] Diesem Zeitraum zuzuordnen ist nach den Forschungen von Friedrich Georg Zeileis und Alan Tyson auch die nur als Fragment überlieferte Kantate 'Dir, Seele des Weltalls, o Sonne' (KV 429),[45] deren Textdichter Lorenz Leopold Haschka, von Kaiser Joseph II. zeitweilig mit einem Publikationsverbot belegt, nach 1785 von der Bildfläche verschwunden war und nun offensichtlich in Freimaurerkreisen wieder Fuß zu fassen versuchte.

Was den Standort Mozarts in der Wiener Freimaurerszene betrifft, ist er ohne Zweifel dem konservativen, sich jeglicher ideologisch-politischer Aktivität enthaltenden Flügel zuzurechnen. Dies erweist sich an der erwähnten Tatsache seines späten Beitrittes erst nach Konstituierung der habsburgischen Nationalloge und an der künstlerischen Absenz in der kritischen Jahren nach dem Freimaurerpatent, in der sich die Krise der Johannis-Freimaurerei und die Verunsicherung der Brüder widerspiegelt, sowie aus seiner späteren engen Bindung an Kaiser Joseph II. als dessen 'Kammermusicus' zu verstehen. Und doch hat er schon im *Figaro*, aber auch im *Don Giovanni* mit seinem Librettisten Da Ponte Zeichen gesetzt für die spürbaren gesellschaftspolitischen Veränderungen seiner Zeit. In der *Zauberflöte* wird dies in der Einschätzung Taminos durch Sarastro noch viel deutlicher: 'Er ist ein Prinz! — Noch mehr, er ist ein Mensch!' Hinter dieser lapidaren Formulierung verbergen sich eine neue Freiheit und Gleichheit aller Menschen im Sinne des Naturrechtes, wie sie bereits 1776 in der amerikanischen Unabhängigkeitserklärung und 1789 auch in Frankreich in der 'Erklärung der Menschen- und Bürgerrechte' aufgegriffen worden waren. Diese Erklärung war als Präambel zum wesentlichen Bestandteil einer neuen französischen Verfassung geworden, die — sechzehn Tage vor der Uraufführung der *Zauberflöte* — König Ludwig XVI. vor der Pariser Nationalversammlung zu beschwören hatte.

Mozarts Loge arbeitete in den Symbolischen Graden nach dem von der Großloge von England anerkannten Zinnendorfschen Ritual, das von christosophischem Gedankengut tief durchdrungen war. Darüber hinaus sind alchemistisch-rosenkreuzerische Einflüsse erkennbar, die von den Rosenkreuzern bereits in dem Circular vom 4. Oktober 1782 als 'Gebräuche von uns' reklamiert wurden.[46] Gleichsam als Vermächtnis hatte 1793 Mozarts einstiger Logenbruder Joseph Baurnjöpel dieses Ritual in den 'Grundlinien eines eifrig arbeitenden Freimaurers' aufgezeichnet und mit dem nur in wenigen Details abweichenden, als 'leichtere, umgeänderte Observanz' bezeichneten Rektifizierten Ritus in Beziehung gebracht.[47] Als Leitspruch ist am Titelblatt vermerkt: 'Liebe Gott über Alles und deinen Nächsten wie dich selbst.' In einer weitschweifigen, mit rosenkreuzerischem Gedankengut vermengten Einleitung wird die Geschichte des Freimaurerordens vom Anbeginn der Welt dargelegt, Moses als Überlieferer der ihm von ägyptischen Priestern anvertrauten Geheimnisse bemüht und letztlich der zur Absicherung der heiligsten Stätten der Christenheit aufgebotene Templer-Ritterorden als Begründer des Freimaurertums benannt. Baurnjöpel bezeichnet Christus als 'den grösten aller Meister'. Und weiter liest man: '. . . der seine Liebe für die ganze Menschheit am Kreuz bewiesen . . . Er ist das Wort, welches Fleisch geworden und unter den Menschen gewandelt hat: — Ihm betten wir in Geist und Wahrheit an.' Im Kreuz aber läge der tiefere Sinn des Freimaurerordens verborgen: 'Endlich wird jeden eifervollen M[aure]r dieses Kreuz, nicht nur auf das große Geheimniß der Erlösung, sondern auf die Gr[un]dlinien des ganzen Baues des F[rei] M[aurer] Ordens hinführen.' In 'Gott', der 'Geheimen Offenbarung' und der 'Natur' sieht Baurnjöpel 'alle . . . unvergänglichen aus dieser reinen Ordenslehre herfliessend unwiderrufflichen Wahrheiten'. In dieser deutlich christlichen Ausrichtung des von den Wiener Logen bearbeiteten Rituals liegt vermutlich einer der Gründe für die Mitgliedschaft manch eines Angehörigen des geistlichen Standes, aber auch für die Tatsache, daß keine der gegen das Freimaurertum gerichteten päpstlichen Bullen in den habsburgischen Ländern veröffentlicht wurde. In letzter Konsequenz war dieses von Baurnjöpel aufgezeichnete Ritual mit seinen zahlreichen Anspielungen auf die Templertradition weitestgehend auf das unter strengster Geheimhaltung bearbeitete Schottische Hochgradsystem des Rektifizierten Ritus ausgerichtet.

Das Wiederaufleben der Templertradition und der Aufbau eines Schottischen Hochgradsystems wurden in der bisherigen Freimaurerliteratur nie klar ausgesprochen, obwohl darin der Schlüssel zur emblematischen Deutung der *Zauberflöte* enthalten ist. Vordergründig läßt das ausgewählte Libretto nur eine Märchenoper und Maschinenkomödie erkennen, eng durchwoben von der berührenden Liebesgeschichte zwischen Tamino und Pamina und einer komödiantisch angelegten Nebenhandlung mit dem Vogelfänger Papageno und seiner gefiederten Gespielin Papagena. Nichts verrät im gewählten Titel den tieferen Sinn, der sich ganz offensichtlich nur Eingeweihten enthüllen sollte.[48] Daß dies dann tatsächlich der Fall war, beweist der 'Stille beifall', von dem Mozart während der ersten Aufführungsserie seiner Frau zu berichten wußte.

Im Kern der Handlung stehen sich in der Königin der Nacht und in dem priesterlichen Sarastro die Hauptprotagonisten gegenüber. Ihre Gegnerschaft erklärt ein Gespräch Paminas mit ihrer Mutter, in dem die Königin der Nacht den Verlust des 'Siebenfachen Sonnenkreises' beklagt, den ihr verstorbener Mann noch kurz vor seinem Tod an seinen Freund Sarastro weitergegeben hatte: 'Mit deines Vaters Tod gieng meine Macht zu Grabe.' Dieses aus ihrer Sicht als 'mächtig' und 'alles verzehrend' charakterisierte Emblem ist für sie nur Symbol der Macht ohne esoterisch-hermetische Bedeutung. Den 'Siebenfachen Sonnenkreis' wiederzu-gewinnen, ist zu ihrem Lebensziel geworden. Hinter dieser scheinbar simplen Erzählung einer enttäuschten, machthungrigen Frau verbirgt sich aber nichts anderes, als der Kampf um den Führungsanspruch einer von der Königin der Nacht repräsentierten und mit den Illuminaten gleichzusetzenden para-maurerischen Geheimgesellschaft gegenüber den Wiener Freimaurern nach dem josephinischen Freimaurerpatent.

Der Schauplatz dieser Auseinandersetzung wird von einem ausgeprägt ägyptischen Kolorit bestimmt. Über das Ägyptische in der *Zauberflöte* ist bereits viel gesagt und noch mehr geschrieben worden. Borns Einfluß durch seine Übungslogen mit den Referaten über die ägyptischen Mysterien sollte dabei nicht überbewertet werden, lagen sie doch neun Jahre zurück, und seit der Drucklegung im *Journal für Freymaurer* waren mittlerweile auch bereits sieben Jahre vergangen. Darüber hinaus war die Behandlung dieses Themenkreises nur Teil eines umfassenden Bildungsprogrammes über die Mysterienbünde in der alten Welt. In gleicher Ausführlichkeit wurde über die Geheimlehren der Inder, Griechen, Perser, Hebräer und Etrusker referiert. Eine gedankliche Verbindung mit dem Sonnengott Osiris besteht lediglich in dem Hauptfest des Freimaurertums, das am Tag der Sommersonnenwende begangen wird. Keinesfalls war das Ägyptische in der freimaurerischen Emblematik ein bestimmendes Element.[49]

Viel eher wollte der Librettist mit 'Ägypten' den tatsächlichen Schauplatz der Oper in verschlüsselter Form benennen. Er hat diese geographische Chiffre dem Sprachgebrauch der Illuminaten entlehnt, die neben Decknamen für ihre Mitglieder auch solche für Städte- und Ländernamen verwendeten.[50] Sonnenfels nannte sich anfangs 'Numa' und dann 'Fabius', Gemmingen verwendete den Decknamen 'Antoninus' und Born hatte den Ordensnamen 'Furius Camillus' angenommen. 'Rom' stand für die kaiserliche Residenzstadt Wien und hinter 'Ägypten' verbargen sich die habsburgischen Länder. In diesem habsburgischen 'Ägypten' findet die Auseinandersetzung zwischen Sarastros 'Frömmlern' und den 'Heuchlern' der Königin der Nacht statt.

Unschwer sind hinter der als 'Frömmler' diskriminierten Priesterschaft Sarastros die in den Hochgraden nach dem christlich orientierten System des Rektifizierten Ritus arbeitenden Wiener Freimaurer zu erkennen. Ihr priesterlicher Habitus findet seine Erklärung im Ritual, in dem der künftige Schottische Meister ausdrücklich als 'hoherpriesterlicher Ordensbruder' angesprochen wird.[51] In einem solchen Kreis würde Sarastro den eine Schottische Loge leitenden Schottischen Obermeister personifizieren. Die Gefolgschaft der Königin der Nacht dagegen wird von Sarastros Priestern als 'Heuchler' bezeichnet, hinter deren Maske sich die auf gesellschaftliche Veränderungen drängende para-maurerische Geheimgesellschaft der Illuminaten verbirgt. Da sich diese Vereinigung der Freimaurerlogen als Pflanzschule bediente, beteuern dann auch die drei Damen heuchlerisch: 'Statt Haß, Verleumdung, schwarzer Galle, / Bestünde Lieb und Bruderbund.' Und selbst die Beschreibung der Königin der Nacht als 'sternenflammende Königin' muß unter diesem Gesichtspunkt als Vereinnahmung des 'Flammenden Sterns', eines der Hauptembleme in einer Freimaurerloge, bewertet werden.[52]

Sarastro trägt als Symbol seiner Würde den 'Siebenfachen Sonnenkreis' auf der Brust. Die Siebenzahl steht ganz allgemein für Vollkommenheit und Harmonie, im Besonderen aber im Baurnjöpel-Codex für die sieben Naturkräfte, aus denen die sieben Welten entstanden waren, die mit den Namen der sieben Planeten benannt wurden.[53] Darüber hinaus findet sich dort ein Vers aus dem Buch des Propheten Jesaias (30:26) zur Deutung dieses ungewöhnlichen Bijous: 'Das Licht des Mondes wird, wie das Licht der Sonne seyn, aber das Licht der Sonne, wird siebenfältig seyn wie das Licht der sieben Tage.' In der freimaurerischen Emblematik symbolisiert die Sonne nicht nur Weisheit und Verjüngung, sie bedeutet auch die Gegenwart des Göttlichen, die Seele des Weltalls, und aus der Sicht eines christlichen Lichtreiches steht die Sonne für den Glauben an die Ewigkeit. Vielleicht kann darüber hinaus der 'Siebenfache Sonnenkreis' auch als Anspielung auf den mit 'Eques a Sole Aureo' (Ritter von der goldenen Sonne) überlieferten Ordensnamen des legendären Großmeisters des Templer-Ritterordens zur Zeit der Entstehung der Strikten Observanz verstanden werden.

Dagegen repräsentiert Sarastros Gegenspielerin durch die bedeutungsvolle Rollenbenennung als Königin der Nacht die Mächte der Finsternis, hinter denen sich jene auf Veränderung der gesellschaftlichen Ordnung drängenden, an dem Dolch-Attribut des Rächergrades erkennbaren Kräfte verbergen. Als Werkzeug ihrer Pläne soll Pamina mit dem Dolch aus der Mutterhand meuchlings den verhaßten Widersacher Sarastro ermorden. Dem Rachebekenntnis in der 'Rachearie' der in ihrem Machtrausch vor nichts zurückschreckenden Königin der Nacht ist in der 'Hallenarie' des Sarastro[54] eine Welt frei von Rache und erfüllt mit Liebe und Vergebung gegenübergestellt. Mit dieser Polarisierung wird die *Zauberflöte* zur emblematischen Standortbestimmung der des politischen Umsturzes bezichtigten und deshalb um ihre Existenz fürchtenden Wiener Freimaurer im letzten Jahrzehnt des 18. Jahrhunderts.

Von einem echten Freimaurer wurden 'unverbrichliche Ergebenheit gegen seine Religion, Obrichkeit, Vaterland und gute Sitten' gefordert, insbesonders jedoch Wachsamkeit auf 'böse Anlagen' gegen Kaiserhaus und Regierung.[55] In Sarastro manifestiert sich ein solches dem Haus Habsburg loyal ergebenes Freimaurertum. Er bekennt, 'im Namen der Menschheit' zu handeln, und er übt Toleranz gegenüber dem Fehlgeleiteten, dem er den Weg zurück zum Bruderbund weist ('. . . Und ist ein Mensch gefallen;/Führt Liebe ihn zur Pflicht'). Unnachsichtig aber ist er auch bereit, sich von Abweichlern zu trennen und jeden Renegaten auszugrenzen ('Wen solche Lehren nicht erfreu'n,/Verdienet nicht ein Mensch zu seyn').

Ein solcher Wendehals wird in der Gestalt des Mohren Monostatos in die Handlung eingeführt. Zuerst in Diensten Sarastros, finden wir ihn später unter den

Gefolgsleuten der Königin der Nacht. Emblematisch erkennbar wird dieser Wandel auf der Bühne in dem Augenblick, als Monostatos den zum Mord an Sarastro bestimmten Dolch aus den Händen Paminas an sich reißt. Man wird nicht fehlgehen, hinter Monostatos den damals pensionierten fürstlich Liechtensteinschen Hausoffizier Angelo Soliman zu vermuten. Der wohl aus Ostafrika stammende Schwarze hatte als junger Mann am fürstlichen Hof der Lobkowitz eine erstklassige Ausbildung erfahren. Vordergründig erweist sich an ihm die traditionelle Einstellung seiner Zeit: 'Weiß ist schön! . . .' und '. . . Weil ein Schwarzer häßlich ist.' Und doch hat das Wiener Freimaurertum an ihm echte Toleranz gelebt: im Jahr 1781 war er – der Andersartige – in die Wiener Loge 'Zur wahren Eintracht' aufgenommen worden, der er bis zum Freimaurerpatent treu blieb. Er ist dann noch in der ersten Mitgliederliste der Sammelloge 'Zur Wahrheit' vom 19. Januar 1786 verzeichnet, in der zweiten, undatierten jedoch bereits gestrichen.[56] Die Gründe für sein Ausscheiden müssen demnach in einer tiefgreifenden Änderung seiner Einstellung gegenüber dem Freimaurertum gelegen haben. Nach Meinung von Hans-Josef Irmen hätte er eine zwielichtige Rolle in der Freimaurerei gespielt und wäre zu den Anhängern des Wiener Fürsterzbischofs Kardinal Christoph Graf Migazzi übergelaufen,[57] was nicht unbedingt der Charakterisierung der Rolle des Monostatos in der *Zauberflöte* entsprechen würde.

Höhepunkt der Handlung ist im zweiten Aufzug das von Sarastros Priesterschaft an Tamino vollzogene Initiationsritual, das bislang wegen der 'Feuer- und Wasserprobe' zur weitverbreiteten Meinung führte, es handle sich um die Aufnahmezeremonien in eine Symbolische Loge. Unbeachtet blieb, daß in einem solchen Fall der Neuaufzunehmende nur drei Proben ('Reisen') bestehen muß, während Tamino im Prüfungstempel von den beiden Geharnischten ganz eindeutig mit eindringlichen Worten auf vier derartige Reisen vorbereitet wird: 'Der, welcher wandert diese Strasse voll Beschwerden,/Wird rein durch Feuer, Wasser, Luft und Erden.' Darin wird das Schottische Meisterritual für den IV. Grad nach dem Schottischen Hochgradsystem des Rektifizierten Ritus erkennbar, in dem der Aufzunehmende noch einmal Proben seiner Standhaftigkeit ablegen muß. Er schreitet durch das Feuer, taucht in das Wasser und durchforscht Luft und Erde. Jedes dieser vier 'Elemente' erfährt im Ritual seine metaphorische, aber auch magische Erläuterung:[58]

. . . und wird der Aufzunehmende mit dem Gesichte gegen den Altar zwischen die beyden Br[üder] Aufsehern gestellt.
Der Br[uder] 2te Aufseher . . . führet den Aufzunehmenden viermal von Süden gegen Norden.

Während dieser 4. Reisen wird von dem Br[uder] 2ten Aufseher dem Aufzunehmenden eine Erklärung der 4. Elemente gemacht, und zwar bey der 1ten des Feuers:

wo er ihn die Eigenschaften eines ätzenden, verzehrenden und zerstöhrenden; eines feuchten, erwärmenden, und belebenden Feuers erklärt.

2ten des Wassers:

wo er ihn nebst den physischen Eigenschaften des Wassers noch jene entdeckt, daß es ein philosophisches Wasser gebe, das die Hände nicht benetzt, und um dessen Känntniß sich ein schottischer Meister hauptsächlich bewerben soll.

3ten der Luft:

Er beweißet ihm unter selber die Nothwendigkeit und Unentbehrlichkeit dieses Elements zum menschlichen Leben; zugleich die Gegenwart des Astralgeistes oder Anaoh Elohim, der sich häufig in selber befinde.

4ten der Erden:

Die er als ein trockenes, festes, fixes Element schildert, zugleich aber ihm den Spruch der Philosophen anführt: Fac Fixum Volatile, et Volatile Fixum; zum Beweiß, daß die Verflüchtung dieser fixen Bestandtheile eines der größten Kunststücke schottischer Meister sey.

Nach geendigter lezter Reise führen beyde Aufseher den Aufzunehmenden über das Tapis ...

Nach Ableistung des Eides, der im hauptsächlichen Verschwiegenheit und Nächstenliebe beinhaltet, wird dem Neuaufgenommenen, der wie im ersten Symbolischen Grad auch die Schottische Loge mit verbundenen Augen betreten hat, das Licht erteilt. Aus der Farbe der Augenbinde ergibt sich ein weiterer Hinweis auf den IV. Grad. Im Alberti-Libretto von 1791 wird nur lapidar vermerkt: 'Zwey bringen eine Art Sack, und bedecken die Häupter der beyden Fremden.' Dagegen ist in dem Handexemplar des Zauberflöte-Librettos von Schikaneders Theaterdichter Karl Ludwig Gieseke an dieser Stelle handschriftlich eine erläuternde Regieanweisung eingefügt:[59] 'die 2. Priester kommen. d[er eine] hat einen grünen Sak [vor] Tamino, der andre hat [eine Kas]perlhaube vor den Papageno, [sie] sezen ihnen selbe auf ...'. Die Farbe 'Grün' war im Gegensatz zum 'Blau' der die Symbolischen Grade bearbeitenden Johannis-Logen die Farbe der Schottischen Logen nach dem Schottischen Hochgradsystem des Rektifizierten Ritus:[60]

Der Tempel muß entweder grün spalliert, oder mit passenden allegorischen Figuren bemahlet seyn. Im Osten befindet sich [der] Altar, welcher mit einem grünen mit Gold besezten Thronhimel versehen ist. Der Altartisch selbst ist mit einem grünen Teppich bedeckt; . . . Zur Rechten des Altars am vordern Tischeck eine Fahne von roth und grünen Taffet.

Neben diesem Altartische sind zwey gleichfalls grün bedeckte Tischel befindlich.

Die Stufe, auf der der Altar steht, ist gleichfalls mit grünen Tuche überzogen; auf dieser liegt ein grüner Kissen.

Dem Aufzunehmenden wird die grüne Farbe als 'das erste Zeichen der wachsenden und fröhlichen Natur' erläutert, und es würde 'das menschliche Aug keine von allen Farben leichter, angenehmer ertragen, als die grüne'. Zur Erklärung wird aber auch Paracelsus (1493–1541) mit seinem Ausspruch 'O Sancta Viriditas' bemüht, ebenso das Vitriol der Alchemisten. 'Schlüßlich . . . ist die grüne Farbe die Farbe der Hoffnung, und eben ist es eines Schottischen Meisters erste Pflicht seine Hoffnung in Gott zu setzen.'

Auch zur Lichterteilung enthält das Alberti-Libretto einen versteckten Hinweis auf das Schottische Hochgradritual: 'Dieser Jüngling will seinen nächtlichen Schleyer von sich reißen, und ins Heiligthum des größten Lichtes blicken.' Nur im Schottischen Meisterritual wird die Lichterteilung im Aller-heiligsten des Tempels vollzogen, nachdem der Aufzunehmende symbolisch Halle, Vorhof und Heiligtum durchschritten hat. In der Regieanweisung am Schluß der 'Feuer- und Wasserprobe' heißt es: 'sogleich öffnet sich eine Thüre; man sieht einen Eingang in einen Tempel, welcher hell beleuchtet ist . . . Dieser Anblick muß den vollkommensten Glanz darstellen.'

Wenn Tamino – 'Hand in Hand' – mit Pamina seine Einweihung erlebt, wird in der *Zauberflöte* auch eine der 'merkwürdigsten neueren Erscheinungen der Maurerwelt' im leopoldinischen Wien in verschlüsselter Form angesprochen:[61] die bisher kaum beachtete Adoptionsmaurerei. Es handelte sich dabei um Frauenlogen, die Männerlogen angegliedert waren, von deren Dignitären das Logenzeremoniell vollzogen wurde. Würden und Ämter waren paritätisch mit Brüdern und Schwestern besetzt. Den Anfang hatte diese Form weiblicher Freimaurerei 1775 in Paris genommen, in der Folge erfreute sie sich in den Österreichischen Niederlanden größter Beliebtheit. Anfang der achtziger Jahre war die Adoptionsmaurerei auch in den habsburgischen Ländern denkmöglich geworden. Bereits 1783 erschien in der Offizin des Prager Freimaurers und Buchdruckers Johann Ferdinand von Schönfeld die deutsche Ausgabe eines mit 'L'adoption ou la maçonnerie des femmes' bezeichneten Rituals unter dem Titel 'Die drei Grade der Freimaurerei des Frauenzimmers, mit allen Gebräuchen und Ceremonien und einem vollständigen Katechismus'. Aber erst durch eine Veröffentlichung der Geschichte und Ziele der

Adoptionsmaurerei im *Journal für Freymaurer* wurde zu Anfang 1785 dieser emanzipatorische Zweig der bisher ausschließlich Männern vorbehaltenen Freimaurerei auch in Wiener Logenkreisen bekannt.

Die Entstehung der Adoptionsmaurerei wird nach den in dem *Wiener Journal* zitierten zeitgenössischen französischen Quellen mit einer neuen gesellschaftlichen Stellung der Frau in Verbindung gebracht: 'Der Augenblick, wo die Tiranney des Feudalsystems seine Macht in Frankreich verlohr, war ohne Zweifel die Epoche, wo die Frauen daselbst die süssen Erstlinge der Freyheit kosteten. Das Zeitalter Ludwigs des Grossen legte die letzte Hand an diese so lichtvolle und gerechte Reforme.' In Wien wird die neue Adoptionsmaurerei in positiver Weise kommentiert: 'Beym ersten Anblick scheint es allerdings ein sehr glückliches Mittel zu seyn, die Kräfte, Talente und Vorzüge der oft so ungerecht vernachlässigten weiblichen Hälfte des menschlichen Geschlechts mit den unsrigen wohlthätig zu vereinigen, um durch ihre bestimmtere und zweckmäßigere Wirksamkeit einen desto grössern Beytrag zur allgemeinen Summe der Menschenglückseligkeit zu gewinnen.'

Die tatsächliche Existenz solcher Adoptionslogen in den habsburgischen Ländern erfährt man aus der zeitgenössischen Chronik der Prager Loge 'Wahrheit und Einigkeit zu drei gekrönten Säulen'.[62] Hier wird von der ersten Arbeit einer solchen Loge in Prag am 10. Juli 1787 berichtet. Schauplatz war das Haus des Grafen Prokop Lazansky, dessen Gemahlin – eine geborene Gräfin Kolowrat – als Logenmeisterin fungierte. In einem Situationsbericht über die Freimaurerei im Prag des Jahres 1792 heißt es darüber hinaus:[63] 'Sie hat hier eben so wie die Gräfin Thun in Wien eine weibliche Maçonnerie gestiftet.' Mit der 'Gräfin Thun' war die Mozart-Gönnerin Wilhelmine Gräfin Thun gemeint, deren Mann als Thaumaturg, Visonär und Mesmerist vor dem josephinischen Freimaurerpatent zu den schillerndsten Persönlichkeiten der Wiener Freimaurerszene gehörte.

Die Thun'sche Loge war wohl die Adoptionsloge von Mozarts Loge 'Zur (neu)gekrönten Hoffnung', ist doch in dem erwähnten Baurnjöpel-Codex von 1793 neben dem Ritual für die Symbolischen Grade einer Männerloge auch das dreistufige Ritual für eine solche Adoptionsloge aufgezeichnet.[64] Baurnjöpel nennt die Reize des schönen Geschlechts, die die Brüder an der Arbeit und bei der Beobachtung der Ordnung hindern könnten, als althergebrachten Ausschließungsgrund für Frauen in der Freimaurerei. Er glaubt aber die Adoptionsmaurerei befürworten zu können, sieht er doch in dem Zusammenwirken von Mann und Frau, die er mit zwei Feuern vergleicht, 'eine einzige würkende Kraft', um dann fortzufahren: 'Mann und Weib, Weib und Mann – gränzen an die Gottheit an.' Dieses Zitat findet sich fast wörtlich im Libretto der *Zauberflöte* am Schluß des Duetts 'Bey Männern, welche Liebe fühlen', in dem der Mensch als

Ebenbild Gottes besungen wird: 'Nichts edleres sey, als Weib und Mann. | Mann und Weib, und Weib und Mann,/Riechen an die Götter an.' Mozart hat die letzte Zeile dann auf den Text 'Riechen an die Gottheit an' vertont.

Allerdings werden auch Vorurteile gegen die Frau in der Freimaurerei in der *Zauberflöte* im Verlauf der Handlung ins Gespräch gebracht, wie etwa 'Bewahret euch vor Weibertücken' und 'Sie ist ein Weib, hat Weibersinn', oder 'Ein Weib thut wenig, plaudert viel.' Sarastro selbst erkennt sehr deutlich die auf Emanzipation hindrängende Stellung der Frau, wenn er mäßigend meint: 'Ein Mann muß eure Herzen leiten,/Denn ohne ihn pflegt jedes Weib/Aus ihrem Wirkungskreis zu schreiten.' Und doch wird der Frau in Gestalt Paminas gegen Ende der *Zauberflöte* im Adoptionsritual Gerechtigkeit zuteil. Sie erfährt ihre Initiation durch die beiden Geharnischten mit den Worten: 'Ein Weib, das Nacht und Tod nicht scheut,/Ist würdig, und wird eingeweiht.' Die dichterische Freiheit des Librettisten erlaubt auf der Bühne die Gleichzeitigkeit des Ungleichzeitigen: Tamino, der sich selbst den Prüfungen für die erste Stufe im Schottischen Hochgradritual unterwirft, geleitet Pamina als 'Adoptivbruder' durch die Prüfungen für den ersten Grad einer Adoptionsloge.

Der wohl deutlichste Hinweis auf das Schottische Meisterritual nach dem Schottischen Hochgradsystem des Rektifizierten Ritus ergibt sich aus dem Auftreten der beiden 'schwarz geharnischten Männer'. Im Anschluß an die Aufnahme-zeremonie wird dem neuen Mitglied eröffnet:[65]

> Sie sind nun schottischer Meister; ich muß Ihnen aber sagen, daß wir insgesamt noch Ritter des heil[igen] Andreas sind . . . Wir haben den heil[igen] Andreas zum allgemeinen Schutzpatron gewählet . . . Der Name Ritter setzet eine edle That voraus . . . In ältern Zeiten machten die Ritter Gelübde, ihr Leben für die Religion zu wagen, und Beschützer der Wittwen, Weisen, Bedrängten und Mühseligen zu seyn, und dieses seye auch von nun an ihre Pflicht.

Gerüstet mit Harnisch, Helm, Sporen und Degen und ausgestattet mit dem feuerfarbenen Ordensband und dem Orden des heiligen Andreas empfängt der Schottische Meister den Ritterschlag. Im Verständnis des Rituals sieht sich der Ritter des heiligen Andreas als Mitglied einer christlichen Ritterschaft, wie sie der Apostel Paulus im Epheserbrief (6: 10–17) fordert:[66] 'Zieht die Waffenrüstung Gottes an, . . . umgürtet mit Wahrheit, gepanzert mit Gerechtigkeit, beschuht mit der Bereitschaft für das Evangelium des Friedens . . . ergreift den Schild des Glaubens . . . und nehmt den Helm des Heiles und das Schwert des Geistes.' In den Geharnischten widerspiegeln sich die beiden, im Rang eines Schottischen Meisters und Ritters des heiligen Andreas stehenden Aufseher, die – dem Ritual entsprechend – den Kandidaten durch die Prüfungen geleiten.

Durch diese deutlich christliche Ausrichtung wird auch die Verwendung des Luther-Chorals 'Ach Gott vom Himmel sieh darein' verständlich, der seit den frühesten reformatorischen Liedpublikationen zum Kernbestand des evangelischen liturgischen Gemeindegesanges zählt. Diese altertümliche Choralmelodie bildet den vokalen Cantus firmus, der vom Orchester mit einer unaufhaltsam schreitenden Achtelbewegung kontrapunktiert wird, die nach Hermann Abert aus dem Kyrie der *Missa Sancti Henrici* von Heinrich I.F. Biber entlehnt zu sein scheint.[67] Durch die Verklammerung dieser Gegenstimmen mit dem liturgischen Gesangsstück bei der Vertonung des zeitentrückten Textes aus Abbé Jean Terrassons Moderoman *Séthos* wollte Mozart ganz offensichtlich über die Begleitung der rituellen 'Reisen' des Aufzunehmenden weit hinausgehen und des Menschen duldend-beschwerliches Durchschreiten der Lebensbahn in seine musikalische Aussage miteinbeziehen, aber auch die religiöse Toleranz innerhalb des Freimaurertums musikalisch unter Beweis stellen.

Das Schlußbild der *Zauberflöte* entwickelt sich dann wie selbstverständlich zur klaren Absage des Wiener Freimaurertums an alle monarchiefeindlichen und antiklerikalen Kräfte. Monostatos entlarvt sich selbst und damit auch die auf Veränderung der gesellschaftlichen Ordnung drängenden Kräfte durch seine eigenen Worte: 'Nur stille! stille! stille! stille!' Dieses 'Nur stille!' ist dem Sprachgebrauch der Deutschen Unionisten entlehnt, die 1787 in den Untergrund abgewandert waren und seitdem dort 'im stillen' und unter größter Geheimhaltung agierten.[68] Nur allzu deutlich wird das angestrebte Ziel von den 'Heuchlern' aus der Umgebung der Königin der Nacht ausgesprochen: 'Die Frömmler tilgen von der Erd / Mit Feuersgluth und mächt'gem Schwerd.'

Der Handstreich mißlingt. Sarastros Hoffnungen hatten sich erfüllt: Gemeinsam mit Tamino war es gelungen, den Tempel der Weisheit gegen Blendwerk und Aberglauben zu befestigen. Mit der Regieanweisung im Alberti-Libretto – 'Das ganze Theater verwandelt sich in eine Sonne' – unterstreicht der Librettist die metaphysische Dimension der Oper. An dieser Stelle wünschte sich Schikaneder nach den Erinnerungen seines Neffen Joseph Carl 'einen imposanten Sonnentempel'.[69] Und er läßt Sarastro verkünden: 'Die Strahlen der Sonne vertreiben die Nacht, / Zernichten der Heuchler erschlichene Macht.' Dieses 'Sonnentheater', wie die Dekoration in Giesekes Handexemplar des *Zauberflöte*-Librettos bezeichnet wird,[70] visualisiert die erste Vision aus der 'Geheimen Offenbarung', in der Christus dem Evangelisten Johannes erscheint, 'wie die Sonne, wenn sie leuchtet in voller Kraft'. Nur für den Eingeweihten begreifbar, reiht sich der christliche Glaube als neuerlicher Hinweis auf das Schottische Meisterritual nach dem Rektifizierten Ritus zu den im Schlußchor von Sarastros Priestern gerühmten Grundpfeilern der Johannis-Freimaurerei: 'Es siegte die Stärke, und krönet zum Lohn / Die Schönheit und Weisheit mit ewiger Kron.'

Auch im Libretto von 1791 verbirgt sich hinter dem von Mozarts Logenbruder Ignaz Alberti gestochenen Frontispiz einer Ruinenlandschaft eine Allegorie auf diesen Schottischen Meistergrad. Achtlos zurückgelassene Grabwerkzeuge erinnern den Eingeweihten zwar an die Suche in den Ruinen des Salomonischen Tempels nach dem 'Verlorenen Meisterwort', dem Profanen gegenüber wird es jedoch nicht preisgegeben. Die Abbildung wird von einer hieroglyphengezierten Pyramide beherrscht, die in der freimaurerischen Emblematik zumeist für das Grabmal des Tempelbaumeisters Hiram steht.[71] Vollendet wird das allegorische Programm durch das Pendant eines mächtigen Urnengefäßes, in dem die Aschenurne des letzten Großmeisters des Templer-Ritterordens Jacques de Molay zu vermuten ist. So wie Hiram hatte auch er sein Geheimnis nicht preisgegeben und es am Scheiterhaufen mit in den Tod genommen. Folgt man der freimaurerischen Legende der Strikten Observanz, dann wäre Molays Asche nicht in alle Winde zerstreut, sondern heimlich von einigen Getreuen über die Auvergne nach Schottland in Sicherheit gebracht worden. Zu Mozarts Zeiten war diese Tradition längst aufgegeben und im Schottischen Hochgradsystem des Rektifizierten Ritus galt dieses Mausoleum nur mehr als 'Todten-Urne', die an 'die Unsterb-lichkeit der Seele und die Auflösung der Materie' erinnern sollte.[72]

Die verschlüsselte Darstellung von Emblemen und Einweihungszeremonien aus dem Schottischen Hochgradsystem des Rektifizierten Ritus setzt wohl die Rezeption Mozarts in die den Symbolischen Graden übergeordnete Erkenntnisstufe des Schottischen Meisters voraus. Dieses Thema ist in der Mozart-Literatur bisher nicht wirklich abgehandelt worden[73] und ist nach dem heutigen Wissensstand nur über Umwege beantwortbar. Während sich Leopold Mozart in einem Brief an den Verleger und Freimaurer Pasquale Artaria vom 8. Juli 1785 sowohl im Text als auch durch die Schreibweise des Datums in Andreaskreuzform und das aus zwei ineinandergeschobenen Dreiecken gebildete Hexagramm hinter seiner Unterschrift als Freimaurer zu erkennen gibt, hat sich Mozart selbst in dieser Frage äußerst bedeckt gehalten.[74]

Zweimal allerdings gibt uns Mozart einen versteckten Hinweis. Am 8. Januar 1787 trägt er sich in das Stammbuch seines angeheirateten Cousins Edmund von Weber ein, wo er seiner Unterschrift ein auf die Spitze gestelltes Dreieck und daneben ein nur mit drei Punkten markiertes Dreieck in normaler Lage beifügt (Abb. 1). Ein aus den beiden Dreiecken zusammengefügtes Hexagramm verwendet

Mozart am 30. März 1787 hinter seiner mit einer 'manu propria'-Paraphe versehenen Unterschrift unter der Stammbucheintragung für Georg Kronauer. Dieses 'gedoppelte Triangel', wie das Hexagramm in der freimaurerischen Emblematik genannt wurde, symbolisiert das durchdringende Wirken von Geist und Materie. Der sich daraus ableitende sechszackige Stern wird – im Gegensatz zum fünfzackigen Stern der Symbolischen Logen – zum Leitmotiv der Schottischen Logen ('Ober den Altar hängt der sechseckigte flammende Stern im vollen Glanz.')[75] und läßt bei Mozart in der Beifügung zur Unterschrift den Schottischen Meister erkennen. Aber auch in der Grußformel von Mozarts Brief vom 27. Juni 1788 an Johann Michael Puchberg findet sich in der Eigendefinition als 'O[rdens] B[ruder]' ein weiterer Hinweis. Da die Symbolischen Grade der Johannis-Freimaurerei keine Ordens-hierarchie kennen, deklariert sich Mozart hier eindeutig als Mitglied des von seiner Loge bearbeiteten Schottischen Hochgradsystems des Rektifizierten Ritus.

Neue Erkenntnisse zu diesem Fragenkomplex bietet eine handschriftliche Eintragung am Innendeckel der 1784 in zweiter Auflage erschienenen 'Briefe aus Berlin . . . An den Verfasser der Briefe aus Wien'.[76] Unter dem Besitzvermerk 'Neumayr Wolfgang' ist von anderer Hand eine zweizeilige Notiz hinzugefügt, von der nur die erste Zeile lesbar geblieben ist: 'Wolfgang Mozart ist . . .' der Rest wurde durch ein dichtes Schlingennetz fast unkenntlich gemacht, doch läßt sich die zweite Zeile durch Ausretouchieren einigermaßen zweifelsfrei mit '. . . Der E[. . .]a B[. . .]d' lesen (Abb. 2). Hier ist ganz offensichtlich Mozarts *nom de guerre* als ritterlicher Ordensbruder vermerkt gewesen. Aus Geheimhaltungsgründen hat der Schreiber ihn nur mit den Anfangsbuchstaben notiert, um ihn dann – aus welchen Gründen immer – ganz zu löschen. Ergänzt müßte die Eintragung bis auf den dem Ritterprädikat beigegebenen, zumeist latinisierten phantasievollen Ortsnamen oder Sachbegriff gelautet haben: 'Wolfgang Mozart ist / Der E[ques] a B[. . .]d'.

Völlig unbeachtet blieb aber bisher, daß die Lösung der Frage nach einer Zugehörigkeit zu einem höheren Grad in der Schlußsequenz der 'Maurerrede auf Mozarts Tod' zu finden ist: 'Bis einst durch drey Mahl drey zur Bruderkette, / Dich Adoniram rufen wird. / Wo wir in sanftern Melodienchören, / Vereint durchs ew'ge Meisterwort – / Das heilig – heilig – heilig werden hören, / Jehova ist der Maurer Gott!!!' Hinter 'Jehova' verbirgt sich nämlich das Meisterwort aus dem Schottischen Meisterritual.[77] So scheint die Verabschiedung Mozarts mit dem unaussprechlichen Namen Gottes ein untrügliches Zeichen für seine Mitgliedschaft im Schottischen Meistergrad zu sein.

Für Mozart war die *Zauberflöte* ganz offensichtlich keine Märchenoper oder Maschinenkomödie. Er hatte sich in einer entscheidenden Phase der österreichischen Freimaurerei ganz in den Dienst der Sache gestellt. Denn wie sonst wäre sein zu

Anfang September 1791 nach Absingen der Kantate 'Die Maurerfreude' (KV 471) in der Prager Loge 'Wahrheit und Einigkeit zu drei gekrönten Säulen' überlieferter Ausspruch zu verstehen, 'er werde demnächst dem Maurerthume eine bessere Huldigung darbringen.'[78] Von einem, knapp zwei Monate später an ihm mit einem Ritualmord gesühnten Verrat an den Geheimnissen des Bruderbundes kann daher keine Rede sein. Denn unter keinen Umständen hätten ihm seine Logenbrüder dann den Kompositionsauftrag aus Anlaß der Einweihung des neuen Logenquartiers am 17. November 1791 anvertraut. Durch die von Mozart – und vor allem seinem Librettisten Schikaneder – vorgenommene Verschlüsselung der Embleme würde nur dem Eingeweihten nach dem oft zitierten Goethe-Wort 'der höhere Sinn nicht entgehen, wie es ja auch bei der *Zauberflöte* und andern Dingen der Fall ist.'[79]

Ganz offensichtlich war man auch bei der Wahl des Theaters für die erste Präsentation der *Zauberflöte* entsprechend umsichtig vorgegangen. Aus

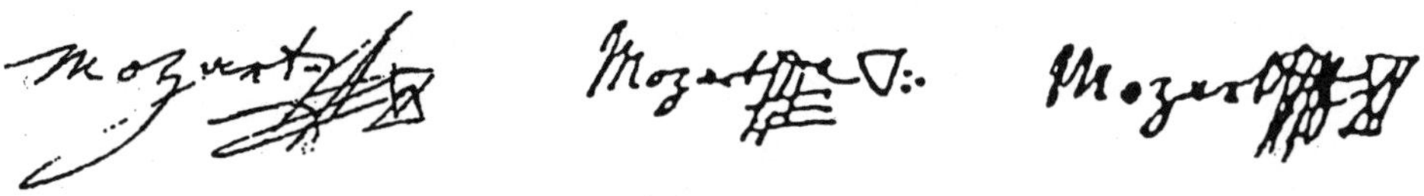

Abb. 1   Masonische Chiffren hinter dem Namenszug von Leopold Mozart (1785) und bei zwei Mozart Unterschriften (1787).

Abb. 2   Ausgetilgter *nom de guerre* Mozarts als Mitglied des Rektifizierten Ritus der Strikten Observanz, mit (unten) Versuch einer Dechiffrierung des unlesbar gemachten Decknamens.

verständlichen Gründen waren dafür die beiden innerstädtischen Bühnen nicht in Frage gekommen. Hingegen sprach vieles für das Wiedner Theater im Starhembergschen Freihaus, das sich allgemeiner Beliebtheit erfreute. Im *Wienerblättchen* war bereits am 24. Juni 1788 kolportiert worden, daß man sich in dem Vorstadttheater nicht wie 'im Nationaltheater bey dem unausstehlichen Gewinsel und Maulaufreissen zu Tode ennujirt'. Daß Ludwig Graf Starhemberg, Sohn des Hauseigentümers, selbst Freimaurer und Logenbruder Mozarts war, spielt sicherlich eine nicht zu unterschätzende Rolle. Darüber hinaus war Schikaneders Theater wiederholt durch die Gegenwart des Wiener Hofes ausgezeichnet worden: So berichtete beispielsweise die *Wiener Zeitung* am 16. Februar 1791 rückblickend von zwei Opernabenden, die vom Kaiserpaar 'mit Allerhöchstdero Beyfall' bedacht worden waren. Am 3. August 1791 besuchte dann Leopold II. mit dem Thron-folger Erzherzog Franz neuerlich das Freihaustheater.

Der Initiator der *Zauberflöte* muß wohl in den vordersten Reihen der Wiener Freimaurer vermutet werden. Man wird ihn unter den Mitgliedern der als Aufsichtsbehörde über die Symbolischen Logen fungierenden Schottischen Loge zu suchen haben, über deren Zusammensetzung im Jahre der Uraufführung der *Zauberflöte* aus Gründen der selbstgewählten Geheimhaltung bisher soviel wie nichts bekannt geworden ist. Der Theaterprinzipal Emanuel Schikaneder ist damit kaum in Verbindung zu bringen. Hingegen ist der routinierte Theaterpraktiker als Verfasser des Librettos nahezu unbestritten. Schikaneder gehörte seit 1788 der Regensburger Loge 'Die Wachsende zu den drei Schlüsseln' an und wird noch in der Mitgliederliste von 1790 unter den Abwesenden im Lehrlingsgrad geführt.[80] Ein Jahr später ist der seit 1789 in Wien weilende Schauspieldirektor letztmals in der Mitgliederliste seiner Loge genannt und wird dabei allerdings bereits als Geselle bezeichnet.[81] Er muß demnach in der Zwischenzeit in den Gesellengrad befördert worden sein. Dies könnte in Wien in der von Regensburg konstituierten Loge 'Zur Liebe und Wahrheit' im Delegationsweg erfolgt sein. Eine Affilierung Schikaneders, verbunden mit einer Meistererhebung, wäre nach Johannis 1791 denkbar, wenngleich durch das Fehlen jeglicher Mitgliederlisten derzeit nicht beweisbar. Hingegen war Schikaneders Theaterdichter Karl Ludwig Gieseke in Mozarts Loge 'Zur gekrönten Hoffnung' gerade zu diesem Zeitpunkt in den Meistergrad erhoben worden.[82] Ihm wird ein gewisser Anteil am Libretto sicherlich nicht abzusprechen sein, da zwangsweise bei einer auf Gewinn orientierten Theaterkompagnie alle Kräfte zum Gelingen einer Aufführung beizutragen hatten.

Ins Spiel zu bringen ist in diesem Zusammenhang aber ein bisher kaum erwähnter Name: Caterino Mazzolà.[83] Der in Dresden engagierte italienische Poeta teatrale hatte ein Jahrzehnt zuvor für die geplante Festoper aus Anlaß der Hochzeit des Herzogs Anton von Sachsen ein Libretto verfaßt, das von dem Hofkapellmeister und Freimaurer Johann Gottlieb Naumann in Musik gesetzt unter dem Titel *Osiride* am 27. Oktober 1781 in Dresden zum ersten und einzigen Mal zur Aufführung gelangte. Dieses zuweilen als Freimaureroper bezeichnete Werk könnte Schikaneder in den Einweihungszeremonien und Priesterchören sowie in der Gegenüberstellung des Elysiums der Isis mit Thyphons Reich der Finsternis durchaus als Vorbild gedient haben.[84] Auch im textlichen Aufbau einiger Arien finden sich anmerkenswerte Übereinstimmungen, etwa in den Arien der entführten Aretea und der verzweifelten Pamina, oder in den Schlußchören mit dem Lobpreis der Standhaftigkeit des Göttersohnes Orus und des Königssohnes Tamino, besonders aber in den 'Bildnisarien' beider Opern.

In der entscheidenden Phase der Entstehung der *Zauberflöte* war Mazzolà dann auch tatsächlich in Wien, als er mit Mozart gemeinsam das Libretto für die Prager Krönungsoper *La clemenza di Tito* einzurichten hatte. Der Dresdner Theaterdichter könnte bei dieser Gelegenheit auch Mozart auf Naumanns 'Vierzig Freimäurerlieder . . . zum Gebrauch der deutschen und französischen Tafellogen' aufmerksam gemacht haben, in dem das Lied 'Stärke' durch Versrhythmus und einzelne musikalische Wendungen eine entfernte Ähnlichkeit mit der Arie des Papageno 'Ein Mädchen oder Weibchen' erkennen läßt. Des weiteren gibt es in der Sammlung aber auch Anklänge an das Mozart zugeschriebene Kettenlied (KV 623a), das nach seinem Tod zusammen mit dem Erstdruck der 'Kleinen Freimaurerkantate' veröffentlicht worden war.[85] Das Liederbuch war 1782 in Berlin erschienen und erlebte 1784 eine zweite Auflage, was auf große Beliebtheit und weite Verbreitung schließen läßt.

Der Zeitpunkt für eine Thematisierung des Freimaurertums auf einer Opernbühne war klug gewählt. Für Kaiser Leopold II. waren die Freimaurerlogen 'gesellschaftliche Verbindungen und Cliquen zur gegenseitigen Unterstüzung und als solche, wie andere Vereinigungen . . . hervorragendes Mittel zur Verbreitung "guter" wie "schlechter" Ideen, Ansichten und Gerüchte, die daher, wie Café und Wirtshäuser und andere Institutionen zur Pflege menschlicher Geselligkeit, von der Regierung aufmerksam beobachtet werden mußten.'[86] Er unterschied demnach zwischen 'guten' und 'schlechten' Freimaurern, wobei unter den letztgenannten wohl jene Kräfte zu verstehen sind, die der Regierung feindlich gesinnt zu sein schienen und einen revolutionären Umsturz der politischen Verhältnisse in Betracht zogen. Ganz offensichtlich wollte der Kaiser durch direkte Einflußnahme die positiven Kräfte des Dritten Standes in der Freimaurerei für sich gewinnen, um deren Abwandern in die Opposition zu verhindern. Diese 'Verstaatlichung' der Freimaurerei sollte − entsprechend seiner auch in anderen Bereichen gepflogenen

Maxime – vorerst nur in Teilbereichen, nämlich in der Residenzstadt selbst und im Königreich Ungarn, probeweise eingeleitet werden.[87] Unter diesem Aspekt werden die Neuzulassungen von Logen in Wien und Pesth verständlich. Darüber hinaus aber sollten staatsbejahende Kräfte aus Verwaltung und Wissenschaft (worunter selbstverständlich auch Freimaurer sein konnten) in eine die gesamte Monarchie umfassende geheime 'Assoziation' mit staatstragender Funktion aufgenommen werden.[88]

Mehrfach ist die Frage nach einer historischen Persönlichkeit hinter der Figur des Sarastro diskutiert worden. Der des öfteren benannte Ignaz von Born hatte zwar in der radikal-aufklärerischen Phase der österreichischen Freimaurerei mit seinen Ideen einer neuen Bildungsgesellschaft maßgeblich für die Aufklärung gewirkt, war aber letztlich gescheitert und nach dem josephinischen Freimaurerpatent dem Bund ferngeblieben.[89] Unbedankt ist Born dann am 24. Juli 1791 in Wien gestorben. Daß Sarastro den neuen Kaiser selbst verkörpern könnte, wie Alfons Rosenberg vermutet hat, findet in der dramaturgischen Anlage der Rolle als Vorsteher einer priesterlichen Gemeinschaft keine Entsprechung.[90] So wie die Königin der Nacht die Mächte der Finsternis und damit aus der Sicht der Zeitgenossen das Illuminatentum verkörpert, so steht Sarastro ganz allgemein für Recht und Ordnung und bürgt für ein regierungstreues Freimaurertum.

Dagegen bietet sich für Tamino eine solche Identifizierungsmöglichkeit. Er – 'ein Königssohn, 20 Jahre seines Alters' – muß sich zwischen den Parteiungen der 'Heuchler' und 'Frömmler' entscheiden.[91] Die 'Eingeweihten' in der *Zauberflöte* sahen in ihm den künftigen Protektor, durch dessen Beitritt die sich häufenden Vorurteile wohl schwinden würden und dem sie schon jetzt ihre Segenswünsche entgegenbrachten: '. . . und wünschest du einst als weiser Fürst zu regieren, so mögen die Götter dich ferner begleiten.' In Taminos Selbstdarstellung gegenüber Papageno heißt es zudem: 'Mein Vater ist Fürst, der über viele Länder und Menschen herrscht.' Mit Tamino war vielleicht Alexander Leopold, der viertgeborene Sohn Leopold II., gemeint gewesen. Schon durch seinen Erzieher Andreas von Riedel, Freimaurer und späterer Jakobiner, könnte der am 14. August 1772 in Florenz geborene Erzherzog möglicherweise mit den Ideen des Freimaurertums konfrontiert worden sein.[92] Nach seiner Wahl am 12. November 1790 durch den ungarischen Reichstag zum Palatin von Ungarn hatte Alexander Leopold auch die dirigistischen Maßnahmen seines Vaters im Bereich des ungarischen Logenwesens mitzutragen. Falls sich der knapp zwanzigjährige Palatin in Ungarn dem Freimaurerbund gegenüber zumindest nicht unfreundlich verhalten würde, so hätte dies auch einen Hoffnungsschimmer für alle anderen habsburgischen Länder bedeuten können.

Die Reaktionen der 'Eingeweihten' unter den Zeitzeugen auf die *Zauberflöte* waren unterschiedlich: Der Obskurant Leopold Alois Hoffmann sah in der Zurschaustellung bislang streng gehüteter Zeremonien lediglich eine Spekulation zur Anlockung neuer Mitglieder.[93] Dagegen bejubelte der Asiatische Bruder Ephraim Joseph Hirschfeld die letzte Oper Mozarts, die er als das 'Canticum canticorum oder Sanctum sanctorum' beschreibt.[94] Aber nicht nur in Freimaurerkreisen war die Botschaft der *Zauberflöte* verstanden worden. Antonio Salieri beurteilte das Werk gegenüber Mozart mit den Worten: 'eine Opera – würdig bey der größten festivität vor dem größten Monarchen aufzuführen.' Am 11. Juni 1792 sollte dann die *Zauberflöte* im Freihaustheater sogar 'Auf hohes Begehren' gespielt werden.[95]

Erstmals nachgespielt wurde die *Zauberflöte* nicht in Prag – wie in der Literatur zumeist behauptet – sondern am 21. September 1792 von der Theaterkompagnie des Franz Bulla in der galizischen Hauptstadt Lemberg.[96] In der *Preßburger Zeitung* war damals zu lesen, daß Bulla 'keine Kosten scheute, um durch Darstellung geschmackvoller Dekoration und prächtige Kleider das Stück zu erheben' und 'Sänger und Sängerinnen sich alle Mühe gaben, die Musick eines so großen Meisters auf das vollkommenste zu exequiren'. Erst vier Wochen später, am 25. Oktober 1792, stand die Oper am Spielplan des Ständetheaters in Prag. Von dieser Inszenierung stammt das älteste bisher bekannt gewordene Szenenbild, das im Fasching 1793 die Einladungskarten zu den beliebten Prager Konviktbällen zierte.[97] Die von Johann Graf Bretfeld veranstalteten Bälle standen unter dem Motto 'Es klinget so herrlich, es klinget so schön!', worin sich der Erfolg der Oper auch in der böhmischen Haupstadt bestätigt.

Bemerkenswert war dann die Aufführung der *Zauberflöte* in einer vieraktigen Fassung am 15. November 1793 im Hamburger Theater am Gänsemarkt, das unter der Leitung des engagierten Freimaurers Friedrich Ludwig Schröder stand. Der Erfolg der Aufführung fand gleichfalls ein illustratives Echo:[98] Der Buchbinder J.C. Zimmer gab sieben kleinformatige Kupferstiche heraus, deren Aktbezeichnungen und Textzitate auf die Schrödersche Bearbeitung Bezug nehmen. In dem einzigen querformatigen Blatt dieser wohl als Kalenderillustration geplanten Folge – Sarastros Einzug im ersten Finale – sind Sarastro und seine Priester, wie schon zuvor in Leipzig und München, nicht in ägyptisierende Gewänder gekleidet, sondern treten – an ihren, der christlichen Ikonographie der Hohenpriester in den Kreuz-wegdarstellungen entlehnten mitraähnlichen Kopbedeckungen erkennbar – als jüdische Tempelpriester auf. Ob daraus geschlossen werden darf, daß Sarastro auch bei der Wiener Uraufführung von 1791 in einer solchen hohepriesterlichen Kleidung auf der Bühne erschienen ist, muß vorerst dahingestellt bleiben. Jedenfalls tragen er und seine Priester auf dem um 1795 entstandenen und immer wieder mit dieser Aufführung in Zusammenhang gebrachten Szenenbild von Joseph Schaffer nicht die beschriebene mitraähnliche Kopfbedeckung, sondern vielmehr die aus der altjüdischen Überlieferung bekannte turbanartige 'Miznefet' eines Hohepriesters. Diese Art der Kopfbedeckung ist ein neuerlicher Hinweis auf das Kernstück der Legende des Schottischen Meistergrades, das den Wiederaufbau des Salomonischen Tempels unter dem Hohepriester Josua während der Amtszeit des Statthalters Zerubbabel zum Inhalt hat.

Aus Anlaß der Hamburger Aufführung kam es 1794 in der Loge 'Zum Pelikan' in Altona zu einem fast völlig vergessenen Vortrag durch den Deputierten Meister vom Stuhl Johann Heinrich Detenhoff, Syndikus beim Hamburger Domkapitel, in dem erstmals unter freimaurerischen Gesichtspunkten 'Zufällige Gedanken über das bekannte Drama der Zauberflöte' dargelegt wurden.[99] Im Gegensatz zu dem im selben Jahr im *Journal des Luxus und der Moden* erschienenen Beitrag 'Ueber Mozarts Oper die Zauber-Flöte' von Ludwig v. Batzko aus Königsberg, der nur ganz allgemein darauf hinwies, daß 'manche Szenen gewisse Anspielungen auf bestimmte Ordensbräuche enthalten', die nur von denjenigen entschlüsselt werden könnten, 'welche Mitglieder des Ordens sind', wird von Detenhoff die *Zauberflöte* unzweifelhaft als freimaurerische Allegorie verstanden.

$$*\quad*\quad*$$

Wie sich indessen zeigte, waren letztlich in Wien aber alle Bemühungen von seiten der nach dem Schottischen Hochgradsystem des Rektifizierten Ritus arbeitenden Freimaurer um Rehabilitierung und Abgrenzung gegenüber para-maurerischen Geheimgesellschaften durch den frühen Tod von Kaiser Leopold II. vergebens gewesen. Während der Regierung von Kaiser Franz II. hatten dann die Geschehnisse in Frankreich mit der Hinrichtung von König Ludwig XVI. am 21. Januar 1793 einen neuen Höhepunkt erreicht. Die Freimaurerlogen in den habsburgischen Ländern mit Ausnahme Ungarns wurden in der Folge durch das Circular vom 13. Mai 1793 aufgefordert, ihre Mitgliederlisten unter Namhaft-machung von Militärpersonen und Angehörigen des geistlichen Standes der Wiener Polizeihofstelle vorzulegen. Insgesamt reagierten neun Logen auf diese Verordnung, darunter die Wiener Logen 'Zur gekrönten Hoffnung' und 'Zum heiligen Joseph'.[100] Die dritte Wiener Loge 'Zur Liebe und Wahrheit' hatte sich auf Anordnung ihrer Regensburger Mutterloge bereits im Frühsommer 1793 aufgelöst, und mit ihr das von Joseph Mesmer geleitete geheime Direktorium.[101]

Die immer vehementer werdenden pauschalen Verdächtigungen nach dem 'Königsmord' in Frankreich führten am 7. Oktober 1793 in der Loge 'Zum heiligen

Joseph' zur Erkenntnis: 'die unselige französische Revolution macht der hiesigen Freimaurerei manche unangenehme Stunde, weil der niedrige Pöbel und die unwissende Geistlichkeit, Illuminatismus und Jacobinismus immer mit der schuldlosen reinen Maurerei verwechseln, und eins wie das andre gänzlich ausgerottet wissen möchten.'[102] Gemeinsam mit der zweiten noch existierenden Wiener Loge 'Zur gekrönten Hoffnung' beschloß sie zwei Monate später ihre Selbstauflösung. Am 8. Dezember 1793 überreichten die Dignitäre dem Kaiser in einer geheimen Audienz ein Memorandum über die Einstellung der Tätigkeit der beiden Logen. Zumindest die Loge 'Zum heiligen Joseph' bezog allerdings die abgegebene Erklärung nur auf die Einstellung der Arbeiten in den Symbolischen Graden und nicht auf solche nach dem Hochgradritual, denn sie wußte in einem Schreiben an die Große Landesloge von Deutschland zu berichten:[103] 'Uns in Wissenschaften zu üben und zu vervollkommnen, ist uns auch nicht von der Landesregierung untersagt worden. Wir bitten daher recht sehr, uns ferner als gute, eifrige, obgleich in der untern Maurerei ruhende Loge zu betrachten.'

Ähnlich verhielt es sich in Prag: Dort hatte bereits am 24. Juni 1791 die Loge 'Zu neun Sternen' schriftlich versichert, 'mit den französischen Logen und allen jenen, die von der Revolutionsseuche Frankreichs angesteckt sind, in keiner Verbindung mehr stehen zu wollen'.[104] Ein Jahr später wurde von ihr gemeinsam mit den Logen 'Wahrheit und Einigkeit zu drei gekrönten Säulen' und 'Zu den drei gekrönten Sternen und Redlichkeit' eine 'Erklärung . . . an das Publikum' mit einer scharfen Zurückweisung aller Verdächtigungen veröffentlicht.[105] Als letzter Versuch erschien 1793 dann noch eine Verteidigungsschrift unter dem Titel 'Die Freimaurer keine Jakobiner'. In einem gemeinsamen Memorandum vom 14. April 1794 sahen sich dann die drei Prager Logen veranlaßt, die Einstellung jedweder Tätigkeiten bekanntzugeben.

In Ungarn wurden dagegen die Freimaurer wohl wegen der Patronanz des habsburgischen Palatins Alexander Leopold über das politische Erbe seines Vaters am längsten geduldet. Unter Franz II. war in Pesth neben den beiden Symbolischen Logen 'Zur Großmut' und 'Zu den sieben Sternen' noch ein in höheren Graden arbeitendes Schottisches Kapitel 'Franz zum wachenden Löwen' entstanden,[106] das sich wohl vor Einbeziehung des kaiserlichen Namens in den Logennamen des Protektoriums des Monarchen versichert haben mußte. Noch im Frühjahr 1793 wurde an die Wiederbegründung einer Provinzialloge von Ungarn gedacht.[107] Aber auch hier waren vor dem politischen Hintergrund Absetzbewegungen deutlich erkennbar, sodaß im Mai 1794 die beiden Symbolischen Logen zu einer einzigen Loge mit dem Namen 'Zu sieben Sternen und Vereinigung' zusammengelegt werden mußten.[108] Die Jakobinerprozesse und der Tod des bei einem alchemistischen Experiment tragisch ums Leben gekommenen Palatins machten dann auch in Ungarn der Freimaurerbewegung ein Ende.

Die nunmehr sinnentleerten freimaurerischen Embleme der *Zauberflöte* erfuhren außerhalb Wiens in der Folge die widersprüchlichsten Deutungen.[109] Auf dem Theater und in Flugschriften kam es sowohl zu jakobinerfreundlichen wie regierungstreuen Demonstrationen. Für Schikaneder und sein Freihaustheater war die *Zauberflöte* mit 223 Aufführungen in elf Jahren das erfolgreichste Stück im Repertoire. Über die ganze Zeit hinweg hatte ihn das Alberti-Frontispiz von 1791 begleitet, das in den Neuauflagen der Textbücher von 1793, 1795 und 1798 stets enthalten war.

Der große Erfolg ermutigte Schikaneder 1798 zu einem zweiten Teil unter dem Titel 'Das Labyrinth oder Der Kampf mit den Elementen' mit der Musik von Peter Winter.[110] Wieder sind freimaurerische Bezüge erkennbar, wenngleich nicht mehr so deutlich wie in der *Zauberflöte*. Zu diesem Zeitpunkt war die Freimaurerei in den habsburgischen Ländern formal nach wie vor nicht verboten, doch durch restriktive Verordnungen zu völliger Stagnation verurteilt. Noch immer steht Sarastro an der Spitze des Bundes der 'Eingeweihten', aus dem der Würdigste und Weiseste erwählt wurde, 'damit er schütze Thron und Vaterland'. Seine mitraähnliche Kopfbedeckung als 'Eingeweihter' und die zum Jagdgewand getragene Brustplatte lassen Sarastro in den überlieferten Figurinen des Innocenzo Chiesa neuerlich als jüdischen Tempelpriester erscheinen, wie schon bei den *Zauberflöte*-Aufführungen in Leipzig, München und Hamburg. Den ersten Auftritt seiner Gegenspielerin, der Königin der Nacht, wie sie 'in Lunas Kleidung' in dem von einer (dem Illuminatentum zuzuordnenden) Eule gezogenen 'Wolkenwagen' erscheint, umgeben von ihren drei Damen und dem mit einem roten Freimaurerschurz bekleideten Monostatos, hat Vincenzo Sacchetti im Deckenfresko in Schikaneders Landhaus in dem Wiener Vorort Nußdorf festgehalten.[110]

Am 4. Januar 1802 zeigte Schikaneder erstmals die *Zauberflöte* in seinem neuen Theater an der Wien, dessen gemalter Hauptvorhang thematisch von Franz Scheyerer auf dieses Werk abgestimmt worden war. Selbst zu diesem späten Zeitpunkt wurde dem Libretto noch immer das Alberti-Frontispiz der Erstausgabe beigebunden.[112] Der Grund hierfür muß weniger in der Ästhetik des Kupferstiches als vielmehr im anhaltenden Bekenntnis zum freimaurerischen Inhalt der Oper gelegen haben. Zehn Jahre später hat dann dem in ärmlichen Verhältnissen lebenden Sechzigjährigen die Direktion seines einstigen Theaters 'von der Einnahme jeder Aufführung der Zauberflöte vier Procente auf Lebenslang bewilligt'.[113] Wie es sich zeigen sollte jedoch zu spät, denn Schikaneder ist bald danach am 21. September 1812 gestorben.

ANHANG

Leopold Alois Hoffmann

Die Einweihung in das Geheimniß der
schreklichen Unbekannten.

(In: *Wiener Zeitschrift*, 1. Jg., 3. Band, 8. Heft, 1792, S. 156f.)

'. . . Wem ist es noch eingefallen, auch unsre
neuern Ritterromane, unsre Volksmährchen,
unsre Zauber- und Feenschauspiele, nicht blos
mit dem Richterblik des Schöngeists und des
Rezensenten, sondern mit der ernsten Prüfung des
Staatsmannes, des Herzenskenners, und in dem
Gesichtspunkte von *Volkslektür und Volksschauspiel*
zu beurtheilen? – Sollte nebst andern nicht die
bekannte *Zauberflöte* eine solche Prüfung ver-
dienen? Es scheint doch in dieser *Volksoper* nicht
blos Auge und Ohr angesehen zu sein.

Man stellt da doch Dinge auf, welche eine
gewisse Tradition immer als heiligste Geheimnisse in
tiefes Dunkel verhüllte. Gehören solche geheime
Heiligkeiten heut zu Tage als Schauspiel für das
große Volk? *Warum* denn?? – – Und *warum* werden
doch diese Heiligkeiten mit einem so ehrwürdigen, anziehenden, einladenden und *höchstkostbaren*
Gepränge dargestellt? – –

Es kann doch, unter solchen Umständen und
bei solchen so ganz *handgreiflichen* Bemühungen,
am Ende wahrlich kein Geheimniß mehr sein,
wie sehr der Ordens- und Fraktionsgeist überall
geschäftigt ist, sein Reich mit immer neuen
Proseliten und neuen – *Betrogenen* zu vermehren.
Man wird bald nicht mehr nöthig haben, über
diese Bemühungen *nur Fingerzeige* zu geben. Die
Anwerbungen und Einladungen an *alle* Klassen
Menschensöhne werden ja schon ohne alles Hehl
und Verborgensein gemacht. Oeffentlich und frei
stellt man ja schon in Volksromanen und
Volksschauspielen die Leimstangen auf, um die
Neugier, die Einfalt und – *die Bosheit* in die
Labirinthe des *Geheimnisses* hinein zu fangen –

Wie lange dies noch so ungeahndet und –
unbemerkt hingehen wird? – Ich – lege die Hand
auf den Mund, und erstaune! – H.'

Johann Detenhoff

Zufällige Gedanken über das bekannte Drama
der Zauberflöte (1794)

(zitiert nach: Paul Nettl, 'Zur Geschichte der freimaurerischen Deutung der "Zauberflöte"', in: *Das Jahrbuch der
Weltfreimaurerei*, Wien 1935, S. 75ff.)

'Zur kurtzen Uebersicht und Zusammenfassung
aller in der Zauberflöte an- und dramatisch aufgeführten sehr wichtigen, einem Freymaurer ein-
leuchtenden, Gegenstände will ich folgendes
bemerken. Ueberhaupt fällt hier so gleich der sehr
große Unterschied zwischen Sarastro und der
Stern Königinn oder der nächtlichen Königinn
einem jeden von selbst schon in die Augen, und
ein Freymaurer betrachtet solche als Bilder, jenes
als das reinste größte Licht, die wahre Licht-
Kraft! dieses Bild als nächtliche Finsterniß in so
weit diese unter dem Gewande eines über die
gantze Menschheit verbreiteten dunkeln Schleyers
aufs einleuchtendste dargestellt und aufgeführtes
ist. Sogar wird auch darüber ein Lichts Strahl
verbreitet, wie und auf welche Art Sarastro als
das Haupt und vorsitzender Meister der eingeweyhten die in Händen habende sehr große
Kraft und Macht / : so in der gantzen dramati-
schen Ausführung sich zeigt: / erlanget, und die
Stern Königinn solche verlohren hat.'

Die Königin eröffnet ihrer Tochter Pamina, daß
ihr Vater bei seinem Tode den Siebenfachen
Sonnenkreis den Eingeweihten übergeben habe,
und daß dieser Sonnenkreis und die mit ihm verbundenen übermenschlichen Kräfte von den
Göttern nur den Eingeweihten bestimmt seien.
Auch habe der sterbende Vater die Warnung
hinzugefügt, sie dürfe nicht nach Wesen oder
wesentlichen Dingen forschen, die dem weiblichen
Geschlecht nicht geziemen, sondern es sei mütter-
liche Pflicht, die Tochter der Führung der weisen
Männer zu überlassen. Bei Betrachtung der

Personen des Kreises um die Königin träfe man Gutes und Böses in vermischtem Zustande 'bis so gar das böse in pur Rache und Bosheit ausartet, und das gute zur völligen Einweyhung gelangt'. Papageno sei ein Mann, der nur an Schlafen, Essen, Trinken und seine Fortpflanzung denkt und sich nur wenig vom Vieh unterscheidet, 'daher auch dieses von allerley Art erscheinet, sich zu ihm gesellet und mit ihm speiset'. Da er weder Gut noch Böse kennt, so ist er auch nicht in der Lage, das Gute erlernen zu können, weshalb ihm auch der Eintritt ins Heiligtum verwehrt sei. Detenhoff hält es für besonders bemerkenswert, daß Papageno 'so bald er dem bösem nur im mindesten beytritt und er anfängt, zu lügen, er sofort unmittelbaar auf der Stelle gestraft und fürs künftige nachdrücklich gewarnt wird'. Er erhält Strafe und Lohn, aber gewissermaßen nur im Rahmen des 'Profanen'. Ein Naturmensch wie Papageno kann unmöglich Freimaurer werden, setzt Detenhoff fort. Ganz anders ist es mit Tamino bestellt, der zwar auch ein Naturmensch ist, der in sich jedoch einen Trieb zu Tugend, Freundschaft und reiner Liebe empfindet, die Götter verehrt und anbetet und schließlich den Tempel der Weisheit aufsucht. Tamino und Papageno werden auf Sarastros Befehl mit bedeckten Häuptern in den Prüfungstempel eingeführt, und es wird ihnen gesagt, daß sie erst gereinigt werden müßten. 'Sodann werden sie weiter vors erste damit getröstet, daß wenn es mit ihrer Aufsuchung des Tugendweges ein rechter Ernst ist, und sie allen Wanderschaften und Gefahren selbst dem Tode sich unterwerfen wollen, sie dazu admittiret werden sollen.'

Nach dieser Versicherung gibt Sarastro, nachdem er den Beifall aller Eingeweihten errungen hat, dem Sprecher als dem Verteidiger der Wahrheit den Auftrag, sein heiliges Amt zu verrichten, Tamino in den Vorhof des Tempels einzuführen, und ihn zu unterrichten, was Menschenpflicht sei. Hiebei wird Verschwiegenheit zur ersten Pflicht gemacht. Den Suchenden, Tamino und Pamina, stellen sich nunmehr allerlei Hindernisse und Beschwerden in den Weg: Es erscheinen die drei Nymphen der nächtlichen Königin und bemühen sich, die Suchenden von ihrer Einweihung abzubringen. Auch Papageno macht allerlei Einwendungen und Pamina sucht das Stillschweigen zu brechen. Blitz und Donner erheben sich, um den Mut Taminos sinken zu lassen, und schließlich macht die Sternenkönigin selbst den Versuch, die Einweihung zu verhin-

dern. Nun erscheint ein Eingeweihter, der Taminos Angesicht bedeckt, ihn bei der Hand faßt und reinen Herzens die Wanderschaft mit ihm fortsetzt. Inzwischen hat Papageno ähnliche Erlebnisse. Nach zurückgelegter Wanderschaft wird ihnen die Bedeckung ihres Angesichtes von einem Priester abgenommen, in einer Halle werden sie sich allein überlassen; sobald die Posaune ertönt, sollen sie ihren Weg dahin nehmen, 'wer hier sein Stillschweigen bricht, werde von den Göttern durch Blitz und Donner gestraft'. Detenhoff fährt dann in der Inhaltsangabe des Dramas fort, verweilt vor allem bei der Feuer- und Wasserprobe. Zum Schluß seines Vortrages sagt er: 'Alles dieses dient einem Freymaurer zu einem sehr nachdenklichen Bilde. Er soll, dem Bilde gemäs, mit der Bearbeitung des rohen – Natur Menschen anfangen, darin beharren, alles äußere sinnliche Lüste und Begierden ablegen und sein inneres intellectuelles Wesen über seine irrdische Natur erheben, wozu der Keim in ihm im innern liegt und verborgen ist, da er dann nach solcher vollbrachten sehr mühseeligen mit vielen Hindernissen und Gefahren begleiteten dreifachen Arbeit und nach bewürckter völliger Reinigung an Leib – Seel – und Geist gäntzlich von dem Druck der Materie frey wird, und zum Heyligthum gelanget, und seine Gattin an der Hand mit einführen kann.

Noch mehr aber sey es uns ins Gedächtniß gerufen, daß wer die Hände in den Schoß legt, dem bloß Natur Menschen folgt, daher auch nicht ins Heyligthum komt, und ferner mercke man des Sarastro Ausspruch: Ein Mann mus Weiber Hertzen leiten, denn ohne ihn pflegt jedes Weib, aus ihrem Würckungskreis zu schreiten.

Außer diesem angeführten mus ich noch einen Blick auf die nächtliche Königinn ihre drey Nymphen und den in Sarastros Dienste befindlichen Mohren werfen, in welchen wir gute und böse Handlungen in einem höchst vermischten Zustande antreffen.

Als gute Menschen zeigen sie sich, indem die drei Nymphen den Tamino von der ihn den Tod drohenden Schlange befreyen, und diese tödten.

Der Mohr bezeigt sich als ein guter Mensch, indem er die Pamina vom Selbst Mord befreyt und ihr den Dolch aus der Hand reißt.

Allein betrachten wir den Grund von diesen vermischten guten Handlungen, so werden wir überzeugt, daß nie ein wahrer Tugend Grund vorhanden, sondern lauter Neben Absichten –

unächte Freundschaft und eine unreine Liebe die etwaigen guten Handlungen zufälliger weise befördern, wie wir an des schwartzen Mohrs Betragen offenbaar sehen, und wovon Sarastro selbst den Ausspruch thut, daß seine Seele so schwartz sey wie seine Farbe! –

Dahero denn auch am Ende so wohl mit der Königinn der Nacht als mit ihren Nymphen und dem Mohr selbst, alles dahin hinausläuft, daß sie sich unter einander gegen die gäntzliche Ausrottung alles guten verbinden, und den Eingeweyhten den Untergang drohen und beschwören.

Ein Bild, welches einen Freymaurer schon bey dem Gedanken eine steten Beharrlichkeit im Bösen Schaudern machen sollte.

Ein Haupt Umstand aus der Königinn der Nacht ihrer Geschichts Erzählung, so sie ihrer Tochter mitgetheilt, kan ich schließlich nicht mit Stillschweigen übergehen, da sie bekennt, daß der Pamina ihr Vater vor seinem Tode den siebenfachen sehr mächtigen auch zugleich alles verzehrenden Sonnenkreis in Händen gehabt und dadurch alles regieret und alle Gewalt exercirt habe, und daß er diese Macht und Gewalt, nach der Götter Willen den Eingeweyhten übergeben habe.

Ein herrliches, hyeroglyphisches Bild für einen ächten Freymaurer! Es hat also die Königinn der Nacht und ihre Tochter, als ein Bild der irrdischen Natur – und der Menschheit einen Vater – Herrscher – und Regierer gehabt, welcher bey seinem Tode, oder möchte ich sagen, bey seiner sich selbst durch den Mißbrauch seines freyen Willens zugezogenen Ohnmacht seine Herschaft vermittelst des Thier Kreises, selbst über Mond und Sterne – über Himmel und Erde abgetreten hat, oder möchte ich sagen hat abgeben müssen, und zwar an die Auserwählten, oder vielmehr deren Haupt, als an den folgenden Stellvertreter des ersteren in Ohnmacht versunkenen Innhabers, dem nunmehro gegeben ist alle Gewalt im Himmel und auf Erden.

Ich will diese Gedanken einem jeden zur weitern Überlegung anheim geben, um die Achtung und das Bestreben zum wahren Heyligthum desto mehr in sich zu beleben, und dazu sich gesetzmäßig zu bilden, sich immer mehr zu verbessern und zur gäntzlichen Vollkommenheit nach Anweisung des Ordens und durch die vorgeschriebenen Hülfs Mittel sich empor zu schwingen.'

EPHRAIM JOSEPH HIRSCHFELD

Brief an [den Leipziger Verleger Adam Friedrich] Böhmen vom 24. Januar 1818

(Den Haag, Archiv des Grootosten der Nederlanden, Handschriften der Klossianischen Bibliothek, Sign. 191 D 29)

'Mein lieber Böhmen!
Hier folgt Ihrem Verlangen gemäß noch ein Heft. Ich muß Ihnen übrigens auch dasjenige, was Ihnen M[olitor] hierüber gesagt hat, in Wahrheit bestättigen: daß über die wichtigsten und interessantesten Stellen ein Schleier gezogen ist, welcher aus guten Gründen, freilich nicht sobald für die Beruffenen, als für die Auserwählten, durch einen systematischen privat-Unterricht aufgezogen werden kann und darf, um klar und deutlich und hell zu sehen. M[olitor] wird Ihnen hierüber mündlich mehr sagen können, als ich aus Mangel an Zeit und Muse, Ihnen desfalls zu schreiben gegenwärtig nicht im Stande bin.

Sie schreiben mir, daß der Hofkapellmeister Hummel so sehr in Frankfurt bewundert wird ... Alles was der unsterbliche Mozart componiert hat, ist ein wahrhaftes Canticum oder besser Sanctum; allein seine Zauberflöte ist und bleibt in alle Ewigkeit: das Canticum canticorum oder Sanctum sanctorum, und demnach kläfften manche Südel-Componisten aus vollem Halse: er hätte in dieser alles übertreffenden Opera himmelschreiend und ganz unverantwortlich gegen die Regeln der Declamation gefehlt. O Sancta Simplicitas. Ich muß schliessen. Kommen Sie doch ja bald! Der Ihrige,

Offenbach, Januar [18]18   Hirschfeld'

Otto Biba

Nachrichten über Joseph Haydn, Michael Haydn und Wolfgang Amadeus Mozart in der Sammlung handschriftlicher Biographien der Gesellschaft der Musikfreunde in Wien

IN DER SITZUNG des Repräsentantenkörpers der Gesellschaft der Musikfreunde in Wien vom 12. Oktober 1825 stellte der Gründer und langjährige Sekretär der Gesellschaft Joseph Sonnleithner (1725–1835) den Antrag,[1]

> Die Nachrichten über das Leben der einheimischen Musiker zu sammeln und zu bewahren, um solche vielleicht in der Folge als Ergänzung des Gerber'schen Lexikons[2] öffentlich bekannt zu machen, zu welchem Zwecke eine eigene Committée gewählt werden dürfte.

Der Antrag wurde von Sonnleithner mit Datum vom 13. Oktober schriftlich ausgefertigt, um dem Sitzungsprotokoll beigelegt zu werden. Seine ausführliche Begründung dieses Projektes, das im Zusammenhang mit einer in Wien bereits länger latent vorhanden gewesenen Idee eines österreichischen Musik- oder Musikerlexikons bzw. einer österreichischen Musikgeschichte zu sehen ist, braucht hier ebensowenig wiedergegeben zu werden, wie die Idee an sich hier weiter verfolgt werden kann.

Die Diskussion dieses Antrages ist im Sitzungsprotokoll der Gesellschaft wie folgt festgehalten:

> Über die Bemerkung des Herrn Hofrathes v. Mosel,[3] daß Herr Abbé Stadler[4] sich bereits mit Sammlung von Materialien zur vaterländischen Geschichte der Tonkunst beschäftige, andere der anwesenden Mitglieder bemerkten daß diese Geschichte sich auf die Epoche bis zu J. Haydn's Tode beschränke: so war man darüber einverstanden, daß über alle nach Haydns Tode verstorbenen und die noch lebenden Tonkünstler die biographischen Nachrichten und Daten, durch eine hierzu zu wählende besondere Committée, gesammelt werden soolen.

Im Protokoll der nächsten Sitzung des Repräsentantenkörpers am 31. Jänner 1826 lesen wir zu diesem Thema:[5]

> Herr Reg[ierungs] Rath v. Sonnleithner erinnert, daß schon in der letzten Repraesentanten-Versammlung beschlossen wurde, eine Committée zu wählen, welche sich mit der Sammlung der Daten über das Leben und Wirken der vater-

ländischen Tonsetzer, Tonkünstler u.a. zu beschäftigen hätte. Der leitende Ausschuß [der Gesellschaft] hat hierzu eine Anzahl von Individuen vorgeschla-gen. Es werden daher diese Nahmenslisten unter die Anwesenden vertheilt und solche ersucht, diese Listen mit ihren Zusätzen Bemerkungen oder Bestätigungen, nach einigen Tagen, in der Gesellschaftskanzley abzugeben.

Das gebildete Komitee stand unter der Leitung Joseph Sonnleithners, der mit Datum vom 20. Juli 1826 über die Arbeit dieses Komitees einen schriftlichen Bericht vorlegte,[6] in dem neunzig bereits gelieferte Biographien und deren Verfasser angeführt sind; 63 stammten von Joseph Sonnleithner selbst, 15 von Johann Baptist Geißler, der Rest von verschiedenen Autoren.

Die bearbeiteten Namen lassen erkennen, daß man für deren Auswahl nicht (wie ursprünglich vorgesehen) Haydns Todesjahr 1809 als *terminus post quem* gewählt, sondern auch einige früher verstorbene Komponisten aufgenommen hat. Daß die Brüder Haydn und W.A. Mozart in dieser Biographien-Sammlung nicht aufscheinen, darf uns nicht wundern; sie hatten ja bis 1826 schon – mehrfache – biographische Würdigungen erfahren.

Die weitere Geschichte des Projekts braucht hier nicht dargestellt zu werden. Die Sammelleidenschaft der Proponenten erlahmte, die Bereitschaft lebender Komponisten, selbst einen biographischen Abriß beizustellen, war gering, aber dennoch wurde das Projekt noch bis in die dreißiger Jahre verfolgt. Zur Publikation eines Lexikons ist es freilich nie gekommen. Jedoch stellt diese Sammlung hand-schriftlicher Biographien in der Bibliothek der Gesellschaft der Musikfreunde in Wien[7] eine erstrangige Quelle dar, die auch als Torso eines größeren Projektes dankenswerte, meist einzigartige Hilfestellungen zu leisten vermag.

Sie wird vornehmlich als biographische Quelle für die in der Sammlung vertretenen Komponisten oder Musiker verwendet. In der Folge werden erstmals die in den Biographien enthaltenen Erwähnungen Joseph und Michael Haydns sowie Wolfgang Amadeus Mozarts gesammelt publiziert. Grundsätzlich wurden alle Erwähnungen aufgenommen, die eine persönliche Beziehung des behandelten Komponisten oder Musikers zu den Brüdern Haydn oder zu Mozart erkennen lassen sowie auch Nachrichten zur fürstlich Esterházyschen Kapelle im allgemeinen sowie zu Musikern, die als fürstlich Esterházysche Untertanen geboren worden waren. Sinnvoll erschien es auch, eine – in der Biographie von Ignaz Holzbauer enthaltene – Detailinformation über künstlerische Aktivitäten im Internat der Wiener Dom-sängerknaben zur Zeit des Domkapellmeisters Johann Georg Reutter d.J. aufzu-nehmen, weil man daraus auch Rückschlüsse für jene Zeit ziehen kann, die die Brüder Haydn dort verbracht haben.

Der Informationscharakter der hier gesammelten Nachrichten über Joseph und Michael Haydn sowie Wolfgang Amadeus Mozart ist verschieden. Bekannte und vielfach belegte Details stehen neben absolut neuen. Deren Kommentierung und Einordnung in die biographische Haydn- und Mozartliteratur konnte nicht die Aufgabe dieser Publikation sein. Sie will als Quellenedition verstanden werden, die einen an sich bekannten, aber für die Haydn- und Mozartforschung noch nicht ausge- werteten Quellenbestand zugänglich macht.

Die Zitate aus den einzelnen Biographien sind genau nach der Vorlage wiedergegeben, auf jede – auch orthographische – Veränderungen wurde verzichtet, lediglich die Verdopplungsstriche über dem Buchstaben m wurden aufgelöst. Zu den Namen, in deren Biographien die wiedergegebenen Zitate gefunden wurden, sind Geburts- und Sterbeort sowie die Lebensdaten so genannt, wie sie in der Quelle angegeben sind, um einen unmittelbaren Eindruck von ihr – allenfalls auch von ihrer Zuverlässigkeit – zu vermitteln. Auch hierbei wurden keine Ergänzungen, Kommentierungen oder Korrekturen vorgenommen. Die Schreibweise der Namen selbst folgt unverändert der vorliegenden handschriftlichen Biographie, auch wenn sie von der heute verbreiteten Schreibweise abweicht. Abkürzungen wurden nur dann – in eckiger Klammer – aufgelöst, wenn ein Un- oder Mißverständnis möglich schien. Auch allfällige andere Ergänzungen zum Verständnis des aus einem größeren Zusammenhang herausgenommenen Zitates stehen in eckiger Klammer.

Die Mehrzahl der Biographien liegt in Reinschriften vor, die nicht vom Verfasser der Biographien vorgenommen wurden. Diese schöne Kanzlei-Handschrift ist aus dem Aktenbestand der Gesellschaft der Musikfreunde bekannt, doch läßt sich ihr Schreiber nicht namentlich identifizieren. In selteneren Fällen stammt die Reinschrift von der Hand Johann Baptist Geißlers,[8] Mitglied des Repräsentantenkörpers der Gesellschaft und des Komitees zur Erstellung der Biographien sowie Verfasser einer Reihe von ihnen; einige hat Geißler signiert, bei anderen ist seine Hand zweifelsfrei zu identifizieren.

Ist der Verfasser genannt oder die Biographie datiert, so werden die entsprechen- den Signatur- und Datierungszitate wiedergegeben. Bietet der Text der Biographie einen Rückschluß auf den Zeitpunkt von dessen Entstehung, so ist auch dies vermerkt. Schließlich wird auch der Verfasser genannt, wenn sich sein Name in jener Liste[9] findet, welche die bis 20. Juli 1826 vorliegenden Biographien und deren Autoren nennt. Handelt es sich um eine eigenhändig geschriebene Selbstbiographie, so ist auch dies vermerkt.

Maria Anna Freyinn Berthold von Sonnenburg
(Salzburg, 1751–keine Angabe)

[. . .] Sie bildete sich im Klavierspiel unter der Leitung ihres Vaters, der sie und ihren Bruder als bewunderungswürdige Klavierspieler in den Jahren 1762–1768 auf einer großen Reise durch Frankreich, Holland, England, Deutschland begleitete. Die beiden kleinen Künstler ließen sich auf dieser Reise auch in Wien hören, und wurden allgemein bewundert. [. . .]

Josepha Barbara Bessenig
(Wien, 25. September 1758–Wien, 30. Jänner 1820)

[. . .] Ihr Hang zur Musik entwickelte sich sehr früh; auf dem Pianoforte machte sie außerordentliche Fortschritte, besonders unter der Leitung des großen Mozart. [. . .]

Anmerkung: Josepha Barbara Bessenig hieß vor ihrer Verehelichung (also zur Zeit des Unter- richtes bei Mozart) Auernhammer.

Elise Beysteiner
(Kleinhöflein bei Eisenstadt 1806–keine Angabe)

[. . .] Es geschah auch sehr bald, daß der Abbate Paolo Bevilacqua, ein Italiener von Geburt, damals einer der vorzüglichsten Tenoristen, und gegenwärtig noch bei der fürstlich Esterhazyschen Kapelle angestellt, nachdem er sich von dem schönen Talent der jungen Beysteiner überzeugt hatte, nicht nur die Sorge für ihre Gesangausbildung, sondern auch für ihre wis- senschaftliche Bildung ohne alles Interesse, über- nommen hatte. [. . .]

Anmerkung: Dazu die von Johann Baptist Geißler signierte Bemerkung 'Zur Sammlung der Biographien; aus der Damenzeitung No. 294 vom 10. Dezember 1830.'

Joseph Carpani
(Villalbese im Bezirke Brianza, 1752–keine Angabe)

[. . .] Er arbeitete in Form von Briefen, die den Nahmen Haydine(*) erhielten, eine Biographie Haydns, und eine Apologie von dessen Compositionen und zugleich eine Art von musikalischer Ästhetik, aus. [. . .]

(*)*Le Haydine, ovvero lettere su la vita e le opere del celebre maestro Giuseppe Haydn*, di Gius. Carpani, dedicate al R. Conservatorio di musica di Milano. Milano, da Candido Buccinelli, Stampatore- Cartaro, contrada di S. Margherita num. 1118. 1812.

Handschrift: Johann Baptist Geißler.

Joseph Drechsler
(Wlachowoberzy/Wällischbürken im Prachiner Kreis, 26. Mai 1782–keine Angabe)

[. . .] Er studirte aber auch während dieser ganzen Zeit eine Menge Werke anderer Compositeurs. Sein Lieblingsautor wurde Mozart, besonders in Opern, und Klavierstücken. Die ganze Partitur von Don Juan lernte er auswendig, und laut Beilage, weiß er eine jede Stelle, wie sie der große Meister instrumentirte, auswendig; Mozarts Concerte größtentheils, und besonders jenes aus D. moll [KV 466] kann ebenfalls auswendig. [. . .] In seinem 20ten Jahre 1802 wählte er Glucks Opern, zu seiner Beschäftigung, und angenehm- sten Unterhaltung; dann Joseph Haydens Messen, und auch Opern. Ein Manuscript von der Haydens[chen] Oper: la virtu praemiata [*La fedeltà premiata* (Hob. XXVIII:10)] darin Haydens eigene Hand Notaten gezeichnet hat, erkaufte er um vieles Geld. Diese Opera ist auser diesem Exemplar kaum mehr vorhanden, da von diesem Schatze in Eisenstadt viel verbrannt worden seyn soll. [. . .]

Anmerkung: Verfasser der Biographie ist Carl Gottfried Salzmann, der sie am Ende signiert und mit dem Datum der Ablieferung, dem 2. April 1826, versehen hat.

Adam Joseph Emmert
(Würzburg, Christnacht 1768–16. April 1812, Wien)

[. . .] Sein Vater, der selbst viele Kirchen- Kompositionen geliefert hatte, bildete ihn schon früh zum Musiker, und Emmert vervollkommnete seine Kenntnisse in Salzburg vorzüglich durch seinen Umgang mit Otter, Marchand, Simoni, Michael Haydn u.s.w. [...]

Karl Friberth
(Wullersdorf, 7. Juni 1736–6. August 1816, Wien)

[...] Seine erste Bedienstung war bey der Kapelle des Prinzen von Sachsen-Hildburghausen, in der Folge wurde er 1759 bey dem Fürsten von Esterhazy als Tenorsänger bey der Kapelle angestellt; dort lernte er Joseph Haydn kennen, und beide wurden die vertrautesten Freunde. Er machte in der Zwischenzeit eine Reise nach Triest und Venedig auf Kosten des Fürsten v. Esterhazy, und erhielt 1796 wegen seinen Verdiensten in der Musik vom Papst Pius VI den Orden des goldenen Sporens. [...]

Anmerkung: Verfasser der Biographie ist Joseph Sonnleithner (Liste Juli 1826).

Johann Evangelist Fuß
(Tolna, Ungarn 1777–7. März 1819, Ofen)

[...] Eine nähere Bekanntschaft mit J. Haydn erwarb F[uß] die Achtung dieses großen Künstlers, der selbst die Partitur des erwähnten Melodrams [*Pyramus und Thisbe*, Melodram in einem Aufzug, komponiert in Preßburg und aufgeführt im dortigen Theater] an seinem Clavier durchspielte, den jungen Mann mit Beyfall und dem Versprechen ehrte, bey der Generalprobe dieses, damals an die Bühne [des Theaters] an der Wien verkauften Melodrams, selbst zu erscheinen, um, wie sich Haydn ausdrückte, dem würdigen aber noch unbekannten jungen Künstler, durch seine Gegenwart im Orchester Achtung zu verschaffen. [...]

Anmerkung: Signiert und datiert von Johann Baptist Geißler, 1828.

Joseph Gelinek
(Selcž im Braunauer Kreis in Böhmen, 3. Dezember 1758–13. April 1825, Wien)

[...] Im Jahre 1783 wurde er als Theolog in das Prager Generalseminarium aufgenommen. Auch hier hatte er Gelegenheit sich immer mehr und mehr in der Musik zu vervollkomnen; denn zu eben der Zeit trafen in dem Seminarium so viele musikalische Theologen zusammen, daß sie mit

vollständig besetztem Orchestre die größten Meisterwerke aufgeführt hatten. Selbst Mozart während [wegen Ausriß im Papier zu ergänzen: seinem] Aufenthalte in Prag ließ keine ihrer Accademien aus, musizirte mit ihnen, und gestand es öffentlich, daß seine Symphonien und Messen eben da am vollkommensten exequirt wurden. Bei diesen Accademien hatte auch der Hr. Abbé Gelinek die Gelegenheit sich öfter vor Mozart auf dem Pianoforte hören zu lassen; und von ihm den Beifall und Aufmunterung zur Composition einzuereden. Im Jahre 1786 erhielt er von der Frau Gräfin Wratislaw als absolvirter Theolog den Titulum mensae, worauf er zum Priester geweiht wurde. Hierauf kam er als Hauskaplan und Fortepianomeister in das Fürst Joseph Kinskische Haus, wo er 13 Jahre blieb, und von demselben bis sein Ende alljährlich eine Pension von 600 fl genoß. Durch eben dieses Haus kam er nach Wien, wo er die Bekanntschaft mit Mozart erneuerte, von demselben und durch den Umgang mit Hrn. Albrechtsberger sich fernerhin in der Theorie der Musik vervollkommnete. [...]

Anton Grams
(Markersdorf in Deutschböhmen, 29. Oktober 1752–18. Mai 1823, Wien)

[...] Im Jahre 1801 wurde er im Orchester des Theaters a. d. Wien angestellt, wo er 9 Jahre blieb. Von hier aus kam er in die fürstl. Esterhazysche Kapelle nach Eisenstadt, wo er einen lebenslänglichen Contract schloß; doch nach Verlauf von 2½ Jahren wurde der größte Theil des Kapelle aufgelöst, worunter auch Grams begriffen war. [...]

Anmerkung: Signiert von Johann Baptist Geißler mit dem Vermerk: 'Nach der Wien. mus. Zeitung 1823'. In der Liste Juli 1826 enthalten; als Autor Johann Baptist Geißler angegeben.

Adalbert Gyrowetz
(Böhmisch Budweis, 1763–keine Angabe)

[...] Bald darauf wurde er zu den Concerten des Herrn Salomon in Hanoversquare engagirt, wo seine Symphonien mit vielem Beyfalle aufgeführt wurden. [...] Gyrowetz blieb drey Jahre in London, wo er mit Haydn zusammen traf und ihm wesentliche Dienste leistete, doch, da das Clima auf seine Gesundheit schädlich einzuwirken begann, verließ er England und reiste nach Deutschland zurück. [...]

Anmerkung: Im Titel der Vermerk 'Biographische Skizze nach autobiographischen Notizen bearbeitet von Freyherrn von Lannoy' [Heinrich Eduard Josef von Lannoy] und in dessen Handschrift.

Peter Haensel
(Leipe, Bezirk Grottkau in Preußisch Schlesien, 29. November 1770–1831, Wien)

[...] bis er im Frühjahre 1791 sich nach Wien verfügte, wo er darauf im November desselben Jahres als Kapellmeister und erster Violinist bey der Fürstin Lubomirska angestellt wurd. Nach der Rückkunft Joseph Haydns aus England im Jahre 1792 fing Hänsel an bey selben Unterricht im Contrapunct zu nehmen, setzte dieses Studium durch einige Jahre fort, worauf im Jahre 1795 seine ersteren Arbeiten im Stiche erschienen. [...]

Anmerkung: Das Todesdatum später in der Handschrift von Johann Baptist Geißler ergänzt. Verfasser der Biographie ist Franz Kirchlehner (Liste Juli 1826).

Gregor Hauer
(Ernstbrunn in Niederösterreich, 3. Februar 1753–6. September 1822, Stift Seitenstetten)

[...] In Salzburg lebte er während der theologischen Studienjahre in herzlicher Freundschaft mit Mich. Haydn. [...]

Anmerkung: Signiert und datiert von Johann Baptist Geißler mit dem Vermerk 'Nach den schriftlichen Mittheilungen des H.P. Carl Stadler, Musikdirektors im Stifte Seitenstätten 1828'.

Ignaz Holzbauer
(Wien, 1711–7. April 1783, Mannheim)

[...] auch machte er, der Absicht seines Vaters gemäß, den juridischen Curs an der hiesigen Universität, aber, sein Hang führte ihn zur Musik, die immer seine Lieblingsbeschäftigung war. Er machte Bekanntschaft mit den Singschülern der Domkirche zu St. Stephan, welche damahls in einem kleinen Hause wohnten, welches an die in der Folge abgebrochene, auf dem jetzigen Stephansplatze befindliche Magdalena Kapelle stieß, in welchem auch der Domkapellmeister wohnte. Georg Albrechtsberger war der letzte Domkapellmeister, welcher darinn wohnte, bevor das ganze Gebäude niedergerissen ward. Diese Schüler führten zur Uibung kleiner Komödien und Operetten auf, wie sie noch unter dem Capellmeister Reutter gegeben wurden. Holzbauer dichtete für die Schüler Komödien, und die Schüler unterrichteten ihn dafür in der Musik, der eine im Gesange, der andere auf dem Klavier, der dritte auf der Violine, dem Violoncell, so daß er endlich mit allen Instrumenten bekannt wurde. Endlich, nach weiterer Ausbildung sich sehnend, ruhte er nicht, bis ihm seine Schwester den Gradus ad Parnassum des Hofkapellmeisters Fux kaufte. [...]

Anmerkung: Verfasser der Biographie ist Joseph Sonnleithner (Liste Juli 1826).

Thaddäus Huber
(Nieder-Hollabrunn in Niederösterreich, 1744–27. Februar 1798, Wien)

[...] Joseph Haydn schätzte seine Arbeiten sehr. Nach seinem Tode hat seinen musikalischen Nachlaß Gottfried Freyherr von Swieten, ein großer Musikkenner und selbst Tonsetzer, gekauft. Diese Nachrichten hat seine Wittwe zweyter Ehe, welche noch jetzt (1826) [...] lebt, mitgetheilt. [...]

Anmerkung: Verfasser der Biographie ist Joseph Sonnleithner (Liste Juli 1826).

Joseph Hugelmann
(Wien, 17. Februar 1768–keine Angabe)

[...] Bemerkenswerth ist, daß er, um auch den Klavierspielern den Genuß der größeren Mozartschen Werke zu verschaffen, die Opern, Symphonien, Quartetten, Quintetten dieses großen Meisters für 4 Hände arrangirte. Die ersten 3 Nummern der Quartetten sind bey Diabelli & Comp., die letzten drey bey Mechetti im Stich erschienen. [...]

Anmerkung: Verfasser der Biographie ist Joseph Sonnleithner (Liste Juli 1826).

Johann Nepomuk Hummel
(Preßburg, 14. November 1778–keine Angabe)

[...] Der siebenjährige Hummel zog die Aufmerksamkeit aller Musikkenner auf sich, und man

kam dem Wunsche seines Vaters, den hoffnungs-
vollen Sohn dem großen Mozart vorzustellen,
entgegen. Mozart's Abneigung vor dem Unter-
richtgeben war bekannt, man rieth Hummeln
daher, seinen Sohn eine Bachsche Sonate ein-
studieren zu lassen. Der Jüngling erhielt den Beyfall dieses großen Mannes in solchem Grade, daß
er sich selbst anboth, sein Lehrer zu werden, jedoch unter der Bedingung, daß ihm der Schüler
gänzlich übergeben werden, und in seinem Hause
wohnen müße. Mozart schrieb damals gerade
seine 3 großen Sonaten [*recte* Symphonien] in Es,
C und G moll [KV 543, 551, 550]. So oft er seine
Freunde etwas davon hören lassen wollte, mußte
Hummel immer à 4 mains mit ihm den doppelten
Baß aus seiner Original-Partitur spielen. Nachdem Hummel durch 2 Jahre Mozart's Unterricht genossen, wollte ihn sein Vater öffentlich
hören lassen; Mozart rieth ihm aber, eine Reise
mit ihm zu machen, weil der Prophet in seinem
Vaterlande nichts gelte. So ging der 9jährige Hummel mit seinem Vater auf Reisen, besuchte ganz
Deutschland, Dänemark, England, Schottland
(wo er seine ersten Compositionen, Variazionen
fürs Pianoforte, ohne die Setzkunst gelernt zu
haben, in Druck gab) und Holland. Uiberall
wurde er mit dem ausgezeichnetsten Beyfalle gehört; außer Mozart selbst hatte es noch niemand
in diesem Alter zu solcher Meisterschaft gebracht.
[. . .] Im Jahre 1803 erhielt Hummel auf Joseph
Haydn's besonderer Empfehlung einen Ruf nach
Stuttgart, aber die Unterhandlungen wurden
wieder abgebrochen; der Herzog wollte keinen
Kapellmeister mehr aus Wien nehmen. Bald darauf, als Fürst Nicolaus von Esterhazy von London nach Paris zurück kam, bothen ihm dieser
Fürst und der damahlige Direktor der k.k. Hoftheater, Peter Freyherr von Braun zu gleicher Zeit
Dienste an; er zog den fürstlichen Dienst als
Concertmeister vor. Joseph Haydn, der schon alt
und schwächlich ward, schlug ihn vor. Er stand
der aus beynahe 100 Personen bestehenden fürstlichen Kapelle bis 1811 vor. Da der Fürst besonders Kirchenmusik liebte, so fand Hummel Gelegenheit, sich auch in diesem Fache zu versuchen,
und that es mit Glück. Schon seine erste Messe
erhielt Joseph Haydn's Beyfall. Als später eine
Gesellschaft von Cavaliere, an deren Spitze der
Fürst Esterhazy stand, die k.k. Hoftheater übernahm, fand er auch Gelegenheit, für das Theater
zu schreiben. Im Jahre 1811 verließ er die fürstlichen Dienste, und privatisirte in Wien. [. . .]

Anmerkung: Am Ende der Biographie der
Vermerk 'Diese Nachricht hat Hummel selbst
mittels Schreibens vom 22. May 1826, welches
aufbewahrt wird, mitgetheilt.'

Robert Kimmerling
(Wien, 8. Dezember 1737–5. Dezember 1799,
Stift Melk)

[. . .] Während der theologischen Studien in
Wien, erhielt er durch Jos. Haydn Unterricht in
der Composition, wurde bald einer seiner innig-
sten Freunde, und als trefflicher Tenorist und
Orgelspieler, ein großer Verehrer Grauns und Ph.
Em. Bach's, deren Werke er unablässig studierte,
machte er darin bald grosse Fortschritte, componirte anfangs mehrere Trio und Quartetten,
dann viele Messen, Vespern, Offertorien, Salve
Regina u.a. [. . .]

Anmerkung: Signiert und mit 1826 datiert von
Johann Baptist Geißler. In der Liste Juli 1826
enthalten; als Autor Johann Baptist Geißler
angegeben.

Simon Thaddäus Kölbl
(Eisenstadt, 6. April 1737–10. Juli 1816, Wien)

[. . .] Simon Thaddäus Kölbl wurde den 6. April
1737 auf dem fürstlich Esterhazyschen Grunde in
Eisenstadt gebohren. Sein Vater Mathias war
Grenadier bey der fürstlichen Garde. Er widmete
sich früh der Musik, und bildete sich vorzüglich
im Orgelspiele so aus, daß er im Jahre 1781 als
Chorregent bey der Kirche des h[eiligen] Karl
Boromäus in der Wiener Vorstadt Wieden
angestellt wurde. [. . .]

Anmerkung: Dazu die Bemerkumg 'Diese
Nachrichten hat seine Wittwe mitgetheilt, welche
jetzt (1826) noch lebt und das 90. Jahr zählt.'
Verfasser der Biographie ist Joseph Sonnleithner
(Liste Juli 1826).

Mathias Kracher
(Mattighofen, 30. Jänner 1752–keine Angabe)

[. . .] Mit 1. May 1772 trat er in Seekirchen als
Stiftsorganist ein. Hier war er ganz in seinem
Elemente, und machte die Bekanntschaft des
Concertmeisters Michael Haydn und des P.
Georg Pasterwitz, Musikdirektors in Krems-
münster. Mit beiden trat er in musikalische Korres-
pondenz, und sammelte einen auserlesenen

Vorrath an Musikalien, die er selbst copirt. [...] So verlebte er 42 Jahre in Seekirchen. Michael Haydn blieb sein treuer Freunde, und besuchte ihn zuweilen. [...]

Anmerkung: Verfasser der Biographie ist Joseph Sonnleithner (Liste Juli 1826).

Anton Kraft
(Rokizan, Böhmen, 1751–28. August 1820, keine Ortsangabe)

[...] Seine nun erreichte Virtuosität auf dem Violoncello veranlaßte seine Freunde, ihn zu bewegen, sich ganz der Musik zu widmen, und da eben die erste Violoncellistenstelle in der dazumahl berühmtesten Kapelle des Fürsten Nicolaus Esterhazy unbesetzt war, so wurde ihm selbe von dem Kapellmeister Jos. Haydn selbst angebothen, worauf Kraft im Jahre 1778 nach Esterhaz reiste, und 13 Jahre daselbst verblieb.

Haydn entdeckte bei Kraft eine besondere Anlage zur Composition, und munterte selben auf, bey ihm Unterricht zu nehmen; dieses Anerbiethen nahm Kraft mit innigstem Danke an, und widmete sich nun der Composition mit solchem Eifer, daß er das Violoncell darüber beynahe vernachlässiget hätte. Um Kraft zu zwingen, wieder zu seinem Instrumente zurück zukehren, brach Haydn mit seinem Unterrichte gänzlich ab, und gab die Versicherung, Kraft wisse nun genug um sich seine Conzerte selbst zu setzen, wodurch aber beynahe die ganze Lust zur Composition bey Kraft wieder erlosch, welche erst in späteren Zeiten wieder erwachte.

Nach dem Tode des Fürsten Esterhazy wurde die Kapelle aufgelöst [...]

Kraft spielte auch den Bariton, und componirte mehrere Trios für 2 Bariton und Violoncello, weil der Fürst Esterhazy selbst dieses Instrument spielte.

Um sich die Zuneigung des Fürstens noch mehr zu gewinnen, studierte er auch dieses Instrument.

Als er es zu einem ziemlichen Fertigkeit gebracht hatte, setzte er auch in einem Trio ein Solo für den zweyten Bariton, welche Parthie er immer spielen mußte.

Kaum hörte dieses der Fürst, so unterbrach er das Stück, und sagte zu Kraft: 'Gieb er mir die Stimme.' spielte das Solo durch, und als er solches einigermassen über seine Kräfte fand, erwiderte er: 'Schreib er nur Solo für meine Stimme; denn

daß er besser spielt wie ich, ist keine Kunst sondern seine Schuldigkeit.' [...]

Anmerkung: Signiert und datiert mit 1826 von Johann Baptist Geißler sowie mit der Bemerkung versehen 'Nach den schriftlichen Mittheilungen seines Sohnes Nicolaus Kraft.' Verfasser der Biographie ist Johann Baptist Geißler (Liste 1826).

Nicolaus Kraft
(Esterhaz in Ungarn, 14. Dezember 1778–keine Angabe)

[...] Im 6ten Jahre seines Alters spielte er sein erstes Conzert, welches sein Vater für ihn componirte; im 8ten Jahre begleitete er seinen Vater auf dessen Kunstreisen nach Berlin, Dresden, Ofen, Gratz, und erhielt von Fürsten Nicolaus Esterhazy, welcher sein Taufpathe war, das Versprechen in dessen Kapelle angestellt zu werden.

In seinem 13ten Jahre wurde er aber, nach Auflösung der Esterhazyschen Kapelle, ganz von der Musik entfernt, und sollte sich nun dem Studium zur Ausbildung eines Geschäftsmannes widmen. [...]

Anmerkung: In der Handschrift von Johann Baptist Geißler und mit dessen Bemerkung. 'Nach den handschriftlichen Mittheilungen des Künstlers.' In der Liste Juli 1826 enthalten; Johann Baptist Geißler als Autor genannt.

Joseph Kratochvill
(Zagesitz, Böhmen, 4. Mai 1763–keine Angabe)

[...] Zufälligerweise veranstaltete Fürst Auersperg in seinem Palais eine Operette, Victorini [der Oboist Victorini, der Kratochvill als Substitut einsetzte und ihm dafür Kost und Quartier gab] nahm mich mit, der Auersperg mich von der Loge erblickend, fragte Victorini warum er seinen Sohn nicht mitgenommen? Dieser antwortete, dieser ist auch mein Sohn und dein Unterthan. Am folgenden Tag nach zuvoriger Anhörung des Victorini mußte ich bey Seiner Durchlaucht erscheinen, wurde gnädig mit dem gütigen Bescheid dahin versichert, seine Durchlaucht, werden für mich die Kost und Quartier bezahlen, ich soll mich unter der Aufsicht des Victorini in allen musikalischen Gegenständen recht qualifiziren, Seine Durchlaucht nehmen mich auf seine Güter als Kapellmeister und werden den alten Pensioniren, zugleich mußte der Kanzellist [. . .] alle Einladungs Bileter herhohlen, und den Befehl befolgen, daß ich zu jeder Academie zugelassen werden sollte, um alles zu sehen, und etwas zu erlernen.

Bey dieser Gelegenheit habe ich die Ehre gehabt, die damahligen großen Männer können zu lernen, als Haydn, Mozart, Salieri, und Hofmeister, Wanhall, Paul Wraniczky kannte ich schon [. . .]

Anmerkung: Eigenhändig geschriebene Selbstbiographie.

Franz Seraph Kurz
(Käfermarkt im Mühlkreise, 2 April 1771–keine Angabe)

[. . .] Hochdieselben würden daraus ersehen, daß der Herr Canonicus Franz Ser. Kurz Fugen schreiben konnte, vor denen Contrapunktisten und Zuhörer Achtung haben mußten; Michael Haydn erklärte die seinige auch frey bey mehr als einer Gelegenheit. [. . .]

Anmerkung: Zitat aus dem Schreiben des Stiftsorganisten zu St. Florian in Oberösterreich Mathias Keinersdorfer an Joseph Sonnleithner vom 16. Juli 1826, mit dem er seine eigene Biographie und die seiner Amtsvorgänger bzw. anderer Stiftsmusiker mitteilt. Es wurde unter Keinersdorfer abgelegt; die übrigen Biographien wurden nicht ausgewertet.

Joseph Lipawsky
(Hosenmauth, Böhmen, 22. Februar 1774–7. Jänner 1810, keine Ortsangabe)

[. . .] Von größtem Nutzen war für ihn die Freundschaft, die er mit Georg Pasterwitz, dem bekannten Componisten im Stifte Kremsmünster, schloß, und sehr nützlich war ihm die Bekanntschaft mit Wanhal und dem großen Mozart. [. . .]

Maria Anna Martinez
(Wien, 1750–1811, keine Ortsangabe)

[. . .] Den Unterricht im Klavier erhielt sie von Joseph Haydn; es ist nicht bekannt, ob er auch ihr Lehrer in der Composizion war, in der sie es gleichfalls weit brachte. [. . .]

Anmerkung: Verfasser der Biographie ist Joseph Sonnleithner (Liste Juli 1826).

Franz Anton Maurer
(St. Pölten, Niederösterreich, 1777–10. April 1803, München)

[. . .] Da er einen sehr schönen Sopran sang, und überdieß eine sehr angenehme Gestalt hatte, suchte ihn Emanuel Schickaneder zu dem von ihm dirigirten Theater im Freyhause in der Vorstadt Wieden zu erhalten. Maurer trat bey der ersten Vorstellung von Mozart's Zauberflöte den 30. September 1791 auf, und gefiel sehr. Ganz falsch ist, was Lipowski in dem Bayerischen Musiklexikon unter dem Artikel Maurer erzählt, daß er nämlich so plötzlich Stimme gewechselt, und vier Wochen später als Sarastro in derselben Oper aufgetreten sey. Es ist bewundernswürdig genug, daß er schon am 8. Oktober 1795 als ein ausgezeichneter Bassist auftreten konnte. [. . .]

Anmerkung: Verfasser der Biographie ist Joseph Sonnleithner (Liste Juli 1826).

Wolfgang Amadeus Mozart Sohn
(Wien, 26. Juli 1791–keine Angabe)

[. . .] Am 8 April 1805, gab er in Wien sein erstes öffentliches Concert, wo eine (auf Haydens Geburtstag von H: Legations Rath von Griesinger gedichtete) von ihm damahls 14: jährigen Jüngling in Musik gesetze Cantate aufgeführt wurde (dieselbe befindet sich bis jetzt noch in den Händen des Compositeurs. [. . .]

Mit der Schlußbemerkung: 'Diese Notizen gab mir der H: Mozart selbst: Pawlikowski 1826.' Geschrieben von Pawlikowski, wohl jener Ritter von Pawlikowsky, der in der Liste Juli 1826 als Verfasser der Biographie von Joseph Hoffmann genannt ist, während die Biographie von Mozart Sohn dort noch nicht angeführt ist. Zu identifizieren ist er wohl mit dem K.k. wirklichen Hofconcipisten Gualbert Edler Ritter von Pawlikowsky, doch war weder dieser, noch ein anderer Träger dieses Namens, Mitglied der Gesellschaft der Musikfreunde.

Franz Karl Ockl
(Maria Kuln, Böhmen, 1759–keine Angabe)

[. . .] Eine Messe hat Ockl an D[oktor]Hayden überschickt, und 2 Briefe von ihm selbst erhalten, einen über die Schöpfung besitzt er noch. [. . .]

Mit der Bemerkung: 'Diese Nachrichten hat H.

Ockl im Jänner 1827 dem Sekretär der Gesellschaft mitgetheilt.'

Georg Pasterwitz
(Bierhütten bei Passau, 8. Juni 1730–26. Jänner 1803, Kremsmünster)

[. . .] Hier [d.i. Wien] kam er mit den berühmtesten Männern in Verbindung, und das enge Band der Freundschaft, welches sich für ihn daraus mit dem K.K. Kapellmeister Salieri, und dem Doctor der Tonkunst Joseph Haydn entspann, war ihm kostbarer Schatz, dessen er sich fortan erfreute. [. . .]

Ambros Rieder
(Döbling bei Wien, 10. Oktober 1771–keine Angabe)

[. . .] Aber, wer kann sich mein Erstaunen vorstellen! als ich so glücklich war, den unsterblichen, großen W.A. Mozart bey einer zahlreich versammelten Gesellschaft auf dem Pianoforte nicht nur variren, sondern auch fantasiren zu hören. – Dieß war mich eine ganz neue Schöpfung mit ganz anderem Wesen, als ich bisher zu hören und zu sehen gewohnt war; den kühnen Flug seiner Fantasie bis zu den höchsten Regionen und wieder in die Tiefen des Abgrundes konnte auch der erfahrenste Meister in der Musik nicht genug bewundern und anstaunen. – Noch jetzt, mit 55 Jahren höre ich diese himmlischen, unvergeßlichen Harmonien in mir ertönen, und gehe mit der vollsten Überzeugung zu Grabe, daß es nur Einen Mozart gegeben habe. – [. . .]

Anmerkung: Eigenhändig geschriebene Selbstbiographie, signiert und datiert mit 6. April 1826. In der Liste Juli 1826 ist Joseph Sonnleithner als Verfasser genannt.

Johann Georg Roser
(Naarn, Oberösterreich, 1740–23. September 1797, Linz)

Eine recht artige Begebenheit mit Mozart verdient hier angemerkt zu werden. Als eben Roser seine erste Funkzion [als Domkapellmeister] mit einer von ihm komponirten Messe mit Doppelchor in der Domkirche [zu Linz] hielt, kam Mozart nach dem Gloria auf das Chor, und ersuchte Roser, ob es ihm nicht vergönnt sey, den Platz an der Orgel einnehmen zu dürfen. Roser, der Mozart nie persönlich kannte, frug ihn, ob er aber auch die Orgel gut spielen könnte, da in dieser Messe mehrere Fugen vorkämen. Mozart verbürgte sich, und nun ging es ans Credo. Als dieses beendigt war, wo das et vitam venturi eine große Fuge war, ging Roser zu dem Orgelhelden, und sagte ihm, er könnte nur Mozart seyn; Mozart's Antwort war: mehr sey er auch nicht. Roser hatte das Glück, Mozart mit seinem Vater durch 11 Tage in seiner Wohnung bewirthen zu können. Eben zu dieser Zeit vollendete Roser das von ihm erfundene Pianoforte, welches er Harmonie pour la parfait nannte. [. . .] Mozart hat während seines Aufenthaltes bei ihm 2 kleine Piecen für dieß Instrument geschrieben; leider aber ist dessen Manuskript bey dem Brande in Linz 1799 ein Opfer der Flamme geworden. [. . .]

Anmerkung: Am Ende die Bemerkung 'Diese Nachrichten theilte sein Sohn Franz de Paula Roser mit [. . .]'.

Franz de Paula Roser von Reiter
(Naarn, Oberösterreich, 1779–keine Angabe)

[. . .] 1796 trat er als Noviz in das Zisterzienser Kloster Wilhering in Oberösterreich unter dem Klosternahmen Nivardus. Er komponirte daselbst 2 Messen a 4 voci et Organo im strengen Styl. Michael Haydn, der eben aus Salzburg hier auf Besuch war, ertheilte ihm viel Lob. [. . .]

Ignaz Ritter von Seyfried
(Wien, 15. August 1776–keine Angabe)

[. . .] Er zeigte schon in früher Jugend eine besondere Neigung für die Tonkunst, und erhielt Unterricht sowohl im Singen, als auf mehreren Instrumenten; vorzüglich wurde er durch Mozart, und nach dessen Tode durch seinen Nachfolger Kozeluch zu einem fertigen Klavierspieler ausgebildet, so wie der geschickte Organist Hayda sein erster Lehrer im Generalbaß war. [. . .]

Anmerkung: Verfasser der Biographie ist Joseph Sonnleithner (Liste Juli 1826).

Anton Heinrich Sigora von Eulenstein
(Wien, 1772–14. November 1821, keine Ortsangabe)

[. . .] Er ward ein sehr guter Violinspieler, studierte eifrig den Generalbaß, und Wolfgang

Amade Mozart selbst war sein Leiter bey dem Studium der Composizion. [...]

Christoph Sonnleithner
(Szegedin, Ungarn, 28. Mai 1734–25. Dezember 1786, keine Ortsangabe)

[...] In den späteren Jahren, als ihm die Aerzte schon die Composition strenge untersagten, schrieb er noch Symphonien für den alten Fürsten Esterhazy und seinen Freund Kees, wie auch 36 Quartetten in kurzen Zwischenräumen für den Kaiser Joseph, der ihn seinen Lieblings-Compositor zu nennen pflegte, und sich seine Quartette gewöhnlich wochentlich ein- oder zwey Mahl vorspielen ließ. [...] Als nach dem Tode des obenerwähnten H v. Kees, eines bekannten Musikfreundes, sein bedeutender Musikalien-vorrath versteigert wurde, fand sich Sonnleith-ner's Sohn Joseph dabey ein, um einige Partituren seines Vaters zu kaufen. Da war aber ein Mann, der ihn jedesmahl überboth. Der Sohn näherte sich endlich diesem Unbekannten, und ersuchte ihn, von der Steigerung abzustehen, weil er als der Sohn die Partituren seines Vaters zu besitzen wünsche. Dieser Unbekannte war Joseph Haydn, der jene Partituren gleichfalls zu besitzen gewünscht hatte. [...]

Anmerkung: Verfasser der Biographie ist Joseph Sonnleithner (Liste Juli 1826).

Maximilian Stadler
(Melk, 4. August 1748–keine Angabe)

[...] Da ich öftern Umgang mit Mozart und Joseph Haydn hatte, so könnte ich Vieles von Ihnen erzählen. Da aber das Wichtigste ohnehin von Ihnen bekannt ist, so halt ich es überflüßig Unbedeutende Dinge anzuführen. Ich hörte Mozart schon in seinem 8ten Jahr auf der Orgel bey einer Vesper im Stifte Melk so spielen, wie man es von einem tüchtigsten Organisten erwarten kann. Als er nach Wien kam und seine 6 Sonaten für das Clavir und Violin [KV 286, 376, 377, 378, 379, 380] bey Artaria stechen und der [Josepha Barbara] Auernhammer widmen ließ, nahm er mich zur Probe mit; Artaria brachte den ersten Abdruck mit, Auernhammer spielte das F[orte] P[iano] – Mozart begleitete es statt der Violine auf einem 2ten nebenstehenden Fortepiano, und ich war ganz entzückt über das Spiel des Meisters und der Schülerin, und habe es niemal

mehr in meinem Leben so unvergleichlich vor-tragen gehört.

Mozart hatte in der freyen Fantasie Kunst Keinen seines Gleichen. Er fantasirte so ordentlich, als wenn er es geschrieben vor sich liegen gehabt hätte. Dieß brachte Mehrere auf den Gedanken, daß, wenn er öffentlich mit einer Fantasie auftratt, er sich vorher alls genau aus-gedacht, und vorbereitet haben müßte. Albrechtsberger dachte ebenso. Einst aber kamen Beyde abends bey einer musikalischen Unter-haltung Zusamm[en]; Mozart war in guter Laune, und begehrte von Albrechtsberger ein Thema. Dieser spielte ihm ein gemeines altes deutsches Lied vor. – Mozart setzte sich, und führte dieses Thema über eine Stunde so durch, daß er alle musikalischen Künste durch Variazionen, oder Fugen ohne vom Thema abzuweichen zur all-gemeinen Bewunderung ganz in seiner Macht zu haben zeigte. Albrechtsberger ward so entzückt, daß er nun vollends überzeigt war, Mozart habe nicht nöthig sich zu einem freyen Spiel aus dem Stegreif vorzubereiten.

Ich lernte Haydn frühzeitig kennen und als er nach Esterhaz als Kapellmeister berufen wurde, besuchte ich Ihn alldort einige Mahle. Das erste Mahl sang er mir seine ersten deutschen Lieder beym Clavier vor, die er kurz darauf in Wien stechen ließ. Das 2te Mahl hatte er eben damals von Spanien aus, den Auftrag erhalten, die 7 Worte instrumentalisch zu setzen. Er war in Verlegenheit und dachte nach, wie er es am besten ausführen könnte. Er fragte auch mich, was ich davon hielt. Ich antwortete: Mir schien es am rathsamsten, wenn anfangs über die Worte eine passende Melodie gesetzt würde, die hernach nur durch die Instrumente ausgeführt würde, in welcher Art er zu setzen ohnehin Meister wäre. Er that es auch, ob er aber nicht selbst schon früher dieß zu thun willens war, weis ich nicht.

Als er seine 4 Jahreszeiten verfertiget hatte, und seine Kräfte ihn sehr verließen, gab er das be-kannte Visitenbillet: Hin ist alle meine Kraft alt und schwach bin ich mit Melodie heraus und vertheilte es unter seine Freunde. Ich antwortete mit beybehaltener Melodie durch eine 2te Stimme, und überbrachte es ihm. Und als er auf die Worte: Hin ist alle meine Kraft, die Antwort, doch, was sie erschuf, bleibt stets, und auf die: alt und schwach bin ich: ewig lebt dein Ruhm, las, fielen ihm die Thränen aus den Augen, dankte mir und sagte nur: Dieß hätte er nicht verdient.

Wir unterhielten uns über musikalische Gegenstände. Bey meinem Abschied bat er mich in-
ständig, ich sollte meine Antworte zum Stich
befördern, weil es zu seinem Ruhm wäre. Ich
konnte seinem Begehren nicht widerstehen. Die
Antwort auf Haydns Visitenbillet wurde ge-
stochen, ausgetheilt, verschickt, in Paris ins
Französische übersetzt, und im Moniteur an-
gezeigt. [...]

Anmerkung: Eigenhändig geschriebene Selbstbiographie.

Gottfried Freiherr van Swieten
(Holland unfern von Leyden, keine Datum-
angabe–29. März 1803, keine Ortsangabe)

[...] Auf van Swieten's Antrieb und Belohnung
komponirte Haydn die Schöpfung und die
Jahreszeiten, wozu Ersterer den Text verfaßte.
[...]

Anmerkung: Verfasser der Biographie ist Joseph
Sonnleithner (Liste Juli 1826).

Joseph Weigl
(Eisenstadt, 28. März 1766–keine Angabe)

[...] Ich bin geboren zu Eisenstadt in Ungarn am
28. März 1766. Mein Vater Joseph Weigl war
damals erster Violoncellist und meine Mutter
Anna geborene Glatz (nach der späteren Angabe
in der zweiten Biographie Scheffstos) erste
Sängerinn im Dienste des Fürsten Nikolaus
Esterhazy, Großvaters des jetzt regierenden.
Joseph Haydn, damals fürstlicher Capellmeister,
hielt mich zur Taufe. [...] Ich wendete mich an
den damaligen Studienpräses Baron Van Swieten
um ein Stipendium; dieser war ein großer
Musikkenner und Schüler Kirnberger's in der
Composition, ich gefiel ihm und er versprach,
meine Bitte zu berücksichtigen, lud mich aber vor
der Hand zu den Musiken ein, die alle Sonntage
von 12 bis 2 Uhr Mittags bey ihm gegeben
wurden. Hier hörte man nur Bachsche,
Händlsche, Graunsche Werke und die
Compositionen der anderen älteren berühmten
Meister. Mozart begleitete auf dem Fortepiano;
Salieri, Starzer, Teiber, der Baron van Swieten
selbst und ich sangen. Da lernte ich, wie man
Partituren spielen sollte. Wer Mozart nicht 16 und
mehrzeilige Händelsche Partituren mit unüber-
trefflicher Fertigkeit spielen, selbst dazu singen
und zugleich die Fehler der anderen Sänger ver-

bessern sah, der kennt Mozart nicht ganz, denn
er war darin eben so groß, als in seiner Composition. Man hörte stets ein ganzes Orchester.
Wie glücklich war ich, um solche Männer zu
seyn. [...] Täglich um 9 Uhr Vormittags gab mir
Salieri eine Stunde Unterricht über das Theater-
fach, die musikalische Deklamation und das
Partiturspielen, nahm mich zu allen Proben und
Vorstellungen und in kurzer Zeit mußte ich an
seiner Statt bey den Proben am Claviere accompagniren. [...] Da ich zu gleicher Zeit mehrer[n]
Sängern und Sängerinnen ihre Partien ein-
studiren half, erhielt ich eine solche Fertigkeit im
Accompagniren, daß ich nun alle Opern gegenwärtiger fremder Meister mit der Gesellschaft
einüben mußte. So begleitete ich am Claviere
Mozart's Figaro, Don Juan u.s.w. bey allen
Proben zu seiner Zufriedenheit und mußte nach
den drey ersten Vorstellungen, die er selbst leitete,
den Platz des großen Meisters am Claviere einnehmen. [...] Später [das ist nach der
Kaiserkrönung in Frankfurt, Oktober 1790]
komponirte ich für ein in Esterhaz gegebenes Fest
die Cantate: Venere ed Adone, die gefiel.
[...]

Anmerkung: Mit der Bemerkung im Titel 'ganz
nach autographischen Nachrichten [wiederge-
geben von] Freiherrn von Lannoy (um so wenig
als möglich fremdartiges hinein zu bringen, lasse
ich den Autobiographen in der ersten Person
von sich sprechen)'. Handschrift von Heinrich
Eduard Joseph Freiherr von Lannoy.

Thaddäus Weigl
(Wien, 1776–keine Angabe)

[...] Weigl, der mit Mozart, Salieri, Haydn, Paer,
Winter und anderen berühmten Meistern einen
vertrauten Umgang pflog [...]

Joseph Widerhofer
(Mariazell, Steiermark, 7. Jänner 1786–keine
Angabe)

[...] Joseph Widerhofer erhielt den Unterricht im
Singen, im Orgelspiel und im Generalbaß von
seinem Vater, und machte hierinn solche
Fortschritte, daß er schon in seinem 7. Jahr
salarirter Discantist [an der Wallfahrtskirche
Mariazell] wurde, in seinem 12. Jahre in
Gegenwart der Wiener Prozession die sogenannte
große Zeller-Messe [Missa Cellensis (Hob.

XXII:5), zum Unterschied von der kürzeren und kleineren Missa Cellensis (Hob. XXII:8)] von Joseph Haydn auf der dasigen großen Orgel spielte, und nach dem in eben diesem Jahre erfolgten Tode seines Vaters die Organisten Stelle daselbst erhielt, wodurch er nicht nur sich, sondern auch seine Mutter und seine noch 4 unmündige Brüder ernährte. [...]

Anmerkung: Im Text der Biographie ist erwähnt, daß sie 1826 geschrieben wurde.

Johann Wittmann
(Weyer, 8. Dezember 1757–keine Angabe)

[...] Nach ein paar hier [im Stift Lambach in Oberösterreich, wo Wittmann seit 1789 tätig war] zugebrachten Jahren hatte er das Vergnügen, Herrn Michael Haydn kennen zu lernen, da dieser von Salzburg, und H: Sießmayr, k.k. Hofkapellmeister von Wien im Stifte zusammen kamen. Da Wittmann mit Letzterem schon früher bekannt war, gab sich die Zuneigung und Freundschaft des Ersteren sehr bald.

Im Jahre 1797 mit 1. März trat Wittmann den Schuldienst zu Lambach an, und benützte nebst dem Schulgeschäfte immer die Zeit mit Abschreiben aus Sparten, wodurch er auch noch mehrere Kenntnisse sich erwarb, und wozu auch die Gewogenheit und Freundschaft des unvergeßlichen Herrn Michael Haydn, welchen er öfters zu sehen und mit ihm umzugehen die Ehre hatte, sehr viel beytrug. [...] Diese erste kirchliche Arbeit [eine Messe in B-Dur] wies er dem hochberühmten unsterblichen Herrn Michael Haydn bey seiner nächsten Anwesenheit in Lambach, wo ihn dann dieser erhabene Mann nichts getadelt, und, nachdem Wittmann sich entschuldigte, daß

er zu wenig muntere Gedanken habe, ihm die treffliche Anleitung gegeben hatte, daß Kirchenmusik Gebeth seyn müße, so schrieb er nach solcher Erinnerung und Anweisung noch 4 Messen [...]

Joseph Wölfl
(Salzburg, 1772–21. Mai 1812, England)

[...] Er bildete sich in der Musik in seiner Vaterstadt unter Leopold Mozart und Michael Haydn aus. [...] Als sich der Ruf des Wolfgang Amade Mozart in ganz Deutschland verbreitete, beschloß Wölfl's Vater, den Sohn zur Vollendung seiner musikalischen Ausbildung zu diesem unsterblichen Componisten zu schicken. Mozart ward Wölfl's treuer Freund, und empfahl den achtzehnjährigen Jüngling dem Pohlnischen Grafen Orginsky als Kapellmeister. [...]

Anmerkung: Verfasser der Biographie ist Joseph Sonnleithner (Liste Juli 1826).

Cajetan Wutky
(Tulln, Niederösterreich, 18. August 1735–27. April 1815, Wien)

[...] Während seines Aufenthaltes in Preßburg leistete er eigentlich die Dienste eines Kapellmeisters, und dirigirte nicht nur die Concerte, welche der Herzog [Albert von Sachsen-Teschen, in dessen Diensten Wutky als Waldhornist und Türhüter stand] gab, sondern auch die großen Concerte des Fürsten Esterhazy. Er genoß damals die vertraute Freundschaft und Achtung des großen Joseph Haydn. Als [Erzherzogin] Maria Christine [die Gattin des Herzogs] als Gouvernante nach den Niederlanden abging, begleitete Wutky die höchste Herrschaft nach Brüßel [...]

GERDA MRAZ

Musikerportraits in der Sammlung Lavater

IN DER ÖSTERREICHISCHEN NATIONALBIBLIOTHEK gibt es eine graphisch-
photographische Sammlung, die weltweit Beachtung findet, obwohl gerade der
graphische Altbestand nur mehr ein Torso ist. Es ist die Doppelsammlung
Porträtsammlung und Bildarchiv, der aus historischen Gründen auch die ehemalige
Fideikommißbibliothek, d.i. die kaiserliche Privatbibliothek, angehört.

Die Anfänge der Sammlung reichen in das ausgehende 18. Jahrhundert zurück,
als der habsburgische Großprinz und Erzherzog Franz aus seiner Vaterstadt Florenz
nach Wien geschickt wurde, um in den Herrscherberuf hineinzuwachsen, der ihm als
ältestem Sohn Leopolds von Toscana als Erbe seines kinderlosen Onkels, Kaiser
Josephs II., zugedacht war. Franz, der lebenslang ein großer Bibliophile war, nahm
seine damals noch bescheidene eigene Bibliothek mit und stellte sie in seinen
Wohnräumen im sogenannten Schweizertrakt der Hofburg auf. Das war 1784, und im
Jahr darauf begann der junge Mann aus einem spontan geweckten Interesse heraus,
Graphik (vor allem Kupferstiche) zu sammeln. Auch diese Neigung war schon
grundgelegt gewesen. Franz zeichnete recht geschickt, und seine Mutter hatte ihm
immer wieder Kupferstiche zum Anmalen geschenkt. Für seine Graphiksammlung,
die er aus den ihm zugewiesenen Mitteln kaufen mußte, erfand er ein eigenes
Ordnungssystem, wie er auch lange Zeit sein eigener Bibliothekar blieb und – nach
Aussagen von Zeitgenossen – bei einem Bestand von 30.000 Bänden immer noch jedes
einzelne Buch ohne Katalog zu finden imstande war.

Franzens besonderes Interesse galt den Portraits; darin war er ganz ein Kind
seiner Zeit, denn die Aufklärung stufte alles Individuelle – und was kann individueller
sein als das Gesicht eines Menschen – besonders hoch ein. Schon in Florenz hatte der
Prinz *das* Modewerk der Zeit, Johann Caspar Lavaters *Physiognomische Fragmente*
kennen gelernt, 1828 ließ er den gesamten graphischen Nachlaß des berühmten
Mannes für seine Privatbibliothek ankaufen.

Bevor von Lavater die Rede ist, noch ein Wort zu dieser Privatsammlung, die
bald recht vielfältig war, das heißt Gemälde, Kunstgegenstände, Globen,
Handschriften, Musikalien, Münzen und anderes mehr umfaßte. Einen Tag vor
seinem Tod im Jahr 1835 faßte der Kaiser alle seine privaten Schätze zu einem
Fideikommiß zusammen, der immer dem Familienoberhaupt anvertraut sein sollte.

Im Laufe der Zeit kamen die Nachlässe mancher Familienmitglieder, wie z.B. die Bibliothek des Kronprinzen Rudolf, hinzu. 1889 wurde die ganze private Sammlung, nicht nur die Bücher, 'k.u.k. Familien-Fideikommiss-Bibliothek' benannt, 1921 in 'Porträtsammlung der Nationalbibliothek' umgewandelt. Die vielfältige Sammlung wurde damals zerschlagen, neue Zuordnungen fanden statt, die Bibliothek aber blieb auch unter dem neuen und nur bedingt zutreffenden Titel mit der Graphik (so weit sie nicht an die Graphische Sammlung Albertina überging) vereinigt. Der Graphik-Bestand der Portraitsammlung und des Bildarchivs der Österreichischen Nationalbibliothek umfaßt heute ca. eine halbe Million Blätter verschiedener Techniken, die 22.065, die Lavater gehört hatten, sind mitinbegriffen.[1]

Von dieser Lavater-Sammlung soll hier die Rede sein, denn sie wird in den nächsten Jahren Gegenstand eines umfassenden Forschungsprojektes sein. Im Jahr 2001 soll aus Anlaß des 200. Todestages J.C. Lavaters seine groß angelegte Sammlung erforscht und erschlossen vorliegen. Ohne Zweifel werden dann für viele Sparten der Kulturwissenschaften neue Erkenntnisse vorliegen. Dieser Beitrag, H.C. Robbins Landon gewidmet, soll den Auftakt signalisieren.[2]

Die Physiognomik ist so alt wie die Menschheit selbst, und bis heute, wenn wir einem Menschen zum ersten Mal gegenübertreten, reagieren wir zuerst auf sein Äußeres, vermuten in ihm bestimmte Eigenschaften lediglich aufgrund seiner Erscheinung, seines Gesichtsschnittes, seiner Körperhaltung. Das belegte Wissen um diese 'Grenzwissenschaft' geht auf eine pseudoaristotelische Schrift, 'Physiognomica', zurück, erlebte einen ersten Höhepunkt in der Renaissance, den nächsten in der Folge der Aufklärung, eine Fortsetzung in der Sturm und Drang-Bewegung, ihren Mißbrauch in den Rassenideologien und scheint heute – wenn man die zunehmende Publikationstätigkeit zum Gegenstand als Gradmesser anerkennen will – wieder an Aktualität zu gewinnen.[3]

Mehr durch Zufall kam Lavater zur Physiognomik. Er war in Zürich im Jahr 1741 geboren worden, Sohn eines Arztes, wenig verstanden von seiner Mutter und auf der Suche nach Geborgenheit fand er die Liebe Gottes, die sich in kleinen, schützenden 'Wundern' manifestierte. Lavater wurde Pastor, wobei die Menschenbeobachtung und die Einfühlungsgabe in menschliches Verhalten sozusagen als berufskohärent angesehen werden kann. Irgendeinmal fiel ihm auf, daß Menschen mit ähnlichen körperlichen Merkmalen ähnliche Charakterzüge aufwiesen, und er begann, diese Beobachtung systematisch zu verifizieren. Nicht nur seine Freunde waren von den Ergebnissen begeistert. Bald war Lavater eine gesuchte und viel besuchte Persönlichkeit, Menschen aller Ränge und Stände kamen auch von weit her, um einen Blick in ihre Seelen tun zu lassen. Auch Kaiser Joseph II. und eine Reihe deutscher Fürsten gehörten zu den Gästen, für die Großfürstin Maria Feodorovna, die Gemahlin des späteren Zaren Paul I., stellte er eine eigene physiognomische Galerie von rund tausend Blättern zusammen, die heute wieder in Zürich sind.[4]

Lavater stand mit den bedeutendsten Geistesgrößen seiner Zeit in Gedankenaustausch, Basedow, Goethe, Herder, Swedenborg und viele andere begeisterten sich für ihn, Goethe arbeitete an den Lavaterschen Werken mit, wollte allerdings — nach dem Zerwürfnis der beiden — nicht als Mitautor genannt sein. Andere, allen voran Lichtenberg, lehnten Lavaters Lehre heftig ab oder fühlten sich von seinem missionarischen Eifer, den er nie ablegen konnte, abgestoßen, wie Moses Mendelssohn.[5]

Lavater hat über 160 physiognomische Schriften verfaßt, am berühmtesten wurden seine *Physiognomischen Fragmente*, die noch zu seinen Lebzeiten in einer französischen Fassung (nicht einfach Übersetzung!) erschienen sind. Neun Jahre nach seinem Tod gab es sechzehn deutsche, fünfzehn französische, zwei amerikanische, zwei russische, eine holländische, eine italienische und zwanzig(!) englische Ausgaben dieses Werkes. Der 8. Abschnitt im 3. Band der *Physiognomischen Fragmente* ist den Musikern gewidmet. Die eingangs geäußerten Selbstzweifel an der eigenen Kompetenz in der Beurteilung musikalischer Qualität ('wie darf ich entscheiden, da ich so wenig Musiker kenne . . . ?') mag Lavaters häufig auftretender phraseologischer Bescheidenheitstopik zugeschrieben werden können, denn gleich geht er daran, die Musiker den Malern gegenüberzustellen: 'Was der Maler sehen muß, muß der Virtuose hören.' Diese Prämisse bekommt nur Sinn, wenn man die zeitbedingte Anschauung zugrunde legt, die die wichtigste Aufgabe des Künstlers darin sieht, Natur möglichst getreu wiederzugeben. Selbstverständlich verlangt Lavater dies von den Portraitmalern, die ihm das Quellenmaterial für seine Schriften zur Verfügung stellen. Und die Musik? 'Musik ist Nachahmung der Naturtöne.'

Damit aber sind die Gemeinsamkeiten von Malern und Musikern erschöpft. Die Aufgabe der Maler ist es, einen Moment dessen, was er sieht, festzuhalten, der Musiker hingegen produziert etwas, was im Moment vergeht, Moment für Moment eine Folge schwindender Wahrnehmungen. 'Physiognomien, die bestimmt sind, Momente zu fixiren — sollten also wesentlich verschiedenen Charakter haben von denen die bestimmt sind, Successionen darzustellen. Die Physiognomie des Mahlers sollte demnach stehender, die des Musikers fließender seyn. . . . Schwebender, unbestimmter, flüßiger, lockerer, wie's die Natur der Empfindungsempfänglichkeit und der Empfindungsmittheilsamkeit zu erfordern scheint — sind alle Musiker-Gesichter — als die der Mahler.'[6] Und anders formuliert: 'Die Natur des Schwebens — des beständigen Schwebens, das Wesentliche der Musik läßt nicht die ruhigstätige — stehende Gesichtsform zu, die zur Schöpfung einer momentanen Welt nöthig ist.'[7]

In den *Physiognomischen Fragmenten* werden zwei 'musikalische Physiognomien' einer Analyse unterzogen: Carl Philipp Emanuel Bach und Niccolò Jomelli. Auf

Jomelli soll näher eingegangen werden, weil er mit zwei qualitätvollen Portraits in der Sammlung Lavaters vertreten ist: das eine ist eine lavierte Bleistiftzeichnung, der Künstler konnte noch nicht identifiziert werden, das andere ein Aquarell von Friedrich Christoph Weisbrod (1739–1803), der in seiner Heimatstadt Stuttgart als Bildnismaler, aber auch zeitweise in Mannheim und in England, tätig war. Die Bleistiftzeichnung (Abb. 1) mißt 244 × 175 mm, rundum ist ein einfacher grüner Rahmen gezogen, dem ein Goldleistchen ein wenig Lebhaftigkeit verleiht, unter dem Bild ist kurz und bündig zu lesen: 'Stirn und Aug Genie das ganze sinnlich und sehr roh. L. 1799.' Die Zeichnung diente als Vorlage für eine druckgraphische Umsetzung und gelangte so (seitenverkehrt) als Illustration in die *Physiognomischen Fragmente*, aller‚ dings mit nicht unmaßgeblichen Veränderungen: Die Konturen sind schärfer heraus‚ gearbeitet, das Gesicht wirkt weniger glatt gerundet und dadurch älter.

Das zweite Portrait (103 × 84 mm) zeigt Jomelli mit Allongeperücke; in den 'Fragmenten' gibt es dazu eine 'zeichnerische' Variante, die bei Lavater beliebte Reduktion auf 'Gesichtslinien' unter Vernachlässigung der Flächen. Weisbrods Bildchen hat Lavater besser gefallen, links neben dem Portrait ist mit Handschrift auf dem Innendeckel vermerkt: 'voller Reichthum, Feuer und Kraft und gewaltsames Leben.' Die Eintragung stammt aus dem Jahr 1796. Dazu ist zu sagen, daß die Bedeutung der Jahreszahlen noch nicht geklärt ist. Sicherlich beziehen sie sich nicht auf die Entstehung der Bilder, wahrscheinlich auch nicht auf deren Erwerb, am ehesten auf die Anbringung der Textnotiz.

Niccolò Jomelli (1714–74), aufgewachsen in Neapel, konnte am Wiener Hof in der Zusammenarbeit mit Pietro Metastasio als Textdichter seiner Opern die schönsten Erfolge feiern. Im Jahre 1753 ging er als Hofkapellmeister nach Stuttgart, blieb dort bis 1769 und verbrachte den Rest seines Lebens, gezeichnet von einem Schlaganfall, wieder in Neapel. Lavater, der für seine *Physiognomischen Fragmente* eine Reihe von Mitarbeitern fand (von Goethe war schon die Rede), zitiert seinen Gewährsmann über Jomelli:

In der bürgerlichen Welt Capellmeister und Director des glänzenden Würtembergischen Orchesters. Seine Opern und sonstige Werke bewundert die Welt, und adelt ihn dafür: Genie. – er bewürkte unter andern neue Gefühle in den Sterblichen, als er die Brüder der Schattirungen in der Malerey, das musikalische Crescendo und Diminuendo, näher ans Licht zog, und auf Beute ausgehen ließ. Italiäner und Deutsche, die vor seinen singenden Welten stunden, wollen sich geweidet haben; sagen ihm nach, daß er die Leidenschaften glücklich auszudrücken gewußt; daß er die Mitwürkung aller Instrumente zu Einem großen Zwecke verstanden ...

Abb. 1.
Niccolò Jomelli von einem
unbekannten Zeichner.
Inv. Nr. LAV 7432

Abb. 2.
Niccolò Jomelli von Friedrich
Christoph Weisbrod.
Inv. Nr. LAV 5999

Abb. 3.
Philipp Christoph Kayser von
Johannes Pfenninger.
Inv. Nr. LAV 9872

Abb. 5.
Ph. Chr. Kayser,
anonyme Gouache.
Inv. Nr. LAV 11763

Abb. 4 (*rechts*).
Ph. Chr. Kayser,
anonyme Zeichnung.
Inv. Nr. LAV 4633

Abb. 6. Ernst Wilhelm Wolf, Ölminiatur. Inv. Nr. LAV 9864

Abb. 7. Johann André, anonyme Bleistiftzeichnung. Inv. Nr. LAV 7055

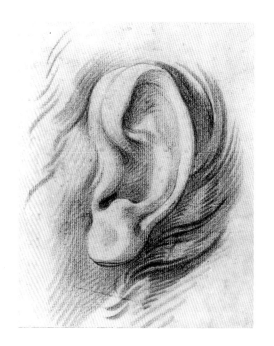
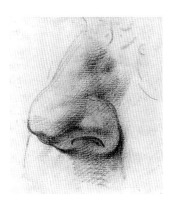
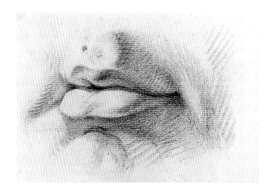
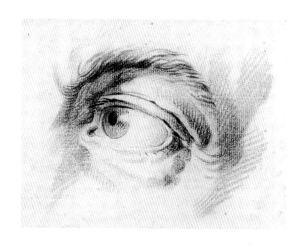

Abb. 8.
Rötelzeichnungen,
Inv. Nr. LAV 3997, 3862,
3634, 3431; 156 × 125 mm,
99 × 90 mm, 87 × 126 mm,
105 × 140 mm

Dem Portrait (Abb. 1) könne man dies allerdings nicht ansehen, und Lavater selbst beurteilt es so: 'Ein Kopf, der allenfalls Genie ist, wenigstens es seyn kann – wenig ruhig forschender stillauseinanderlesender Verstand – Mehr Feuer als Genauheit in seinen Werken; mehr Pomp als Eleganz; mehr hinreissende Gewalt, als sanft anziehende Zärtlichkeit – das scheint mir wenigstens dieß Gesicht deutlich genug zu sprechen. Die Stirne nicht schwer suchend – vorgreifend! Muthiges, festfassendes, ganz zurückgebendes Auge. Kräftige, markige Nase; ohne Adel und Feinheit. Mund voll sinnlichen Gefühles; Kraft unterm Munde. Reichthum und Ueberfluß leicht empfangener, leicht zurückgegebener Gefühle im Kinne – und gute Nahrung im Unterkinne. Schade, daß gerade das Ohr eines Virtuosen so unbestimmt gezeichnet ist, doch, so viel man sieht – frey, stark, markig.'[8]

Lavater schätzt das Portrait von Weisbrod aus seiner physiognomischen Sicht höher: 'Im Umrisse ist noch mehr vom musikalischen Genie sichtbar, als im schattirten Bilde. Das Aug in 1. ist verstaunt und in 2. treffender' (Abb. 2 zeigt die Originalvorlage). Viel mehr aber bewegt ihn interessanterweise ein sozialer Aspekt, wenn er schreibt: 'Hier [in Weisbrods Portrait] der wahrhaft verdeutschte Jomelli! hier steht oder sitzt der Virtuose in politischer Würde; das Gesicht in producirende Ordnung gelegt – der vorige [= die Bleistiftzeichnung] war der Tonschöpfer in seiner unraubbaren Freyheit; dieser ist der Tonkünstler am Hofe! Entfaltet und ausgekehrt – wie im Gallakleide, rasirt und gewaschen in glücklicher Uebereinkunft mit Parucke und Haarbeutel.'[9] – Wer dächte hier nicht an Joseph Haydn und die Diskussion, inwieweit ihn die Esterházysche Hofuniform zum Diener degradiert habe!

Am interessantesten, weil Lavater den Musiker persönlich kannte, sind seine Bemerkungen über 'Ein schattirtes männliches Porträt im Profil. K.': 'Wieder eins von denen Gesichtern, die man nie ähnlich und nie unähnlich nachzeichnen kann, und einer von den Charaktern, von welchen man so viel und so wenig zu sagen weiß. . . . Ich bin leider nicht Tonverständiger, . . . doch sagt mir, so oft ich ihn, oder nach ihm andere höre – mein ungelehrtes Menschengefühl, daß Simplicität, schnelles Treffen und Ergreifen der reinen wahren Naturreinheit und Drang tief heraus quillender Empfindung – mit der wenigsten Manier – Charakter seines Genies sey.' Worauf ein vernichtendes Urteil über das Profilportrait (Abb. 3) folgt, das von Johannes Pfenninger[10] stammt: 'Gegenwärtiges Bild – ist so wunderbar aus Trübsinn, Übellaune, und einer gewissen Knäblichkeit, wenn ich so sagen darf, zusammengesetzt, zusammengeflickt sollt' ich sagen, die im Urbilde nicht ist, und nicht sehn kann. So was Zaghaftes, Eingedrücktes, Unfestes, das ganz wider den Naturcharakter ist. So ist dieß Aug im Mißverhältnis des Ausdrucks zu dieser kraft- und bangreichen Stirne! So die Vertiefung bei der Nasenwurzel – wieder heterogen mit der Stirne! Um ein Haar auch die Spitze aber der Knopf der Nase – Allzuausgerundet die Höhlung der

Oberlippe von der Nase zur eigentlichen Lippe. Die eigentliche Oberlippe, aus der noch viel tiefe, innige Empfindsamkeit und poetischer Geist – nein poetische Seele hervorleuchtet – ebenfalls gegen das Ende zu abgeschnitten. Das Kinn – zu virtuosisch – aber merkwürdig und sprechend das obenher sehr dünne und breite, unten äußerst zarte spitzige Ohr'.[11]

Die Originalvorlage (Medaillonform, D. 145 mm) befindet sich ebenfalls in Lavaters Bildernachlaß und dabei sein Text (datiert vom 29. August 1793):

> Zaghaft soll Dich nicht zeichnen – die Hand
>   der Bildenden Kunst, Dich . . .
> Kraftmann . . . Reicher Dich, nicht ärmlich
>   an geistigen Zügen.
> Kaum im Auge noch schwebt, in der Stirn
>   und dem Munde –
> Geniekraft –
> Kraft zu männlichem Sinn und den
>   allerzärtsten Gefühlen.

Hinter K. verbirgt sich Philipp Christoph Kayser, geboren 1755 in Frankfurt am Main, gestorben am 24. Dezember 1823 in Zürich, ein heute vergessener Komponist. In Zürich lernte ihn Goethe kennen, es ergab sich eine jahrelange Zusammenarbeit, ja fast eine Freundschaft. Kayser vertonte eine Reihe von Gedichten sowie Singspieltexte Goethes, der ihn auch beauftragte, eine Bühnenmusik für *Egmont*(!) zu schreiben. Über Goethe ergibt sich die Verbindung zu Lavater und auch zu dem Kreis der Schwestern Schulthess. Der Dichter lud Kayser nach Weimar ein und nahm ihn auf eine Rom-Reise mit. Dann aber hat er sich von ihm Ende der 80er Jahre wie auch von Lavater getrennt. Kayser war nicht der Mensch, der am höfischen Leben Gefallen fand, und es machte ihm weniger Ehre als Mühe, für die Herzogin Anna Amalia den Reisebegleiter zu machen. Goethe hat für eine solche Haltung sicherlich viel weniger Verständnis aufbringen können als Lavater. Kayser jedenfalls kehrte nach Zürich zurück.[12]

In der Sammlung finden sich noch weitere vier Profilzeichnungen, die Kayser darstellen, und keine stellte Lavater zufrieden, wie seine Texte beweisen:

> 1794.
> Allzu kleinlich gezeichnet ein
>   mächtiges, geistiges,
>   Starkes
> Feines Profil voll Verstand, voll
>   Sinn für Schönes und Grosses.   [vgl. Abb. 4, 118 × 90 mm]

Zu einem ganz ähnlichen:

> Fester sollte die Stirn, das Aug
> bestimmter, die Lippe
> Etwas breiter sogar – doch zeigt
> auch dies das Genie noch.
> 1797.

Dann zu einem, das Kayser älter zeigt:

> Diesem Profile fehlt das Genie
> des kraftvollen
> Urbilds.
> 1797.

Eine Gouache schließlich bezeichnet er als 'Carricatur des Musikers Kayser' (Abb. 5, 78 × 62 mm), wobei der Begriff der Karikatur jedoch nicht mir unserem heutigen gleichzusetzen ist.[13] Lavater vermerkt dazu:

> Originelles Gesicht voll Kraft verkleinlicht
> durch Zagsinn...
> Dennoch blickt hindurch Gefühl und des
> Genius Kunstsinn.
>
> [datiert: 30. 1. 1789]

In den 'Goethe‑Umkreis' lassen sich noch zwei weitere Portraits der Sammlung einordnen. Das eine ist eine Ölminiatur (oval, 190 × 160 mm), die den Weimarer Hofkapellmeister und besonderen Protegé der Herzogin Anna Amalia, Ernst Wilhelm Wolf (1735–92) darstellt und die Lavater wie folgt kommentiert: 'Viel Talent und Kunst und Fertigkeit, Festigkeit, Feuer.'[14]

Eine feine Bleistiftzeichnung (oval, 95 × 75 mm) zeigt das Profilbild des Musikers und Musikverlegers Johann André (1741–99). Goethe beschrieb ihn in *Dichtung und Wahrheit* als 'Mann von angeborenem lebhaftem Talente', Lavater notiert unter das Portrait: 'Zartes, helles Profil, dem's nicht an Geist und Talent fehlt.' Die Auswahl der Musikerbilder soll damit fürs erste beendet sein. Die beiden Zitate stehen für ein wichtiges Kapitel in Lavaters, aber auch in Goethes Leben. Was mit gegenseitiger schwärmerischer Begeisterung begonnen hatte (Goethe über Lavater: 'Er ist der beste, größte, weiseste, innigste aller sterblichen und unsterblichen Menschen . . .'), eine intensive Kooperation mit sich brachte, Lavater erhielt u.a. von Goethe eine Reihe von Portraits, schlug ihn schwere Differenzen um (Goethe über Lavater: 'Ich bin Haß und Liebe auf ewig los'). Erst 1814 gelangte Goethe in *Dichtung und Wahrheit* doch wieder zu einem abschließenden positiven Urteil: 'Ein Individuum,' schreibt er über den Verstorbenen, 'einzig, durchgezeichnet, wie man es nicht gesehen hat und nicht wieder sehen wird, sah ich lebendig und wirksam vor mir.'[15]

Daß bei dem Gesicht eines Malers das Auge und bei dem des Musikers das Ohr Träger der entscheidenden Persönlichkeitsmerkmale ist, nähert sich der Banalität. Das war Lavater auch klar. Er selbst machte die Beobachtung, daß die Ohren der Virtuosen 'sehr dünn und fast ohne Rand' seien, gesteht aber die zu schmale Basis seines Vergleichsmateriales ein.[16] Wie das physiognomische Detailmaterial beschaffen ist, mit dem Lavater experimentierte, soll eine zusammengehörige Serie von Ohr, Nase, Mund und Auge abschließend illustrieren (Abb. 8), die – so scheint es mir – dem Bleistift-Portrait Jomellis entnommen sein dürfte und folgende Unterschriften trägt: 'Vergrössertes Ohr [bzw. Nase, Mund] eines musikalischen Genies'. 'Vergrössertes Musikalisches Genieaug'.

Robert Münster

Bestände mit mehrstimmigen Musikhandschriften aus Kloster-, Stifts- und Domkirchen in Bayern seit dem 16. Jahrhundert

DIE HIER VORGELEGTE ERSTE ÜBERSICHT über erhaltene umfangreichere Bestände an Musikhandschriften vorwiegend des 17. und 18. Jahrhunderts aus dem Besitz ehemaliger und bestehender Klöster, Kollegiatstifte und Domkirchen in Bayern erhebt keinen Anspruch auf Vollständigkeit. Sie versucht Erkenntnisse aus der von 1967 bis 1990 von der Musikabteilung der Bayerischen Staatsbibliothek mit finanzieller Unterstützung durch die Deutsche Forschungsgemeinschaft durchgeführten Erfassung und Katalogisierung bayerischer Kirchenmusikbestände und diejenigen der Katalogisierungsaktion des RISM in Bayern zusammenzufassen.[1]

Vor der Säkularisation von 1802/3 wurde die Musik vor allem in den Prälatenklöstern mit Nachdruck gepflegt. Fast in jedem Kloster gab es eigene Hauskomponisten.[2] Von den umfangreichen Musikbeständen, die 1803 noch vorhanden waren, ist der überwiegende Teil verloren. Dies weniger durch Beschlagnahme, da die vorhandenen, bis zum Zeitpunkt der Aufhebung der Klöster gebrauchten Musikalien für die Hofbibliothek nicht von Interesse waren. Die Musikbestände aus früherer Zeit waren mit Ausnahme kostbar ausgestatteter Handschriften und einem Teil der Chorbücher bis auf wenige Reste zuvor schon in den Klöstern im Zuge des Stilwandels ausgeschieden und durch neuere Kompositionen ersetzt worden. In der Regel blieben Musikalien etwa ein halbes Jahrhundert in Gebrauch und galten dann als veraltet.

Im Zuge der Säkularisation sind die in den Klosterkirchen vorgefundenen Musikalien häufig den ehemaligen Klosterpfarreien zum weiteren Gebrauch überlassen worden, doch nun bestanden nicht mehr die Besetzungsmöglichkeiten und nicht mehr die zahlreichen Anlässe, sie weiter zu verwenden. Die Handschriften und Drucke wurden zum großen Teil nicht mehr gebraucht, galten als veraltet, gelangten in andere Hände oder sie wurden vernichtet. Was davon seit 1967 noch vorgefunden werden konnte, ist nur ein bescheidener Prozentsatz des einstigen Repertoires. An Musikalienbeständen sind allein diejenigen der Benediktinerabtei Ottobeuren und des Augustiner-Chorherrenstifts Weyarn in größerem Umfang erhalten geblieben.

Zusätzlich zu den festgestellten Beständen oder Resten derselben können sich heute an nicht vermuteten Orten noch weitere Handschriften aus ehemaligem Klosterbesitz befinden. Eine zu Beginn der Erfassungsaktion vom Erzbischöflichen Ordinariat München-Freising veranstaltete Umfrage war ohne jedes Ergebnis geblieben. So mußten eigene Nachforschungen angestellt werden, die zum heutigen Wissensstand geführt haben.

Neben den Handschriften aus Prälatenklöstern wurden auch solche aus Klöstern der Mendikanten mit ihrer bescheideneren Musikübung, aus Kollegiatstiften und von Domkirchen verzeichnet, wobei Bestände in den letztgenannten mit am besten überliefert sind, da sie durch die Säkularisation nicht berührt worden waren.

In der Übersicht folgen dem Namen des Klosters oder des Stiftes und dem Zeitraum von dessen Bestehen kurze Angaben über Anzahl und Art der erhaltenen Handschriften und die zugänglichen thematischen Kataloge (Kat). Auf gedruckte Kataloge, wie die Reihe Kataloge Bayerischer Musiksammlungen (*KBM*), und auf den gegenwärtigen Aufbewahrungsort (Fundort) wird verwiesen. Genannt sind namentlich eruierte Komponisten in den betreffenden Klöstern (K), wobei vermerkt ist, ob von diesen zeitgenössische Drucke (+) oder nur handschriftlich überlieferte Werke (*) festgestellt wurden. Werke von Klosterkomponisten befinden sich heute häufig nicht in den Beständen des Ursprungsortes, sondern an anderen Orten, auch außerhalb Bayerns. Sie waren im 18. Jahrhundert zwischen den Klöstern ausgetauscht worden. Weltliche Komponisten in klösterlichen Diensten (Stiftskapellmeister, Chorregenten, Organisten etc.) sind in der Regel nicht mit aufgenommen.[3]

Soweit Musikaufnahmen aus den genannten Klöstern in der wesentlich darauf spezialisierten Reihe *Musica Bavarica* erschienen sind, ist die zutreffende Bestell-nummer angegeben (T). Die in Aufnahmen berücksichtigten Komponistennamen sind durch Kursivdruck gekennzeichnet. Am Ende des Abschnitts über ein Kloster oder eine Kirche ist die wichtigste auf die Musikpflege bezogene Literatur verzeichnet.

Choralhandschriften und Musikdrucke wurden nicht berücksichtigt. Die Drucke vor 1803 sind bereits im Internationalen Quellenlexikon der Musik (*Répertoire International des Sources Musicales*) erfaßt.[4] Nachstehend folgt eine Liste der Sigel der Fundorte und der Abkürzungen der genannten thematischen Kataloge.

ABKÜRZUNGEN

Fundorte

AÖhk	Altötting, Heilige Kapelle, Archiv
As	Augsburg, Staats- und Stadtbibliothek
Asa	Augsburg, Stadtarchiv
ASsb	Aschaffenburg, Stiftsbibliothek
Au	Augsburg, Universitätsbibliothek
BB	Benediktbeuern, Kath. Pfarramt
DTF	Dietfurt, Franziskanerkloster
DWc	Donauwörth, Pädagogische Stiftung Cassianeum
EB	Ebrach, Kath. Pfarramt
Ed	Eichstätt, Dom
Ew	Eichstätt, Benediktinerinnenabtei St. Walburg
FS	Freising, Dombibliothek
FÜS	Füssen, Kath. Pfarramt St. Mang
FW	Frauenwörth, Benediktinerinnenabtei
LaM	Landshut, Stadtpfarrkirche St. Martin
LDB	Landsberg am Lech, Kath. Pfarramt
LF	Laufen, Stiftsarchiv
Mbs	München, Bayerische Staatsbibliothek
Mf	München, Dom
Mm	München, St. Michael
MS	Münsterschwarzach, Benediktinerabtei
NT	Neumarkt-St. Veit, Kath. Pfarramt
OB	Ottobeuren, Benediktinerabtei
Po	Passau, Bischöfliches Ordinariat
POL	Polling, Kath. Pfarramt
Rp	Regensburg, Bischöfliche Zentralbibliothek (Proske Musikbibliothek)
SCHEY	Scheyern, Benediktinerabtei
TEG	Tegernsee, Kath. Pfarramt
TEGha	Tegernsee, Herzogliche Hauptverwaltung
TEI	Teisendorf, Kath. Pfarramt
TIT	Tittmoning, Kath. Pfarramt
URS	Ursberg, St. Josefs-Kongregation
WALL	Walleshausen, Kath. Pfarramt
WS	Wasserburg am Inn, Kath. Pfarramt

Kataloge Bayerischer Musiksammlungen (KBM)
Herausgegeben von der Generaldirektion der Bayerischen Staatlichen Bibliotheken, Henle-Verlag, München

KBM 1 Die Musikhandschriften der ehemaligen Klosterkirchen Weyarn, Tegernsee und Benediktbeuern. Bearbeitet von Robert Münster und Robert Machold, 1971.

KBM 2 Die Musikhandschriften der Benediktinerinnenabtei Frauenwörth und der Pfarrkirchen Indersdorf, Wasserburg am Inn und Bad Tölz. Unter der Leitung von Robert Münster bearbeitet von Ursula Bockholdt, Robert Machold und Lisbet Thew, 1975.

KBM 3 Die Musikhandschriften der Fürstlich Oettingen-Wallerstein' schen Bibliothek Schloß Harburg. Bearbeitet von Gertraut Haberkamp.

Mit einer Geschichte des Musikalienbestandes von Volker von Volckamer, 1976.

KBM 4 Die Musikhandschriften in der Theatinerkirche St. Kajetan in München. Bearbeitet von Siegfried Gmeinwieser, 1979.

KBM 5 Die Musikhandschriften der Bayerischen Staatsbibliothek.
Bd. 1: Chorbücher und Handschriften in chor-buchartiger Notierung. Beschrieben von Martin Bente, Marie Louise Göllner, Helmut Hell und Bettina Wackernagel. Mit einem Anhang: Nachträge zu den Tabulaturen und Stimmbüchern in *KBM* 5/2, 1989.
Bd. 2: Tabulaturen und Stimmbücher bis zur Mitte des 17. Jahrhunderts. Beschrieben von Marie Loise Göllner, 1979.

KBM 7 Die Musikhandschriften der St. Michaelskirche in München. Bearbeitet von Hildegard Herrmann-Schneider, 1985.

KBM 8 Die Musikhandschriften aus dem Dom zu Unserer Lieben Frau in München. Anhang: Ein Chorbuch aus St. Andreas in Freising. Bearbeitet von Helmut Hell, Monika Holl und Robert Machold, 1987.

KBM 9 Die ehemaligen Musikhandschriften-sammlungen der Königlichen Hofkapelle und der Kurfürstin Maria Anna in München. Herausgegeben von Gertraut Haberkamp und Robert Münster, 1982.

KMB 10 Die Musikhandschriften der Kollegiatsstifte Laufen und Tittmoning und der Pfarrkirchen Aschau, Berchtesgaden, Neumarkt-St. Veit und Teisendorf (in Vorbereitung).

KBM 11 Die Musikhandschriften in Eichstätt.
Bd. 1: Benediktinerinnenabtei St. Walburg und Dom. Bearbeitet von Hildegard Herrmann-Schneider, 1991.

KBM 13 Die Musikhandschriften Herzog Wilhelms in Bayern mit einem Restbestand aus der Benediktinerabtei Banz, der Grafen zu Toerring-Jettenbach und der Fürsten Fugger zu Babenhausen. Bearbeitet von Gertraut Haberkamp und Barbara Zuber. Geschichte und Inhalt des Musikalienbestandes von Robert Münster, 1988.

KBM 14 Die Musikhandschriften der Bischöflichen Zentralbibliothek Regensburg.
Bd. 1: Sammlung Proske. Manuskripte des 16. und 17. Jahrhunderts aus den Signaturen A.R., B, C, AN. Beschrieben von Gertraut Haberkamp. Mit einer Geschichte der Proskeschen Musiksammlung von August Scharnagl und einem Vorwort von Paul Mai, 1989.
Bd. 2: Sammlung Proske. Manuskripte des 18. und 19. Jahrhunderts aus dem Signaturen A.R., C, AN. Beschrieben von Gertraut Haberkamp und Jochen Reuter, 1989.
Bd. 4: Kollegiatstift Unsere Liebe Frau zur Alten Kapelle, Dom St. Peter und Kollegiatstift

zu den Heiligen Johann Baptist und Johann Evangelist in Regensburg. Beschrieben von Christofer Schweisthal, 1994.

KBM 15   Die Musikhandschriften der St. Josefs‑ Kongregation Ursberg, des Cassianeum Donauwörth und der Malteser‑ Studienbibliothek Amberg. Bearbeitet von Nicole Schwindt‑Gross und Barbara Zuber, 1992.

KBM 16   Die Musikhandschriften der Pfarrkirchen Polling, Walleshausen, Aichach, Landsberg, Erpfting, Lindau und des Franziskanerklosters Dietfurt (in Vorbereitung).

KBM 18   Die Musikhandschriften der Stifskirche Altötting, des Kollegiatstifts Landshut und der Pfarrkirchen Beuerberg, Schnaitsee und St. Mang in Füssen. Bearbeitet von Nicole Schwindt‑Gross, 1993.

KBM 21   Die Musikhandschriften der Dommusik St. Stephan im Archiv des Bistums Passau. Bearbeitet von Gertraut Haberkamp, 1993.

Sonstige Kataloge

Gottwald A   Die Musikhandschriften der Staats‑ und Stadtbibliothek Augsburg. Beschrieben von Clytus Gottwald, Wiesbaden 1974 (Handschriften‑Kataloge der Staats‑ und Stadtbibliothek Augsburg, 1).

Gottwald M   Die Musikhandschriften der Universitätsbibliothek München. Beschrieben von Clytus Gottwald, Wiesbaden 1968 (Die Handschriften der Universitätsbibliothek München, 2).

BESTÄNDE
(alphabetisch geordnet)

ABENSBERG
Kloster der unbeschuhten Karmeliten, 1389–1802 Musikalien verschollen.

K: +Justinus a Desponsatione BMV=Johann Justus Will (1675–1747).

Lit: Paul Ruf, *Säkularisation und Bayerische Staats‑ bibliothek*, Bd. 1: *Die Bibliotheken der Mendikanten und Theatiner*, Wiesbaden 1962, S. 104.

ALDERSBACH
Zisterzienserabtei, 1123–1803 Der laut Inventar von 1803 umfangreiche Musikalienbestand ist verschollen.

K: *Balduin *Wurzer* (1738–1809), *Vinzenz *König* (1748–1804).

T: Mc MB 75052.

Lit: R. Münster, 'Die Musik in den Klöstern um Passau zur Zeit Mozarts', in: *20. Deutsches Mozartfest der Deutschen Mozartgesellschaft*, Programmheft, Passau 1971, S. 48ff.; Robert Klugseder, 'Geschichtliche Abhandlung über das Musikleben im ehemaligen Zisterzienser‑ stift Aldersbach . . .' in: *Musica sacra in der Zisterzienserkirche Aldersbach*, Aldersbach 1992, S. 2ff.

ALTÖTTING
Kollegiatstift, 1231–1803, 1930– Nach einer größeren Vernichtungsaktion noch vorhandener Restbestand, insgesamt 237 Hand‑

schriften: vorwiegend Kirchenmusik 18./19. Jh., sowie 1 Orgeltabulatur (1588–ca. 1610) und 12 Salzburger Abschriften, darunter die Opern *L'isola disabitata* 1774 von L. Gatti und *L'isola disabitata* 1782 von D. Fischietti. – Außerdem 625 autographe Kompositionen des Kapell‑ organisten Max *Keller* (1770–1854).

Kat: *KBM 18* (Fundort: *AÖhk*).

K: +Abraham *Megerle* (1607–80), +Georg Christoph Leuttner (1644–1703).

T: MB 70311 (auch als MC: MB 75056 oder CD: MB 75102).

Lit: Max Moesmang, *Geschichte der Altöttinger Stifts‑ und Kapellmusik*, Altötting 1909; Nicole Schwindt‑Gross, Einleitung zu *KBM 18*.

ALTOMÜNSTER
Birgittenkloster, 1497–1803, 1842– Gemäß der Ordensregel nur Choralgesang. Erst in den letzten Jahrzehnten vor der Aufhebung gele‑ gentlich Figuralmusik. Musikalien verschollen.

Lit: R. Münster, 'Musik und Musiktheater in Altomünster im 18. Jahrhundert', in: *Festschrift Altomünster 1973*, Aichach 1973, S. 309ff.

AMORBACH
Benediktinerabtei, um 1700–1803 Musikalien verschollen. Der Musikalienbestand im Fürstlich Leiningenschen Archiv Amorbach

enthält keine Musik aus dem Kloster. Ein Folio-
band mit Kirchensonaten von Coelestin Mann in
Mbs (Mus. ms. 88a).

K: *Coelestin Mann (1674–1713), +Romanus
Hoffstetter (1742–1815).

Lit: Ernst Fritz Schmid, *Die Orgeln der Abtei
Amorbach*, Buchen 1938, Mainz ²1963; Hubert
Unverricht, *Die beiden Hoffstetter*, Mainz 1968
(Beiträge zur mittelrheinischen Musik-
geschichte, 10).

ANDECHS

Benediktinerabtei, 1455–1803, 1850–
Musikalien von Andechser Hauskomponisten
außer einem Offertorium von Placidus Scharl im
Kloster nicht erhalten. Ein noch unkatalogisierter
Musikalienstand im Klosterarchiv ist eine
Schenkung um 1830, ohne Bezug zum
Andechser Musikrepertoire.

K: Otto Ameis (gest. 1660); +Cajetan *Kolberer*
(1658–1732), Meinrad Moosmiller (1717–67),
+Gregor *Schreyer* (1719–67), *Johann
Nepomuk Trost (1729–83), +Nonnosus
Madlseder (1739–97), *Placidus Scharl
(1731–1814), *Benedikt *Holzinger*
(1747–1815), +Johann Baptist Randl
(1770–1801).

T: MB 201, CD MB 75107, CD MB 75111.

Lit: Max Schreiber, *Beiträge zur Musikpflege im
Kloster Andechs vor 1803*, Birkeneck 1932; R.
Münster, 'Thematisches Verzeichnis der erhal-
tenen Kompositionen von P. Nonnosus
Madlseder OSB . . .', in: *Musik in bayerischen
Klöstern* I, Regensburg 1986, S. 225ff.
(Schriftenreihe der Hochschule für Musik in
München. 5); ders., 'Musik im Kloster
Andechs', in: *Andechs. Der Heilige Berg*, hrsg.
von Karl Bosl u.a., München 1993. S. 219ff.;
ders., Art. 'Andechs' in *MGG*, 2. Ausg.,
Sachteil I (1994).

ASBACH

Benediktinerabtei, um 1090–1803
Musikalien verschollen.

K: +Carlmann Kolb (1703–65).

Lit: Ulrich Siegele, Art. 'Kolb' in *MGG* 7
(1958).

ASCHAFFENBURG

Kollegiatstift St. Peter und Alexander, um
950–1802
Musikalien, abgesehen von Choralhandschriften

und einer Orgeltabulatur um 1590 in *ASsb*,
verschollen.

Lit: W. Gleissner, 'Kirchenmusiktradition des
Kollegiatstifts St. Peter und Alexander zu
Aschaffenburg', in: *Kirchenmusikalisches
Jahrbuch* 68, 1984, S. 89f.

ATTEL

Benediktinerabtei, um 1040–1803
Musikalien verschollen. 3 Ms. in *FS*, Bestand
Wasserburg, St. Jakob (Ae. Holler, F.X Brixi, F.
Gleissner), s. *KBM 2*; 1 Sinfonie (Leopold
Mozart) in *Mbs*.

K: *Aegidius Holler (1751–?, seit 1788 in Siena,
St. Urban), *Ildephons Kyrmayr (1741–nach
1802), *Leonhard Hueber (1746–1823).

T: MB 201.

AU AM INN

Augustiner-Chorherrenstift, 784–1803, 1853–
(Franziskanerinnen)
Musikalien verschollen. 2 Orgeltabulaturen
(Mus. ms. 1640 und 1641) und – möglicherweise
– 1 fragmentarischer Stimmensatz (Mus. ms.
6485) mit Messen und Motetten, beide um 1600,
in *Mbs*, s. *KBM 5/2*.

AUGSBURG

Augustiner-Chorherrenstift Heilig-Kreuz,
1154–1802, 1936– (Dominikaner)
Der zum Teil erhaltene Musikalienbestand und
ein Inventar von 1855 in *Asa*.

K: +Melchior Dürr (um 1700), +Ludwig
Zoeschinger (1731–1806), Fortunat Schoedl
(1749–1818), +Matthäus Fischer (1763–1840).

T: MB 70313.

Lit: Ernst Fritz Schmid, 'Mozart und das
geistliche Augsburg, insonderheit das
Chorherrenstift Heilig Kreuz', in: *Zeitschrift
des historischen Vereins für Schwaben* 55/56,
1942/43, S. 104ff.; ders., *Ein schwäbisches
Mozartbuch*, Lorch 1948, S. 442; Walter Senn,
'Die Mozart-Überlieferung im Stift Heilig
Kreuz zu Augsburg', in: *Zeitschrift des
Historischen Vereins für Schwaben* 62/63, 1962, S.
333ff.

AUGSBURG

Benediktinerabtei St. Ulrich und Afra,
1012–1802
Musikalien weitgehend verschollen. 21
Chorbücher, ca.1580–1630, in *As*, s. *Gottwald A.*

Ungeklärt ist die Provenienz der angeblich aus St. Ulrich und Afra stammenden Manuskripte in *Rp*, s. *KBM 14/2*, S. xxv (Motetten in Stimmbüchern, 16. Jh.).

K: *Georg Gastel (1537–1616), Wolfgang Schorrmaier (1. Hälfte 18. Jh.), Nonnosus Pitzenberger (1699–1749), Ulrich Beitinger (1743–72), *Nitgar Fichtl (1748–1817), *Placidus Braun (1756–1829), Rupert Streicher (1766–1837).

Lit: Adolf Layer, 'Benediktinisches Musikerbe in Schwaben', in: *Jahrbuch des Historischen Vereins Dillingen*, 86, 1984, S. 96 und 100f.; Josef Mančal, Art. 'Augsburg, Kloster St. Ulrich und Afra', in *MGG*, 2. Ausg., Sachteil I (1994).

AUGSBURG
Kollegiatstift St Moritz, um 1020–1803
Musikalien verschollen.

Lit: Richard Schaal, 'Zur Musikpflege im Kollegiatstift St. Moritz zu Augsburg', in: *Die Musikforschung* 7, 1954, S. 1ff.; Josef Mančal, Art. 'Augsburg' in *MGG*, 2. Ausg., Sachteil I (1994).

BANZ
Benediktinerabtei, um 1070–1803
Einige Handschriften aus der 2. Hälfte des 18. Jh. in der Musiksammlung von Herzog Wilhelm in Bayern (1752–1837), der das Kloster 1814 erwarb: Kompositionen von P. Roman Schad, P. Andreas Daum, P. Romanus Hoffstetter, A.L. Fracassini, F.X. Brixi, Rüll (Johann Baptist Rill?) und geistliche Kontrafakturen von Opernarien (Grétry, Piccini, Mysliveček).
Kat: *KBM 13* (Fundort: *TEGha*).

K: +Valentin Rathgeber (1682–1750), *Roman Schad (1758–1834).

Lit: Wilfried Dotzauer, 'Die kirchenmusikalischen Werke Johann Valentin Rathgebers', Diss. Erlangen 1976; R. Münster, 'Die Musiksammlung Herzog Wilhelms in Bayern', in *KBM 13*, S. xiff.; Franz Krautwurst, 'Valentin Rathgeber', in: *Fränkische Lebensbilder* 14, 1993, S. 141ff.; R. Münster, Art. 'Banz', in: *MGG*, 2. Ausg., Sachteil I (1994).

BAUMBURG
Augustiner-Chorherrenstift, 1107/9–1803
Musikalien verschollen.

K: +Gaudentius *Lenghamer* (1699–1733).
T: CD MB 75107.

Lit: R. Münster, 'Zur Musikpflege des Augustiner Chorherrenstift Baumburg im 18. Jahrhundert', in: *Traunwalchener Musiktradition*, hrsg. von Siegrid Düll und Hans Lauber, Traunreut 1995, S. 32ff.

BENEDIKTBEUERN
Benediktinerabtei, um 740–1803, 1930– (Salesianer)
Erhalten nur 239 Handschriften nach 1803, ohne Musik aus dem alten Kloster. Darunter Abschriften von Werken aus Weyarn (s.d.) und ein fragmentarischer Nachlaß des Chorregenten Erasmus Vogel (1760–1816), der Frauenkirche München, mit 16 Handschriften. 4 Handschriften aus dem Kloster vor 1803 in *FS*, Bestand Wasserburg, St. Jakob (Franz Feuchtmayr, J.M. Haydn), s. *KBM 2*. 1 Chorbuch, 1609, in *Mbs*, s. *KBM 5/1*.
Kat: *KBM 1* (Fundort: *BB*).

K: Corbinian Carl (1643–1713), Gregor Zoedl (1682–1721), Udalrich Waldenberger (1721–83), Heinrich Gassler (1722–74), Columban Kern (1741–96), Bonifaz Koller (1752–99), *Martin *Gebhard* (1770–1836).
T: CD MB 75 101.

Lit: R. Münster, Einleitung zu *KBM 1*; Josef Hemmerle, *Die Benediktinerabtei Benediktbeuern*, Berlin u.a. 1991, S. 278ff. (Germania sacra, NF 28).

BERCHTESGADEN
Gefürstetes Augustiner-Chorherrenstift, um 1102–1803
Der nach vorausgegangener Dezimierung vorgefundene Bestand umfaßt noch 174 Handschriften. In seiner Zusammensetzung dokumentiert er u.a. die Verbindung mit Salzburg und Wien. Kirchenmusik, 2. Hälfte 18. und 1. Hälfte 19. Jh.
Kat: *KBM 10*, in Vorbereitung (Fundort: *BGD*).

Lit: Hans Bruckner, 'Die Kirchenmusik in der Fürstpropstei Berchtesgaden', in: *Kunst und Kultur der Fürstpropstei Berchtesgaden*, Ausstellung Berchtesgaden 1988, S. 122ff.; R. Münster, Einleitung zu *KBM 10*.

BERNRIED
Augustiner-Chorherrenstift, 1121/22–1803
Reiche Pflege der Musik und des Theaters. Musikalien verschollen.

K: *Herkulan *Glück* (1776–1860).

T: MB 211.

Lit: R. Münster, 'Mozarts Bernrieder Kanon. Die Geschichte einer Legende', in: *Mozart-Jahrbuch* 1962/63, S. 178ff. Repr. in: R. Münster, *"Ich bin hier sehr beliebt". Mozart und das kurfürstliche Bayern*, Tutzing 1993, S. 322ff.

BEUERBERG

Augustiner-Chorherrenstift, 1120–1803, 1835–(Salesianerinnen)

Im vorhandenen Musikalienbestand (167 Handschriften) nur 14 Manuskripte aus der Klosterzeit vor 1803, darunter Joseph Haydn, Serenata (Hob. II:17; Fassung ohne Oboen), Sinfonie (Hob. I:89) und – fragmentarisch – Mozart KV 250/248b (Sinfoniefassung) und Sinfonie KV 319. Übrige Handschriften 19. Jh.

Kat: *KBM 18* (Fundort: *FS*).

K: Bernhard Perghofer (1. Hälfte 18. Jh.).

Lit: R. Münster, 'Die Musik im Augustiner-Chorherrenstift Beuerberg von 1768 bis 1803 und der thematische Katalog des Chorherrn Alipius Seitz', in: *Kirchenmusikalisches Jahrbuch* 54, 1970, S. 47ff.; ders., Art. 'Beuerberg' in *MGG*, 2. Ausg., Sachteil I (1994); Nicole Schwindt-Gross, Einleitung zu *KBM 18*.

BEYHARTING

Augustiner-Chorherrenstift, um 1130–1803

Musikalien verschollen. Sie wurden 1803 der Klosterpfarrkirche überlassen. Ein kursorisches, sicherlich unvollständiges Inventar von 1803 nennt 11 Messen, 15 Litaneien und 7 Sinfonien. 2 Gradualien von Michael Haydn in *LDB*, s. *KBM 16*.

K: *Joseph Neumayr (1755–1822), +Johann Nepomuk Furthner (1776–1820).

Lit: R. Münster, 'Zur Musikpflege im Augustiner-Chorherrenstift Beyharting' (in Vorbereitung).

DIESSEN

Augustiner-Chorherrenstift, 1114–1803

Bestand im 20. Jh. vernichtet. Einst reiche Musikpflege, von Kurfürst Karl Albrecht 1726 bei einem Besuch gerühmt. 1 Messe von Cavo in *FS* (Bestand Wasserburg, St. Jakob), s. KBM 2. Orgelhandschrift von Rathard Mayr im Pfarramt Dießen. 1 Chorbuch, 1603, in *Mbs*, s. *KBM 5/1*.

K: Michael Vishaber (Mitte 18. Jh.), *Rathard

Mayr (1737–1805), Joseph Weinmayr (1778–1844).

T: MB 207.

DIETFURT

Franziskanerkloster, 1660–1802, anschließend Zentralkloster, 1827–

Musikalienbestand mit 251 Handschriften, Ende 18. und 19. Jh.

K: u.a. Dalmatius Scheck (1750–1822).

Kat: *KBM 16*, in Vorbereitung (Fundort: *DTF*).

Lit: Hildegard Herrmann, 'Die Musikpflege der bayerischen Franziskaner von der Gründung der Provinz bis zur Säkularisation (1625–1802)', in: *Musik in bayerischen Klöstern* I, Regensburg 1986, S. 280 (Schriftenreihe der Hochschule für Musik in München, 1); R. Münster, Einleitung zu *KBM 16*.

DIETRAMSZELL

Augustiner-Chorherrenstift, 1098–1803

Musikalien verschollen. 107 Kompositionen wurden 1803 nach München verbracht. Ein Requiem (Haydn, Hob. XXIIa:C4) und eine fragmentarische deutsche Messe von Wieser nebst späteren Werken desselben heute in *TEG*, s. *KBM 1*.

K: *Herkulan Wieser (1775–1839).

Lit: R. Münster, 'Die Musik in Dietramszell', in: *Oberbayerischer Gebirgsbote* 1961, Nr. 268; ders., Artikel 'Wieser, Herkulan', in *MGG* 14 (1968); Edgar Krausen, *Das Augustiner-chorherrenstift Dietramszell*, Berlin u.a. 1988, S. 175ff.

DONAUWÖRTH

Benediktinerabtei Heilig Kreuz, um 1040–1803

Restbestände der Musikalien in *Au* (Bestand Fürstlich Oettingen-Wallersteinsche Musiksammlung, s. *KBM 3*, S. XVII Anm. 60 und Münster, S. 157f., in *DWc* (s. *KBM 15*, S. XXIIff.) und *URS* (s. *KBM 15*, S. 11: Franz Bühler, Singspiel *Der letzte Rausch*).

Kat: *KBM 3* (Fundort: *Au*) und *KBM 15* (Fundort: *URS*).

K: +Magnus *Häußler* (1725–83), Benno Gorhan (1744–94), Willibald Zeiller (1745–89), +Gregor (Franz) *Bühler* (1760–1823), +Johann *Brandl* (1750–1837, Novize 1779/80).

T: MB 70313, CD MB 75112.

Lit: Adolf Layer, 'Benediktinisches Musikerbe in

Schwaben', a.a.O., S. 102ff.; R. Münster, 'Die Musik im Kloster Heilig Kreuz', in: *Heilig Kreuz in Donauwörth*, hrsg. von Werner Schiedermair, Donauwörth 1987, S. 155ff.; Nicole Schwindt-Gross, Einleitung zu *KBM 15*.

EBRACH

Zisterzienserabtei, 1127–1803
Musikalienbestand mit 215 Nummern und 45 Drucken erhalten.
Kat: Dennerlein, s.u. (Fundort: *EB*).
Lit: Hans Dennerlein, *Musik des 18. Jahrhunderts in Franken. Die Inventare der Funde von Ebrach, Burgwindheim, Maria Limbach und Iphofen*, Münsterschwarzach 1953, S. 7ff. (Bericht des Historischen Vereins Bamberg, 92); Rudolf Laugg, 'Studien zur Instrumentalmusik im Zisterzienserkloster Ebrach in der zweiten Hälfte des 18. Jahrhunderts', Diss. Erlangen 1953.

EGGENFELDEN

Franziskanerkloster, 1649–1802, 1832–
Die erhaltenen Musikalien seit 1968 nach Ankauf in *Mbs*: Mus. ms. 8647 bis Mus. ms. 8705, darunter zwei Foliobände 1770 (Mus. ms. 8704) und 1800 (Mus. ms. 8705) mit Messen u.a., übriges meist 19. Jh.
K: u.a. Johannes Columbinus Putzmann (1759–1820).
Kat: Zettelkatalog *Mbs*.

EICHSTÄTT

Benediktinerinnenabtei St. Walburg, 1035–1806, 1835–
Musikalienbestand mit 347 Handschriften aus den Jahren von ca. 1745 bis 1900. Kirchenmusik u.a. von Komponisten der fürstbischöflichen Hofmusik, Orgel- und Klaviermusik.
Kat: *KBM 11/1* (Fundort: *Ew*).
T: MB 809, CD MB 75112.
Lit: Hildegard Herrmann-Schneider, Einleitung zu *KBM 11/1*.

EICHSTÄTT

Dom St. Willibald
Bestand mit 534 Handschriften: Repertoire 18. und 19. Jh. u.a. mit Kirchenwerken Eichstätter Hofkomponisten (Bachschmidt, Meck, Schermer, Schlecht) und Vertretern des Cäcilianismus.

Kat: *KBM 11/1* (Fundort: *Ed*).
Lit: Hildegard Herrmann-Schneider, Einleitung zu *KBM 11/1*.

ELCHINGEN

Benediktinisches Reichsstift, um 1120–1803, 1921– (Oblaten der Unbefleckten Jungfrau Maria)
Musikalien verschollen.
K: Magnus Dürrbeck (2. Hälfte 17. Jh.), +Ambrosius *Lutzenberger* (1767–1834).
T: MB 70305.
Lit: Adolf Layer, 'Benediktinisches Musikerbe in Schwaben', a.a.O., S. 104f.

ENSDORF

Benediktinerabtei, 1121–1802, 1920– (Salesianer)
In der ehemaligen Klosterkirche befand sich 1967 ein kleiner Bestand mit z.T. fragmentarischen Messen (Brixi, Wiest, Giulini, Ivanschiz, Loos, Königsberger, Lohelius), Offertorien (u.a. Michl, Pichl) und einer Vesper von Schaller (1772).
K: Franz Xaver Pellet (1735–1805).
Lit: Dominikus Mettenleiter, *Musikgeschichte der Oberpfalz*, Amberg 1867, S. 223f.

ETTAL

Benediktinerabtei, 1330–1803, 1900–
Dernach dem Brand von 1744 neu beschaffte, umfangreiche Musikalienbestand ist verschollen.
K: Placidus Wild (1694–1768), *Anselm Achmiller (1777–1833).
T: MB 70301.
Lit: Angelus Waldstein OSB, 'Franz Xaver Richter an der Ettaler Ritterakademie', in: *Ettaler Mandl* 45, 1965/66, S. 145ff.; ders., 'Das Ettaler Oratorium von der Ausgrabung bis zur Aufführung', in: *Ettaler Mandl* 48, 1968/69, S. 49ff.

FRAUENWÖRTH

Benediktinerinnenabtei, Mitte 7. Jh.–1803, 1836–
Musikalienbestand mit 224 Handschriften: Kirchenmusik zwischen 1765 und 1815, darunter 42 Abschriften und ein Autograph Michael Haydns. Musikalische Kontakte bestanden zu Seeon und Herrenchiemsee. Einige Handschriften aus dem Kloster heute in *FS* (Bestand Wasserburg, St. Jakob), s. *KBM 2*, S. XVIII.
Kat: *KBM 2* (Fundort: *FW*).

T: MB 206, MB 70304, CD MB 75104.
Lit: R. Münster, Einleitung zu *KBM 2*.

FÜRSTENFELD

Zisterzienserabtei, 1278–1803
Musikalien verschollen. Der Nachlaß von P. Benedikt Pittrich mit zahlreichen Autographen aus der Zeit nach 1803 blieb in dem vor mehreren Jahren aufgelassenen Pfarrhof Erpfting bei Landsberg erhalten. 2 Mensural-Codices in *Mu* (2° Cod. 166/167) um 1600, mit Motetten und einer Messe.
Kat: *KBM 16*, Nachlaß Pittrich im Bestand *ERP* (Fundort: Augsburg, Ordinariatsarchiv); *Gottwald M.*
K: Engelbert Asam (1683–1752), ⁺Remigius *Falb* (1714–70), Benedikt Lindinger (ca. 1725–74), *Maximilian von *Schönberg* (1737–92), ⁺Benedikt *Pittrich* (1758–1827).
T: CD MB 75 102, Mc 75 056.
Lit: R. Münster, Art. 'Pittrich' und 'Fürstenfeld' in *MGG* 10 (1962) und 16 (1979); Hans Schmid, 'Zur Musikgeschichte des Klosters Fürstenfeld', in: *700 Jahre Fürstenfeld*, München u. Zürich 1978, S. 46ff. (Große Kunstführer, 39); Klaus Mohr, *Die Musikgeschichte des Klosters Fürstenfeld*, Regensburg 1987 (Schriftenreihe der Hochschule für Musik in München, 8).

FÜRSTENZELL

Zisterzienserabtei, 1274–1803
Musikalien verschollen.
K: *Franz Xaver Hochmayr (1724–80).
Lit: Franz Xaver Rixinger, 'Musikpflege am ehemaligen Zisterzienser-Kloster Fürstenzell', in: *Die ostbairischen Grenzmarken* 18, 1929, S. 209ff.; R. Münster, 'Die Musik in den Klöstern um Passau zur Zeit Mozarts', in: *20. Deutsches Mozartfest der Deutschen Mozart-Gesellschaft*, Programmheft, Passau 1971, S. 42ff.

FÜSSEN

Benediktinerabtei St. Mang, um 850–1802
Bestand mit 236 Handschriften: Kirchenmusik, ca. 1770 bis Mitte 19. Jh. und einige Instrumentalwerke, in *FÜS*. Weitere 15 Handschriften aus dem Klosterbestand in *Au* (Bestand Fürstlich Oettingen-Wallersteinsche Musiksammlung), s. *KBM 3*, S. XIII.
Kat: *KBM 18*.
K: ⁺Gallus *Zeiler* (1705–55), *Leopold Natterer

(1732–1805), *Gallus Weiß (1742–91), *Magnus *Schnitzer* (1755–1827).
T: MB 501.
Lit: Adolf Layer, 'Zur Musikpflege des Benediktinerklosters St. Mang in Füssen', in: *Jahrbuch des Historischen Vereins für Augsburger Diözesangeschichte* 6, 1972, S. 241ff.; Margarete Löschberger-Holzer, 'P. Gallus Zeiler – Ein Komponist am Kloster St. Mang in Füssen', in: *Musik in bayerischen Klöstern* I, Regensburg 1986, S. 139ff.; Nicole Schwindt-Gross, Einleitung zu *KBM 18*.

FULTENBACH

Benediktinerabtei, um 739–1803
Musikalien verschollen.
K: ⁺Benedikt Fasold (1718–66); ⁺Amandus Schwarz (1773–1815).
Lit: August Hefner, 'Geschichte des Klosters Fultenbach', in: *Jahrbuch des historischen Vereins Dillingen an der Donau* 27, 1914, S. 1ff. und 29, 1915, S. 255ff.

GARS

Augustiner-Chorherrenstift, um 764–1803
Musikalien verschollen, nur 6 Handschriften (B. Buchwieser, V. Hösl) in *FS* (Bestand Wasserburg, St Jakob), s. *KBM 2*, S. XVIII.
K: *Virgil Hösl (1757–1819).

GEISENFELD

Benediktinerinnenabtei, 1030–1803
Ein erhaltener Teil der Musikalien (mindestens 42 Handschriften 17. und 18. Jh.) heute in *Rp*, vgl. *KBM 14/2*, S. XXXII.
Lit: Gertraut Haberkamp, Einleitung zu *KBM 14/2*.

GOTTESZELL

Zisterzienserabtei, 1285–1803
Musikalien verschollen. Werke des Klosterrichters Ignaz Gullingstein (gest. nach 1807) u.a. in *Mbs* und *BG*, s. *KBM 18*, S. 126.
Lit: R. Münster, 'Nachrichten zur Musikpflege in der Zisterzienserabtei Gotteszell in der 2. Hälfte des 18. Jahrhunderts' (in Vorbereitung).

HEIDENFELD

Augustiner-Chorherrenstift, 1069–1803
Reste der Musikalien in *MS*.
Kat: Dennerlein (s. unten).

K: +Joseph Krafft (1750–1812).

Lit: H. Dennerlein, 'Der Musikalien-Bestand Heidenfeld/Wipfeld', in: *Bericht des Historischen Vereins Bamberg* 109, 1973, S. 285ff.

HERRENCHIEMSEE

Augustiner-Chorherrenstift, um 765–1803

Einzelne Handschriften aus dem Musikalien-bestand heute in *Mbs* (F. Chr. Neubauer: Messe) und in *FS* (Bestand Wasserburg, St. Jakob, 10 Mss.: F.X. Brixi, Conrad Gassler, J.M. Haydn, Joseph Neumayr).

K: +Norbert Hauner (1743–1827), *Conrad Gassler (1762–1805).

Lit: R. Münster, Einleitung zu *KBM 2*, S. XVIIf.; ders., Artikel 'Herrenchiemsee' in *MGG* 16 (1979); ders., 'Thauet, Himmel, den Gerechten', in: *Weihnachten in den Bergen*, hrsg. von Hans Heyn, München 1983, S. 38ff.; ders., 'Musik in den Chiemseeklöstern', in: *Lesebuch aus der Provinz Chiemgau*, Rosenheim 1988, S. 244ff.; ders., 'Eine neuentdeckte Kantate Michael Haydns für den letzten Fürstbischof des Bistums Chiemsee', in: *Begegnung* 1/1994, München 1994, S. 55ff.

HÖGLWÖRTH

Augustiner-Chorherrenstift, 1125–1817

Musikalien weitgehend vernichtet. 5 Mss. (J.M. Haydn, B. Stoeckl, F. Lipp) in *TEI*, s. *KBM 10* (in Vorbereitung).

K: Virgil Unterrainer (1781–1849).

Lit: R. Münster, Einleitung zu *KBM 10*.

HOLZEN

Benediktinerinnenabtei, 1152–1802, 1927–
(St. Josefs-Kongregation)

450 Handschriften: 2. Hälfte 18. Jh. bis Mitte 20. Jh. Zum kleineren Teil aus dem alten Benediktinerinnenkloster, wo die Nonnen ihr Ordensleben bis etwa 1830 weiterführen konnten: Kirchenmusik sowie einige der sonst selten über-lieferten klösterlichen Kantaten und Singspiele. Der größere Teil umfaßt Kammermusik mit Klavier und Liedern aus der Musikbibliothek der Grafen Fischler von Treuberg, der Klosterbesitzern von 1802 bis 1927.

Kat: *KBM 15* (Fundort: *URS*).

Lit: Nicole Schwindt-Gross, Einleitung zu *KBM 15*.

INDERSDORF

Augustiner-Chorherrenstift, 1126–1783

Restbestand mit 48 Handschriften Mitte 18. Jh. bis ca.1900, darunter Fragmente aus einer Münchner Fastmeditation 1772 von J.G. Holzbogen. 28 alte Drucke Anfang 17. Jh. in *Mbs*, einzelne Stimmen dazu noch im Bestand Indersdorf.

K: *KBM 2* (Fundort: *FS*).

Lit: R. Münster, Einleitung zu *KBM 2*; ders., 'Die Münchner Fastenmeditationen von 1724 bis 1774 und ihre Komponisten', in: *Quaestiones in Musica. Festschrift für Franz Krautwurst zum 65. Geburtstag*, Tutzing 1989, S. 413ff.

IRSEE

Reichsunmittelbare Benediktinerabtei, 1182–1802

Musikalien weitgehend verschollen. 3 Orgel-tabulaturen zwischen 1596 und 1610 in *Mbs* (Mus. ms. 263–265), s. *KBM 5/2*; Chorbücher des 17. Jh. in *As* (Tonk. Schl. 95 und 96), s. *Gottwald A*, und in *Rp* (4 Chorbücher), s. *KBM 14/1*, S. 275ff.

K: *Joannes Seytz (17. Jh.), *Gregor Stemmele (gest. 1619), *Carl Andreae (gest. 1627), +Meinrad *Spieß* (1683–1761), Anselm Schwink (1725–93).

T: MB 70 311, CD MB 75 115.

Lit: August Scharnagl, Art. 'Stemmele' in *MGG* 12 (1966); Alfred Goldmann, Art. 'Andreae' in *MGG* 15 (1973); ders., 'Musikpflege im Kloster Irsee', in: *Das Reichsstift Irsee*, Weissenhorn 1981, S. 235ff.; ders., *Meinrad Spieß, der Musikprior von Irsee*, Weissenhorn 1987; Gertraut Haberkamp, Einleitung zu *KBM 14/2*, S. XXVIII; Clytus Gottwald, Einleitung zu *Gottwald A*.

LANDSHUT

Kollegiatstift St. Martin, 1598–1803, 1937–

Der Hauptteil der 111 Handschriften stammt aus dem 19. Jh., verwendet etwa seit 1835. Von besonderer Bedeutung sind 17 Handschriften Salzburger Provenienz mit Kirchenwerken von W.A. Mozart und J.M. Haydn, die, wie sieben weitere, geschrieben vom Seeoner Abt Lambert Neisser (1748–1817), aus dem 1803 aufgehobenen Kloster Seeon stammen.

Kat: *KBM 18* (Fundort: *LAm*).

Lit: R. Münster, 'Mozart in Seeon', in: *Schönere*

Heimat 80, 1991, S. 159ff.; Nicole Schwindt-Gross, Einleitung zu *KBM 18*.

LANDSHUT-SELIGENTHAL
Zisterzienserinnenkloster, 1231–1803, dann 'Absterbekloster', 1835–
Ein nicht erfaßter Bestand (vor allem Drucke) im Kloster.

LANGHEIM
Zisterzienserkloster, 1132/33–1803
Musikalien verschollen.
K: *Andreas Daum (gest. 1801): 1 Requiem in *KBM 13*.

LAUFEN
Kollegiatstift, 1334 (*de jure* 1621) –
Der Bestand mit 288 Handschriften spiegelt vor allem die engen Beziehungen zur Musik in Salzburg. Laufen gehörte, wie Tittmoning, zum Erzbistum Salzburg. 1 Chorbuch mit Werken von Peter Guetfreund, 17. Jh.
Kat: *KBM 10* in Vorbereitung (Fundort: *LF*).
Lit: R. Münster, 'Seltene Musikdrucke des 17. Jh. im Stiftsarchiv Laufen an der Salzach', in: *Die Musikforschung* 20 (1967), S. 284ff.; ders., 'Die Musiküberlieferung im Kollegiatstift Mariae Himmelfahrt in Laufen', in: *Das Salzfaß*, NF 26, 1992, S. 128ff.

MAIHINGEN
Minoritenkloster, 1607–1803
6 Handschriften und 20 Drucke in *Au* (Bestand Oettingen-Wallerstein), s. *KBM 3*.
Lit: Volker von Volckamer, Einleitung zu *KBM 3*, S. XIV.

MALLERSDORF
Benediktinerabtei, 1107–1803, 1869– (Franziskanerinnen)
Musikalien verschollen.
K: *Bonifaz Stoeckl (1747–84), Bernhard Vitzthum (1757–1816).
Lit: R. Münster, Art. 'Stoeckl' in *MGG* 12 (1965).

METTEN
Benediktinerabtei, um 766–1803, 1830–
Ein umfangreicher Musikhandschriftenbestand, z.T. aus dem 18. Jh., im Kloster.
Kat: unvollständiger Zettelkatalog in der Klosterbibliothek.

K: +Lambert *Kraus* (1728–90), Amand Steigenberger (1741–1809), +Johann Baptist Sternkopf (1753–1817), Gamulbertus Holzhauser (1763–1833), Lambert Faerber (1774–1821), Roman Raith (1774–1855).
T: MB 70 312.
Lit: Bertha Antonia Wallner, 'Beiträge zur Musikgeschichte von Metten', in: *Alt und Jung Metten* 11, H. 3, 1936/37, S. 1ff.

MICHELFELD
Benediktinerabtei, 1119–1803
Aus dem einst reichen Bestand befinden sich heute noch 7 Handschriften, 2. Hälfte 18. Jh., im Pfarrarchiv St. Leonhard, Michelfeld. Eine umfangreiche Sammlung (84 Komponisten) gelangte nach 1803 aus Michelfeld in das Schullehrer-Seminar Eichstätt.
K: Maurus Rambsmoser (1708–74), Innocentius Burger (1745–1805), Wolfgang Liber (1758–1840), Benedikt Gulder (1761–1830).
Lit: Dominikus Mettenleiter, *Musikgeschichte der Oberpfalz*, Regensburg 1867, S. 224f.; Fritz Schnelbögl und Theodor Wohnhaas, 'Zur Geschichte von St. Leonhard in Michelfeld', in: *Ostbairische Grenzmarken* 19, 1977, S. 888f.

MÖNCHSDEGGINGEN
Benediktinerabtei, 1138–1803
55 Handschriften, 18. Jh., in *Au* (Bestand Oettingen-Wallerstein), s. *KBM 3*.
K: Michael Dobler (1704–77), Martin Haugg (Mitte 18. Jh.).
Lit: Volker von Volckamer, Einleitung zu *KBM 3*, S. XIII; Adolf Layer, Benediktinisches Musikerbe in Schwaben, a.a.O., S. 104.

MÜHLDORF
Kollegiatstift, 1610–1803
Mühldorf war bis 1810 Enklave des Fürsterzbistums Salzburg. Ein Teil der Musikalien gelangte 1968 durch Ankauf an die Bayerische Staatsbibliothek (Mus. ms. 8371–8491), ca. 1750–1840.
Kat: Zettelkatalog *Mbs*.

MÜNCHEN
Franziskanerkloster, 1221–1802, 1827–
5 Foliobände mit Messen, Litaneien, Hymnen etc. 1791 (Mus. ms. 83–87) in *Mbs*.
Lit: Paul Ruf, *Säkularisation und Bayerische Staatsbibliothek*, Bd. 1, a.a.O., S. 357f.

MÜNCHEN

Hieronymitenkloster, 1727–1805

Bestand 1805 aufgelöst. 13 Handschriften in *Mf* (s. *KBM 8*, S. 422), *Mbs* (Mus. ms. 280/7, 282/1, 283/6 und 7) und *URS* (s. *KBM 13*, S. 167).
K: *Joseph [Tafferner] (1739–1815).

MÜNCHEN

Jesuitenkirche St. Michael 1559–1773, 1921–
17 Chorbücher, 1561–1. Hälfte 17. Jh., in *Mbs*, s. *KBM 5/1*. Aus der Zeit vor 1773 sonst keine Quellen. Anschließend war die Kirche bis 1918 'große Hofkirche'. Vorhanden sind 1270 Individual- und Sammelhandschriften mit dem Repertoire vom Ende des 18. bis zum Anfang des 20. Jh., dabei zahlreiche Werke von Caspar Ett und solchen der von ihm eingeleiteten Renaissance der klassischen Vokalpolyphonie. Umfangreicher Bestand an Abschriften von Kirchenwerken Johann Michael Haydns.
Kat: *KBM 7* (Fundort: *Mm*).
K: +Johann Paullinus (1604–1671), +Ferdinand Hueber (1679–1762).
Lit: Adalbert Schulz, *Die St. Michaels-Hofkirche in München*, München 1897; Otto Ursprung, *Münchens musikalische Vergangenheit*, München 1927, S. 241ff.; Hildegard Herrmann-Schneider, Einleitung zu *KBM 7*; R. Münster, 'Caspar Ett (1788–1847)', in: *Christenleben im Wandel der Zeit*, hrsg. von Georg Schwaiger, II, München 1987, S. 92ff.

MÜNCHEN

Kloster der Augustiner-Eremiten, 1294–1803

Bestand 1803 aufgelöst, einige Handschriften in *Mbs* (Joh. Zach, J.M. Haydn, W.A. Mozart) und in *Mf* (s. *KBM 8*, S. 424).
K: +Bruno Holzapfel (Mitte 18. Jh.), +Gregor Rösler (ca. 1714–1775), *Remigius Rigauer (1746–1827), +Theodor Grünberger (1756–1820), *Georg Weissinger (1766–1843).
T: MB 312, CD MB 75 107.
Lit: Paul Ruf, *Säkularisation und Bayerische Staatsbibliothek*, Bd. 1, a.a.O., S. 293; Eberhard Kraus, 'Augustiner-Kloster – Pflegestätte der Musica sacra', in: *Alt-Bayerische Heimat* H. 6, 1964, S. [1f.]; R. Münster, 'Mozarts Kirchenmusik in München im 18. und beginnenden 19. Jh.', in: *Festschrift Erich Valentin zum 70. Geburtstag*, Regensburg 1976, S. 146ff.; ders., Art. 'Grünberger' in *MGG* 15 (1979).

MÜNCHEN

Kollegiatstift zu Unserer Lieben Frau, 1495–1803, seit 1817 Dom

Umfangreicher Bestand: (1.) Chorbücher und Handschriften bis zur Mitte des 18. Jh. (13 Nummern), (2.) Handschriften 2. Hälfte 18. und 19. Jh. (1634 Handschriften).
Kat: *KBM 8* (Fundort: *FS*).
K:*Christoph Martin (gest. 1610), *Christoph Perckhofer (gest. 1612), +Franz Xaver *Murschauser* (1663–1738), *Christoph Hirschberger (gest. 1756), *Joseph Adam *Obermüller* (1729–1769), Erasmus Vogel (1760–1816). Komp. des 19. u. 20. Jh., s. Münster.
T: MB 802, CD MB 75114.
Lit: Helmut Hell und Monika Holl, Einleitung zu *KBM 8*; R. Münster, '500 Jahre Pflege der Musik in der Frauenkirche', in: *Monachium sacrum. Festschrift zur 500-Jahr-Feier der Metropolitankirche Zu Unserer Lieben Frau in München*, München 1994, S. 593ff.

MÜNCHEN

Theatinerkirche St. Kajetan (1663ff.)

Aus dem Theatinerkloster (1662–1801) keine Musik erhalten.
In der Kirche fanden vor allem größere Hof-Gottesdienste statt. Der Bestand von 1915 Individual- und Sammelhandschriften enthält den nach empfindlichen Kriegsverlusten verbliebenen neueren Teil der Musikalien der Allerheiligen-Hofkirche, einen Teil der Musiksammlung der Stiftspropstes Michael Hauber (1778–1843) und Musikalien aus dem Kirchenmusik-Repertoire von St. Kajetan im 19. Jh. Der ältere Bestand der Hofkirchenmusik des 18. Jh. (vgl. den Thematischen Katalog in *KBM 9*) ist im 2. Weltkrieg weitgehend verbrannt.
Kat: *KBM 4* (Fundort: Theatinerkirche).
Lit: Siegfried Gmeinwieser, Einleitung zu *KBM 4*; ergänzend dazu R. Münster, Einleitung zu *KBM 9*.

NEUMARKT/OBERPFALZ,

Kapuzinerkloster, ?–1802

1 Chorbuch, 1597, in *Mbs*, s. *KBM 5/1*.

NEUSTADT AM MAIN

Benediktinerabtei, um 770–1803

Musikalien verschollen.
K: +Aemilian Hön(n)inger (1694–1757), +Peregrinus Poegel (1711–88), Karl Leim (18. Jh.).

Lit: Adelhard Kaspar, 'Zur innern Geschichte der Abtei Neustadt am Main', in: *Würzburger Diözesan-Geschichtsblätter* 30, 1968, S. 225f.

NEUSTIFT BEI FREISING

Prämonstratenserabtei, 1141/42–1803
Musikalien verschollen.
K: *Hugo Rehrnböck (Rehrnpeck) (1742–76), Norbert Friedl (1778–1835).
Lit: R. Münster, 'Die Musikalien- und Instrumenteninventare der Prämonstratenserabtei Neustift von 1803' (in Vorbereitung).

NIEDERALTAICH

Benediktinerabtei, 1741–1803, 1918–
Musikalien verschollen. Ein unkatalogisierter Bestand aus der Klosterpfarrei Spitz/Niederösterreich im Kloster Niederaltaich.
K: *Kilian *Krauter* (1706–42), Heinrich Doppelhammer (gest. 1770), Franz Xaver Maichl (gest. 1793), + Coelestin Jungbauer (1747–1823), Anselm Weiß (Mitte 18. Jh.), + Anselm Loibl (1776–1822).
T: MB 402.
Lit: Georg Stadtmüller, *Geschichte der Abtei Niederaltaich*, Augsburg 1971, S. 264 u. 267f.

OBERALTAICH

Benediktinerabtei, um 1080–1803
Musikalien verschollen.
K: +Balthasar Regler (1627–1694), Franz Keser (1694–1724), Basilius Driendl (1704–54), +Bruno Lehner (1721–64), Bonifaz Wenzel (1737–63), *Angelus Lang (1754–98), +Lambert Knittelmair (1769–1845).
Lit: Gerold Huber, 'Die Musikpflege der Benediktinerabtei Oberaltaich', in: *Musik in bayerischen Klöstern* I, Regensburg 1986, S. 61ff.

OBERSCHÖNENFELD

Zisterzienserinnenkloster, 1211–1803, 1836–
Musikalienbestand mit rund 150 Handschriften im Kloster, wo die Nonnen noch 1803 weiter in klösterlicher Gemeinschaft bleiben konnten. Enge Verbindung zu Abtei Kaisheim. Der dortige Abt war Vaterabt von Oberschönenfeld.
Kat: Linsenmayer (s.d.).
Lit: Jürgen Linsenmayer, 'Studien zur Musiküberlieferung im Zisterzienserinnenkloster Oberschönenfeld in der 2. Hälfte des 18. Jahrhunderts, Phil. Diss. Augsburg 1990;

'Musiküberlieferung und Musikpflege in Oberschönenfeld', in: *Kloster Oberschönenfeld*, hrsg. von Werner Schiedermair, Donauwörth 1995, S. 144ff.

OTTOBEUREN

Reichsunmittelbare Benediktinerabtei, 764–1802, 1835–
Umfangreicher Bestand, vorwiegend 18. Jh., dabei Kompositionen aus der Wiener Hofmusik zur Zeit Karl VI. Kirchen- und Orgelmusik: 1205 Handschriften.
Kat: *KBM 12* (Fundort: OB, Kath. Pfarramt).
K: Joseph Magg (ca. 1630–1705), *Joseph Christadler (1687–1730), *Maurus Klöck (1694–1736), *Johann Chrysostomus Kolbinger (1703–58), Nikolaus Maichelbeck (1716–56), *Benedikt Vogel (1718–90), Hieronymus Hornstein (1721–58), +Franz *Schnitzer* (1740–85), *Konrad Bagg (1747–1810), *Carl Eberle (1751–1811), *Theodor Clarer (1766–1820), Placidus Feyerabend (1777–1855).
T: MB 70 308.
Lit: Theodor Wohnhaas, Art. 'Ottobeuren' in *MGG* 10 (1962); Willi Pfänder, 'Das Musikleben der Abtei Ottobeuren vom 16. Jahrhundert bis zur Säkularisation', in: *Ottobeuren 764–1964. Beiträge zur Geschichte der Abtei*, Augsburg 1964, S. 45ff. (Studien und Mitteilungen zur Geschichte des Benediktinerordens, 73); Siegfried Michl, 'Theatermusik Ottobeurer Hauskomponisten im 18. Jahrhundert', in: *Musik in bayerischen Klöstern* I, Regensburg 1986, S. 189ff.; R. Münster, 'Wiener Kirchenmusik im Reichskloster Ottobeuren zur Zeit Karl VI.', in: *Mitteleuropäische Kontexte der Barockmusik*, Bratislava (im Druck).

PASSAU

Augustiner-Chorherrenstift St. Nikola, um 1070–1803
Musikalien verschollen. Einige wenige Kirchenwerke von Floridus Syccora in Passau, St. Paul und im Dom Passau (vgl. *KBM 21*).
K: *Floridus Syccora (1726–89), *Valentin (Dionys d.J.) Grotz (1773–1833).

PASSAU

Dom St. Stephan, 1407–
Umfangreicher Bestand des Repertoires der

Dommusik des 18. und 19. Jahrhunderts, in dem auch die Beziehungen zu Salzburg und Wien deutlich werden. Die frühesten Werke sind rund 70 Kompositionen von Benedikt Anton Auffschnaiter (1665–1742). Insgesamt ca. 1300 Handschriften.

Kat: *KBM 21* (Fundort: *Po*).

Lit: Wolfgang Maria Schmid, 'Zur Passauer Musikgeschichte', in: *Zeitschrift für Musikwissenschaft* 13, 1931, S. 89ff.; Elisabeth Krems, 'Passaus Musikkultur von den Anfängen bis zur Auflösung der geistlichen Fürstentums (1803)', in: *Ostbairische Grenzmarken* 4, 1960, S. 155ff., und 5, 1961, S. 130ff.; ausführliche Bibliographie von Herbert W. Wurster als Einleitung zu *KBM 21*.

PLANKSTETTEN

Benediktinerabtei, 1129–1806, 1904–

Musikalien verschollen.

K: Roman Reutter (1753–1806).

POLLING

Augustiner-Chorherrenstift, 1010–1803, 1892– (Dominikanerinnen)

In *Mbs* 1 Chorbuch, 1623, ferner 1 Partitur nach Herrer: *Hortus musicalis 1609,* 1628, s. *KBM 15/1.* Der Bestand an 267 Individual- und Sammelhandschriften in der Pfarrkirche Polling stammt bis auf eine Ausnahme (Gregor Schreyer, Andechs) aus der Zeit nach 1803. In der ehemaligen Klosterpfarrei Walleshausen befindet sich ein weiterer Bestand mit 129 Handschriften, ebenfalls nach 1803, darin vorwiegend deutsche Kirchenmusik.

Kat: *KBM 16,* in Vorbereitung (Fundorte: *POL, WALL*).

K: [+]Wilhelm Krumper (1. Hälfte 17. Jh., Mathias Resch (1. Hälfte 18. Jh.), Mansuet Braun (1725–86), Alipius Wäßler (gest. 1809), [+]Andreas Neumair (1750–1828), [+]Franz Xaver *Weinzierl* (1757–1833).

T: MB 209, MB 70 603, MB Mc 75 055.

Lit: George Rückert, 'Pflege der Musik im ehemaligen Kloster Polling', in: *Zeitschrift für Bayerische Landesgeschichte* 6, 1933, S. 113ff.; Eberhard Dünninger und R. Münster, 'Liberalitas Bavarica. Das Kloster Polling und sein Schicksal', in: Josef und Eberhard Dünninger, *Erlebtes Bayern*, Rosenheim 1978, S. 82ff.; R. Münster, 'Die Musik im Augustiner-Chorherrenstift Polling vor der Säkularisation', in: *10 Jahre Pollinger Bibliothekssaal*, Polling 1985, 5 ungez. S.; ders., 'Die Kirchenlieder-Sammlung des Walleshausener Kooperators Peter Forer Socher', in: *Walleshausen, "Das kleine Polling"*, hrsg. von Walter Brandmüller, Weissenhorn 1985, S. 140ff.

PRÜFENING

Benediktinerabtei, 1117–1803

Musikalien verschollen.

K: [+]Marianus Königsperger (1708–69).

Lit: Friedhelm Zwickler, 'Frater Marianus Königsperger (1708–1769). Ein Beitrag zur süddeutschen Kirchenmusik des 18. Jahrhunderts', Diss. Mainz 1964.

RAITENHASLACH

Zisterzienserabtei, 1143–1803

Musikalien verschollen.

K: [+]Albericus *Hirschberger* (1709–45), Albericus Haas (1724–81), Theobald von Cröner (1763–1806), *Blasius (= Anton) Diabelli (1781–1758, Novize 1798–1802).

T: MB CD 75 107.

Lit: Edgar Krausen, *Zisterzienserabtei Raitenhaslach*, Berlin 1977, S. 164f. (Germania sacra, NF 11, 1)

REBDORF

Augustiner-Chorherrenstift, 1153/59–1806

Musikalien verschollen.

K: [+]Floridus Ott (1681–1736).

REGENSBURG

Dom St. Peter (ca. 1250ff.)

Umfangreicher Bestand mit 449 Handschriften instrumental begleiteter Kirchenmusik ab 1810; ferner 389 Vesperpsalmen, hauptsächlich im Falsobordone-Satz, 686 a-capella-Messen und 173 a-capella-Motetten in Abschriften des 19. Jh.

Kat: *KBM 14/4* (Fundort: *Rp*; die a-capella-Hss. im Archiv der Regensburger Domspatzen).

Lit: August Scharnagl, 'Beiträge zur Musikgeschichte der Regensburger Domkirche', in: *Der Regensburger Dom*, hrsg. von Georg Schwaiger, Regensburg 1976, S. 657ff. (Beiträge zur Geschichte des Bistums Regensburg, 22/24); Thomas Emmerig, 'Die Musik im Regensburger Dom vor der Verwirklichung der Reformpläne Proskes', in: *Verhandlungen des Historischen Vereins für*

Oberpfalz und Regensburg 124, 1984, S. 421ff.;
Christofer Schweisthal, 'Die Wiederaufnahme
des A-capella-Gesangs in das Chorrepertoire
der Regensburger Stiftskirchen (Dom, Alte
Kapelle, St. Johann) im 19. Jahrhundert', in:
Musica Divina, Regensburg 1994, S. 89ff.
(Bischöfliches Zentralarchiv und Bischöfliche
Zentralbibliothek Regensburg. Kataloge und
Schriften, 11).

REGENSBURG
Kollegiatstift Alte Kapelle, 875–

Das Stift war wegen seiner Musikpflege berühmt.
Dort wurde seit ca. 1840 vor allem die cäciliani-
sche Reform praktiziert. Hier wirkten Dr. Carl
Proske (1794–1861) als Kanoniker, Dominikus
Mettenleiter (1822–68) als Stiftsvikar und
Michael Haller (1840–1915) als Kapellmeister.
Erhalten sind rund 100 Handschriften mit instru-
mental begleiteter süddeutsoher Kirchenmusik
und etwa 660 Abschriften von a-capella-Messen
und -Motetten des 16. und 17. Jh.
K: *KBM 14/4* (Fundort: *Rp*).
Lit: Christofer Schweisthal, 'Die Wieder-
aufnahme des A-capella-Gesangs . . .' a.a.O.,
S. 91ff.; ders., Einleitung zu *KBM 14/4*.

REGENSBURG
Kollegiatstift St. Johann, 1127–   (ursprünglich
Augustimer-Chorherrenstift)
Erhalten sind 62 Handschriften (instrumental
begleitete Kirchenmusik und a-capella-Motetten
in Abschriften), um 1800–ca. 1870.
K: *KBM 14/4* (Fundort: *Rp*).
Lit: Christofer Schweisthal, 'Die Wieder-
aufnahme des A-capella-Gesangs . . .' a.a.O.,
S. 92; ders., Einleitung zu *KBM 14/4*.

REGENSBURG
gefürstete Benediktinerabtei St. Emmeram, vor
739–1810
Musikalien verschollen. Bedeutsamer Mensural-
codex, 15. Jh., in *Mbs* (Clm 142274), s. *KBM 5/1*.
K: +Sebastian Prixner (1744–99), Coelestin
Steiglehner (1738–1819).
Lit: Dominikus Mettenleiter, *Musikgeschichte der
Stadt Regensburg*, Regensburg 1966, S. 136ff.

REICHENBACH
Benediktinerabtei, 1118–1802, 1675–1803
Musikalien verschollen.
K: Joseph Prixner (1743–1804).

Lit: Dominikus Mettenleiter, *Musikgeschichte der
Oberpfalz*, Amberg 1867, S. 227.

ROHR
Benediktinerabtei, 1133–1804
Musikalien verschollen.
K: Ildephons Koch (gest. 1781).

ROTT AM INN
Benediktinerabtei, 1081/85–1803
Musikalienbestand verschollen.
K: +Severin Conradi (ca. 1620–1672),
Columban Praelisauer (1703–52), +Placidus
Metsch (1700–68).
T: MB 203, MB 70 312, CD MB 75 107.
Lit: R. Münster, 'Streiflichter aus der
Musikpraxis in Rott am Inn vom 17. bis zum
19. Jahrhundert', in: *Rott am Inn, Beiträge zu
Kunst und Kultur der ehemaligen Benediktinerabtei*,
Weissenhorn 1983, S, 229ff.

ROTTENBUCH
Augustiner-Chorherrenstift, 1073–1803
Bestand in den 30er Jahren des 20. Jh. vernichtet.
Einzelne Handschriften in *Mbs* (B. Pittrich) und
in *Mf* (R. Dedler, s. *KBM 8*).
K: +Augustin *Grieninger* (1638–92), *Prosper
Staudinger (ca. 1698–1752), *Gelasius *Hiebler*
(1716–80).
T: MB 208, Mc MB 75 055.
Lit: R. Münster, 'Aus dem Rottenbucher
Musikleben im 17. und 18. Jahrhundert', in:
*Rottenbuch. Das Augustinerchorherrenstift im
Ammergau*, hrsg. von Hans Pörnbacher,
Weissenhorn ²1980, S. 136ff.

ST. VEIT bei Neumarkt
Benediktinerabtei, 1121–1802
248 Handschriften blieben erhalten: 18. und 19.
Jh., darunter frühe Abschriften Salzburger
Provenienz (u.a. J.M. Haydn, W.A. Mozart).
Kat: *KBM 10*, in Vorbereitung (Fundort: *NT*).
K: *Vitus Rost (1767–1802), Coelestin Weighart
(1745–1804).
Lit: R. Münster, 'Mozarts "Tantum ergerl" KV
142 und 197', in: *Acta Mozartiana* 10, 1963, S.
54ff. Repr. in: R. Münster, *"Ich bin hier sehr
beliebt". Mozart und das kurfürstliche Bayern*,
Tutzing 1993, S. 274ff.

ST. ZENO/REICHENHALL
Augustiner-Chorherrenstift, 1136–1803
Musikalien verschollen. Eine Sammelhandschrift

mit 196 z.T. unvollständigen Motetten (1583) in *Mbs* (Mus. ms. 1536), dort auch 4 Chorbücher (1619–1622/23), s. *KBM 5/1* und *2*.

K: Georg Pfingstl (16. Jh.), ⁺Johann Staindl (1713–82).

T: MB 205.

SCHÄFTLARN

Praemonstratenserabtei, um 762–1803, 1866 – (Benediktiner)

Der einst ca. 1000 Kompositionen umfassende Musikalienbestand ist verschollen Je eine Handschrift von Stollreiter in Schäftlarn und Beuerberg.

K: Hugo Ponrad (1737–1804), Ludolph Stollreiter (1752–1807), Marian Denni (1752–1834), ⁺Evermod Groll (1755–1810), Otto Schwab (1770–1810).

Lit: R. Münster, 'Evermod Groll und die Musikpflege in Schäftlarn im Ausgang des 18. Jahrhunderts', in: *1200 Jahre Kloster Schäftlarn*, hrsg. von Sigisbert Mitterer, Schäftlarn 1962, S. 123ff. Musikinventar 1803: S. 108ff.

SCHEYERN

Benediktinerabtei, um 1119–1803, 1838–

Umfangreicher Musikalienbestand im Kloster, nach 1838 erworben, doch z.T. mit Handschriften aus dem 18. Jh. Die Scheyerner Klostermusikalien vor 1803 sind verschollen. Katalogisiert ist nur ein Teil der vorhandenen Musikalien.

Kat: Juranek (s.d.). (Fundort: *SCHEY*)

K: Marian Gulder (1757–1809), Bonifaz Pokorny (1758–89), Emmeram Resch (1769–1815), Ulrich Achter (1777–1803).

Lit: Rudolf Quoika, *Musik und Musikpflege in der Benediktinerabtei Scheyern,* München 1958 (Studien und Mitteilungen zur Geschichte des Benediktinerordens, Ergänzungsheft 16), dazu Rezension von R. Münster in: *Zeitschrift für Bayerische Landesgeschichte* 23, 1960, S. 188ff.; Nikolaus Juranek, *Die geistlichen Musikhandschriften der Benediktinerabtei Scheyern.* Thematischer Katalog, Scheyern 1985 (Facharbeit Musikerziehung, Gymnasium Pfaffenhofen a.d. Ilm).

SCHLEHDORF

Augustiner-Chorherrenstift, 1140–1803, 1892– (Dominikanerinnen)

Musikalien verschollen. 2 Handschriften

(Hueber, W. Pichl) in *FS* (Bestand Wasserburg, St. Jakob), s. *KBM 2*, S. XVIII (*WS* 422 und 530).

SEEON

Benediktinerabtei, 994–1803

Die Musikalien wurden 1803 der Klosterpfarrkirche überlassen, doch heute ist am Ort keine Handschrift mehr vorhanden. In den vergangenen Jahren wurden Teile in *WS* (37 Handschriften, s. *KBM 2*, S. XVII), in *Mbs* (J.M. Haydn: 4 Handschriften), *LAm* (s. oben, Landshut, Kollegiatstift St. Martin) und Trostberg, Heimatmuseum (W.A. Mozart: Messe KV 140) wiedergefunden. Liederhandschrift von Johannes Werlin (1645/46) in *Mbs*.

K: *Johannes Werlin (1588–1666), Rufinus *Sigel* (1601–75), ⁺Romanus *Pinzger* (1714–55), *Aegidius Strasser (1730–88), Romanus König (1750–1801), Virgilius Kiermayer (1759–1800).

T: CD MB 75 110.

Lit: R. Münster, 'Die Musik im Kloster Seeon', in: *Kloster Seeon. Beiträge zu Geschichte und Kultur der ehemaligen Benediktinerabtei*, Weissenhorn 1994, S. 347ff.

SPEINSHART

Prämonstratenserabtei, um 1145–1803, 1921–

Nur eine Messe von Vanhal im Pfarrarchiv Speinshart, neben einer Sammlung von 26 Musikdrucken des 18. Jh.

K: Augustin Klier (1744–1816).

Lit: Dominikus Mettenleiter, *Musikgeschichte der Oberpfalz*, Amberg 1867, S. 242f.; Theodor Wohnhaas, 'Zur Kirchenmusik der Praemonstratenserabtei Speinshart im 18. Jahrhundert', in: *Musik in Bayern*, H. 12, 1976, S. 43f.; Gustav Motyka, *Das Kloster Speinhart*, Weiden 1963, S. 33f. (Weidener Heimatkundliche Arbeiten, 6).

STEINGADEN

Praemonstratenserabtei, 1147–1803

Musikalien verschollen. Ein Requiem des letzten Abtes Gilbert Michl in *FS* (Bestand Wasserburg, St. Jakob), s. *KBM 2* (WS 485).

K: *Gilbert *Michl* (1750–1828).

T: MB 202a, MB 70 301, CD MB 75 109.

TEGERNSEE

Benediktinerabtei, 746–1803

Erhalten sind 12 Handschriften vor 1803:

Kirchenmusik und 3 Sinfonien (Pleyel, Sterkel), sowie 26 Handschriften aus der 1821 errichteten Kantoreistiftung, z.T. Kompositionen und Bearbeitungen des ersten Kantors Herkulan Wieser (1775–1839). In *Mbs* 5 Chorbücher, ca. 1570–1600, und 1 Orgelpartitur, Ende 16. Jh., s. *KBM 15/1*.

Kat: *KBM 1* (Fundort: *TEG*).

K: +Gotthard *Wagner* (1678–1738), +Marian *Praunsperger* (1682–1742), +Leonhard *Trautsch* (1693–1762), Coelestin Praelisauer (1694–1745), Gotthard Durmayr (1725–1783), +Tegurini = Chrysogonus *Zech* (1728–1804), Leonhard Buchberger (1740–1806), Joseph Pronath (1745–87), Nonnosus Brand (1755–93), Godehard Gloggner (1765–1832), Anton Schneider (1766–1822).

T: MB 204.

Lit: R. Münster, 'Fragmente zu einer Musikgeschichte der Benediktinerabtei Tegernsee', in: *Studien und Mitteilungen zur Geschichte des Benediktinerordens 79*, 1968, S. 66ff.; ders., Einleitung zu *KBM 1*; ders., Art. 'Tegernsee' in *MGG 13* (1966), 'Wagner' und 'Wieser' in *MGG 14* (1968).

THIERHAUPTEN

Benediktinerabtei, um 750–1803
Musikalien verschollen. 2 Chorbücher (1596/97 und 1622) in *Mbs*, s. *KBM 5/1*.

TITTMONING

Kollegiatstift, 1633–
Der erhaltene Bestand mit 246 Handschriften wurde nach dem Brand von 1815 neu beschafft, z.T. aus Nachlässen und aus St. Peter in Salzburg. Er enthält wichtige Quellen aus dem 18. Jh.

Kat: *KBM 10*, in Vorbereitung (Fundort: *TIT*).

Lit: R. Münster, 'Das Musikrepertoire des Kollegiatstifts Tittmoning zur Zeit des Frühbarock', in: *Das Salzfaß*, NF 24, 1990, S. 24ff.; ders., Einleitung zu *KBM 10* (in Vorbereitung).

TRIEFENSTEIN

Augustiner-Chorherrenstift, 1102–1803
Musikalien verschollen.

K: +Benedikt Geisler (1696–1772), +Franz Xaver Bitthauser (1727–nach 1800).

Lit: R. Walter, 'Benedikt Geisler, ein fränkischer Klosterkomponist des 18. Jahrhunderts', in: *Mainfränkisches Jahrbuch 42* (1990), S. 168ff.

URSBERG

Praemonstratenserabtei, 1125–1802
Musikalien verschollen. Nur ein Cembalokonzert von P. Isfried Kettner im Bestand der Pädagogischen Stiftung Cassianeum Donauwörth, s. *KBM 15*, S. 181. Zu dem heute in Ursberg verwahrten Bestand s. oben Holzen.

K: Isfried Kettner (1756–1820).

Lit: Alfred Lohmüller, *Das Reichsstift Ursberg. Von den Anfängen 1125 bis zum Jahre 1802*, Weissenhorn 1987, S. 179f., 216–51.

T: CD MB 75112.

VORNBACH

Benediktinerabtei, 1094–1803
Musikalien weitgehend verschollen. 7 Handschriften (Dionys Grotz, J.M. Haydn) wurden 1963 aus dem Antiquariatshandel von der Bayerischen Staatsbibliothek erworben (Mus. Ms. 5594–5600). Weitere Handschriften möglicherweise in Oberaltaich.

K: *Berengar Perfaller (1632–95) sowie weltliche Klosterorganisten: Crudeli = Mathias Grausahm (1713–70), Dionys (d.Ä.) Grotz (1748–1813).

Lit: R. Münster, 'Die Musik in den Klöstern um Passau zur Zeit Mozarts', in: *20. Deutsches Mozartfest der Deutschen Mozartgesellschaft*, Programmheft, Passau 1971, S. 50; Helmut Wagner, 'Musik im Kloster Vornbach', in: *900 Jahre Benediktinische Kultur am unteren Inn*, hrsg. von Joseph Eschl und Joseph Duschl, Vornbach 1994, S. 33ff.

WALDERBACH

Zisterzienserabtei, 1143–1563, 1669–1803
Musikalien verschollen.

K: +Eugen Pausch (1758–1838).

WALDSASSEN

Zisterzienserabtei, 1131/32–1803, 1863–
(Zisterzienserinnen)
Musikalien verschollen. Im Schwäbischen Landesmusikarchiv Tübingen, Bestand Gutenzell, 3 Kirchenwerke eines 'B. von Waldsassen'.

Lit: Dominikus Mettenleiter, *Musikgeschichte der Oberpfalz*, Amberg 1867, S. 232ff.

WEIHENSTEPHAN
Benediktinerabtei, 1021–1803
Musikalien verschollen. 1 Pergament-Chorbuch,
1. Hälfte 16. Jh., in *Mbs*, s. *KBM 5/1*.
K: +Sebastian Ertel (1550/60–1618), Johann
   Baptist Schmidhueber (18. Jh.), +Coelestin
   (Franz Christian) Hochbrucker (1727–1805),
   *Joseph Schreiner (1744–1800), Joseph
   Knaup (1778–1837).
Lit: Heinrich Gentner, *Geschichte des Benediktiner-
   Kloster Weihenstephan bei Freysing*, München
   1854, S. 221f.

WELTENBURG
Benediktinerabtei, um 763–1803, 1842–
Musikalien verschollen.
K: Bernhard Aiba (1724–ca. 1759); *Maurus
   Pauli (1747–86), Benedikt Werner
   (1748–1830), Ildefons Hefele (1756–1807),
   *Benno Grueber (1759–96).
T: MB 401, MB 70 210.
Lit: R. Münster, 'Benno Grueber und das
   Schultheater in Weltenburg in der 2. Hälfte des
   18. Jahrhunderts', in: *Unser Bayern. Beilage zur
   Bayerischen Staatszeitung* 1995 (im Druck);
   Wolfgang Wagner, 'Die Musik im Kloster
   Weltenburg', in: *Schriftenreihe der Hochschule für
   Musik in München* (in Vorbereitung).

WESSOBRUNN
Benediktinerabtei, 753–1803
Musikalien verschollen.
K: Coelestin Leuttner (1695–1759), Bernhard
   Lienhard (1696–1734), Maurus Bayrhamer
   (1721–87).

WETTENHAUSEN
Augustiner-Chorherrenstift, 1130–1802, 1865–
(Dominikanerinnen)
Musikalien verschollen.

K: *Michael Kriener (1759–1818).

WEYARN
Augustiner-Chorherrenstift, 1133–1803
Im größeren Umfang erhaltener Bestand mit 592
Nummern, vorwiegend 2. Hälfte 18. Jh.:
Kirchenmusik, Sinfonien, Trompetenaufzüge.
Verbindung zur Münchner Hofmusik im
Repertoire dokumentiert.
Kat: *KBM 1* (Fundort: *FS*).
K: *Patritius *Perchtold* (1721–91), *Benedikt
   Haltenberger (1748–80), *Lorenz Justinian *Ott*
   (1748–1805), *Herkulan *Sießmayr* (1761–
   1832), Hartmann Enk (1766–1814), *Floridus
   Hottner (1772–1836).
T: MB 201, MB 70 303, MB 70 701, CD MB 75
   105, 75 107 und 75 114.
Lit: Richard Schmied, 'Bayerische Schuldramen
   des 18. Jahrhunderts. Schule und Theater der
   Augustiner-Chorherren in Oberbayern unter
   besonderer Berücksichtigung des Stiftes
   Weyarn', Phil. Diss. München 1964; R.
   Münster, Art. 'Weyarn' in *MGG* 14 (1968);
   ders., Einleitung zu *KBM 1*; Matthias Mayer,
   'Die Seelsorge der Weyarner Chorherren im
   ausgehenden 18. Jahrhundert nach den
   Tagebüchern des Chorherrn L.J. Ott', in:
   Beiträge zu altbayerischen Kirchengeschichte 30,
   1976, S. 115ff.

WÜRZBURG
St. Stephan, Benediktinerabtei, 1013–1803
Musikalien verschollen.
K: *Stephan Hammel (1756–1830).
Lit: P. Weissenberger, 'Beiträge zur Kunst- und
   Kulturgeschichte mainfränkischer Benedik-
   tiner- und Zistersienserklöster', in: *Main-
   fränkisches Jahrbuch* 3, 1951, S. 216.

Jiří Sehnal

Die adeligen Musikkapellen im 17. und 18. Jahrhundert in Mähren

In der Geschichte der tschechischen Musik pflegte man das 17. und 18. Jahrhundert als Epoche der Schloßkapellen zu bezeichnen, da diese die wichtigsten Zentren der Pflege der weltlichen Musik darstellten. Diese These implantierte eine naive Vorstellung, nach der in jedem Schloß in Mähren, deren es mehr als hundert gibt, eine Musikkapelle existierte. Im Verlaufe weiterer Forschung erwies sich diese Vorstellung als falsch. Es gibt zwar große Schlösser, wie z.B. Lysice, Vranov nad Dyjí, Telč, Velké Losiny, in deren Räumen wir die Musik eher voraussetzen als konkret beweisen können. Daneben gibt es oft in architektonischer Hinsicht merkwürdige Schlösser, wie z.B. Branná, Bučovice, Plumlov, von denen wir wissen, daß in ihnen die Musik nie gepflegt wurde und daß diese architektonischen Denkmäler nur wirtschaftlichen Zwecken dienten. Das Musikleben eines Schlosses hing immer von dem persönlichen Interesse seines Besitzers an der Musik ab und endete mit dessen Tode, was mit der nachfolgenden Dokumentation veranschaulicht werden wird. Die Musik stellte für den Adeligen, auch wenn es sich um eine Kapelle aus Livreebedienten handelte, eine Art aufwendiger Unterhaltung dar. Aus diesen Gründen waren nicht alle Adeligen bereit, Mittel für eine Privatkapelle zu opfern. Manche Adeligen zogen verschiedene Spiele und die Jagd dem Musikgenuß vor. Richtig erfaßt die Einstellung mancher Adeligen zu Kunst eine Episode aus dem Besuch des Grafen Dietrichstein im Kloster Hradisko den 21. Juli 1693. Nachdem der Graf den Konvent, die Sakristei und den Kirchenschatz besah, ließ er fallen: '*Ad quid huic Ecclesiae tantus thesaurus?*' Der Chronist kommentierte die Bemerkung des Grafen: '*Forte iudicabat, melius futurum fuisse, si pro equis aut canibus venaticis impensae haec factae fuissent. Melius scilicet aedificare tabernas, quam exornare ecclesias.*'[1]

In unserer Übersicht der adeligen Musikkapellen in Mähren führen wir nur die wichtigsten Angaben mit der sie betreffenden Literatur bzw. mit den Quellen an. Die Kapellen sind nach ihrem Wirkungsort gereiht, wobei die Ortsnamen in Berücksichtigung der heutigen Situation erst tschechisch angeführt sind, dann aber auch mit der alten deutschen Bezeichnung. Manchmal läßt sich der Wirkungsort nicht eindeutig bestimmen, da mehrere Orte in Betracht kommen. In diesen Fällen werden zwei bis fünf Orte genannt, wobei der vermutlich wichtigste Ort an der ersten Stelle steht.

Eine der bedeutendsten Musikkapellen in Mähren war jene der Olmützer Bischöfe in ihrer Residenzstadt Kroměříž (Kremsier). Sie war ohne Zweifel eines der wichtigsten Vorbilder für die Kapellen von einigen musikfreudigen Adeligen in Mähren. Man darf sich die bischöfliche Kapelle keineswegs als eine ständige, der kaiserlichen Musikkapelle ähnliche Institution vorstellen. Es wäre am Platz, eher von einer Reihe von Kapellen einzelner Bischöfe zu sprechen, da sie manchmal an die vorherigen Kapellen weder in der Personalbesetzung noch im Repertoire anknüpften. Da wir die Reihe der bischöflichen Kapellen mit kleinen Unterbrechungen durch ganze zwei Jahrhunderte verfolgen können, widmen wir ihnen unsere Aufmerk- samkeit an erster Stelle. Informationen über die übrigen adeligen Kapellen folgen dann in alphabetischer Ordnung nach ihrem Wirkungsort.

Kroměříž – Olomouc – Brno – Vyškov – Mikulov – Mírov (Kremsier – Olmütz – Brünn – Wischau – Nikolsburg – Mirau)

Bereits am Anfang des 17. Jahrhunderts begegnen wir Musikern an dem Hof des Kardinals Franz von Dietrichstein (1599–1636). Die Tatsache, daß der Kardinal Trompeter, Lautenisten, Organisten und Tanzmeister beschäftigte, ist noch kein genü- gender Beweis dafür, daß er ein wirkliches Musikerensemble hielt. Die Trompeter stell- ten eine besondere Musikkategorie dar, weil sie vor allem wegen der für den höheren Adel verbindlichen höfischen Repräsentation und nicht wegen der musikalischen Unterhaltung engagiert waren. Die Olmützer Bischöfe gehörten zum höchsten Adel in Mähren, da ihnen mit der geistlichen Würde zugleich der Fürstentitel zufiel. Der Lautenist und der Tanzmeister waren am Hofe des Kardinals wegen der Ausbildung der hier als Pagen weilenden jungen Adeligen unentbehrlich. Doch muß der Kardinal eine persönliche Beziehung zur Musik gehabt haben, da er bereits im Jahr 1616 ver- suchte, fünf italienische zum polnischen König reisende Musiker für seine Dienste zu gewinnen,[2] und da ihm im Jahr 1631 ein Musiker namens Marc' Antonio Rossini vom Laibacher Bischof zum Engagement empfohlen wurde.[3] Zum Unterschied von seinen Nachfolgern hielt sich Kardinal Dietrichstein meist in seiner Heimatstadt Mikulov und aus politischen Gründen in Brno und nicht in Kroměříž auf. Unter den hundert Personen seines Hofstaates treffen wir die italienische Komponisten Carolo Abbate, Giovanni Battista Aloiisi, Claudio Cocchi und Vincenzo Scapitta, die dem Kardinal sowie seinen Verwandten ihre geistlichen Werke widmeten.[4] In Mikulov sorgten für die Musik neun Knaben des im Jahr 1625 errichteten Lauretanischen Seminars und zehn Knaben des St. Wenzel-Seminars bei der Kollegiatkirche des hl. Wenzel. Dazu kamen noch Musiker des im Jahre 1631 in Mikulov vom Kardinal Dietrichstein gegründeten Piaristenkollegiums,[5] des ersten in Mitteleuropa. Der

Kardinal verfügte also in Mikulov über so viele Musiker, daß er kein eigenes Musikensemble zu halten brauchte.

Während der Regierung des Bischofs Erzherzog Leopold Wilhelm (1637–62) gab es in Mähren keine bischöfliche Musikkapelle, da der Erzherzog gleichzeitig Bischof von Passau und Breslau war und außerdem die Funktionen des Oberbefehlshabers der kaiserlichen Armee und des Statthalters in Niederlanden ausübte und die Olmützer Diözese nur zweimal kurz besuchte. Nur sein ehemaliger Generaladjutant Johann Nikolaus Reiter von Hornberg, der von ihm 1644 zum Oberregenten der bischöflichen Güter in Mähren bestellt wurde, war der Musik sehr geneigt und unterhielt Kontakte mit mehreren bedeutenden Musikern seiner Zeit.[6]

Von internationaler Bedeutung wurde erst die Musikkapelle des Bischofs Karl von Liechtenstein-Castelcorno (1664–95). Dieser Bischof brachte aus seiner früheren Wirkungsstätte Salzburg, wo er in den Jahren 1654–65 das Amt eines Kapiteldekans bekleidete, die Vorstellungen mit, wie ein Bischof leben müsse um seine geistliche Stellung würdig zu repräsentieren. Aus diesem Grund beauftragte er einen seiner Angestellten den Trompeter Pavel Vejvanovský (1639–93) ein Ensemble von Musikern zusammenzustellen, das die Musik bei den bischöflichen Gottesdiensten und bei den gesellschaftlichen Anlässen in den bischöflichen Residenzen in Vyškov, Brno, Kroměříž, Olomouc und Mírov zu besorgen hatte. Der Bischof war besonders an der Musik zu den Faschingsbällen interessiert, die er jedes Jahr für den mährischen Adel in einer seiner Residenzen prunkvoll veranstaltete. Aus diesem Anlaß knüpfte der Bischof einen brieflichen Kontakt mit dem Komponisten und späteren Kapellmeister der Kaiserlichen Hofkapelle in Wien Heinrich Schmelzer an. In den Jahren 1668–70 war Heinrich Ignaz Biber Konzertmeister und Kammerdiener des Bischofs.

Die genaue Zusammensetzung der Liechtensteinschen Musikkapelle ist zwar nicht bekannt, aber wir wissen, daß an der Musik einige bischöfliche Trompeter, Hofangestellte, Choralisten und Organisten der Kremsierer Kirchen, Lehrer der Stadtschule und vielleicht auch einige Bürger teilnahmen. Die Kapelle verfügte über erstklassige Musikinstrumente von Meistern wie Nicolo Amati und Jacobus Stainer. Keines davon erhielt sich, obwohl sie der Bischof zusammen mit allem seinen Besitz testamentarisch seinen Nachfolgern hinterließ. Ein glücklicheres Schicksal ereilte die Musiksammlung Liechtensteins, die im Jahr 1695 insgesamt 1397 Posten zählte. Noch heute sind davon 1152 Werke meist komplett erhalten. Die Liechtensteinsche Musiksammlung stellt die bedeutendste Musiksammlung des 17. Jahrhunderts in Mitteleuropa und ein Gegenstück der berühmten Sammlung G. Dübens in Uppsala dar. Sie ist eine einzigartige Quelle zur Kenntnis der Musik am Hofe Kaiser Leopold I., da sie viele Werke von G. Valentini, A. Bertali, G.F. Sances, A. Poglietti und vor allem von J.H. Schmelzer enthält. Sie ist aber auch für die Salzburger Dommusik wichtig, da sie als Unika Werke von Andreas Hofer und H.I.F. Biber beinhaltet. Von dem Leiter der Kapelle P. Vejvanovský sind in der Sammlung an die 150 Werke zu finden. Von den übrigen tschechischen Komponisten dieser Zeit sind besonders A. Michna, A. Mazák, J. Melcelius und J. Pecelius vertreten. Das Schwergewicht der Sammlung liegt in der Kirchenmusik, die Kirchensonaten eingerechnet. Die weltliche Musik ist hauptsächlich von den Tanzsuiten – *Balletti* genannt – repräsentiert. Die internationale Musiköffentlichkeit wurde auf die Liechtensteinsche Musikkapelle zum ersten Mal von P. Nettl im Jahr 1921 aufmerksam gemacht.[7] Der Geschichte der Kapelle widmete sich eingehend der Autor dieses Beitrags.[8] Das erste Verzeichnis der Musiksammlung veröffentlichte im Jahr 1928 der erzbischöfliche Archivar Antonín Breitenbacher, der die Sammlung von weiteren Verlusten rettete und nach dem Inventarverzeichnis aus dem Jahr 1695 in Ordnung brachte.[9] Den wissenschaftlichen thematischen Katalog der Sammlung erstellte der Autor dieses Beitrags mit Jitřenka Pešková.[10] Mehrere Handschriften der Sammlung dienten als Vorlagen zu wissen, schaftlichen und praktischen Editionen (z.B. Denkmäler der Tonkunst in Österreich, Musica antiqua Bohemica, Denkmäler der Musik in Salzburg, Monumenta artis musicae Sloveniae, Musica rara, Diletto musicale u.a.).

In der Zeit des Nachfolgers Liechtensteins Karl von Lothringen (1695–1710) ging die Musikkapelle ein, da dieser Bischof gleichzeitig das Amt eines Bischofs zu Osnabrück ausübte und dort residierte.

Der Bischof Kardinal Wolfgang Hannibal von Schrattenbach (1711–38) hatte wieder eine Musikkapelle, obwohl er oft in verschiedenen politischen und diplomati, schen Missionen des Kaisers außerhalb seiner Diözese weilte. In den Jahren 1719–22 wirkte er als Vizekönig in Neapel, wo er sich für die italiensische Oper begeisterte. An seinem Hof in Neapel hielt er eine Kapelle von 43 Musikern, über die wir leider nichts weiteres wissen.[11] Während seines Aufenthalts in Mähren ließ er in Kroměříž, Vyškov und Brno italienische Opern und Oratorien aufführen.[12] Mit der Organisation dieser Aufführungen wurde ein nicht näher bekannter Abbate Leporati aus Neapel und nach ihm der Komponist Václav Matyáš Gurecký beauftragt, dem der Kardinal das Studium bei A. Caldara in Wien ermöglichte. In Kremsier beschäftigte der Kardinal eigene Musiker, von denen zehn namentlich bekannt sind.[13] Bei den Opern, aufführungen war er jedoch von der Hilfe des von P. David Kopecký geleiteten Musikensembles der Kremsierer Piaristenkollegiums abhängig.[14] In den Jahren 1734–38 stand Carlo Fornarini aus Urbino in Schrattenbachs Diensten und in den Jahren 1736–38 Carlo Tessarini, der dem Kardinal sein Op. 4 *La Stravaganza* (Amsterdam, sine dato) widmete. Von den Musikalien Schrattenbachs ist nichts erhalten geblieben.

Aus der Zeit des Bischofs Jakob Ernst Liechtenstein (1738–45) und des Kardinals Julius Troyer (1745–58) besitzen wir – abgesehen von den üblichen Trompetern – keine Nachrichten über die Musikkapelle und keine Musikalien. Wir wissen nur, daß es unter den Angestellten des Kardinals Troyers Personen gab, die in der Ära seines Nachfolgers Leopold Egk als Klarinettisten bezeichnet waren. Daraus könnte man schließen, daß Julius Troyer bereits um das Jahr 1750 ein Harmonieensemble hatte.[15]

Der Bischof Leopold Egk von Hungersbach (1758–60) besaß während seines kurzen Episkopats eine Kapelle, die nur Instrumentalmusik (Symphonien, Trios und Harmoniemusik) pflegte. Sein Kapellmeister war Anton Neumann (gest. 1776). Von den Musikern zeichnete sich der Waldhornist Karl Franz (1738–1802) aus, der später in der Esterházyschen und danach in in der Batthyánischen Kapelle in Preßburg als Virtuose auf dem Baryton Berühmtheit erlangte. Die Musiker der Egkschen Kapelle sind unter den sieben Livreebedienten genannt. Es handelte sich um einen Geiger, einen Violonisten, zwei Oboisten, zwei Hornisten und einen Fagottisten. Das Repertoire kennen wir an Hand des erhaltenen thematischen Verzeichnisses der Musikalien aus dem Jahr 1795, in dem 124 Symphonien, acht Konzerte und 56 Streichtrios verzeichnet sind. Unter den Symphonien ist an erster Stelle die erste Symphonie von Joseph Haydn (Hob. I:1) angeführt, die der Bischof am 25. November 1759 in Wien anschaffte. Vom stilistischen Standpunkt zeichnet sich das Repertoire durch ausgeprägte frühklassische Züge aus. Unter den Autoren ist am meisten der Kapellmeister Neumann mit 62 Kompositionen vertreten. Von den übrigen Komponisten seien I. Holzbauer mit zehn, G. Chr. Wagenseil mit zehn, Carlo Antonio Campioni mit neun, Le Roy mit neun und G.B. Sammartini mit neun Werken genannt. Ein Teil der Musikalien Egks soll in die Musiksammlung seines Nachfolgers Hamilton übergegangen sein, aber die Bestimmung der Egk/schen Musikalien in den Kremsierer Beständen ist sehr schwierig. Wahrscheinlich erhielten sich nur einige Harmonie/Stücke, die im Egks Inventar nicht spezifiziert sind. Es ist anzunehmen, daß die Mehrzahl der Werke aus Egks Kapell/Repertoire nicht erhalten blieb.[16]

Bischof Maximilian Hamilton (1760–76) war ein großer Liebhaber der Musik und begann im Jahr 1771 in Olmütz einmal pro Woche musikalische Akademien zu veranstalten, die auch den anständig gekleideten Bürgern für Eintrittsgeld zugänglich waren.[17] Er übernahm einige Musiker aus der Kapelle seines Vorgängers und auch einen Teil seiner Musikalien. Auch Anton Neumann blieb bis 1762 sein Kapellmeister. Nach dessen Abschied leitete die Musik ein nicht näher bekannter Jacob Vegini; eine wichtige Rolle spielten in der Kapelle der Oboist Josef Premoti, Bassanini genannt, und Anton Roller (gest. 1801).[18] Unter den erhaltenen Musikalien des Schlosses in Kroměříž läßt sich nur selten feststellen, welche Handschriften aus der Zeit Hamiltons stammen, da die meisten Musikalien nicht datiert sind. Zu diesen gehören besonders einige Kompositionen von K. Dittersdorf, J. Haydn, L. Hofmann, J.A. Štěpán und G. Chr. Wagenseil. Es scheint, daß in der Ära Hamiltons die Vorliebe für Harmoniemusik noch stieg. Dies wird sowohl durch das Vorkommen der Bläser im Aktenmaterial wie auch durch die erhaltenen Musikalien bestätitgt, unter welchen an die 80 Manuskripte von Harmoniemusiken in die Zeit Hamiltons zu datieren sind.[19]

Der erste Olmützer Erzbischof und seit 1803 Kardinal Anton Theodor Colloredo-Waldsee (1777–1811) übernahm gleichfalls einige Musiker und die Musikalien seines Vorgängers. Im Jahre 1780 führte er an seinem Hof die Funktion eines Musikdirektors ein, mit der er Ignaz Küffel beauftragte, dessen Name unter den Orchestermusikern J. Haydns am Esterházyschen Hof in den Jahren 1768–70 erscheint.[20] Wegen seines unordentlichen Lebens wurde I. Küffel 1780 entlassen. Ein neuer Musikdirektor wurde merkwürdigerweise erst im Jahr 1788 aufgenommen. Es war der Violinvirtuose, erfahrene Kapellmeister und Komponist Franz Götz (1755–1815), der unter Dittersdorf in Jánský Vrch spielte und einige Jahre die Oper in Brno dirigierte. In der Zeit Colloredos wurde das Repertoire der Kapelle um Werke von J. Chr. Bach, L. Boccherini, K. Ditters von Dittersdorf, J. Haydn, L. Hofmann, F.A. Hoffmeister, J. Jelínek, L. Koželuh, Kužník, V. Mašek, W.A. Mozart, G. Paisiello, I.J. Pleyel, F.A. Rössler, F. Schraub, J.A. Štěpán, F. Urban, J.K. Vaňhal, G. Chr. Wagenseil, F. Weigert und A. Zimmermann bereichert. Da die Handschriften nicht datiert sind, läßt es sich manchmal nicht bestimmen, aus welcher Zeit sie stammen. Außer den Symphonien und Kammermusik enthält die Colloredo'sche Sammlung zahlreiche Kompositionen mit konzertierendem Klavier. Manche Handschriften stammen aus den Wiener Kopistenwerkstätten des L. Lausch, J. Schmutzer, Radnitzky und J. Harold. Die Bestände der Hamilton'schen und Colloredo'schen Musiksammlung wurden oft als Vergleichsmaterial zu den kritischen Ausgaben der Werke J. Haydns, L. Hofmanns, W.A. Mozarts und J.A. Štěpáns gebraucht. Wegen Lücken im Aktenmaterial bleiben viele die Musiker und Musikalien betreffenden Fragen offen.[21]

Wie wir oben andeuteten, wirkten die bischöflichen Musiker nicht nur in Kroměříž, sondern überall, wo sie der Bischof benötigte. Die meisten Kapellenmitglieder sind unbekannt, da sie im Hofstaat verschiedene nichtmusikalische Funktionen als Kammerdiener, Livreebediente und Beamte ausübten. Einem besonderen Status erfreuten sich stets die Trompeter und seit der zweiten Hälfte des 18. Jahrhunderts auch die Waldhornisten. Die Streichinstrumentenspieler werden im Aktenmaterial nur ausnahmsweise genannt. Seit Ende der fünfziger Jahre stieg die

Bedeutung der Harmonie, die während der Regierung des Erzbischofs Maria Thadäus Trautmannsdorf (1811–19) die ursprüngliche Musikkapelle völlig ablöste. Einige Ausnahmen ausgenommen bestand das Repertoire der bischöflichen Kapelle seit der Ära Egks (1758) nur aus weltlichen Kompositionen.[22]

Die größeren Musikveranstaltungen fanden im Kroměříž offensichtlich im heutigen prunkvollen Reichstagsaal statt, der nach der im Jahr 1752 erfolgten Feuerbrunst des Schlosses unter der Regierung des Bischofs Hamilton um das Jahr 1770 renoviert wurde und die heutige Gestalt erhielt. In diesem Ort befand sich angeblich auch der große Speisesaal des Bischofs Karl Liechtenstein-Castelcorno, in dem sich P. Vejvanovský produzierte. Der Reichstagsaal zeichnet sich trotz seiner künstlerischen Schönheit durch eine schlechte Raumaukustik aus, was angeblich durch die in den letzten Jahren durchgeführte Rekonstruktion der die großen Deckengemälde tragenden Elemente verursacht wurde. Vermutlich konnten die Musikaufführungen im Sommer auch im Schloßgarten, bzw. in der Sala terrena des Schlosses oder in der Rotunde des Ziergartens stattfinden.

Blansko
(Blansko)

Am 5. Mai 1702 verstarb in Blansko Graf Ernst Leopold Gellhorn, der diesen Ort seit 1694 besaß. 29 Musikinstrumente (Dudelsack eingerechnet), die in seinem Nachlaßinventar verzeichnet sind, zeugen davon, daß der Graf in Blansko eine Kapelle unterhielt. Über die Musikalien gibt es im Inventar keine Erwähnung.[23] Die Familie Gellhorn hatte enge Beziehung zum Olmützer Domherr Alexander Rudolph Herzog von Schleswig-Holstein.

Brno
(Brünn)

Am 19. März 1772 bewarb sich um die Stelle eines Domchoralisten in Olmütz Anton Albrechtsberger *Virtuos* der Reichsgräfin Pamphili in Brünn.[24] Über diese Dame und ihre Musiker näheres zu ermitteln, gelang es uns bis heute nichts.

Brno – Boskovice
(Brünn – Boskowitz)

In Brno bzw. auch in Boskovice hatte der Graf Johann Leopold Dietrichstein (1703–73) eine Musikkapelle. Es wurden ihm seit 1737 einige Karnevalopern in Brno gewidmet.[25] In seinen Diensten stand der Komponist Joseph Umstatt, der in den

Jahren 1741 bis 1747 in den Matrikeln der dortigen St. Jakob-Kirche abwechselnd *Capellmeister, magister musicae, praefectus musicae, musicae instructor apud ill. comitem Dittrichstein* tituliert wurde.[26] In der Musiksammlung der Augustiner in Brno sind von Umstatt mehrere Kompositionen erhalten, darunter auch *Oratorio della Cor[on]atione B.V.M.*, das am 15. August 1745 anläßlich der Hundertjahr-Feier der Befreiung der Stadt von der schwedischen Belagerung aufgeführt wurde.[27] Von den übrigen Musikern des Grafen Dietrichstein sind Karel Suchánek,[28] Reymund Albertini (geb. 1701 in Olomouc), der früher beim Grafen Rottal in Holešov tätig war,[29] und der Fagottist Ludwig Detri[30] bekannt. Nach diesen Nachrichten sind wir berechtigt anzunehmen, daß der erwähnte Graf eine eigene Musikkapelle in Brno hielt.

Brtnice
(Pirnitz)

Seit dem Jahr 1623 gehörte Brtnice der italienischen Familie Collalto. Eine kleine Musikkapelle dürfte bereits Graf Anton Franz Collalto (1630–96) gehabt haben. Als hoher Beamte der mährischen Landesregierung beschäftigte er Trompeter, deren Anzahl um 1690 bis zu sieben stieg. Die Trompeter betrifft auch seine reiche, leider schwer lesbare Korrespondenz, die er mit dem Olmützer Bischof führte. Er nahm auch regelmäßig an den vom Bischof veranstalteten Faschingsbällen teil. Nach dem Nachlaßinventar hatte der Graf in Brtnice 19 Musikinstrumente (überwiegend Streichinstrumente) und wir können vermuten, daß er in seinem Sitz ähnliche Tanzmusik aufzuführen pflegte, wie wir sie aus der Liechtensteinschen Musiksamm-lung kennen. Er kannte persönlich den kaiserlichen Organisten Alessandro Poglietti, für dessen Kindern er in Wien einigemal die Patenschaft übernahm. In den neunziger Jahren beschäftigte er einen Bassisten und zwei Sopranistinen(!).[31]

Nach Anton Franz übernahm die Regierung Anton Rombald Collalto (1681–1740), der um das Jahr 1730 zum kaiserlichen Gesandten beim päpstlichen Stuhl in Rom ernannt wurde und viele Jahre in Venedig und in seinem Familiengut San Salvatore bei Treviso verbrachte. Da er sich in Brtnice nur wenig aufhielt, bediente er sich eher gedungener Musiker. Von Interesse ist seine Korrespondenz mit dem Poeten Apostolo Zeno.

Ihren Höhepunkt erreichte die Musikkapelle in Brtnice unter der Regierung des Grafen Thomas Vinciguerra Collalto (1710–69), eines Sohnes des Anton Rombald. Seine Kapelle leitete der Komponist Karel Welz (gest. nach 1769) aus Brtnice, während sein Bruder Silvestr Welz die Musik in der Schloßkirche besorgte. Auch die übrigen Kapellenmitglieder, unter welchen sich als Komponist besonders Jan Šrámek (Schrammek) auszeichnete, stammten aus der Herrschaft. Der Musik widmete sich aktiv auch die Gräfin und ihre Kinder. Die Komtesse Caecilia wurde am Cembalo in Wien von Matthäus Schlöger unterrichtet. Der Graf hatte persönliche Kontakte mit den Komponisten C. d'Ordoñez, J.G. Orsler, N. Porpora, A. Vivaldi und G. Chr. Wagenseil, mit der Sängerin Violante Masi und dem Tenoristen J. Meisner.[32] Das wertvollste Denkmal der Collaltschen Kapelle stellt das nach 1750 entstandene thematische Musikalieninventar der Brtnicer Kapelle dar, das 1059 Instrumental- (Symphonien, Konzerte, Kammermusik) und Kirchenwerke von 130 Autoren beinhaltet. Vom Kapellmeister K. Welz sind da 118, von Šrámek 80 Kompositionen verzeichnet. Von den übrigen Komponisten sind vor allem A. Caldara, J.A. Hasse, I. Holzbauer, A. Laube, Mikulecký, J.F. Novák(?), L.A. Predieri, J.L. Oehlschlägel, J.G. Orsler, A. Ragazzi, J.A. Sedláček, J.V. Stamic, C. Tessarini, F. Tůma, A. Vivaldi (15 unbekannte Violinkonzerte), G. Chr. Wagenseil, A. Zani, J.G. Zechner vertreten. Es hat sich bedauerlicherweise keine von den im Inventar verzeichneten Kompositionen erhalten.[33]

Dřevohostice – Hodonín
(Drewohostitz – Göding)

Der königliche Obrist Landrichter in Mähren Graf Friedrich von Oppersdorf (um 1620–1696?) muß in seinem Schloß in Dřevohostice oder in seinen Gütern in Schlesien eine Musikkapelle gehabt haben, da uns bereits aus dem Jahre 1642 der Name seines Kapellmeisters Stephan Wilkowski bekannt ist.[34] Dem Namen nach kam dieser wahrscheinlich aus Schlesien; er kann mit Johann Georg Wilkowski verwandt gewesen sein, der in den Jahren 1672–1711 Choralist der Olmützer Kathedrale war und aus Glogau stammte.[35] Im dem am 19. Juni 1696 verfassten Testament des Grafen Oppersdorf kommt ein Sekretär eines ähnlichen Namens Joseph Ignaz Walkowski(!) vor.[36]

Frýdek
(Fridek)

Graf Jan Nepomuk Pražma (1726–1804) hatte in den Jahren 1749–98 in seinem Schloß in Frýdek eine Musikkapelle, der sein Kanzellist František Weigert vorstand, von dem in den historischen mährischen Musiksammlungen einige Symphonien erhalten sind. Von den übrigen Kapellenmitgliedern sind überwiegend nur Bläser und ein *Klavirschleger* bekannt. Als der Graf Pražma im Jahr 1798 die Herrschaft Frýdek verkaufte, sicherte er seinen langjährigen Musikern eine Lebensrente und auch František Weigert lebte hier bis zu seinem Tode 1804 als pensionierter Obrigkeitskapellmeister.[37]

Holešov
(Holeschau)

Holešov war seit 1650 im Besitz der Grafen Rottal. Die Musik wurde hier wahrschein‐ lich schon in der Zeit des Johann Christoph (1635–99) und des Johann Siegmund Rottal (gest. 1717) gepflegt. Die größte Entfaltung erreichte hier das Musikleben aber in den Jahren 1731 bis 1740 unter der Regierung des Grafen Franz Anton Rottal (1690–1762). In der Leitung der Kapelle folgten aufeinander Reymund Albertini, Johann Georg Orsler und in den Jahren 1736 bis 1740 (1742?) Ignaz Holzbauer, der sich mit dem Titel *componista ducalis* schmückte. Von den übrigen Kapellisten sind Tenorist Karel Beer, Violoncellist Ignác Mara, Johann Joseph Monse, Sänger Václav Pischl, Johann Ferdinand Seidl, Jan Tuček u.a. bekannt. Als Tanzmeister wirkte hier in den Jahren 1737–48 Johann Baptist Danese (1700?–post 1748), dessen Tochter Johanna Theresia eine berühmte Opernsängerin war.[38] Vom bunten Opernleben in Holešov zeugen hauptsächlich Libretti der in den Jahren 1733–39 aufgeführten Opern von G.N. Alberti, E. Bambini, J.A. Hasse, I. Holzbauer J.G. Orsler, G. Porta und J.F. Seidl. Auf der Holešover Opernbühne traten auch Sänger der damals in Brünn wirkenden Operngesellschaften des Angelo Mingotti (1733–36), Filippo Neri del Fantasia (1736–37) und Alessandro Manfredi (1737–40) auf. Selbst Mitglieder der gräflichen Familie wirkten in einigen Opern mit. Das Musikleben in Holešov brach nach dem Tode der Gräfin Caecilia im Jahr 1740 plötzlich ab. Doch können auch andere Gründe, wie Staatstrauer nach dem Tode Karl VI. und die nach dem Einfall des Friedrich des Großen in Mähren entstandenen ökonomischen Schwierigkeiten zur Auflösung der Musikkapelle geführt haben. Einige Rottalsche Musiker kamen bald in den Diensten des Grafen Leopold Dietrichstein in Brünn zur Geltung.[39] Im Jahr 1761 soll Gräfin Maria Theresia Rottal alle Theaterkostüme und Musikalien (*cum partibus musicis*) an das Piaristenkollegium in Kroměříž verschenkt zu haben,[40] aber im dortigen Musikarchiv ist davon nichts erhalten geblieben.[41] Einige Oratorien schenkte Graf Rottal dem Olmützer Bischof Egk.[42] In Holešov, der noch im 18. Jahrhundert in Hände einer anderen Familie kam, erhielt sich kein Andenken an die ruhmvolle Musikära. Der berühmte Komponist František Xaver Richter (1709–89), der angeblich in Holešov geboren ist, war von der im Schloß gepflegten Musik nicht beeinflußt. Der Aufenthalt seiner Eltern in Holešov läßt sich annähernd in die Jahre 1720–1727? datieren, da ihr Sohn in den Jahren 1722–27 am Jesuitengymnasium in Uherské Hradiště studierte. Es scheint, daß seine Eltern nach dem Jahr 1727 aus Holešov wegzogen und deshalb die prunkvolle Ära der Rottalschen Oper nicht miterleben konnten.[43]

Das Schloß wurde im 19. Jahrhundert so weit umgebaut, daß wir uns über das Innere nur schwer eine Vorstellung machen können. Im ersten Stock gibt es einen ziemlich großen Saal, der mit zwei Pilasterreihen verziert ist, deren Kapitelle von kräftigen Halbfiguren der Atlanten getragen sind. Die Opernaufführungen können in diesem Raum oder in dem schönen Park hinter dem Schloßgebäude stattgefunden haben.

Hoštálkovy
(Gotschdorf)

Die Musikkapelle existierte hier vielleicht bereits in der ersten Hälfte des 18. Jahrhunderts, da im Jahr 1718 in Hoštálkovy der ehemalige *magister capellae aulicae* aus Slezské Rudoltice Math. Auschieldt die Stelle eines Kammerdieners antrat. Den Höhepunkt erreichte das Musikleben unter Baron Karl Traugott Skrbenský (gest. 1783). Die Kapelle wurde in den Jahren 1763–1767(?) von Joseph Puschmann und in den Jahren 1777–87 von Anton Johann Höflich geleitet. In der Kapelle wirkte auch Christian Anton Roller, der mit dem als Livreebedienter in den Diensten des Erzbischofs Colloredo in Kroměříž gestandenen Komponisten Anton Roller (gest. 1801) identisch sein könnte. Die Musikkapelle in Hoštálkovy bestand angeblich als Harmonie noch in den neunziger Jahren.[44]

Hradec nad Moravicí
(Grätz bei Troppau)

Die Musikkapelle existierte hier ungefähr in den Jahren 1770–78 unter dem Grafen Karl Wolfgang Neffzern (1738–78) und führte angeblich auch Opern auf. Im Jahr 1771 wird als *capellae magister* ein nicht näher bekannte Matthäus Santer angeführt.[45]

Jánský Vrch
(Johannisberg)

Der unter Druck des preußischen Königs gegen Willen des Kapitels und des Papstes zum Fürstbischof von Breslau erwählte Graf Philipp Gotthard Schaffgotsch (1716–95) machte sich während der preußischen Kriege durch sein doppelsinniges Benehmen den König zum Feind und wurde seit dem Jahr 1766 gezwungen, in Jánský Vrch zu leben. Gewöhnt an die große Musikkapelle in Breslau, beauftragte er im Jahr 1769 den berühmten, erfolgreichen Komponisten Karl Ditters (später: von Dittersdorf), eine kleine Kapelle zusammenzustellen. Ditters gelang es in kurzer Zeit, ein kleines Orchester aus meist in Prag engagierten Musikern von hoher Qualität aufzustellen, das im Jahr 1772 zwölf, in den achziger Jahren fünfzehn bezahlte Mitglieder zählte. Gleichzeitig wurde eine kleine Opernbühne im Schloß errichtet und Sängerinnen und Sänger aufgenommen. Nur von Dittersdorf wurden hier nicht weniger als zehn Opern aufgeführt. Bis 1773 war Dittersdorfs Librettist der italienische Priester Salvatore Ignazio Pinto (1714–86), den der Bischof im Jahr 1759 aus Rom mitbrachte. Die Musikkapelle in Jánský Vrch stand in regem Kontakt mit der erzbischöflichen Kapelle in Kroměříž und mit den Kapellen in Slezské Rudoltice, Velké Hoštice, Hošťálkovy und Linhartovy in Schlesien. Von den Kapellmitpliedern zeichneten sich besonders der Violinvirtuose und Komponist Franz Götz, der später in Kroměříž Kapellmeister des Erzbischofs Colloredo wurde, der Fagottist und Komponist Christoph Schimke, der Oboist Joseph Červenka (1759–1835), der später in Eisenstadt, Preßburg und Wien wirkte, Joseph Puschmann (1738–94), seit 1778 Kapellmeister der Olmützer Kathedrale, und der bekannte Komponist Wenzel Müller (1759–1835) aus. Das Theater und Opernleben wurde im Jahre 1785 durch das infolge der Übernahme der bischöflichen Güter in staatliche Verwaltung geschmälerte Einkommen des Bischofs lahmgelegt. Jedoch setzten sich die Theatervorstellungen in der Schießhalle des örtlichen Schützenvereins in begrenztem Maße fort. Erst der Tod des Bischofs Schaffgotsch brachte den definitiven Untergang der Kapelle, da sein Nachfolger Christian Hohenlohe Bartenstein für sie kein Interesse hatte. Von den Musikalien der Musikkapelle auf Jánský Vrch erhielt sich nichts.[46]

Jaroměřice nad Rokytnou
(Jaromeritz)

Das Musikleben in Jaroměřice wurde von Vladimír Helfert entdeckt, der ihm in den Jahren 1916 und 1924 eine umfangreiche zweiteilige Monographie widmete.[47] Helfert standen jedoch einige Archivquellen nicht zur Verfügung, die erst nach seinem Tode im Jahr 1945 zugänglich worden sind. Eine außerordentliche Stellung erreichte die Musik und insbesonders die Oper in Jaroměřice in der Zeit des Grafen Johann Adam Questenberg (1678–1752). Die Leidenschaft des allseitig gebildeten und vielgereisten Grafen für Musik und für die Oper wuchs besonders nach dem Jahr 1735, als er aus kaiserlichen Diensten wegen den Finanzskandale seiner Frau entlassen wurde und sich nur dem Aufbau seines Schlosses und der geliebten Musik ganz widmen konnte. Er ließ Theatersäle nicht nur in Jaroměřice sondern auch in seinen Herrschaften Rappoltenkirchen bei Tulln und in Bečov (Petschau) bei Karlovy Vary (Karlsbad) errichten. Er selbst beherrschte virtuos die Laute und ließ seine Tochter Karoline von Gottlieb Muffat in Wien auf dem Cembalo unterrichten. Der Graf unterhielt rege Kontakte mit den Mitgliedern der Wiener Hofkapelle, verkehrte persönlich mit Antonio Caldara, Francesco und Ignazio Conti und lud Nicolà Porpora und Giuseppe Bononcini nach Jaroměřice ein. Er bevorzug die solistische Oper des sogenannten Neapolitaner Typs und das Wiener Singspiel. Vielleicht aus diesem Grund war ihm der Stil von Johann Joseph Fux fremd; der Graf versuchte nie, Kontakte mit diesem Meister anzuknüpfen. Desto mehr überraschen jüngste Ermittlungen, wonach der Graf mit J.S. Bach verkehrte.[48] Er war auch mit Giuseppe Galli da Bibiena befreundet, von dem er sich szenische Entwürfe für seine Opernbühne erbat.

Questenberg begann sich bereits seit 1706 mit Bediensteten umzugeben, die er als Musiker gebrauchen konnte. Seit 1732 war sein Kapellmeister der in den Besoldungslisten als Kammerdiener geführte František Václav Míča (1694–1744). Die Hauptpflichten von Míča waren, die neuen Opern einzustudieren und sie nach den Bedürfnissen der Bühne in Jaroměřice umzuarbeiten. Schließlich hatte Míča auch die Aufgabe, Gelegenheitskompositionen, wie Gratulationskantaten und Festopern zu komponieren. Von den wenigen erhaltenen Werken dieser Art sei die Oper *L'origine di Jaromeriz in Moravia* erwähnt, die im Jahr 1730 sogar tschechisch für die Stadtbewohner und Untertanen aufgeführt wurde.[49] Während Míča für die Musik im Schloßtheater sorgte, leitete die Kirchenmusik seit 1697 der Schulrektor Václav Frey-Svoboda. Nach Míčas Tod übernahm die Leitung der Kapelle Karel Müller (1729–1803). Mit seiner Entlassung 1765 ging die ruhmreiche Zeit der Musikkapelle in Jaroměřice zu Ende.

Graf Questenberg hatte in Jaroměřice ein mit ungefähr 30 Spielern besetztes Orchester, ein Waldhornensemble, Sänger und Sängerinen, einen Chor von Erwachsenen und einen Kinderchor und auch ein Tanzensemble, das abwechselnd Johann Baptist Danese[50] und Franz Joseph Scotti[51] leiteten. Alle Musiker, Sänger und Tänzer rekrutierten sich entweder aus Livreebedienten oder aus Bürgern des Städtchens und Untertanen von Questenbergs Gütern. Die Intensität des Theaterbetriebs in Jaroměřice war verblüffend. In den Jahren 1722–44 wurden mehr als 200 szenische Werke einstudiert. Jedes Jahr gelangten an die 30 Bühnenwerke zur Aufführung, z.B. im Jahr 1738 achtzehn Opern und sechszehn Komödien. Es gibt schwerwiegende Gründe für die Annahme daß die stetige Überlastung zum vorzeitigen Tod des Kapellmeisters Míča wesentlich beitrug.

Die Opernpartituren besorgte der Graf aus Wien, Venedig, Rom und Neapel. Es wurden Opern von E. Bambini, A. Bioni, A. Caldara, A. Constantini, B. Galuppi, G. Giacomelli, J.A. Hasse, L. Leo, M. Lucchini, G.B. Pergolesi, D. Sarri und L. Vinci aufgeführt. Die Kapelle hatte Beziehungen vor allem zur Wiener Hofkapelle und zu den Opernensembles in Kuks, Prag, Holešov und Brno.

Nach dem Tode des Grafen Questenberg erbte die Herrschaft der Neffe seiner zweiten Frau, Graf Dominik Ondřej Kounic (Kaunitz; 1739–1812), weil er aber noch unmündig war, wurden sie vorerst von der Witwe Gräfin Maria Antonia geb. Kounic verwaltet. Im Jahr 1752 wurde von ihr Karel Müller mit der Liquidierung des Theaters und der Musikpflege überhaupt beauftragt, der aber bald um Entlassung aus der Leibeigenschaft ersuchte und im Jahr 1765 die Stelle eines Organisten in Vyškov (Wischau) antrat. Die Musikkapelle, allmählich auf ein Harmoniemusikensemble reduziert, lebte bis in die achtziger Jahre fort. Einige Musiker fanden in anderen Musikkapellen Betätigung: Peregrin Gravani wurde 1762–1815 Chorrektor der Stadtpfarrkirche St. Jakob in Brno, Josef Nagel wurde in der Oettingen-Wallersteinschen Musikkapelle tätig, Jan Palsa wirkte erfolgreich in Kassel, Paris, London und Berlin, Jan Pfaff in der königlichen Kapelle in Kopenhagen, Karel Pfaff in Colmar, Václav Apolinarius Růžička in Wien. Der berühmte Wiener Komponist Leopold Hofmann war Sohn des gräflichen Hofmeisters in Wien und gleichzeitig wichtigsten Beraters Questenbergs in den Kunstangelegenheiten Georg Adam Hofmann.[52]

Zur Musikkapelle in Jaroměřice erhielten sich reiche archivalische Quellen, aber fast keine Musikalien. Von den Opernaufführungen zeugen nur einige gedruckten Libretti. Mit Ausnahme einiger szenischen Werke F. V. Míčas verschwanden die Musikalien ohne Spur. Die im Jahr 1936 auf dem Kirchenchor in Pelhřimov entdeckte Sinfonia in Re erregte nach dem 2. Weltkrieg großes Aufsehen, da sie im ersten Satz eine ausgeprägte Sonatenform aufwies. Es zeigte sich jedoch bald, daß sie weder ein Werk des František Václav Míča noch des in Wien lebenden Jan Adam František Míča (1746–1811) sein kann.[53]

Die Musikaufführungen fanden in Jaroměřice entweder im Schoß oder im Schloßgarten statt. Es wurde manchmal auch auf den Schiffen auf dem den Schloßgarten durchfließenden Flüßchen Rokytná musiziert. Die Oratorien und Sepolcri erklangen in der prachtvollen Pfarrkirche, die gleich wie das Schloß nach den Plänen Jakob Prandtauers gebaut worden war. Im Schloß ist ein prachtvoller mit feinen Fresken geschmückter Festsaal im Originalzustand erhalten, an dessen Ende sich oben ein kleiner mit verglasten Fenstern versehener Raum befindet, der vermutlich für die Musiker bestimmt war. In diesem relativ niedrigen Raum konnten acht bis zehn Musiker Platz finden. Es ist interessant, daß die Fenster dieses Raumes sich nur etwa 40 cm über dem Fußboden befinden, so daß die im Saal zur Tafel oder zum Tanz versammelte Gesellschaft die Füße, aber kaum Gesichter der spielenden Musiker sehen konnte. Da auch das Schloß in Jaroměřice im 19. Jahrhundert zu anderen Zwecken umgebaut wurde, erhielt sich der Theatersaal nicht. Es gibt nur Vermutungen, wo er sich befand.

Linhartovy
(Gippersdorf b. Freudenthal)

Eine Kapelle oder eher ein Harmoniemusikensemble gab es ungefähr in den Jahren 1780–1805 während der Regierung des Grafen Josef Sedlnický z Choltic

(1751–1839). Ihre Kapellmeister waren der Oboist Wolfgang Bohmann (1742–1814) in den Jahren 1781–1787(?), Josef Souček in den Jahren 1787–1800 und schließlich Josef Bulík.[54] In den Jahren 1777–87 war hier als junger Knabe Gottfried Rieger (1764–1855) tätig, der sich später als Kapellmeister des Grafen Haugwitz in Náměšt nad Oslavou und als Musikpädagoge und Komponist in Brünn auszeichnete. Den Dienst in Linhartovy trat er schon mit 13 Jahren an.[55]

Náměšt nad Oslavou
(Namiest)

Náměšt nad Oslavou gehörte seit 1685 dem Grafen Johann Philipp Werdenberg (gest. 1733). Graf Werdenberg war offensichtlich ein guter Lautenist, da sich eine Lautentabulatur aus seinem Besitz erhalten hat.[56] In seinen Diensten standen vor 1725 der Bassist und Trompeter Bedřich Karel Felix und der Bassist und Geiger Fabián S. Milický.[57]

Eine Kapelle muß auch der nachfolgende Besitzer der Herrschaft Náměšt Graf Wenzel Adrian Enckevoirt (gest. 1738) gehabt haben, da er im Jahr 1734 Anton Wolbert aus Prag als einen *director musicae* beschäftigte.[58]

Im Jahr 1795 übernahm Graf Heinrich Wilhelm Haugwitz (1770–1842) von seinem Vater Karl Wilhelm die Verwaltung der Herrschaft Náměšt. Graf Heinrich Wilhelm war ein unglaublich leidenschaftlicher Verehrer der Musik, besonders der Oper und des Oratoriums. In den Jahren 1795–1800 begann er, Musikinstrumente und Musikalien anzukaufen und Musiker zu gelegentlichen Musikproduktionen aufzunehmen. Seit August 1799 stand ihm schon eine Anzahl von Musikern aus Náměšt und Umgebung zur Verfügung, die bereit waren, an jährlich 30 bis 40 symphonischen Konzerten und Schloßbällen gegen Bezahlung mitzuwirken. Im Jahr 1800 ließ der Graf ein kleines Theater im Schloß errichten, wo regelmäßig Opern und Oratorien aufgeführt wurden. Dieses Kapitel der Musikgeschichte von Náměšt liegt jedoch außerhalb des zeitlichen Rahmens unserer Studie.[59] Die Musikalien der Haugwitzer Kapelle – an die 2000 Werke – erhielten sich fast komplett in der Abteilung für Musikgeschichte des Mährischen Landesmuseums in Brünn.

Nová Horka
(Neuhübel)

Das Musikleben blühte in diesem Schloß in der Zeit des Grafen Karl Joseph Vetter von Lilie (geb. um 1719–1792), der die Herrschaft seit 1742 im Besitz hatte. Nach der Zeugnis des Vincenc Janáček (1821–1901), des Onkels des Komponisten Leoš Janáček, führte Graf Karl Joseph seinen Hof mit aufwendigem Luxus, wozu auch zwölf Livreebediente gehörten, von denen jeder ein Handwerk und ein Musikinstrument beherrschen mußte. Es scheint, daß in Nová Horka meist wenig anspruchsvolle Musik zum Tanz gepflegt wurde. In den Verlassenschaftsakten des Grafen vom Jahr 1792 wurden die Musikinstrumente summarisch mit 193 fl. 35 kr. und die Musikalien mit 122 fl. 35 kr. geschätzt. Die Kapelle leitete in den Jahren 1784–92 der Violinist, Cellist, Klavierspieler und Komponist Anton Bayer, dessen zweiter Beruf das Tischlerhandwerk war. Bemerkenswerterweis hat er sich im Jahr 1794 sogar um die Kapellmeisterstelle an der Olmützer Kathedrale beworben.[60]

Olomouc–Brno
(Olmütz–Brünn)

Im Jahr 1709 wurde der Olmützer Domherr Graf Johann Matthias von Turn und Valessassina (1683–1747) zu neuem infulierten Propst am Petersberg in Brünn installiert. Der Chronist des Klosters Hradisko charakterisierte ihn im Jahr 1722 zutreffend mit den Worten *'singularis amator et fautor musicorum'*.[61] Der Propst zog nicht nur die Kirchenmusiker zu seinen Musikproduktionen heran, er hat auch grundsätzlich bei der Auswahl seiner Bediensteten den musikalisch Begabten den Vorzug gegeben, um diese auch in einem Musikensemble beschäftigen zu können. Über die Musikpflege in seiner Residenz legt sein Nachlaßinventar Zeugnis ab, in dem an 50 Musikinstrumente (davon 24 Streicher) und 61 Instrumentalwerke, Opern, Oratorien und Serenaden von A. Bencini, F. Conti, M. Finazzoli, M. Fini, A. Fiore, A. Fiorilli, P. Franchi, V. Gurecký, L. Leo, F.V. Míča, J.G. Orsler, G.B. Pergolesi, G. Porsile und Camilla Rossi genannt werden. Leider erhielt sich von diesen Musikschätzen nichts.[62]

Olomouc–Peterswaldau (Schlesien)
(Olmütz–Peterswaldau)

Am 2. Mai 1727 starb in seiner Olmützer Residenz der Domherr Alexander Rudolph, Erbe von Norwegen und Herzog von Schleswig-Holstein (geb. 1651), und wurde den 4. Mai als confrater des Prämonstratenserordens in der Gruft der Kirche in Hradisko beigestzt.[63] Ähnlich wie der Propst Turn und Valessassina gehörte auch er zu den musikliebenden Würdenträgern des Olmützer Domkapitels. Davon zeugt wieder ein im Jahr 1690 im Schloß Peterswaldau bei Schweidnitz verfaßtes Inventar, in dem mehr als 20 Musikinstrumente genannt sind.[64] Wir sind also berechtigt anzunehmen, daß der Herzog auch in seiner Olmützer Residenz die Musik pflegte. Die Musikinteressen dürfen wir auch bei seinem Bruder Ferdinand Leopold (1647–1702), gleichfalls Domherr in Olmütz, voraussetzen.[65]

Oslavany
(Oslawan)

Nach dem Jahr 1620 erhielt die Herrschaft Oslavany der Feldherr und kaiserliche Diplomat Graf Michael Adolph von Althan (1574–1636). Zusammen mit Carolo Gonzaga Herzog von Nevers gründete er im Jahr 1618 in Olmütz einen christlichen Orden (*Ordo equitum militiae Christianae* oder *Confraternitas militiae Christianae pro redimendis captivis*). Die Hauptbedingung für die Mitgliedschaft war die adelige Herkunft bis hinauf in das vierte Glied oder des Vaters Verdienst als Kriegsmann. Nach der Genehmigung des Ordens wurde Graf Althan dessen erster Großmeister. Der Orden verbreitete sich vor allem in Bosnien, in der Walachei und in den griechischen Provinzen, ging aber schon um das Jahr 1680 wieder ein. Im Jahr 1631 errichtete der Graf in Wien eine Stiftung für zehn studierende arme Knaben im Seminarium St. Pankraz in Oslavany.[66] Graf Althan muß eine Beziehung zur Musik gehabt haben, da er im Jahr 1626 in Oslavany ein Lehrbuch *Regulae contrapuncti excerptae ex operibus Zerlini et aliorum* von dem Kapellan des Kardinals Dietrichstein Carolo Abbate drucken ließ.[67] Nach der Vorrede war das Lehrbuch für die Musikausbildung der 33(!) Seminaristen im Wiener und zehn Seminaristen im Oslavaner Seminar bestimmt. Es muß in Oslavany einen beachtlichen Musikchor gegeben haben, da hier eine *Missa concertata 8 voci* komponiert wurde.[68] Der Graf muß auch offensichtlich großartige Editionspläne gehabt haben, da er im Jahr 1629 wieder in Oslavany den ersten Teil einer neunteiligen Sammlung *Flores verni ex viridiario Oslaviensi* drucken ließ.[69] Die Dedikation an den Grafen Althan unterschrieb der *Chorus Musicorum Oslaviensium* und als Autor dreier Kompositionen ist 'M. *Oslaviensis Stephano Bernardi*' angeführt. War Steffano Bernardi tatsächlich Magister oder Musicus der Kapelle des Grafen Althan in Oslavany, wenn er zu gleicher Zeit in Salzburg nachweisbar ist? Die hohe politische Stellung des Grafen und seine zahlreichen Fundationen könnten diese Hypothese nur unterstützen. Es wurden leider bis heute keine weiteren Dokumente zur Musiktätigkeit des Seminars in Oslavany entdeckt.

Sádek u Třebíče – Veselí nad Moravou
(Sadek b. Trebitsch – Wesseli)

Es ist anzunehmen, daß hier eine Musikkapelle in der Zeit der Regierung des Grafen František Ignác Chorynský (1759–1821) existierte. Der einzige Beweis dafür stellen 31 Konzerte und Divertimenti für konzertantes Cembalo mit Begleitung verschiedener Instrumente, die in der Burg Sádek aufgefunden wurden und jetzt im Bezirksarchiv in Třebíč aufbewahrt sind. Unter den Komponisten kommen F. Arbesser, K. Ditters, F.X. Dušek, L. Hofmann, F. Klein, J. Puschmann, J.A. Štěpán, G. Chr. Wagenseil und A. Zimmerman vor. Es scheint, daß es sich um ein Torso einer umfangreicheren Musikaliensammlung handelt, die nicht nur in Sádek, sondern auch in Veselí nad Moravou, wo der Graf im Jahr 1780 den neun Musikern ein Deputat in Geld einlöste, Verwendung fand. Das Vorkommen des Namens Puschmann weist auch nach Velké Hoštice.[70]

Slezské Rudoltice
(Roßwald)

In Slezské Rudoltice existierte eine Musikkapelle bereits im Jahr 1688, derer Leitung Bohumir Gabriel (gest. 1709), Mathäus Auschieldt (1715), Johann Georg Kolbe (1720), Godefridus Porsch (1734) und Antonín Gruška (1748) innehatten. Den Höhepunkt erreichte das Kulturleben unter dem Grafen Albert Josef z Hodic a Olbramovic (1706–78), der das Schloß in einen prachtvollen Rokokositz umbauen ließ, den die Zeitgenossen 'schlesische Versailles' zu nennen pflegten. An der Spitze der Kapelle stand in den Jahren 1754–71 Heinrich Schön aus Mödling, dem Karl Hanke in den Jahren 1772–1778(?) nachfolgte. Der Graf pflegte enge Kontakte mit der bischöflichen Kapelle zu Janský Vrch und mit dem dortigen Dichter S.I. Pinto. In Slezské Rudoltice wurden sogar Opern aufgeführt; die erste Oper *Die vergötterte Sophie* komponierte im Jahr 1748 der damalige Kapellmeister Antonín Gruška (1716?–1772). Später gelangten besonders Dittersdorfs Opern zur Aufführung.[71]

Strážnice
(Straßnitz)

Die Herrschaft Strážnice gehörte seit dem Jahr 1629 den Grafen Magnis, die in einem befestigten Schloß außerhalb der von zahlreichen Feuerbrunsten und feindlichen Überfällen der Türken und ungarischen Aufständischen heimgesuchten Stadt lebten, sofern sie sich überhaupt auf ihrer Herrschaft aufhielten. Über das Musikleben im Schloß das ganze 17. und 18. Jahrhundert hindurch fehlen alle Berichte, Daß hier zu Ende des 18. Jahrhunderts eine Musikkapelle existierte, können wir aufgrund einer Sammlung von 320 Instrumental-Kompositionen annehmen, die sich in der Schloßbibliothek erhielt. Die meisten handschriftlich überlieferten Werke stammen aus dem letzten Viertel des 18. Jahrhunderts und aus der ersten Hälfte des 19. Jahrhunderts und auf einigen Manuskripten ist als Besitzer ein nicht näher bekannter Ripamonti angeführt. Der ältere Teil der Sammlung bilden Symphonien und Kammerwerke italienischer Komponisten, den jüngeren Teil Salonmusik für Klavier oder für ein Soloinstrument mit Klavierbegleitung. Die Musiksammlung gewann V. Helfert als ersten Zugang für die von ihm gegründete Abteilung für Musikgeschichte des Mährischen Landesmuseums in Brünn. Die Entstehung der erwähnten Musiksammlung wird mit dem Namen des Grafen Franz Anton von Magnis und Strážnice (1773–1848) verbunden, aber genauere Informationen darüber, wer die Musikalien gebrauchte, fehlen.[72] Es wurden selbst Vermutungen ausgesprochen, daß die Musiksammlung von anderswo nach Strážnice gebracht wurde.

Telč
(Teltsch)

Die musikalische Vergangenheit des Renaissanceschlosses in Telč bleibt wohl für immer unbekannt. In den Räumen, die in der 2. Hälfte des 16. Jahrhunderts mit Frescos ausgeschmückt wurden, sind auffällig viele Motive mit Musikinstrumenten zu sehen. Im sogenannten Goldenen Saal gibt es eine spezielle – gemauerte – Musikertribüne. Seit 1604 befand sich das Schloß im Besitz der gräflichen Familie Slavata. Mit der Gräfin Marie Barbara Slavata vermählte sich im Jahr 1669 der Neffe des Olmützer Bischofs Karl Liechtenstein-Castelcorno Graf Christoph Philipp (1641–85). Es gibt einige Anzeichen dafür, daß der berühmte Violinvirtuose und Komponist H.I.F. Biber vor dem Jahr 1668 in seinen Diensten stand.[73] Biber ist nämlich in dem Ort Stráž pod Ralskem (früher Wartenberg) geboren, der damals dem Vater des Grafen Christoph Philipp gehörte. Aus der Zeit des Grafen Christoph Philipp sind nur Nachrichten über Trompeter erhalten.[74]

Tovačov
(Tobitschau)

Tovačov befand sich in den Jahren 1671–97 im Besitz des Grafen Ferdinand Julius Salm (1650–96). Der Graf war ein sehr frommer Katholik und unterhielt rege Beziehungen mit dem Olmützer Bischof Karl Liechtenstein und mit den Jesuiten in Olmütz. Im Jahr 1683 empfahl er dem Olmützer Bischof seinen Musiker Martin Habermayer und noch kurz vor seinem Tode ließ er in Wien zwei silberne Trompeten für seine Kapelle herstellen.[75] Seine Kapelle besorgte die Musik sowohl im Schloß wie auch in der Kirche und war so berühmt, daß sie selbst bei der Eröffnung der vierzigstündigen Andacht auf dem Heiligenberg bei Olmütz auftrat.[76] Das einzige Zeugnis von der Musikkapelle des Grafen Salm stellt das Hinterlassenschaftsinventar des Grafen dar, in welchem neun Musikinstrumente am Kirchenchor und 392 kirchliche und weltliche Kompositionen verzeichnet sind.[77] Eine enge Verbindung mit der bischöflichen Musikkapelle in Kroměříž ist durch das zahlreiche Vorkommen derselben Autoren und sogar einiger Werke, die auch in der Liechtensteinschen Musiksammlung erhalten sind, evident. Unter den Dedikatoren von Kompositionen sind Pavel Vejvanovskýund der Kremsierer Schulrektor Jan Škaretka (um 1645–1710) genannt. Unter den Komponisten überwiegen Bertali, Biber, Carissimi, G. Götzl, I. Reinold (Organist des Klosters Hradisko), Schmelzer und Vejvanovský. Auch die Musiksammlung des Grafen Salm verschwand nach seinem Tode ohne Spur.

Valašské Meziříčí
(Walachisch Meseritsch)

Die Herrschaft Valašské Meziříčí gehörte der gräflichen Familie Žerotín. Das Kulturleben im Schloß begann erst nach 1756, als die Herrschaft Graf Michal Josef ze Žerotína (geb. vor 1731, gest. 1779) übernahm, der das Schloß umbauen und darin ein Theater errichten ließ. Während seiner Regierung wirkte als Lehrer und Regens chori in Valašské Meziříčí der fruchtbare Kirchenkomponist František Navrátil (1732–1802), der sich im Jahr 1770 auf Empfehlung des Grafen um die Kapell/meisterstelle in der Olmützer Kathedrale bewarb. Da dieses Amt J. Puschmann anvertraut wurde, blieb Navrátil weiterhin – auch während der Regierung des Grafen Ludvík Antonín ze Žerotína (gest. 1808), eines Bruders des Michal Josef – Schulrektor und Regens chori Valašské Meziříčí.[78]

Valtice
(Feldsberg)

Nach Hannes Stekl[79] beteiligten sich die Fürsten Liechtenstein 'erst verhältnismäßig spät an der Statuskonkurrenz, die die adeligen Privatkapellen darstellten.' Seine Worte verstehen wir in dem Sinne, daß die Fürsten Liechtenstein keine Privatkapelle vor der Gründung ihrer Harmonie im Jahr 1789 besaßen. Trotz Mangel an weiteren Dokumenten scheint diese Vermutung nicht berechtigt zu sein. Vor dem Jahr 1718 bewarb sich um die Tenoristenstelle am Petersberg in Brünn ein gewißer Anton Lux, der behauptete, er hätte mit seiner Stimme dem Fürsten Maximilian von Liechtenstein in Moravský Krumlov (Mährisch Kromau) gedient.[80] Am 17. Juni 1748 heiratete in Podivín (Kostel) Laurentius Pommo de Wayerthal *Serenissimi Ducis ac Principis Joannis Caroli Lichtenstein Majoratus Capellae Welspergensis Capellae Musicus in Welsper* Marianna Schütt, Tochter des Bassisten der St. Jakob/Kirche in Brünn, wobei *Joannes Georgius Orsler ejusdem Principis Capellae Magister* Trauzeuge war.[81] Dem Namen J.G. Orsler begegneten wir in Holešov und in Brtnice. Über sein Wirken bei den Fürsten Liechtenstein wurde bis heute fast nichts bekannt. In diesen kleinen Informationen sehen wir Beweise dafür, daß bereits vor dem Jahr 1789 eine Musikkapelle in Valtice existiert haben muß.

Im prächtigen Liechtensteinschen Schloß in Valtice gibt es eine geräumige

Kapelle, in der sich auf dem kleinen Chor ein Torso einer kleinen Orgel von Lothar Franz Walter aus dem Jahr 1729 befindet.[82] Diese Kapelle zeichnet sich durch hervorragende Akustik durch. Einer von den Schloßsälen wird für den Musiksaal gehalten, da er mit musikalischen Motiven in Stuckarbeit ausgeschmückt ist.

Velké Hoštice
(Groß Hoschitz)

Die Herrschaft Velké Hoštice war im Besitz des Landeshauptmanns des Fürstentums Opava und Krnov Ignác Dominik Chorynský 1729–92. In den Jahren 1767–77 leitete seine Kapelle Josef Puschmann (1738–94), der im Jahr 1778 Kapellmeister der Kathedrale in Olmütz wurde, und in den Jahren 1781–87 František Silvestr. Über die Tätigkeit der Kapelle sind wir nur ungenügend informiert. Wir wissen bloß, daß der Graf Josef Puschmann nur ungern aus seinen Diensten entließ und daß Puschmann noch aus Olmütz dem Grafen seine Instrumentalkompositionen lieferte. Auch die Kapelle in Velké Hoštice unterhielt enge Beziehungen zu Dittersdorf und zu seiner Kapelle in Jánský Vrch sowie zum dortigen Poeten S.I. Pinto.[83]

Velké Losiny–Olomouc–Brno
(Groß Ullersdorf–Olmütz–Brünn)

Die Grafen Žerotín hatten eine Musikkapelle, die nicht nur in Velké Losiny, sondern auch in ihren Residenzen in Olomouc und Brno tätig war. Bereits Přemyslav ze Žerotína (1629–73) hat nachweislich Musiker beschäftigt, da im Jahr 1673 sein ehemaliger Instrumentalist den Olmützer Bischof um einen Musikerposten ersuchte.[84] Der jüngere Sohn des Přemyslav Jan Jáchym (1667–1716) besaß angeblich eine gute Musikkapelle,[85] über die wir jedoch keine konkreten Angaben haben. Man kann ein tieferes Interesse für die Musik bei diesem Grafen voraussetzen, da sich aus seiner Zeit in der Žerotínschen Schloßbibliothek in Bludov gedruckte Partituren zweier Opern von J.B. Lully und handschriftliche Stimmen mit Stücken aus Opern und Balletten desselben Autors erhielten.[86] Der Graf Jan Jáchym beschäftigte sogar Trompeter und die Familie hatte ihre Musiker auch in Brno.[87] Vor 1732 wirkte bei den Grafen Žerotín Johann Ferdinand Seidl aus Falkenberg in Schlesien.[88]

Vranov nad Dyjí–Jaroslavice
(Frain an der Thaya–Joslowitz)

Die Musik wurde in diesem Schloß besonders unter Grafen Michal Johann III. von Althan (1679–1722) und seiner schönen, gebildeten Frau Maria Pignatelli

(1689–1755) gepflegt. Zu den Bewunderern dieser Dame gehörte auch Kaiser Karl VI., der manchmal im Sommer mit einigen Musikern seiner Hofkapelle auf dem Schloß Vranov weilte. Das Schloß wurde auch von den Poeten Apostolo Zeno und Pietro Metastasio besucht, und der letztere ließ sich nach dem Tode des Michal Johann III. mit Maria Pignatelli geheim trauen. Seine eigene Kapelle hatte der Graf Michal aber wohl in Jaroslavice, da sich im dortigen Schloßinventar aus der Zeit um 1720 elf Musikinstrumente befanden.

Graf Michal Johann IV. (1710–78) war ein leidenschaftlicher Opernliebhaber und ließ in seinem Wiener Palais, wo er sich meist aufhielt, Opern von Broschi, Caldara, Conti und J.J. Fux aufführen. Die Partituren beschaffte er direkt aus Italien nicht nur für sich selbst, sondern auch für den Grafen Questenberg in Jaroměřice. Er spielte ausgezeichnet die Violine und wirkte im Jahre 1737 zusammen mit anderen Adeligen anläßlich der Geburtstagsfeier der Kaiser in einem eigens dafür zusam/mengestellten Orchester mit. Seit dem Jahr 1762 war Carlos d'Ordoñez Mitglied seiner Wiener Kapelle.

Der letzte Besitzer von Vranov aus dem Hause Althan war Michal Anton (1716–74), der als Inhaber eines Dragonenregiments größtenteils in Wien lebte. Seinem Musiker Anton Rosetti,[89] der in seinem Dienst seit 1766 stand, hinterließ er eine Jahresrente von 200 fl.[90] Mit Ausnahme einer kleinen Orgel aus der Mitte des 18. Jahrhunderts in der Schloßkirche, die – wie das ganze Schloß – nach den Plänen des J.B. Fischer von Erlach errichtet worden war, erhielt sich aus der musikalischen Vergangenheit der Grafen Althan nichts.

*   *   *

Die oben skizzierte Übersicht unserer Kenntnisse über die adeligen Musikkapellen in Mähren beweist, daß relativ viele Adelige ein Musikensemble besaßen. Besitzveränderungen und das Aussterben der Adelsfamilien führten zur Verlust oder Vernichtung des Aktenmaterials, vor allem der Musikalien. Oft beweisen die Existenz einer Schloßkapelle nur zufällige kurze Erwähnungen der Musikernamen in den Kirchenmatrikeln. Die Lücken in unseren Kenntnissen sind deshalb sehr groß und können kaum geschlossen werden. Besonders bedauerlich ist, daß Musikalien einiger bedeutenden Kapellen, die manchmal mehr als 1000 Kompositionen zählten, wie z.B. Brtnice, Holešov, Jaroměřice, und Werke von Bedeutung sowohl für die mährische, wie auch für die europäische Musikgeschichte enthielten, definitiv verloren sind.

Unsere Übersicht deutet auch an, daß die adeligen Musikkapellen in keiner Isolation lebten, sondern mit den Klöstern und Kirchen ein mit zahlreichen persön/lichen Verbindungen durchwebtes Musiknetz bildeten. Eine umfassende Aufdeckung dieser Verbindungen könnte zur Lösung der oft gestellten Frage beitragen, ob die Schloßkapellen nur einem streng begrenzten Umkreis der Adelsfamilie oder auch einem breiteren Gesellschaftskreis von Zuhörern dienten. Es gibt unter unseren Musikhistorikern eine verlockende Hypothese, daß manche adeligen Musikkapellen die Musikalität der Bevölkerung einer Herrschaft sogar nach ihrem Erlöschen noch beinflußt hätten. Trotz der Ausnahme des aufgeklärten Grafen Questenberg in Jaroměřice, der tatsächlich seinen Untertanen den Besuch seines Theaters zeitweise gestattete und der dafür von J.B. Danese in Wien sogar verleumdet wurde, daß seine Opernvorstellungen nur Schweinhirten und Bauern besucht hätten,[91] vertreten wir die Ansicht, daß die soziale Bedeutung und Wirkung der Schloßkapellen eher in ihren Verbindungen zu anderen Musikinstitutionen als in ihren direkten Leistungen für die breite Öffentlichkeit bestand. Die Antwort auf diese Frage überlassen wir aber der weiteren musikhistorischen Forschung.

Nikolaus Harnoncourt

Wissen – Intuition – Mode:
Faktoren der Interpretation

Intuition und Wissen – das sind wohl die Pole, zwischen denen jeder Musiker, ja jeder Musikhörer eingespannt ist. Alle Probleme der Aufführung, alle Fragen der Hörerfahrung werden im Spannungsfeld dieser Begriffe behandelt. Das musikalische *Wissen* wird normalerweise verkörpert durch den Musikwissenschaftler. Er verfügt prinzipiell über die Kenntnisse und die spekulative Denkweise, die alle Arten von Werkanalysen und vergleichenden Untersuchungen erfordern. Darüber hinaus weiß er normalerweise einiges über die historischen und gesellschaftlichen Zusammenhänge der untersuchten Werke. Die musikalische *Intuition* wird eher durch den praktischen Musiker, den Podiumskünstler verkörpert. Wenn er auch nur ausnahmsweise an Werkanalysen interressiert ist, so hat er doch in der Regel einen sehr direkten, gefühlsmäßigen Zugang zur Musik. Er 'weiß' wie er phrasieren muß, wie ein Werk zu gestalten ist; bei Großwerken wie Oratorien und Opern empfindet er die großen Zusammenhänge so zwingend, daß seine Aufführungen auch dann mitreißend und packend sind, wenn er sich überhaupt keine ernsthaften analytischen Gedanken macht. Es ist auffallend, wie desinteressiert viele solcher Instinkt-Musiker an wissen schaftlicher Information sind, ja, sie verachten 'wissende' Kollegen als trocken, temperamentlos und uninspiriert. Es ist geradezu peinlich für einen Dirigenten, dem Orchester einen Triller, einen Trillernachschlag, oder gar eine Appoggiatur zu erklären: der notorische 'Vollblutmusiker' kann leicht durch eine Demonstration seines Wissens die Aura verlieren; Wissen gilt als Eigenschaft eines trockenen, niemals eines 'musikalischen' Menschen.

Bedeutet dies, daß in der Musik Theorie und Praxis wirklich getrennt sind? Daß sie einander nicht brauchen, ja geradezu abstoßen? Ich glaube, daß Musik klingen muß um zu existieren, und daß rein abstrakte Studien für die Praxis nur insoferne einen Wert haben, als sie zu einer besseren Aufführung beitragen können, also dem ausführenden Musiker Informationen bieten, die entweder seine Inspiration beflügeln oder sein technisches Wissen erhöhen (etwa bezüglich der Tempi oder formaler Zusammenhänge, etc.). Natürlich muß das auch für den Hörer gelten: wenn er durch wissenschaftliche Information ein Werk besser verstehen – das heißt tiefer empfinden – könnte, wäre für ihn musikwissenschaftliche Arbeit sinnvoll und fruchtbar. Andernfalls würde solche Arbeit nur die Bibliotheksstellagen bereichern, bzw. die forschenden Musikwissenschaftler selbst – sie wäre eine Art interner Denksport, der mit Musik nur insofern zu tun hat, als er sie als 'Turngerät' benützt.

Dennoch glaube ich, daß ein Instinktmusiker zwar sehr eindrucksvolle Aufführungen zustande bringen kann, daß es aber im Grunde unprofessionell ist, Fehler nur deshalb zu machen, weil einem das nötige Wissen fehlt. Wenn man überhaupt *das Werk* eines bestimmten Komponisten aufführen will und nicht lediglich eine persönlich nachempfundene Paraphrase (laut Meyer ca. 1900: phantasieartig ausgeschmückte Bearbeitung), dann sollte man schon das Fachwissen haben, um die Äußerungen des Komponisten überhaupt zu verstehen. Man sollte also die von Generation zu Generation wechselnden Bedeutungen der Notenschrift ebenso kennen, wie die verbalen Erklärungen (Ausdrucks-, Tempobezeichnungen, Spielanweisungen, etc.). Wenn man schon Fehler macht, also Anweisungen des Komponisten nicht befolgt, dann sollte man das bewußt tun und nicht aus Unwissenheit.

Einige Beispiele zu Fragen, die häufig falsch beantwortet oder überhaupt nicht gestellt werden: ist Andantino schneller oder langsamer als Andante? Was bedeutet ¢? Soll man bei 'più Andante' schneller oder langsamer werden? . . . Wie verpflichtend sind Metronombezeichnungen? Wie sehr kann man einer Druckausgabe trauen? (Bis heute steht in der verbreitetsten Ausgabe der großen C-Dur Symphonie von Schubert vor der Einleitung c, obwohl Schubert ¢ schreibt – das daraus resultierende zu langsame Tempo wird dann meist beim Übergang durch ein [unnatürliches] Accelerando korrigiert.) . . . Was spricht, rein historisch, für Verdopplung der Bläser, was dagegen? . . . Welche Bedeutung hat die ursprüngliche Besetzungsstärke? . . . Wie wurde ein Rezitativ ursprünglich ausgeführt – wie soll man es heute tun? . . . Hat man Tempi früher (wann?) durchgehalten oder hat man sie modifiziert, indem man bald langsamer, bald schneller wurde – was soll man heute tun? . . . Der Komponist hatte Musikinstrumente zur Verfügung, die anders klangen als die heutigen – angesichts der Möglichkeit, heute wieder solche Instrumente auf hohem technischen Niveau einzusetzen, stellen sich viele Fragen . . . soll man es also tun? Warum?

So eine Frageliste ließe sich beliebig fortsetzen, letztlich bis zur Hauptfrage, ob es überhaupt eine *richtige* Interpretation gibt; es ist ohne Zweifel sehr interessant und auch wichtig, die Anordnungen und Wünsche des Komponisten herauszufinden und zu verstehen – ob man sie unbedingt erfüllen muß, auch lange, lange nach seinem Tode noch, ist eine andere Frage. Meine persönliche Antwort auf diese Frage ist ein kompliziert schillerndes Nein: die Interpretation, und mit ihr vielleicht sogar die Werke selbst verändern sich von Generation zu Generation: Alle Interpreten benützen seit jeher dieselben Quellen, dieselben Noten – wie sie gelesen werden verändert sich; wie sie gehört werden verändert sich.

Die Uraufführung etwa der g-Moll Symphonie (KV 550) Mozarts oder der Eroica war eine aufwühlende Sensation, jede Wiederaufführung vor einem Publikum, das diese Werke kennt, mag andere, möglicherweise neue Aspekte bringen, die Beunruhigung, ja den Schock des Unerhörten aber kann sie nie wieder auslösen. Musik will überraschen, dem Hörer etwas nie gehörtes sagen, seine mithörende Erwartung einmal erfüllen, das nächste Mal täuschen: sie ist für den Hörer geschrieben, der sie nicht kennt, der in ein Abenteuer, in eine echte 'Sensation' gezogen werden soll. Schon beim zweiten Mal erlebt man das Werk ganz anders, jetzt geht es schon nicht mehr in erster Linie um das 'was', sondern um das 'wie'. Nach wenigen Jahren ist das Werk 'alt', seine einst aufregenden Neuheiten sind Allgemeingut. Heute hören wir also die Kompositionen der Klassiker völlig anders, es ist, als hätten *sie* sich verändert. In Wahrheit liegt es an uns, es ist einerseits das erwartende Hören von Bekanntem, andrerseits die Entwicklung der Musik seit damals, die den Eindruck verändern. Mozarts g-Moll Symphonie, ca. 1788 zum erstenmal gehört, ist etwas gänzlich anderes als heute, wo man das Werk 'kennt' und seine Sensationen durch die 'modernen' Kompositionen zahlreicher Generationen 'überholt' sind. Das Werk sagt also heute ganz Anderes. Welchen Wert hätte es daher, es wieder so aufzuführen wie einst? Einen rein historischen . . . also keinen.

Wir können wahrscheinlich aus eigener Hörerfahrung die Interpretations-geschichte von ungefähr zwei Generationen überblicken. (Ich selbst erinnere mich deutlich an Aufführungen seit etwa 1946). Dabei zeigt es sich, daß es auch in der Interpretation so etwas wie eine Mode gibt, wobei die Menschen nachfolgender Generationen fast immer verächtlich auf ältere Interpretationen reagieren. Beim Anhören alter Schallplatten – etwa vom Beginn unseres Jahrhunderts – fällt auf, daß viele heutige Hörer alles was anders ist als man es jetzt gewohnt ist, schlecht und lächerlich finden. Belacht werden ungewöhnliche Tempi und Tempomodifikationen, hörbare Lagenwechsel bei Streichern, glissando-artige Tonverbindungen bei Sängern, Auszierungen des Notentextes, etc. Bedenkt man, daß diese Interpretationen einmal gefeierte Spitzenleistungen waren, muß man erkennen, daß unsere herabsetzende Ablehnung nicht dem jeweiligen Künstler, sondern dem damaligen Zeitgeschmack gilt, und dieser ändert sich eben, ständig!

Das Phänomen des Zeitgeschmackes betrifft ja nicht nur die Musik, sondern alle Künste. Wie herabsetzend wurden etwa in Italien im 16. Jahrhundert die Tafelbilder des 14. Jahrhunderts beurteilt, sie wurden damals stapelweise verbrannt, um das Gold der Grundierung herauszuschmelzen. Stilbegriffe wie 'Gotik' und 'Barock' sind Schimpfausdrücke der nachfolgenden Generation. Die Kunst vergangener Zeit inter-essierte nur insoferne, als sie dem gerade gängigen Zeitgeschmack entsprach; man kann den Wandel des Geschmackes ähnlich dem von Modeströmungen verfolgen. Beispiele:

Raffael mußte, als er seine Fresken in den Stanzen des Vatikans malte, Fresken von Piero della Francesca – die er so bewunderte, daß er sie kopieren ließ – herausschlagen. Sie waren schon ca. 50 Jahre alt, also altmodisch (etwa im Verhältnis: Mendelssohn–Mozart). Oder: die Vorliebe der Romantik für das 'Einfache', Farblose: ursprünglich waren die griechischen Skulpturen und Marmorbauten bunt – sie hatten nun Marmorweiß zu sein; die bunten Statuen der Gotik und viele Flügelaltäre wurden bis aufs bloße Eichen- oder Lindenholz abgelaugt, weil man das 'natürliche' Holz liebte, und die originale Farbfassung als geschmacklos ablehnte. Beides Manifestationen unbegründeten Selbstbewußtseins: das modisch Aktuelle und Gefällige wird über die künstlerische Wahrheit gestellt.

In der Musik gab es um 1800 eine große Begeisterung für Händel – weniger für Bach, später wieder umgekehrt mehr für Bach . . . Das Klanggewand, die Instrumentation wurde sowieso jeweils angepaßt: jede Generation hatte ihre Händel-Bearbeitungen, seit Mendelssohn auch ihre Bach-Bearbeitungen, gegen Ende des 19. Jahrhunderts gab es die Matthäuspassion in der Bach-Stadt Leipzig mit Pauken, Trompeten, Hörnern und Klarinetten und mit orchestrierten Secco-Rezitativen. Auch darüber meinen wir herablassend lächeln zu dürfen, als wären die Zeitgenossen Brahms', Bruckners und Johann Strauß' weniger musikalisch gewesen oder hätten weniger Geschmack besessen als wir heute.

Die Beobachtung der Modetrends sagt mir: Niemand ist im Besitz einer allge-mein gültigen musikalischen Wahrheit. Man ist nicht in der Lage, die Werke der Vergangenheit in all ihren Aspekten zu überblicken, zu verstehen – man greift unbewußt jene Aspekte heraus, die dem gegenwärtigen Zeitgeschmack entsprechen. Die ganz große Kunst ist derart reich, daß sie nahezu jedem Zeitgeschmack etwas zu bieten hat; so überdauerten die großen Klassiker das 19. Jahrhundert und einen Großteil des 20. Jahrhunderts, stets von einer anderen Seite beleuchtet, stets ihr Gesicht wechselnd, immer wieder andere Teilaspekte für das Ganze darbietend. Was hat man mit Haydn, Mozart, Beethoven und Schubert allein in den letzten 80 Jahren gemacht, seit es Schallplatten gibt! Auf jede Modeströmung gabs eine Reaktion: zu romantisch, zu objektiv, zu frei, zu streng, zu groß besetzt, zu klein besetzt; und immer wieder behauptete man, so und nicht anders müße es sein, und was die Vorgänger machten, fand man lächerlich und falsch.

In diesem abwechslungsreichen, wenn nicht gar von Heiß-Kalt-Schocks durch-setzten Konzert durch die Generationen spielte die Musikwissenschaft zuerst über-haupt nicht mit. Sie begnügte sich damit zu forschen, die Ergebnisse zu publizieren und im praktischen Bereich dem allgemeinen Trend zu folgen. Das änderte sich nach und nach, als in den 20er und 30er Jahren dieses Jahrhunderts einzelne Musiker sich bei Wissenschaftlern Rat holten. Man begann von Stil auch bei der Interpretation zu sprechen. Nun, den Zielort dieser Reise kennt jeder: heute gibt es viele Aufführungen klassischer Musik, die als 'authentisch' und wissenschaftlich untermauert bezeichnet werden. Vor 40 Jahren waren die Anfänge dieser Richtung überhaupt nicht ernst genommen worden – heute streitet man darüber, ob es 'richtig' ist, diese oder jene Mozart-Symphonie mit vier oder sechs 1. Violinen zu spielen, wer das a = 430 Hz für diese Musik nicht anwendet, wird von Manchen als arger Verfälscher angeprangert. Es gibt eine 'Szene' des historischen Musikmachens, die fast so ausgebreitet ist wie das alteingesessene Konzertleben. Hier 'kennt' jeder alle erreichbaren Quellen und möglichst alle Forschungsergebnisse. Die doch erheblichen Unterschiede der Interpretation ergeben sich aus der verschiedenen Auslegung der Quellen und aus dem persönlichen Temperament der Interpreten.

Haben wir also jetzt das reine, wirkliche Musikmachen gefunden, ist die schwankende Reise der Interpretation durch Willkür und Modetrend zu Ende? Wissen wir jetzt endgültig wie es gemacht werden muß, was richtig und was falsch ist? Oder sind wir am Ende noch immer auf der Reise und unsere Nachfolger lachen genauso über uns, wie wir über unsere Vorgänger gelacht haben? Sind wir nicht besonders lächerlich geworden dadurch, daß wir uns, auf Grund unserer kleinen Entdeckungen über die Orchestersitzordnung und all die anderen Sachen, einbilden, jetzt wüßten wir es *wirklich*? Ja, wir wissen einiges, was man vor 50 oder 100 Jahren nicht wußte, aber wir wissen auch einiges nicht mehr, was sie damals noch wußten. Hoffentlich hält es sich einigermaßen die Waage und wir haben nicht mehr verloren als wir gewonnen haben.

Auf jeden Fortschritt ist man stolz; ich habe seit jeher gefunden, daß man diesen Schritten sehr skeptisch gegenüberstehen sollte, da man ja wohl mit jeder Errungenschaft auch etwas aufgeben muß, und es sich erst irgendwann nachträglich herausstellen wird, ob der Gewinn bedeutender ist oder der Verlust.

Als Beispiel nenne ich die immer größere Präzision im Zusammenspiel, die man in den letzten 20 Jahren anstrebt; soll wirklich *alles* so toll genau zusammen sein? Jeder Ton genau zugleich mit den darüber und daruntergeschriebenen Tönen? Was ist, wenn der Komponist in seiner Phantasie manches ganz genau und anderes etwas verschwommen sich vorgestellt hat? Wenn das nicht nur viel schöner, sondern auch richtiger wäre? Unser vermeintliches Wissen ist also sehr relativ. Der Großteil unserer Kenntnisse über die Musik vergangener Zeiten stammt ja aus Beschreibungen; – musikalische Vorgänge lassen sich aber nicht eindeutig beschreiben. So entnehmen verschiedene Menschen *denselben* Quellen total verschiedene Resultate.

Versuchen wir uns ein paar Details genauer anzusehen: es wird von einigen Komponisten (etwa Händel oder Schubert) berichtet, sie hätten, anders als ihre Zeitgenossen, Temposchwankungen abgelehnt. Das kann bedeuten, daß sie tatsächlich in 'metronomischem' Tempo spielten, aber es könnte ebenso bedeuten, daß man damals an derart große Temposchwankungen gewöhnt war, daß die ihren – mögen sie aus heutiger Sicht auch beachtlich gewesen sein – nicht als solche empfunden wurden. Oder: Zahlreiche Quellen seit dem 16. Jahrhundert sprechen über das Vibrato von Sängern, Streichern und Bläsern; einige geben genaue, gut verständliche Kriterien an, wo es anzuwenden sei. Bedeutet das nun, daß alle anderen Stellen ohne Vibrato zu spielen seien? Es wäre ja immerhin denkbar, daß man eine leichte Bebung gar nicht als 'Vibrato' bezeichnete und als selbstverständlich voraussetzte . . . Die Quellen behandeln ja nur das, was den Autoren wichtig erschien, Selbstverständlichkeiten – die allerdings heute meist nicht mehr bekannt sind – werden gar nicht behandelt.

Was die historischen Klänge betrifft: Ich glaube, daß wir ziemlich genau wissen, wie gewisse Orgeln und Blockflöten des 16. bis 19. Jahrhunderts geklungen haben (wie sie wirklich gespielt wurden, werden wir nie mehr erfahren), aber alle jene Instrumente, deren Tonbildung vom Spieler wesentlich bestimmt wird, können *so*, aber auch ganz anders geklungen haben. Ich habe oft mit Staunen zugehört, welche Klänge Oboisten verschiedener Schule aus verschiedenen Instrumenten hervorbringen: Oboist A (ein Wiener) und Oboist B (ein Kölner) vergleichen erst ihre 'modernen' Instrumente, dann verschiedene Barockoboen. Es zeigt sich, daß der vom Spieler verursachte Unterschied viel größer ist als der der Instrumente.

Ich meine zu wissen, wie ein Walzer oder eine Schnellpolka um 1860 in Wien getanzt und gespielt wurde – aber *weiß* ich es wirklich? Man kennt die Tanzschritte und es gibt eine lückenlose Überlieferung durch mehrere Musikergenerationen, wie man diese Musik spielt – dennoch, es sind juristisch gesprochen, lediglich Indizien, die mir sagen, es müßte wohl so gewesen sein, aber ein hieb- und stichfestes, beweisbares Wissen ist es nicht. Tänzer aus der Zeit würden uns wahrscheinlich klarmachen, daß die bekannten Schritte, von Generation zu Generation fast unmerklich verändert, heute, nach mehr als hundert Jahren, eben doch anders ausgeführt werden. Das gilt, noch eingreifender, auch für die Musik: wir *wissen* nicht genau, wie die Kriterien, die damals wie heute für eine gute Aufführung gelten, jeweils beurteilt wurden: die Stetigkeit des Tempos; die Exaktheit der Notenwerte; die Intonation (also die Feinabstufung der Tonhöhen), die Artikulation und die Tonbildung; Tonqualität, Tonschönheit, Vibrato, etc. Es spricht vieles dafür, daß sich die Maßstäbe innerhalb dieser relativ kurzen Zeit (ca. 130 Jahre) stark verändert haben. Also etwa: daß man ein stark modifiziertes, schwankendes Tempo damals als Gleichmäßig bezeichnete; daß die gespielten Noten*werte* damals viel weniger mit dem Notenbild übereinstimmten als heute; daß hingegen die Intonation genauer war, aber nicht der gleichmäßigen Temperatur folgte, sondern anderen Systemen; daß die einzelnen Töne ganz anders angespielt und miteinander verbunden wurden als man dies heute macht, und daß auch die Tonqualität selbst sowohl der Streicher als auch der Bläser eine ganz andere war, aufgrund einer anderen Klangvorstellung und eines anderen Vibratos.

Wir versuchen also, einen Strauß-Walzer genau nach den Absichten des Komponisten zu spielen; wir wählen die authentische Besetzungsstärke, denselben Saal (denn die Besetzungsstärke ergibt nur einen Sinn im Zusammenhang mit der Saalakustik), dieselben Instrumente, die geforderten und überlieferten Tempi, befolgen die von Strauß eingeschriebenen Tempomodifikationen, und dennoch ... Strauß persönlich betritt den Saal, lacht 'Was spielt's Ihr denn da . . .'. Er bringt sein Orchester und spielt uns den Walzer so vor, wie sie ihn damals gespielt haben, wirklich 'authentisch'. Jetzt wundern wir uns, lachen vielleicht auch, jedenfalls sind wir höchst überrascht, weil es völlig anders ist, als wir es uns vorgestellt haben, und weil es so gar nicht unserem Geschmack entspricht (etwa der vibratofreie Klang der Geigen, die hörbaren Lagenwechsel, die Tempoveränderungen, etc.) 'Das kann man ja einem *heutigen* Publikum nicht zumuten' sagt jede der beiden Gruppen. Den Menschen von 1865 ist unsere Aufführung ebensowenig zumutbar, wie uns 1995 die von damals. Sehr merkwürdig, fast unglaublich, aber ich müßte mich sehr täuschen, wenn's nicht wahr wäre.

Das hat meines Erachtens überhaupt nichts mit 'besser' und 'schlechter' zu tun, sondern mit prinzipiellen Unterschieden. Eben mit dem, was ich vorhin als 'Mode' bezeichnet habe. Wir sind geneigt, auf Grund der Erfahrungen der letzten 80 Jahre, eine ständige Verbesserung der Interpretationskunst vorauszusetzen. (Die Orchester fanden ursprünglich etwa Bruckners Symphonien unspielbar, heute spielen sie sie problemlos, etc.) Ich will in diesem Rahmen nicht näher auf solche Hypothesen eingehen und nur behaupten, daß ich auf Grund meiner Quellenstudien (dieselben Quellen wie sie alle Anderen haben, auf meine Art gelesen) glaube, die führenden Orchester (die Hofkapelle Maximilians I. um 1500; Monteverdis Mantuaner Gruppe um 1610; die Erzbischöfliche Kapelle in Kremsier um 1660; die Hofkapelle in Köthen um 1720; Haydns Orchester um 1760; Mendelssohns Orchester um 1840, etc. etc.) seien seit einigen hundert Jahren auf einem gleichmäßig hohen Niveau. Was sich ändert, ist der Geschmack und die Mode – im Spielen und im Hören.

Ein anderes Beispiel: (1) Bach spielt sein 5. Brandenburgisches Konzert mit seinen Kollegen in Köthen. Alle sind zutiefst aufgewühlt, man hat so etwas noch nie gehört, weder technisch noch emotional. Diese leidenschaftliche und zugleich so rührend empfindsame Musik bewegte Musiker und Hörer, man ist außer sich, erschüttert, ergriffen (und alles wurde richtig gemacht, nach den damaligen Regeln der Kunst, wie sie jedem Musiker geläufig waren – und wie man sie dann, 230 Jahre später, wieder aus den 'Quellen' zu destillieren versucht). (2) Ein großer Pianist spielt mit seinen Kollegen dasselbe Stück 1950. Die Spieler und Hörer sind zutiefst ergriffen . . . (so ziemlich alles wurde 'falsch' gemacht, weil keiner der Musiker sich um 'Regeln' gekümmert hat, man wußte ja gar nichts von solchen, man hat einfach intuitiv diese große Musik gespielt). (3) Eine Gruppe mit 'historischen Instrumenten' spielt dasselbe Stück 1985 (alles wurde 'richtig' gemacht, korrekt nach den jetzt allgemein bekannten und ziemlich verbindlich ausgelegten Quellen). Es gibt keine Zweifel – so gehört es, nur *so* soll man es machen.

Was war 'richtig' und was 'falsch' an diesen drei Aufführungen? Die Intuition sagt: Aufführung Eins und Zwei waren gut (weil sie bewegten), Aufführung Drei war schlecht (weil kalt). Das Wissen sagt: Aufführung Eins und Drei waren gut (weil 'richtig'), Aufführung Zwei war schlecht (weil voll stilistischer Fehler). Natürlich war nur Aufführung Eins wirklich richtig. Aufführung Drei hatte gewiß nicht weniger Fehler als Aufführung Zwei, nur daß sie sich arrogant als richtig bezeichnete und den hohen emotionalen Wahrheitsgehalt von Aufführung Zwei nicht erkannte. Natürlich wäre auch eine sehr kalte Aufführung in der Art der zweiten denkbar, und eine sehr emotionsstarke in der dritten Art. Nur, die Zweite mißachtete ja prinzipiell das Wissen und setzte *nur* auf Intuition, während die Dritte auf ihre Wissenschaftlichkeit pocht – es ist ein anderer Anspruch.

Man sieht, das Thema ist kompliziert, und es ist kaum möglich, zu verbindlichen Schlußfolgerungen zu kommen. Das Problem scheint nämlich darin zu liegen, daß die abendländische Musik von ihrem Wesen her in ihre Entstehungszeit gehört. Sie ist eigentlich zum einmaligen Hören bestimmt wie eine Rede. Jede Zeit hat also im Grunde nur ihre eigene Musik. Da gibt es keine Probleme der Aufführungspraxis und keine Notwendigkeit der Auslegung und Erklärung – der Zeitgenosse versteht sie, weil er mit ihr lebt.

Die Musik hat ihre alte, unmittelbar sprachliche Funktion verloren. Heute will man immer wieder dieselben Stücke hören, man weiß schon, wie schön sie sind; die andere, dialoghaft, oft auch erschreckende Seite, ist durch das oftmalige Hören verloren gegangen. Ein Repertoire, wie wir es heute haben, mit einem Grundstock von so und so vielen Werken, die immer wieder gespielt werden, widerspricht allerdings der Grundidee dieser flüchtigen Kunst: Die Forderung nach stets neuer Musik galt ja auch mit wenigen Ausnahmen bis ins vorige Jahrhundert, und die Komponisten (bis Haydn und Mozart) haben nicht damit gerechnet, daß ihre Werke noch nach 200 Jahren gespielt werden. Die Geschichte hat sich dann anders entwickelt; aus Gründen, die hier nicht zu erörtern sind, und die *alle* Künste betreffen, gibt es nun ein 'Repertoire', wird vorwiegend 'Alte' Musik gespielt. Heute, da die meisten der gespielten Werke den meisten Hörern bekannt sind, überraschen sie nicht mehr.

Für die Musiker gibt es die Möglichkeit, dieser musealen Einstellung zu entsprechen und die Schönheiten der Vergangenheit möglichst 'authentisch' anzubieten – 'so war es damals'. Abgesehen davon, daß dies ein Trugschluß ist, weil wir ja niemals erfahren können, wie es damals wirklich war – kann dies, meiner Ansicht nach, dieses aufwendige Musikleben nicht rechtfertigen.

*   *   *

Ein Resumée: Geschichte – natürlich besonders Kunst und Musikgeschichte – ist immer Zeitgeschichte, das heißt, sie erzählt nur scheinbar vom historischen Gegenstand, in Wahrheit behandelt sie die Gegenwart. Daraus könnte man für die heutigen Musiker einiges ablesen: da man ja die Werke ohnehin in die Gegenwart transponiert, ist die paraphrasierende Interpretation des Instinktmusikers durchaus vertretbar – man darf sie nur nicht als 'richtig' bezeichnen, was immer das heißen mag. Man könnte auch, und dies entspricht meinem Standpunkt, als Basis jeder Interpretation eine umfassende Kenntnis aller erreichbaren Grundlagen, die das Werk betreffen, fordern. Also das geistesgeschichtliche Umfeld, die Geschichte der Entstehung, die Umstände der ersten Aufführungen, deren Wirkung, die erklärten Absichten des Komponisten . . . und viele technische Details, von der historischen Bedeutung der Notation, der verbalen Erläuterungen, der Tempobezeichnungen, etc. bis zu den Eigenheiten der historischen Instrumente und der sie seinerzeit spielenden Musiker. Auf Intuition, also den gesamten Emotionsbereich kann man auch hier nicht verzichten, er ist immerhin auch 'historisch' und er ist überhaupt das Wichtigste. – Die daraus resultierende Interpretation darf man auch nicht als 'richtig' bezeichnen, selbst wenn sie alle historischen Informationen umzusetzen versucht. Sie kann ebenso berührend – vielleicht sogar noch intensiver – sein, als die der reinen Instinktmusiker, ja sie sollte wohl näher an das Werk heranführen als diese – aber, sie bleibt, wie diese, eine Interpretation *unserer* Zeit. Sie hat ebensowenig endgültigen Charakter als jede andere Interpretation, kommende Generationen werden sie genauso behandeln und beurteilen, wie wir die Interpretationen unserer Vorgänger.

Ich glaube, daß sich in den letzten 100 Jahren nach und nach herausstellt, daß es Meisterwerke gibt, die nicht altern, die über Generationen hinweg aktuell bleiben, deren Inhalte so wichtig sind, daß sie immer wieder vermittelt werden müssen. So könnte es sein, daß wir all die Informationen über die 'richtige' Darstellung doch sehr nötig haben, um wieder über das *Wie* hinaus zur Substanz zu kommen. Das Wissen – das ja letztlich nur ein Scheinwissen ist – kann uns zu Erkenntnissen führen, die in jeder Zeit eine aktuelle, gegenwärtige Interpretation aus dem ursprünglichen Geist des Werkes möglich machen. Vielleicht sogar mit Mitteln, die weit jenseits des Historischen sind. Hier ist die Synthese des Wissens mit der Intuition gefordert – denn diese ist schließlich die einzige tragfähige Brücke, die uns mit den Meisterwerken verbinden kann.

CHRISTOPHER RAEBURN

H.C. Robbins Landon and the Haydn Society:
a pioneering musical adventure

H.C. ROBBINS LANDON is one of the most open and unsecretive people you are likely to meet, yet parts of his early career are seemingly shrouded in obscurity. It is generally known that in his early twenties he founded the Haydn Society, but the history and achievements of this organization are unfamiliar, even to those of us who have known Robbie for forty years or more.

His enthusiasm for Haydn dates back to his schooldays, and he subsequently chose to study music at Boston University precisely because the head of the music faculty was Karl Geiringer, a world authority on Haydn. While still a university student, Robbie created a local sensation by being the moving spirit behind the first modern performance in Boston of Handel's *Messiah* in the composer's own instru- mentation; it was conducted by Samuel Adler with Robbie playing the continuo. He also took part in a trumpet and organ recital in spring 1947 in which he played the 'Purcell' Trumpet Voluntary. His instrument was specially fashioned for him by his father, a distinguished locomotive designer and highly inventive man, who used a tubular curtain rod to convert a Confederate Army bugle into a D trumpet.

But it was after his graduation in June 1947, when Robbie came to Europe, that the potential of his influence on musical scholarship began to become clear. While in Vienna as a young US Army officer, he devoted his spare time to researching Haydn and other musical activities. At that time no complete edition of Haydn's music existed and performances and recordings were confined to a very limited repertoire. In 1948, having embarked on postgraduate work at Boston, Robbie decided to set up the Haydn Society. In a foreword to the society's prospectus, issued in February 1949, he outlined why such an organization was needed:

> The necessity of forming a Haydn Society one hundred and forty years after the composer's death seems at first glance preposterous, for surely no group of musi- cians and musicologists should be needed to spread the gospel of a man who is ranked with the dozen greatest musicians of all time.

He then pointed out that the works included in the complete edition planned by Breitkopf & Härtel and begun in 1907 were limited to the first forty-nine symphonies, the complete piano sonatas, *The Creation*, *The Seasons* and a volume of songs – in short, only a dozen volumes out of a projected set of ninety. He continued:

> Barely one-seventh of Haydn's music has ever been printed at all, and most of what was actually published has been unavailable for a hundred years. Performances of his more than 1,000 works are limited, except in Central Europe, to a few symphonies, a handful of piano sonatas and string quartets, and a very occasional performance of *The Creation*. With the single exception of the string quartets, only a tiny fragment of his compositions has been recorded. Authoritative studies of his music (not his life) are limited to a half dozen treatises published in Germany, and no one has dared, or perhaps wanted, to publish definitive studies of the symphonies, the string quartets, the piano sonatas, the divertimenti, the concerti, the oratorios, etc. in any language whatever.
>
> It is this lamentable condition which the Haydn Society wishes to remedy. For the time being, it is the plan of the Society to issue an album of records three or four times a year; to print studies on various phases of the composer's music, in addition to publishing scores which have been either unpublished or out of print for many years. The Society will make a practice of issuing each item first by advance subscription, at a cost substantially lower than when made available through ordinary commercial channels. Since the Haydn Society is a non-profit organization, all funds will be used for the preparation of future material.

With a number of colleagues from Boston, in particular Bernhard Schwartz, Robbie organized the society's first commercial record, a performance of Haydn's 'Harmoniemesse', taken from a tape recording made at the Salzburg Festival in 1947 and broadcast by Austrian Radio; it was issued in April 1949 and proved to be an instant success. The records were 78s, but pressed on red vinyl, and were presented in a lavish album containing copious notes plus a facsimile of the entire first edition published by Breitkopf & Härtel in 1808.

The society was run by a board of directors that included Alan Forbes, son of the director of the State Street Trust in Boston, and Vose Grenough who owned a small firm in Cambridge, Massachusetts, called Technichord Records. It was this firm that packed and dispatched the records to subscribers.

In 1949 Robbie decided to abandon his doctoral studies in order to concentrate on the work of the Haydn Society. Armed with a grant from the Library of Congress, he moved to Europe so that the research and recording activities of the society could be more closely co-ordinated. The following year, Ernst Hartmann of Universal Edition became the director of the publishing activity of the society; the central office was run by Gertrude Meister from Rot Weiss Rot Radio, with Virginia Pleasants, the well-known harpsichordist, as her supervisor. Numerous research trips were undertaken, systematically exploring the libraries of Austrian monasteries. Robbie was assisted by Christa Fuhrmann (later his wife) and the photographer Josef Vouk, who painstakingly worked his way through pages of material that had lain unused since the eighteenth century. In the first year a set of manuscript parts of Haydn's previously lost Violin Concerto in A (Hob. VIIa:3) was discovered in Melk Abbey; and in 1957 I joined the group on a visit to Göttweig, where a copy of the *Missa brevis alla cappella*: 'Rorate coeli desuper' (Hob. XXII:3), a youthful work by Haydn that had been presumed lost, was uncovered. The then abbot of Göttweig was well known for his good living, and these trips were accompanied by the warmest hospitality. But any voyage of discovery with Robbie was unusual. I even initiated one myself in 1956, when I was in a group of correspondents taken to Eisenstadt for the first time since the Allied forces had left Austria. In Schloß Esterházy we were shown a library that was of no special interest to my colleagues, but I noticed that behind the lattice wire doors to the shelves were rows of manuscript books that looked like large school exercise books. I saw the names of several composers, and told Robbie that I thought they would be worth investigating. The Russians had taken anything of obvious intrinsic value years before, but he was convinced that we would find something of musicological interest, and excitedly speculated on what might be uncovered. We made an appointment, but when we arrived the key was missing; the cupboards had not been opened for at least a decade. The padlocks were eventually broken and Robbie found various treasures, including parts corrected by Haydn for all six of the late masses. In addition, the cupboards contained parts for Beethoven's Mass in C, heavily corrected and annotated by the composer, presumably at the time of the first performance in Eisenstadt in 1807.

Robbie would never use dry academic terminology on these travels. For him research was a great game. His perpetual sense of fun allowed him to mix the most serious aspects of his work with colourful commentary in pastiche Damon Runyon. An unexpected harmony or a striking change of key, not to mention a newly discovered manuscript, was, as in contemporary cereal advertisements, 'real crunchy stuff'.

Four volumes of the Haydn Society's collected edition were prepared and published between 1949 and 1951, with Jens Peter Larsen as the General Editor.

Series I, vol. 5	Symphonies nos. 50–57 (ed. Helmut Schultz, 1951).
Series I, vol. 9	Symphonies nos. 82–87 (ed. Robbins Landon, 1950).
Series I, vol. 10	Symphonies nos. 88–92 (ed. Robbins Landon, 1951).
Series XXIII, vol. 1	*Missa brevis* in F, *Missa in honorem BVM* ('Große Orgelsolomesse'), *Missa Sanctae Caeciliae* and *Missa Sancti Nicolai* (ed. Carl Maria Brand, 1951).

But the publishing side of the society's activity was very costly, and volumes 9 and 10 of the symphonies were published only with the timely support of Robbie's aunt Louise, a bequest of $15,000 from the estate of her husband (and Robbie's namesake), Howard Chandler Robbins. It was becoming clear that a complete edition would not be financially feasible and publication was suspended.

The recording side of the society started in earnest in 1950 with Vose Greenough closing down his company, Technichord, and moving to Vienna to become the society's chief recording engineer, duties he carried out voluntarily. This was typical of all those involved with the Haydn Society. Its work was highly professional, but it had also the zeal of the committed amateur. Most of the recordings were made in a studio in the Konzerthaus and were pressed by Columbia. The business manager for the recording projects in Vienna was Otto Preiser, an acquaintance from Robbie's army days. He went on to found Preiser Records, a firm that specializes in re-issues of recordings made by great singers and conductors of the past.

Financed by a legacy of $5,000 that Robbie had received from his uncle Francis Le Baron Robbins, the recording projects started with a flourish. The *Nelson* Mass, with Lisa della Casa and George London amongst the soloists, was a first recording, as were those of the *Missa Cellensis* ('Mariazellermesse') and Symphonies nos. 1, 13, 28, 44 and 48. The society spread beyond Haydn to record what was then comparatively unfamiliar music by Mozart; the *Coronation* Mass (K.317) was recorded for a total cost of $400, with the Vienna Philharmonic Orchestra having, for contractual reasons, to be renamed the Mozart Festival Orchestra. The society acquired the rights from Austrian Radio for the tapes of *The Creation*, conducted by Clemens Krauss with the Vienna Philharmonic and soloists Trude Eipperle, Julius Patzak and Georg Hann. Unbelievably, this too was a première commercial recording and in 1950 it won the Grand Prix du Disque in Paris. The recording of Haydn's Trumpet Concerto, with Helmut Wobisch of the Vienna Philharmonic Orchestra as soloist, sold 30,000 copies in the first year.

Robbie remained in touch with old friends from the former headquarters of the US Army in Vienna, including Richard Wadleigh, who joined the society, and a colleague of his, Erhard Jaeger, the son of a Harvard professor of philosophy, who decided to invest $50,000 in the society. Other new members included Thomas Crowder, whose sister invested significantly in the society, enabling it to make the first recording of Mozart's Mass in C minor (K.427), a complete *Don Giovanni* (with Mariano Stabile in the title role) and Haydn's *Orfeo ed Euridice*.

Contemporary remarks from *The Record Year* (1952), written by Edward Sackville-West and Desmond Shawe-Taylor, indicate the standing of the society and its recordings:

In America the recorded repertory of Haydn's music has been increased enor-
mously by the LP discs issued by the Haydn Society of Boston . . . It is heartening
to see so many Haydn symphonies, never before recorded, finding their way to the
catalogues. The authors describe the recording of Haydn's 'Orfeo' as "one of the
most ambitious enterprises in the whole gramophone repertory".

The most valuable contribution to the discography of Mozart for many years is
the complete *Idomeneo* of the Haydn Society . . . When we heard that Mariano
Stabile had been selected for the role of Don Giovanni, we feared that he might
prove too old for the part; but in fact he sounds amazingly youthful, and sings the
music, especially the recitatives, with such infectious charm as to ensure the
prompt capitulation, not only of Zerlina and Elvira, but also of the listener. The
performance is complete and scholarly.

The increasing prestige of the recording output of the society demanded a more
efficient distribution in Europe, and Walter Legge of EMI undertook this task; but he
was still suspicious of the merits of LPs and distributed the material as 78s. He tried to
persuade Richard Wadleigh to join EMI but in the event Wadleigh stayed with the
society. The recording industry was evolving at an unprecedentedly rapid pace and by
1952 it was becoming increasingly clear that a specialist label with limited financial
resources would not be able to compete with the large companies, many of which were
beginning to issue recordings of Haydn's music. In a sense the original goal of the
society's missionary work had already been achieved: there was undoubtedly a market
for Haydn on LPs. Robbie left the society in order to devote all his energies to his first
major book, *The Symphonies of Joseph Haydn*, and the organization was eventually
wound up. The whole enterprise had been significant not only for Haydn's reputation
but in the general development of the commercial recording industry. It was founded
on Robbie's initiative and enthusiasm, and had flourished with the extraordinary
generosity and commitment of his family and friends.

APPENDIX

COMPLETE LP RECORD CATALOGUE OF THE HAYDN SOCIETY
(SPRING 1951)

This catalogue contains the recordings prepared under the supervision of H.C. Robbins Landon, together with those issued from material supplied by Austrian Radio. The gaps in the sequence of catalogue numbers represent projected recordings that were never made.

'Let's listen to Haydn.' Instrumental music with narration by Louise Robbins. 10-inch LP. $3.85. HSC-1

Haydn: Symphonies no. 1 in D, no. 13 in D and no. 28 in A. Vienna Symphony Orchestra. Conductor: Sternberg, 12-inch LP. $5.85. HSLP 1001

Haydn: Symphonies no. 31 in D and no. 34 in D minor. Vienna Symphony Orchestra. Conductor: Sternberg. 12-inch LP. $5.85. HSLP 1002

Haydn: Symphonies no. 44 in E minor and no. 48 in C. Vienna Symphony Orchestra. Conductor: Sternberg. 12-inch LP. $5.85. HSLP 1003

Haydn: Symphony no. 82 in C. Vienna Symphony Orchestra. Conductor: Sternberg.
Haydn: Symphony no. 85 in B flat. Orchestra of the Vienna State Opera. Conductor: Baltzer. 12-inch LP. $5.95. HSLP 1008

Haydn: Symphonies no. 22 in E flat and no. 35 in B flat. Vienna Symphony Orchestra. Conductor: Sternberg. 12-inch LP. $5.95. HSLP 1009

Haydn: Symphonies no. 38 in C and no. 39 in G minor. Vienna Symphony Orchestra. Conductor: Sternberg. 12-inch LP. HSLP 1010

Mozart: Serenade in D (K.320). Orchestra of the Vienna State Opera. Posthorn: Wobisch. Conductor: Sternberg. 12-inch LP. $5.95. HSLP 1012

Haydn: Violin Concerto in G; Harpsichord Concerto in G. Collegium Musicum of Vienna. Violin: Bertschinger. Harpsichord: Erna Heiller. Conductor: Anton Heiller. 12-inch LP. $5.95. HSLP 1014

Haydn: Symphonies no. 83 in G minor and no. 84 in E flat. Collegium Musicum of Vienna. Conductor: Heiller. 12-inch LP. $5.95. HSLP 1015

Haydn: Symphonies no. 7 in C and no. 8 in G. Vienna Chamber Orchestra. Conductor: Litschauer. 12-inch LP. $5.95. HSLP 1016

Haydn: Violin Concerto in A. Collegium Musicum of Vienna. Violin: Bertschinger. Conductor: Heiller. 10-inch LP. $4.75. HSLP 1017

Haydn: Symphonies no. 87 in A and no. 89 in F. Orchestra of the Vienna State Opera. Conductor: Swarowsky. 12-inch LP. $5.95. HSLP 1018

Haydn: Symphonies no. 26 in D minor and no. 36 in E flat. Vienna Chamber Orchestra. Conductor: Heiller. 12-inch LP. $5.95. HSLP 1019

Haydn: Dances for the Redoutensaal [Hob. IX:11]. Orchestra of the Vienna State Opera. Conductor: Gillesberger. 12-inch LP. $5.95. HSLP 1022

Haydn: Four Notturni for the King of Naples (nos. 1, 2, 4 and 7). Vienna Chamber Orchestra. Conductor: Litschauer. 12-inch LP. $5.95. HSLP 1023

Bach: Concerto in C for three harpsichords and orchestra (BWV 1064); Concerto in A minor for four harpsichords and orchestra (BWV 1065). Vienna Chamber Orchestra. Conductor: Heiller. 12-inch LP. $5.95. HSLP 1024

Haydn: Symphonies no. 6 in D and no. 21 in A. Vienna Chamber Orchestra. Conductor: Litschauer. 12-inch LP. $5.95. HSLP 1025

Haydn: Symphonies no. 42 in D and no. 47 in G. Vienna Chamber Orchestra. Conductor: Litschauer. 12-inch LP. $5.95. HSLP 1026

Haydn: Horn Concerto in D; Trumpet Concerto in E flat. Horn: Koch. Trumpet: Wobisch. Conductor: Heiller. 12-inch LP. $5.95. HSLP 1038

Haydn: Symphony no. 52 in C minor. Orchestra of the Vienna State Opera. Conductor: Heiller. Haydn: Symphony no. 56 in C. Vienna Symphony Orchestra. Conductor: Heiller. 12-inch LP. $5.95. HSLP 1039

Mozart: Violin Concerto in D (K.218); Piano Concerto in G (K.453). Violin: Schneider. Piano: Kirkpatrick. Dumbarton Oaks Chamber Orchestra. 12-inch LP. $5.95. HSLP 1040

Haydn: Symphonies no. 43 in E flat and no. 50 in C. Chamber Orchestra of the Danish State Radio. Conductor: Wöldike. 12-inch LP. $5.95. HSLP 1041

Haydn: Mass in D minor (*Nelson*). Soloists: Della Casa, Höngen, Taubmann, London. Akademie Kammerchor. Orchestra of the Vienna State Opera. Conductor: Sternberg. 12-inch LP. $5.95. HSLP 2004

Haydn: *Die Schöpfung*. Soloists: Eipperle, Patzak, Hann. Chorus of the Vienna State Opera. Vienna Philharmonic Orchestra. Conductor: Krauss. Recording from Austrian Radio. Three 12-inch LPs. $17.84. HSLP 2005

Mozart: Mass in C minor (K.427). Soloists: Schwaiger, Töpper, Meyer-Welfing, London. Akademie Kammerchor. Vienna Symphony Orchestra. Conductor: Von Zallinger. Two 12-inch LPs. $11.90. HSLP 2006

Mozart: Mass in C (K.317). Akademie Kammerchor. Mozart Festival Orchestra. Conductor: Gillesberger. 10-inch LP. $4.75. HSLP 2007

Haydn: *Missa Cellensis* in C ('Mariazellermesse'). Soloists: Rathauscher, Janacek, Equiluz, Berry. Akademie Kammerchor. Vienna Symphony Orchestra. Conductor: Gilles-berger. 12-inch LP. $5.95. HSLP 2011

Mozart: *Idomeneo*. Soloists: Hopf, Taubmann, Heiller, Handt, Majkut, Grob-Prandl.

Chorus of the Vienna State Opera. Orchestra of the Vienna State Opera. Conductor: Von Zallinger. Four 12-inch LPs $23.80. HSLP 2020

Haydn: *Missa in tempore belli*. Soloists: Toplitz, Milinkovic, Handt, Braun. Akademie Kammerchor. Orchestra of the Vienna State Opera. Conductor: Gillesberger. 12-inch LP. $5.95. HSLP 2021

Haydn: *Die Jahreszeiten*. Soloists: Eipperle, Patzak, Hann. Chorus of the Vienna State Opera. Vienna Philharmonic Orchestra. Conductor: Krauss. Recording from Austrian Radio. Three 12-inch LPs. $17.85. HSLP 2027

Haydn: *Missa Sanctae Caeciliae*. Soloists: Schwaiger, Handt, Wagner, Berry. Akademie Kammerchor. Vienna Symphony Orchestra. Conductor: Gillesberger. Two 12-inch LPs. $11.90. HSLP 2028

Haydn: *Orfeo ed Euridice*. Soloists: Handt, Poell, Berry, Hellwig, Heusser, Wadleigh. Chorus of the Vienna State Opera. Orchestra of the Vienna State Opera. Conductor: Swarowsky. Three 12-inch LPs. $17.85. HSLP 2029

Mozart: *Don Giovanni*. Soloists: Stabile, Pernerstorfer, H. Konetzni, Heusser, Poell, Grob-Prandl, Czerwenka, Handt. Chorus of the Vienna State Opera. Vienna Symphony Orchestra. Conductor: Swarowsky. Four 12-inch LPs. $23.80. HSLP 2030

Mozart: Arias from *Don Giovanni*. Singers as in HSLP 2030. Vienna Symphony Orchestra. Conductor: Swarowsky. 12-inch LP. $5.95. HSLP 2031

Haydn: Piano Sonata in C minor [Hob. XVI:20]; Piano Sonata in C [Hob. XVI:50]. Piano: Pleasants. 10-inch LP. $4.75. HSLP 3031

Haydn: Piano Sonata in C [Hob. XVI:48]; Piano Sonata in D [Hob. XVI:51]. Piano: Pleasants. 10-inch LP. $4.75. HSLP 3032

Haydn: Piano Sonata in G minor [Hob. XVI:44]; Piano Sonata in E flat [Hob. XVI:45]. Piano: Pleasants. 10-inch LP. $4.75. HSLP 3033

H.C. Robbins Landon: A Bibliography

THIS BIBLIOGRAPHY includes most of H.C. Robbins Landon's published work on music to mid-1995. It omits newspaper articles, programme notes, reviews of recordings and performances, sleeve notes, lectures, television and radio broadcasts, correspondence and some minor articles. It is arranged in nine sections: Books; Edited Books; Editor; Articles in Dictionaries and Encyclopaedias; Articles in Journals and Contributions to Composite Volumes; Editions of Music; Reviews of Books; Reviews of Music; and Videocassettes. Each section is in chronological order with items published in the same year arranged alphabetically. Editions of music and reviews are divided by name of composer and title of periodical respectively.

BOOKS

1   *The Symphonies of Joseph Haydn*, London, Universal Edition, Rockliff, 1955; New York, Macmillan, 1956 (see nos. 213–14)

2   *The Symphonies of Joseph Haydn: Supplement*, London, Barrie and Rockliff, 1961; New York, Macmillan, 1961. Includes *Addenda and Corrigenda* (see nos. 1, 67, 74)

3   *Haydn Symphonies* (BBC Music Guides), London, BBC, 1966, 1975. Reprint ed., Seattle, University of Washington Press, 1969; London, Ariel Music, 1986

4   *Das kleine Haydnbuch*, Salzburg, Residenz, 1967. Swedish trans., Stockholm, Generalstabens Litografiska Anstalt, 1968. German trans., Stuttgart, Europäische Bildungsgemeinschaft, 1977; Hamburg, Rowohlt, 1979

5   *Beethoven: Sein Leben und seine Welt in zeitgenössischen Bildern und Texten*, Zurich, Universal, 1970. Abridged ed., Vienna, Universal, 1974 (see nos. 6, 23)

6   *Beethoven: a Documentary Study* (compiled and ed.), trans. from the German, London, Thames and Hudson, 1970; New York, Macmillan, 1970. Japanese trans., Tokyo, Shinjidai-sha, 1970. Abridged ed., London, Thames and Hudson, 1974; New York, Collier

Macmillan, 1975; Toronto, Oxford University Press, 1975 (see nos. 5, 23)

7   *Essays on the Viennese Classical Style: Gluck, Haydn, Mozart, Beethoven*, London, Barrie and Rockliff – The Cresset Press, 1970; New York, Macmillan, 1970. (Includes nos. 58, 104, 110 and trans. of no. 108)

8   *Haydn* (with Henry Raynor) (The Great Composer Series), London, Faber and Faber, 1972; New York, Praeger, 1972

9   *Haydn: Chronicle and Works*, vol. III: *Haydn in England, 1791–1795*, London, Thames and Hudson, 1976; Bloomington, Indiana University Press, 1976 (see nos. 11–14, 27)

10   *Das kleine Verdibuch*, Salzburg, Residenz, 1976; Hamburg, Rowohlt, 1982

11   *Haydn: Chronicle and Works*, vol. IV: *Haydn: the Years of 'The Creation', 1796–1800*, London, Thames and Hudson, 1977; Bloomington, Indiana University Press, 1977 (see nos. 9, 12–14, 27)

12   *Haydn: Chronicle and Works*, vol. V: *Haydn: the Late Years, 1801–1809*, London, Thames and Hudson, 1977; Bloomington, Indiana University Press, 1977 (see nos. 9–11, 13–14, 27)

13   *Haydn: Chronicle and Works*, vol. II: *Haydn at Eszterháza, 1766–1790*, London, Thames and

Hudson, 1978; Bloomington, Indiana University Press, 1978 (see nos. 9, 11–12, 14, 27)

14   *Haydn: Chronicle and Works*, vol. I: *Haydn: the Early Years, 1732–1765*, London, Thames and Hudson, 1980; Bloomington, Indiana University Press, 1980 (see nos. 9, 11–13, 27)

15   *Haydn: a Documentary Study*, London, Thames and Hudson, 1981; New York, Rizzoli, 1981. German trans., Vienna, Munich, Fritz Molden, 1981. French trans., Paris, Chêne/Hachette, 1981

16   *Mozart and the Masons: New Light on the Lodge 'Crowned Hope'*, London, Thames and Hudson, 1982; New York, Thames and Hudson, 1983. 2nd ed. (pbk), London, Thames and Hudson, 1991. Italian trans., Milan, Garzanti, 1990. French trans., Paris, Thames and Hudson, 1991

17   *Handel and his World*, London, Weidenfeld and Nicolson, 1984; Boston, Little Brown, 1984. New pbk ed., London, Fontana, 1992

18   *Haydn: His Life and Music* (with David Wyn Jones), London, Thames and Hudson, 1988; Bloomington, Indiana University Press, 1988. Italian trans., Milan, Rusconi, 1988

19   *1791: Mozart's Last Year*, London, Thames and Hudson, 1988; New York, Macmillan-Schirmer, 1988. 2nd ed., London, Thames and Hudson, 1989. Pbk ed., New York, Schirmer, 1990. Pbk ed., London, Harper Collins (Fontana), 1990. French trans., Paris, J. Lattès, 1988, 1990. Spanish trans., Madrid, Ediciones Siruela, 1989. Italian trans., Milan, Garzanti, 1989. Japanese trans., Tokyo, Chuokoron-Sha, 1989. Swedish trans., Stockholm, Natur och Kultur, 1990. Portuguese trans., Rio de Janeiro, Nova Fronteira, 1990. Dutch trans., Baarn, Bosch & Keuning, 1990. German trans., Düsseldorf, Claassen, 1991. Pbk ed., Munich, Deutscher Taschenbuch Verlag, 1991; Kassel, Bärenreiter, 1991. Danish trans., Copenhagen, Munksgaard, 1991

20   *Mozart: the Golden Years, 1781–1791*, London, Thames and Hudson, 1989; New York, Schirmer, 1989. French trans., Paris, J. Lattès, 1989. Italian trans., Milan, Garzanti, 1989. German trans., Munich, Droemer Knaur, 1990. Spanish trans., Barcelona, Ediciones Destino, 1990. Dutch trans., Baarn, Bosch & Keuning,

1990. Danish trans., Copenhagen, Gyldendal, 1991. Slovenian trans., Ljubljana, Drzavna zalozba Slovenije, 1991. Swedish trans., Stockholm, Norstedt, 1991. Japanese trans., Tokyo, Chuokoron-Sha, 1991

21   *Five Centuries of Music in Venice* (with John Julius Norwich), London, Thames and Hudson, 1991; New York, Schirmer, 1991. French trans., Paris, J. Lattès, 1991. Italian trans., Milan, Rizzoli, 1991. Spanish trans., Barcelona, Ediciones Destino, 1992 (see no. 515)

22   *Mozart and Vienna: Including Selections from Johann Pezzl's 'Sketch of Vienna' (1786–1790)*, London, Thames and Hudson, 1991; New York, Schirmer, Maxwell Macmillan International, 1991. Dutch trans., Baarn, Bosch & Keuning, 1991. Pbk ed., London, Thames and Hudson, 1994

23   *Beethoven: His Life, Work and World* (compiled and ed.), rev. ed., London, Thames and Hudson, 1992; New York, Thames and Hudson, 1993. German ed., Stuttgart, Gerd Hatje, 1994. Italian trans., Milan, Rusconi, 1995 (see nos. 5, 6)

24   *Haydn schreibt Briefe* (selected letters, with commentary), Vienna, Doblinger, 1993

25   *Mozart: Samedi 12 Novembre 1791: une journée particulière*, Paris, J. Lattès, 1993. Spanish trans., Barcelona, Ediciones Destino, 1994.

26   *Vivaldi: Voice of the Baroque*, London, Thames and Hudson, 1993. French trans., Paris, J. Lattès, 1994

27   *Haydn: Chronicle and Works* (5 vols.), reprint ed., including *Addenda and Corrigenda* in vol. V, London and New York, Thames and Hudson, 1994 (see nos. 9, 11–14)

28   *The Mozart Essays*, London and New York, Thames and Hudson, 1995. (Includes nos. 186, 193)

EDITED BOOKS

29   *The Mozart Companion* (with Donald Mitchell), London, Rockliff, 1956; New York, Oxford University Press, 1956; London, Faber and Faber, 1965, 1968. Corrected ed., New York, W.W. Norton, 1969; Westport, Connecticut, Greenwood Press, 1981 (see no. 53)

30   *The Collected Correspondence and London Notebooks of Joseph Haydn*, London, Barrie and Rockliff, 1959; Fair Lawn, New Jersey, Essential Books, 1959

31   Prüller, Wilhelm, *Diary of a German Soldier*, ed. by H.C. Robbins Landon and S. Leitner, London, Faber and Faber, 1963

32   *Studies in Eighteenth-Century Music: a Tribute to Karl Geiringer on his Seventieth Birthday* (in collaboration with Roger E. Chapman), London, Allen and Unwin, 1970; New York, Oxford University Press, 1970. Reprint ed., New York, Da Capo Press, 1979

33   *The Mozart Compendium: a Guide to Mozart's Life and Music*, London, Thames and Hudson, 1990; New York, Schirmer, 1990. Braille ed., New York, Schirmer, 1990. French trans., J. Lattès, 1990. German trans., Munich, Droemer Knaur, 1991. Dutch trans., Baarn, Tirion, 1991. Spanish trans., Barcelona, Editorial Labor, 1991. Japanese trans., Tokyo, Heibonsha, 1992 (see no. 177)

34   *Mozart à Paris* (Nicole Salinger with H.C. Robbins Landon), exhibition catalogue, Paris, Paris-Musées/Francis Van de Velde, 1991 (see nos. 28, 186)

EDITOR

35   *Haydn Yearbook* (ed. with others):
Vols. I–VIII, Bryn Mawr, Pennsylvania, Theodore Presser Company; Vienna, London, Zurich, Mainz, Milan, Universal Edition, 1962–71
Vols. IX–X, Vienna, Universal Edition for the Verein Internationale Joseph Haydn Stiftung Eisenstadt, 1975–78
Vols. XI–XVI, Cardiff, University College Cardiff Press, 1980–86
Vol. XVII, Eisenstadt, Joseph Haydn Stiftung, distributed by Thames and Hudson, 1992
Vols. XVIII–XIX, Foncoussières, Rabastens (Tarm), H.C. Robbins Landon, distributed by Thames and Hudson, 1993–94

36   *Eighteenth Century Studies: An Interdisciplinary Journal*, (advisory editor), University of California Press, 1970–74

ARTICLES IN DICTIONARIES AND ENCYCLOPAEDIAS

37   *Die Musik in Geschichte und Gegenwart*, vol. III, ed. Friedrich Blume (Kassel, Bärenreiter, 1954): 'Elssler, Joseph', cols. 1316–19

38   *Die Musik in Geschichte und Gegenwart*, vol. V, ed. Friedrich Blume (Kassel, Bärenreiter, 1956): 'Gyrowetz, Adalbert', cols. 1146–58

39   *Die Musik in Geschichte und Gegenwart*, vol. V, ed. Friedrich Blume (Kassel, Bärenreiter, 1956): 'Haydn, Franz Joseph' (with Jens Peter Larsen), cols. 1857–1933

40   *Encyclopédie de la Musique*, vol. II, ed. François Michel in collaboration with François Lesure and Vladimir Federov (Paris, Fasquelle, 1959): 'Haydn, Franz Joseph', 439–47

41   *Die Musik in Geschichte und Gegenwart*, vol. X, ed. Friedrich Blume (Kassel, Bärenreiter, 1962): 'Ordoñez, Carlos d'', cols. 194–6

42   *Encyclopaedia Britannica*, 15th ed., vol. XXIV (Macropaedia), (New York, 1985): 'Mozart', 445–8 (in part)

43   *Collier's Encyclopaedia*, vol. XI, (New York, Macmillan, 1992): 'Haydn, Franz Joseph', 726–8

44   *Collier's Encyclopaedia*, vol. XVI, (New York, Macmillan, 1992): 'Mozart, Wolfgang Amadeus', 683–9

ARTICLES IN JOURNALS AND CONTRIBUTIONS TO COMPOSITE VOLUMES

45   'New Complete Haydn Edition', *Notes*, vi/4 (September 1949), 537–8

46   'The Haydn Society', *Music and Letters*, xxxii (1951), 199–200

47   'True and False in Haydn', *Saturday Review*, xxxiv (25 August 1951), 35–8

48   'On Haydn's Quartets of Opera 1 and 2; Notes and Comments on Sondheimer's Historical and Psychological Study', *The Music Review*, xiii (1952), 181–6

49   'Eine neue Mozartquelle', *Österreichische Musikzeitschrift*, ix (1954), 42–4

50 'The Original Versions of Haydn's First Salomon Symphonies', *The Music Review*, xv (1954), 1–32

51 'Die Verwendung gregorianischer Melodien in Haydns Frühsymphonien', *Österreichische Musikzeitschrift*, ix (1954), 119–26

52 'Haydn and Authenticity: Some New Facts', *The Music Review*, xvi (1955), 138–40

53 'The Concertos: Their Musical Origin and Development' in *The Mozart Companion*, ed. H.C. Robbins Landon and Donald Mitchell (London, Rockliff, 1956), 234–82 (see no. 29)

54 'Die Symphonien: Ihr geistiger und musikalischer Ursprung und ihre Entwicklung' in *Mozart-Aspekte*, ed. P. Schaller and H. Kühner (Freiburg, Olten, 1956), 39–62

55 'Two Orchestral Works Wrongly Attributed to Mozart', *The Music Review*, xvii (1956), 29–34

56 'Eine aufgefundene Haydn-Messe', *Österreichische Musikzeitschrift*, xii (1957), 183–5

57 'Doubtful and Spurious Quartets and Quintets Attributed to Haydn', *The Music Review*, xviii (1957), 213–21

58 'The *Jena* Symphony', *The Music Review*, xviii (1957), 109–13 (see no. 7)

59 'Mozart fälschlich zugeschriebene Messen', *Mozart-Jahrbuch*, (1957), 85–95

60 'Ein neuentdecktes Bildnis Joseph Haydns', *Österreichische Musikzeitschrift*, xii (1957), 381–3 (see no. 61)

61 'Ein neuentdecktes Bildnis Joseph Haydns' in *Studien aus Wien (Wiener Schriften, 5)*, (Vienna, Verlag für Jugend und Volk, 1957), 103–8 (see no. 60)

62 'Witt – nicht Beethoven, das Rätsel der Jenaer Symphonie', *Phono*, iv/2 (1957/1958), 9

63 'La Crise romantique dans la musique autrichienne vers 1770: Quelques précurseurs inconnus de la "Symphonie en sol mineur" (KV 183) de Mozart' in *Les Influences étrangères dans l'œuvre de W.A. Mozart. International Colloquium, Paris, 1956*, (Paris, 1958), 27–47

64 'Deutsch und Haydn', *Österreichische Musikzeitschrift*, Sonderheft (special number, 1958), 21–2

65 'Opera in Esterháza', *The Listener* (1 May 1958), 753

66 'Scheinwerfer auf Vater Mozart', *Phono*, iv/3 (1958), 9–10

67 'The Symphonies of Joseph Haydn: Addenda and Corrigenda', *The Music Review*, xix (1958), 311–19 (see nos. 1, 2, 74)

68 'Haydn: Die Salomon-Symphonien (Nr. 93–98). Einleitung zu einer vergleichenden Discographie', *Phono*, vi/1 (1959), 3–5

69 'Haydn's Esterháza is Still There', *High Fidelity/Musical America*, ix/8 (1959), 32–5

70 'Haydns Opern', *Musica*, xiii (1959), 286–9

71 'Neue Haydn-Quellen', *Österreichische Musikzeitschrift*, xiv (1959), 213–16

72 'Problems of Authenticity in Eighteenth-Century Music' in *Instrumental Music; a Conference at Isham Memorial Library, May 4, 1957*, ed. David G. Hughes (Cambridge, Mass., Harvard University Press, 1959), 31–56. Reprint ed., New York, Da Capo Press, 1972

73 'Survey of the Haydn Sources in Czechoslovakia' in *Bericht über die Internationale Konferenz zum Andenken Joseph Haydns, Budapest, 17–22 September 1959*, ed. Bence Szabolcsi and Dénes Bartha (Budapest, Akadémiai Kiadó, 1959), 69–78

74 'The Symphonies of Joseph Haydn: Addenda and Corrigenda', *The Music Review*, xx (1959), 56–70 (see nos. 1, 2, 67)

75 'Wurst and Beethoven: an Un-Baedeker-like Guide', *High Fidelity/Musical America*, ix/11 (1959), 58–62, 160–64

76 'The Haydn Sesquicentennial', *Gramophone*, xxxviii (June 1960), 7–8

77 'Haydn's *St. Anthony* Divertimento', *The Musical Times*, ci (1960), 433

78 'It All Began in Bonn', *High Fidelity/Musical America*, x/4 (1960), 40–3

79 'The Red Priest of Venice' [Antonio Vivaldi], *High Fidelity/Musical America*, x/8 (1960), 30–5

80 'Musical Sleuthing Uncovers Haydn Opera', *Musical Courier*, clxiii/9 (August 1961), 10–11, 45

81 'A Pox on Manfredini', *High Fidelity/Musical America*, xi/6 (1961), 38–9, 87

82 'Some Notes on Haydn's Opera *L'infedeltà delusa'*, *The Musical Times*, cii (1961), 356–7 (see no. 83)

83 'Zu Haydns *L'infedeltà delusa'*, *Österreichische Musikzeitschrift*, xvi (1961), 481–4 (German trans. of no. 82)

84 'Das brennende Haus', *Phono*, viii/4 (1962), 12–15

85 'Haydn's Marionette Operas and the Repertoire of the Marionette Theatre at Esterház Castle', *Haydn Yearbook*, i (1962), 111–97 (see no. 119)

86 'Joseph Martin Kraus', *The Musical Times*, ciii (1962), 25–6

87 'Monteverdi and Mantua', *High Fidelity/ Musical America*, xii/2 (1962), 48–53, 129, 135

88 'Tagebuch einer sentimentalen Reise ins Land hinter der Klassik auf alten Poststationen: Plattenstatt Pferdewechsel', *Phono*, viii/4 (1962), 75–7

89 'The Theater an der Wien', *High Fidelity/Musical America*, xii/6 (1962), 28–31

90 'The Baffling Case of Anton Bruckner', *High Fidelity/Musical America*, xiii/2 (1963), 46–8, 120

91 'Portrait of the Conductor as Celebrity' [Herbert von Karajan], *High Fidelity/Musical America*, xiii/9 (1963), 52–5, 131

92 'Einiges zur Aufführungspraxis von Haydn-Symphonien durch Liebhaber- und Schulorchester', *Das Liebhaberorchester*, xii/3 (September 1964), 43–50

93 '*Gloria in Excelsis Deo*. The Haydn Masses', *High Fidelity/Musical America*, xiv/12 (1964), 56–9

94 'The Haydn Masses on Records', *High Fidelity/Musical America*, xiv/12 (1964), 105–7

95 'Haydn's *Bear* and Haydn's *Hen* . . . the Right Scores Make All the Difference', *High Fidelity/Musical America*, xiv/11 (1964), 89–90

96 'Who Composed Haydn's Opus 3?' (with Alan Tyson), *The Musical Times*, cv (1964), 506–7

97 'Haydn and his Operas', *Opera*, xvi (1965), 557–64

98 'The Honorable Tradition of Englishmen', *High Fidelity/Musical America*, xv/4 (1965), 44–50

99 'Mozart on the Eighteenth Century Stage. How did Mozart's Contemporaries View the Operas which We Now Consider Immortal?', *High Fidelity/Musical America*, xv/11 (1965), 62–4, 183

100 'Haydn's Castle', *HiFi/Stereo Review*, xvi/5 (1966), 48–53

101 'Haydn's Younger Brother. H.C. Robbins Landon on Michael Haydn', *The Listener* (4 August 1966), 172–3

102 'Foreword' and 'Corrigenda' in C.S. Terry, *Johann Christian Bach*, 2nd ed. (London, Oxford University Press, 1967), xvii–xxv

103 'Haydn und die Oper', *Österreichische Musikzeitschrift*, xxii (1967), 253–7

104 'Music of the Rococo', *HiFi/Stereo Review*, xix/11 (1967), 64–70 (see no. 7)

105 'Music's St. Cecilia', *HiFi/Stereo Review*, xviii/4 (1967), 59–63

106 'Box-Office Failure', *The Listener* (22 August 1968), 249

107 'Haydniana (I)', *Haydn Yearbook*, iv (1968), 199–206

108 'Das Haydn-Porträt von Loutherbourg', *Österreichische Musikzeitschrift*, xxiii (1968), 185–9 (see no. 7)

109 'Haydn's Newly Discovered *Responsorium ad Absolutionem: Libera me Domine*', *Haydn Yearbook*, iv (1968), 140–7 (Facsimile and modern ed., pp. 228–35)

110 'The Viennese Classical Era', *HiFi/Stereo Review*, xxi (July 1968), 50–5 (see no. 7)

111 'Archaism and Authenticity. The Real Composers and What They Actually Wrote', *The Times Literary Supplement* (9 October 1969), 1165–6

112 'Haydn's Opera *L'infedeltà delusa*', *The Listener* (30 October 1969), 609

113 'Beethoven – a Pictorial Essay', *High Fidelity/Musical America*, xx (January 1970), 69–76

114 'Beethoven on Records: the Choral Music', *High Fidelity/Musical America*, xx (February 1970), 70–2

115 'Haydniana (II)', *Haydn Yearbook*, vii (1970), 307–19

116 'A Haydn Jewel Recovered', *Opera*, xxi (1970), 499–505

117 'Due Nuovi Ritratti di Mozart', *Nuova Rivista Musicale Italiana*, v (1971), 669–72

118 'Haydns erste Erfahrungen in England. Von der Ankunft in London bis zum ersten Salomon-Konzert', *Jahrbuch für österreichische Kulturgeschichte*, i (1971), 154–81

119 'Das Marionettentheater auf Schloss Esterház', *Österreichische Musikzeitschrift*, xxvi (1971), 272–80 (trans. of part of no. 85)

120 'A New Authentic Source for *La fedeltà premiata* by Haydn', *Soundings*, ii (1971–2), 6–17

121 'Two New Mozart Portraits', *Eighteenth Century Studies*, v/2 (1971–2), 256–60

122 'Haydn in 1772', *The Listener* (6 July 1972), 24–5

123 'Haydn's *fedeltà premiata*', *HiFi Stereophonie*, xi (August 1972), 696

124 'Haydn's Pianos', *The Listener* (20 July 1972), 90–1

125 'H.C. Robbins Landon on the First Performance of Haydn's *Creation*', *The Listener* (30 November 1972), 761

126 'Two Research Lacunae in Music of the Classic Period' in *Perspectives in Musicology: the Inaugural Lectures of the Ph.D. Program in Music at the City University of New York*, ed. Barry S. Brook (New York, Norton, 1972), 136–50

127 'H.C. Robbins Landon Writes About Haydn's Oratorio *Il Ritorno di Tobia*', *The Listener* (14 June 1973), 809

128 'The Operas of Haydn' in *The New Oxford History of Music*, vol. VII: *The Age of Enlightenment 1745–1790*, ed. Egon Wellesz and Frederick W. Sternfeld (London, New York, Oxford University Press, 1973–4), 172–99

129 'Haydns Oper *La fedeltà premiata*: Eine neue authentische Quelle' in *Beiträge zur Musik-dokumentation. Franz Grasberger zum 60. Geburtstag*, ed. Günther Brosche (Tutzing, Hans Schneider, 1975), 213–32

130 'The Newly Discovered Autograph to Haydn's *Missa Cellensis* of 1766 (formerly known as the *Missa Sanctae Caeciliae*)', *Haydn Yearbook*, ix (1975), 306–27

131 'Towards a New Edition of Verdi', *Saturday Review*, iii (1 November 1975), 41–3

132 'Auf den Spuren Joseph Haydns', *Österreichische Musikzeitschrift*, xxxi (1976), 579–81

133 'Joseph Haydn in Vienna – Life and Works' in *The Haydn Museum*, ed. Adelbert Schusser (Museums of the City of Vienna, [1978]), [2–5]

134 'A New Haydn Portrait', *Soundings*, viii (1979–80), 2–5 (see no. 147)

135 'A New Authentic Manuscript Source for Beethoven's Wind-Band Sextetto, Op. 71' in *Music East and West: Essays in Honor of Walter Kaufman*, ed. Thomas Noblitt (Pendragon Festschrift Series no. 3) (New York, Pendragon, 1981), 261–71

136 'The Acta Musicalia of the Esterházy Archives (nos. 1–35)' (with Else Radant and Ian M. Bruce [eds.]), *Haydn Yearbook*, xiii (1982), 5–96

137 'Bringing Haydn's Operas to Life', *Ovation*, iii (March 1982), 20–1

138 'Four New Haydn Letters', *Haydn Yearbook*, xiii (1982), 213–19

139 'Haydn: a Celebration of his 250th Birthday', *Ovation*, iii (March 1982), 16–19, 44

140 'Haydn on Record. I: Symphonies and Vocal Music', *Early Music*, x (1982), 351–60

141 'Haydn on Record. II: Concertos and Other Instrumental Music', *Early Music*, x (1982), 505–12

142 'Haydns Platz im *Pantheon der Bestseller*', *Hi Fi Stereophonie*, xxi (August 1982), 902–5

143 'Joseph Haydn als Opernkomponist und Kapellmeister' in *Joseph Haydn in seiner Zeit, Eisenstadt, 20. Mai–26. Oktober 1982*, ed. Gerda Mraz, Gottfried Mraz and Gerald Schlag (Eisenstadt, Amt der Burgenländischen Landesregierung, 1982), 249–54

144 'Joseph Haydn: a Sketch to *Piano Trio No. 30* [Hob. XV:17]', *Haydn Yearbook*, xiii (1982), 220–7

145 'Joseph Haydns Popularität anno 1982', *Österreichische Musikzeitschrift*, xxxvii (1982), 137–8

146 'Der junge Haydn und Eisenstadt in Haydn Gedenkstätten' in *Burgenland – Jahrbuch für ein Land und seine Freunde* (Vienna, 1982), 57–8

147 'Ein neues Haydn-Porträt' in *Festakt am 250. Geburtstag Joseph Haydns*, ed. Günther Brosche (Vienna, Österreichische Nationalbibliothek, 1982), 12–14 (see no. 134)

148 'Out of Haydn: the Composer's Operas 250 Years After His Birth', *Opera News*, xlvii/2 (August 1982), 9–11

149 'The Place of Haydn in Early Music and the Challenge He Presents to the Early Musician', *Early Music*, x (1982), 298–9

150 'The Acta Musicalia of the Esterházy Archives (nos. 36–100)' (H.C. Robbins Landon and others [eds.]), *Haydn Yearbook*, xiv (1983), 9–128

151 'A Commentary on the Score' in *Wolfgang Amadeus Mozart: Così fan tutte*, ed. Nicholas John (London, John Calder, 1983; New York, Riverrun Press, 1983), 17–32

152 'A Lost Autograph Re-discovered: Missa Sunt Bona Mixta Malis by Joseph Haydn', *Haydn Yearbook*, xiv (1983), 5–8

153 'More Haydn Letters in Autograph', *Haydn Yearbook*, xiv (1983), 200–5

154 'The Acta Musicalia of the Esterházy Archives (nos. 101–152)' (H.C. Robbins Landon and others [eds.]), *Haydn Yearbook*, xv (1984), 93–180

155 'Innenansicht der Wiener Loge "Zur Gekrönten Hoffnung" 1790. Bildstudie und Porträtvergleiche' in *200 Jahre Große Landesloge der Freimaurer*, ed. Zirkel and Winkelmass (Vienna, Museen der Stadt Wien, 1984), 25–31

156 'New Haydn Letters', *Haydn Yearbook*, xv (1984), 214–18

157 'New Manuscript Sources of Works by Joseph Haydn, Johann Michael Haydn and their Austrian Contemporaries', *Haydn Yearbook*, xv (1984), 199–213

158 'Rediscovering Rameau (Recordings)', *Ovation*, v (June 1984), 54–5

159 'Two New Beethoven Letters' in *Festschrift Albi Rosenthal*, ed. Rudolf Elvers (Tutzing, Hans Schneider, 1984), 217–20

160 'The Acta Musicalia of the Esterházy Archives (nos. 153–174)' (H.C. Robbins Landon and others [eds.]), *Haydn Yearbook*, xvi (1985), 99–207

161 'Foreword' in S. Hodges, *The Creation and The Seasons: the Complete Authentic Sources for the Word-Books* (Cardiff, University College Cardiff Press, 1985), 5–12

162 'Foreword' in S. Hodges, *Lorenzo da Ponte: the Life and Times of Mozart's Librettist* (London, Granada, and New York, Universe, 1985), ix–x

163 'George Frideric Handel 1685–1759', *Ovation*, v (January 1985), 14–19

164 'George Szell 1897–1970', *Ovation*, vi (July 1985), 18

165 'A Haydn Letter to Dr. Burney', *Haydn Yearbook*, xvi (1985), 247

166 'The Ovation Record Review', *Ovation*, vi (December 1985), 34

167 'The Newly Discovered Authentic Scores of Haydn's "London" Symphonies from the Library of Johann Peter Salomon' in *Bericht über den Internationalen Joseph Haydn Kongress, Wien, 5.–12. September 1982*, ed. Eva Badura-Skoda (Vienna, Munich, Henle, 1986), 549–50

168 'Wolfgang Amadeus' Last Year', *Austria Today*, ii (1986), 34–7

169 'Zu den Haydn-Autographen der Sammlung Paul Sacher' in *Komponisten des 20. Jahrhunderts in der Paul Sacher Stiftung*, ed. Felix Meyer, Jörg Meyer Jans and Ingrid Westen (Basle, Paul Sacher Stiftung, 1986), 31–6

170 'Controversial Köchels (Authenticity of Mozart's *Sixth* and *Seventh Violin Concertos*)', *The Strad*, xcix (1988), 571–2

171 'Haydn und die Familie Bertie', *Österreichische Musikzeitschrift*, xliii/1 (1988), 21–4

172 'Mozart and the Salzburg Festival', *Music & Musicians International*, xxxvi/13 (September 1988), 14–17

173 'The Pre-Classical Concerto and the Concerto Parallel to Mozart' in *A Companion to the Concerto*, ed. Robert Layton (London, Christopher Helm, 1988), 57–74

174 'The Haydn Quartets', *The Strad*, c (1989), 222

175 *In Memoriam Anton Heiller (1923–1979)*, ed. Thomas Schmögner (Publikationen des Österreichischen Orgelforums, 1) (Vienna, Österreichisches Orgelforum, 1989), [A chronology of his life and recollections by H.C. Robbins Landon and others is included]

176 'Introduction' to E. Baillie, *Haydn: a Graded Practical Guide* (The Pianist's Repertoire) (London, Novello, 1989), v

177 'Doubtful and Spurious [Works]' in *The Mozart Compendium: a Guide to Mozart's Life and Music*, ed. H.C. Robbins Landon (London, Thames and Hudson, 1990), 351–5 (see no. 33)

178 'Mozart's Mass in C minor K427' in *Studies in Musical Sources and Styles: Essays in Honor of Jan LaRue*, ed. Eugene K. Wolf and Edward H. Roesner (Madison, A-R Editions, 1990), 419–23

179 'Mozart und Haydn' in *Zaubertöne. Mozart in Wien, 1781–1791* (Ausstellung des Historischen Museums der Stadt Wien im Künstlerhaus, 6. Dezember 1990–15. September 1991) (Vienna, Museen der Stadt Wien, 1990), 485–6

180 'Warum blieb Mozart in Wien?' in *Zaubertöne. Mozart in Wien 1781–1791* (Ausstellung des Historischen Museums der Stadt Wien im Künstlerhaus, 6. Dezember 1990–15. September 1991) (Vienna, Museen der Stadt Wien, 1990), 586–90

181 'Music' in *The Cambridge Guide to the Arts in Britain*, vol. 6: *Romantics to Early Victorians*, ed. Boris Ford (Cambridge, Cambridge University Press, 1990), 226–53

182 'Delirium und Streptokokken' in *Memorial Mozart. Magazin für das Mozartjahr 1991* (Vienna, Verlag für Kunst & Kultur, 1991), 4, 6–7

183 'Foreword' in G. Brace, *Anna . . . Susanna; Anna Storace, Mozart's first Susanna: Her Life, Times and Family* (London, Thames Publishing, 1991), [5]

184 'Neues zum Requiem', *Sovjetskaja Muzyka*, 12 (1991), 13–19

185 'Mozart's Stay in Vienna and its Ramifications', *Österreichische Musikzeitschrift*, xlvi (1991), 23–6

186 'La Place de Paris dans la vie et l'œuvre de Mozart' in *Mozart à Paris*, ed. N. Salinger in collaboration with H.C. Robbins Landon (Paris-Musées/Francis Van de Velde, 1991), 13–19 (see nos. 28, 34)

187 'Les Symphonies de Mozart', *Diapason-Harmonie*, ccclxxii (June 1991), 18–20

188 'A Letter from Dr. Burney to Longman, Clementi & Co.', *Haydn Yearbook*, xvii (1992), 170–4

189 'The Bohemians c1730–1850', *BBC Music Magazine*, i/5 (January 1993), 29–32

190 'An Englishman in Vienna and Eisenstadt Castle in 1748 and 1749', *Haydn Yearbook*, xviii (1993), 197–212

191 'Haydn's Oratorios', *BBC Music Magazine*, i/8 (April 1993), 65–7

192 'Hidden Delights', *BBC Music Magazine*, i/10 (June 1993), 26–9

193 'The Symphonies of Mozart' in *A Companion to the Symphony*, ed. Robert Layton (London, New York, Simon and Schuster, 1993), 53–79. (Pbk ed., Oxford, Oxford University Press, 1995) (see no. 28)

194 'Documents from the Esterházy Archives in Eisenstadt and Forchtenstein' (edited by János Hárich II) (commentary by Else Radant and H.C. Robbins Landon), *Haydn Yearbook*, xix (1994), 1–359

195 'Haydn Scoop of the Century: Six "lost" Haydn Piano Sonatas have surfaced in Germany. H.C. Robbins Landon reveals the Immense Significance of the Find', *BBC Music Magazine*, ii/5 (January 1994), 11

196 'A Musical Joke in *nearly* Perfect Style. H.C. Robbins Landon on Why There's More to a Recent Find than Meets the Eye', *BBC Music Magazine*, ii/6 (February 1994), 10

EDITIONS OF MUSIC

BACH, JOHANN CHRISTIAN

197 —*Temistocle. Dramma per musica in tre atti di Pietro Metastasio* (with E.O.D. Downes), Vienna, Universal Edition, 1965

198 —*La clemenza di Scipione. Overture*, Vienna, Doblinger, 1970

[EDITIONS OF MUSIC: Franz Joseph Haydn – *continued*]

228 —*Concertino per il Cembalo*, [Hob. XIV:11], Vienna, Wiesbaden, Doblinger, 1959

229 —*Divertimento in E. Klaviertrio*, [Hob. XV:34], Vienna, Wiesbaden, Doblinger, 1959

230 —*Lo Speziale. Dramma giocoso. Sinfonia (Overtura)*, [Hob. Ia:10], Vienna, Munich, Doblinger, 1959

231 —*Ouvertüre in D*, [Hob. Ia:4], Vienna, Munich, Doblinger, 1959

232 —*Overture to the Azione teatrale L'isola disabitata*, [Hob. Ia:13], London, Eulenburg, 1959

233 —*Sämtliche Divertimenti für Blasinstrumente*, [Hob. II:3, 7, 14, 15, 23, D18 and two works in D and G], Vienna, Doblinger, 1959–60

234 —*Sinfonia in D*, Overture [Hob. Ia:7], Vienna, Munich, Doblinger, 1959

235 —*Sinfonia No. 60*, Salzburg, Haydn-Mozart Presse, 1959; Vienna, Universal Edition, 1969

236 —*Sinfonia No. 61*, Salzburg, Haydn-Mozart Presse, 1959; Vienna, Universal Edition, 1969

237 —'*Son pietosa, son bonina*', [Hob. XXXII:1b], in Cimarosas '*La Circe*', Vienna, Doblinger, 1959

238 —*Symphony No. 98, B♭ major*, London, Eulenburg, 1959

239 —*Te Deum in C*, [Hob. XXIIIc:2], Vienna, Munich, Doblinger, 1959

240 —*Cassatio in D*, [Hob. II:D22], Vienna, Doblinger, 1960

241 —*Lirenkonzerte*, nos. 1–5, [Hob. VIIh:1–5], Vienna, Doblinger, 1960

242 —*Litaniae de Beata Maria Virgine in C*, [Hob. XXIIIc:C2], Vienna, Munich, Doblinger, 1960

243 —*Märsche (für Blasinstrumente)*, [Hob. VIII:1–4, 6–7 and one work in G], Vienna, Doblinger, 1960

244 —*Miseri noi, misera patria (Cantata)*, [Hob. XXIVa:7], Vienna, Doblinger, 1960

245 —*Orlando Paladino. Sinfonia. (Overtura)*, [Hob. Ia:16], Vienna, Munich, Doblinger, 1960

246 —*Sinfonia 'B' ('Parthia') in B*, [Hob. I:108], Vienna, Munich, Doblinger, 1960; Vienna, Universal Edition, 1969

247 —*Six Allemandes. Sechs deutsche Tänze*, [Hob. IX:9], Vienna, Munich, Doblinger, 1960

248 —*Symphony No. 26 ('Lamentatione'), D minor*, London, Eulenburg, 1960

249 —*Symphony No. 39, G minor*, London, Eulenburg, 1960

250 —*Zwei italienische Duette (1796)*, [Hob. XXVa:2,1], Vienna, Munich, Doblinger, 1960

251 —*Divertimento a sei. ('Der Geburtstag')*, [Hob. II:11], Vienna, Doblinger, 1961

252 —*L'infedeltà delusa (Untreue lohnt sich nicht/Deceit Outwitted)*, [Hob. XXVIII:5], Salzburg, Haydn-Mozart Presse, 1961; Vienna, London, Universal Edition. 1968

253 —*March. For the Royal Society of Musicians*, [Hob. VIII:3 *bis*], Vienna, Munich, Doblinger, 1961

254 —*Notturno No. 1 in C*, [Hob. II:25], Vienna, Munich, Doblinger, 1961

255 —*Scherzando No. 1 [–6]*, [Hob. II:33–38], Vienna, Munich, Doblinger, 1961

256 —*Sinfonia No. 98*, Salzburg, Haydn-Mozart Presse, 1961; Vienna, Universal Edition, 1969

257 —*13 Arien für Sopran*, [Hob. XXIVb:1, 2, 3, 7, 9, 12, 13, 15, 17, 18, 20, XXX:5b, XXXIc:5], Salzburg, Haydn-Mozart Presse, 1961–2 (see no. 372)

258 —*Cassatio (Divertimento a nove stromenti)*, [Hob. II:20], Vienna, Munich, Doblinger, 1962

259 —*Concerto per l'Organo No. 2*, [Hob. XVIII:8], Vienna, Doblinger, 1962

260 —*L'infedeltà delusa. Overtura*, [Hob. Ia:1], Salzburg, Haydn-Mozart Presse, 1962

261 —*Sinfonia No. 1*, Vienna, Munich, Doblinger, 1962; Vienna, Universal Edition, 1969

262 —*Sinfonia No. 2*, Vienna, Munich, Doblinger, 1962; Vienna, Universal Edition, 1969

263 —*Sinfonia No. 9*, Vienna, Munich, Doblinger, 1962; Vienna, Universal Edition, 1969

[EDITIONS OF MUSIC: Franz Joseph Haydn – *continued*]

264 —*Sinfonia No. 10*, Vienna, Munich, Doblinger, 1962; Vienna, Universal Edition, 1969

265 —*Sinfonia No. 32*, Vienna, Munich, Doblinger, 1962; Vienna, Universal Edition, 1969

266 —*Sinfonia No. 92 ('Oxford')*, Salzburg, Haydn-Mozart Presse, 1962; Vienna, Universal Edition, 1969

267 —*Sinfonia No. 96 ('The Miracle')*, Salzburg, Haydn-Mozart Presse, 1962; Vienna, Universal Edition, 1969

268 —*La fedeltà premiata. Sinfonia (Overtura)*, [Hob. I:73 (XXVIII:10)], Vienna, Munich, Doblinger, 1963

269 —*Die Feuerbrunst (Das abgebrannte Haus/The Burning House). Opera in Two Acts*, [Hob. XXIXb:A], London, Schott, 1963

270 —*Die Feuerbrunst. Overture*, [Hob. XXIXb:A], London, Eulenburg, 1963

271 —*Mass in D minor ('Missa in angustiis'/ 'Nelson Mass')*, [Hob. XXII:11], London, Schott, 1963; London, Eulenburg, 1965

272 —*Sinfonia No. 13*, Vienna, Munich, Doblinger, 1963; Vienna, Universal Edition, 1971

273 —*Sinfonia No. 14*, Vienna, Munich, Doblinger, 1963; Vienna, Universal Edition, 1971

274 —*Sinfonia No. 15*, Vienna, Munich, Doblinger, 1963; Vienna, Universal Edition, 1971

275 —*Sinfonia No. 16*, Vienna, Munich, Doblinger, 1963; Vienna, Universal Edition, 1971

276 —*Sinfonia No. 17*, Vienna, Munich, Doblinger, 1963; Vienna, Universal Edition, 1971

277 —*Sinfonia No. 18*, Vienna, Munich, Doblinger, 1963; Vienna, Universal Edition, 1971

278 —*Sinfonia No. 19*, Vienna, Munich, Doblinger, 1963; Vienna, Universal Edition, 1971

279 —*Sinfonia No. 20*, Vienna, Munich, Doblinger, 1963; Vienna, Universal Edition, 1971

280 —*Sinfonia No. 21*, Vienna, Munich, Doblinger, 1963; Vienna, Universal Edition, 1971

281 —*Sinfonia No. 22 ('Philosoph')*, Vienna, Munich, Doblinger, 1963; Vienna, Universal Edition, 1971

282 —*Sinfonia No. 23*, Vienna, Munich, Doblinger, 1963; Vienna, Universal Edition, 1971

283 —*Sinfonia No. 24*, Vienna, Munich, Doblinger, 1963; Vienna, Universal Edition, 1971

284 —*Sinfonia No. 25*, Vienna, Munich, Doblinger, 1963; Vienna, Universal Edition, 1971

285 —*Sinfonia No. 26 ('Lamentatione')*, Vienna, Munich, Doblinger, 1963; Vienna, Universal Edition, 1971

286 —*Sinfonia No. 27*, Vienna, Munich, Doblinger, 1963; Vienna, Universal Edition, 1971

287 —*Sinfonia No. 33*, Vienna, Munich, Doblinger, 1963; Vienna, Universal Edition, 1969

288 —*Sinfonia No. 37*, Vienna, Munich, Doblinger, 1963; Vienna, Universal Edition, 1969

289 —*Sinfonia No. 39*, Vienna, Munich, Doblinger, 1963; Vienna, Universal Edition, 1969

290 —*Symphony No. 70 in D major*, London, Eulenburg, 1963

291 —*Sinfonia No. 75*, Salzburg, Haydn-Mozart Presse, 1963; Vienna, Universal Edition, 1969

292 —*Sinfonia No. 82 ('L'Ours')*, Salzburg, Haydn-Mozart Presse, 1963; Vienna, Universal Edition, 1969

293 —*Sinfonia No. 83 ('La Poule')*, Salzburg, Haydn-Mozart Presse, 1963; Vienna, Universal Edition, 1969

294 —*Sinfonia No. 84*, Salzburg, Haydn-Mozart Presse, 1963; Vienna, Universal Edition, 1969

295   —*Sinfonia No. 85 ('La Reine')*, Salzburg, Haydn-Mozart Presse, 1963; Vienna, Universal Edition, 1969

296   —*Sinfonia No. 86*, Salzburg, Haydn-Mozart Presse, 1963; Vienna, Universal Edition, 1969

297   —*Sinfonia No. 87*, Salzburg, Haydn-Mozart Presse, 1963; Vienna, Universal Edition, 1969

298   —*Symphony No. 89 in F major (1787)*, London, Eulenburg, 1963

299   —*Kritische   Ausgabe   Sämtlicher Symphonien/Critical   Edition   of   the   Complete Symphonies*, 12 vols. (vol. V, nos. 50–57, ed. by H. Schultz), Vienna, Universal Edition, 1963–8. 2nd rev. ed., Vienna, Universal Edition, in association with Doblinger, 1981

300   —*4 Arien für Tenor*, [Hob. XXIVb:10, 14, 16, XXVIII:7], Salzburg, Haydn-Mozart Presse, 1964 (see no. 372)

301   —*L'incontro improvviso. Dramma giocoso. Sinfonia (Overtura)*, [Hob. Ia:6], Vienna, Munich, Doblinger, 1964

302   —*Salve Regina in G-moll*, [Hob. XXIIIb:2], Vienna, Munich, Doblinger, 1964

303   —*Sinfonia No. 29*, Vienna, Munich, Doblinger, 1964; Vienna, Universal Edition, 1969

304   —*Sinfonia No. 31 ('Hornsignal')*, Vienna, Munich, Doblinger, 1964; Vienna, Universal Edition, 1969

305   —*Sinfonia No. 34*, Vienna, Munich, Doblinger, 1964; Vienna, Universal Edition, 1969

306   —*Sinfonia No. 35*, Vienna, Munich, Doblinger, 1964; Vienna, Universal Edition, 1969

307   —*Sinfonia No. 36*, Vienna, Munich, Doblinger, 1964; Vienna, Universal Edition, 1969

308   —*Sinfonia No. 38*, Vienna, Munich, Doblinger, 1964; Vienna, Universal Edition, 1969

309   —*Sinfonia No. 40*, Vienna, Munich, Doblinger, 1964; Vienna, Universal Edition, 1969

310   —*Sinfonia No. 63 ('La Roxelane')*, Salzburg, Haydn-Mozart Presse, 1964; Vienna, Universal Edition, 1969

311   —*Sinfonia No. 72*, Salzburg, Haydn-Mozart Presse, 1964; Vienna, Universal Edition, 1969

312   —*Sinfonia No. 88*, Salzburg, Haydn-Mozart Presse, 1964; Vienna, Universal Edition, 1969

313   —*Sinfonia No. 89*, Salzburg, Haydn-Mozart Presse, 1964; Vienna, Universal Edition, 1969

314   —*Sinfonia No. 90*, Salzburg, Haydn-Mozart Presse, 1964; Vienna, Universal Edition, 1969

315   —*Sinfonia No. 91*, Salzburg, Haydn-Mozart Presse, 1964; Vienna, Universal Edition, 1969

316   —*3 Arien für Bariton*, [Hob. XXIVb:5, 11, XXVIII:1], Salzburg, Haydn-Mozart Presse, 1964 (see no. 372)

317   —*Motetto di Venerabili Sacramento*, [Hob. XXIIIc:5], Vienna, Munich, Doblinger, [1965]

318   —*Le Pescatrici, dramma giocoso in tre atti*, [Hob. XXVIII:4], 3 vols., Salzburg, Haydn-Mozart Presse, 1965, f.s., 1971, v.s. (Italian and German)

319   —*Scena di Berenice*, [Hob. XXIVa:10], Vienna, Munich, Doblinger, 1965

320   —*Sinfonia 'A'*, [Hob. I:107], Vienna, Munich, Doblinger, 1965; Vienna, Universal Edition, 1969

321   —*Sinfonia Concertante*, [Hob. I:105], Salzburg, Haydn-Mozart Presse, 1965; Vienna, Universal Edition, 1969

322   —*Sinfonia No. 3*, Vienna, Munich, Doblinger, 1965; Vienna, Universal Edition, 1969

323   —*Sinfonia No. 4*, Vienna, Munich, Doblinger, 1965; Vienna, Universal Edition, 1969

324   —*Sinfonia No. 5*, Vienna, Munich, Doblinger, 1965; Vienna, Universal Edition, 1969

325   —*Sinfonia No. 6 ('Le Matin')*, Vienna, Munich, Doblinger, 1965; Vienna, Universal Edition, 1969

326 —*Sinfonia No. 7 ('Le Midi')*, Vienna, Munich, Doblinger, 1965; Vienna, Universal Edition, 1969

327 —*Sinfonia No. 8 ('Le Soir')*, Vienna, Munich, Doblinger, 1965; Vienna, Universal Edition, 1969

328 —*Sinfonia No. 11*, Vienna, Munich, Doblinger, 1965; Vienna, Universal Edition, 1969

329 —*Sinfonia No. 12*, Vienna, Munich, Doblinger, 1965; Vienna, Universal Edition, 1969

330 —*Sinfonia No. 28*, Vienna, Munich, Doblinger, 1965; Vienna, Universal Edition, 1969

331 —*Sinfonia No. 30 ('Alleluja')*, Vienna, Munich, Doblinger, 1965; Vienna, Universal Edition, 1969

332 —*Sinfonia No. 41*, Vienna, Munich, Doblinger, 1965; Vienna, Universal Edition, 1969

333 —*Sinfonia No. 43 ('Merkur')*, Vienna, Munich, Doblinger, 1965; Vienna, Universal Edition, 1969

334 —*Sinfonia No. 49 ('La Passione')*, Vienna, Munich, Doblinger, 1965; Vienna, Universal Edition, 1969

335 —*Sinfonia No. 64*, Salzburg, Haydn-Mozart Presse, 1965; Vienna, Universal Edition, 1969

336 —*Sinfonia No. 66*, Salzburg, Haydn-Mozart Presse, 1965; Vienna, Universal Edition, 1969

337 —*Sinfonia No. 70*, Salzburg, Haydn-Mozart Presse, 1965; Vienna, Universal Edition, 1969

338 —*Sinfonia No. 74*, Salzburg, Haydn-Mozart Presse, 1965; Vienna, Universal Edition, 1969

339 —*Sinfonia No. 76*, Salzburg, Haydn-Mozart Presse, 1965; Vienna, Universal Edition, 1969

340 —*Sinfonia No. 77*, Salzburg, Haydn-Mozart Presse, 1965; Vienna, Universal Edition, 1969

341 —*Sinfonia No. 78*, Salzburg, Haydn-Mozart Presse, 1965; Vienna, Universal Edition, 1969

342 —*Sinfonia No. 79*, Salzburg, Haydn-Mozart Presse, 1965; Vienna, Universal Edition, 1969

343 —*Sinfonia No. 80*, Salzburg, Haydn-Mozart Presse, 1965; Vienna, Universal Edition, 1969

344 —*Sinfonia No. 81*, Salzburg, Haydn-Mozart Presse, 1965; Vienna, Universal Edition, 1969

345 —*Sinfonia No. 93*, Salzburg, Haydn-Mozart Presse, 1965; Vienna, Universal Edition, 1969

346 —*Sinfonia No. 94 ('Surprise')*, Salzburg, Haydn-Mozart Presse, 1965; Vienna, Universal Edition, 1969

347 —*Sinfonia No. 95*, Salzburg, Haydn-Mozart Presse, 1965; Vienna, Universal Edition, 1969

348 —*Sinfonia No. 42*, Vienna, Munich, Doblinger, 1966; Vienna, Universal Edition, 1969

349 —*Sinfonia No. 44 ('Trauersymphonie')*, Vienna, Munich, Doblinger, 1966; Vienna, Universal Edition, 1969

350 —*Sinfonia No. 45 ('Abschiedssymphonie')*, Vienna, Munich, Doblinger, 1966; Vienna, Universal Edition, 1969

351 —*Sinfonia No. 46*, Vienna, Munich, Doblinger, 1966; Vienna, Universal Edition, 1969

352 —*Sinfonia No. 47*, Vienna, Munich, Doblinger, 1966; Vienna, Universal Edition, 1969

353 —*Sinfonia No. 48 ('Maria Theresien-Symphonie')*, Vienna, Munich, Doblinger, 1966; Vienna, Universal Edition, 1969

354 —*Sinfonia No. 67*, Salzburg, Haydn-Mozart Presse, 1967; Vienna, Universal Edition, 1969

355 —*Sinfonia No. 68*, Salzburg, Haydn-Mozart Presse, 1967; Vienna, Universal Edition, 1969

356 —*Sinfonia No. 69 ('Laudon')*, Salzburg, Haydn-Mozart Presse, 1967; Vienna, Universal Edition, 1969

357 —*Sinfonia No. 71*, Salzburg, Haydn-Mozart Presse, 1967; Vienna, Universal Edition, 1969

358 —*Sinfonia No. 73 ('La Chasse')*, Salzburg, Haydn-Mozart Presse, 1967; Vienna, Universal Edition, 1969

359 —*Te Deum*, [Hob. XXIIIc:1], Vienna, Munich, Doblinger, 1967

360 —*Sinfonia No. 99*, Salzburg, Haydn-Mozart Presse, 1968; Vienna, Universal Edition, 1969

361 —*Sinfonia No. 100 ('Military')*, Salzburg, Haydn-Mozart Presse, 1968; Vienna, Universal Edition, 1969

362 —*Sinfonia No. 101 ('The Clock')*, Salzburg, Haydn-Mozart Presse, 1968; Vienna, Universal Edition, 1969

363 —*Sinfonia No. 102*, Salzburg, Haydn-Mozart Presse, 1968; Vienna, Universal Edition, 1969

364 —*Sinfonia No. 103 ('Drum Roll')*, Salzburg, Haydn-Mozart Presse, 1968; Vienna, Universal Edition, 1969

365 —*Sinfonia No. 104*, Salzburg, Haydn-Mozart Presse, 1968; Vienna, Universal Edition, 1969

366 —*Applausus: Cantata*, [Hob. XXIVa:6], Vienna, Munich, Doblinger, 1969

367 —*Concerto per il Cembalo, C-Dur*, [Hob. XIV:12], Vienna, Munich, Doblinger, 1969

368 —*Concerto per il Clavicembalo*, [Hob. XVIII:F2], Vienna, Munich, Doblinger 1969

369 —*Divertimento per il Clavicembalo, C-Dur*, [Hob. XIV:C2], Vienna, Munich, Doblinger, 1969

370 —*Libera me, Domine*, [Hob. XXIIb:1], Salzburg, Haydn-Mozart Presse, 1969

371 —*Missa Sancti Nicolai*, [Hob. XXII:6], London, Faber Music, 1969; London, Eulenburg, 1976

372 —*Arien mit Orchester für Sopran/Tenor/Bass (Bariton)*, rev. ed., Salzburg, Haydn-Mozart Presse, 1970 (see nos. 257, 300, 316)

373 —*Klaviertrios. Urtext Ausgabe, Trio No. 1–7, 10–45*, [Hob. XIV:6, c1, XV:1, 2, 5–32, 34–41, c1, f1 and one work in D], Vienna, Doblinger, 1970–88

374 —*Lo speziale. Dramma giocoso*, [Hob. XXVIII:3], Salzburg, Haydn-Mozart Presse, 1970, v.s. (Italian and German)

375 —*Raccolta de Menuetti Ballabili*, [Hob. IX:7], Vienna, Munich, Doblinger, 1970

376 —*Missa Brevis Sancti Joannis de Deo 'Small Organ Mass'*, [Hob. XXII:7], New York, Schirmer, 1972 (see no. 220)

377 —*Missa Cellensis in C 'Mariazellermesse'. For Four-Part Chorus of Mixed Voices with Piano or Organ Accompaniment*, [Hob. XXII:8], New York, Schirmer, 1972 (see no. 220)

378 —*Missa Sancti Bernardi de Offida 'Heiligmesse'. For Four-Part Chorus of Mixed Voices with Piano or Organ Accompaniment*, [Hob. XXII:10], New York, Schirmer, 1972 (see no. 220)

379 —*Dr. Harington's Compliment*, ['What art expresses'; Hob. XXVIb:3], New York, Broude Brothers, 1974

380 —*24 Menuetti*, [Hob. IX:16], Vienna, Munich, Doblinger, 1974

381 —*Creation Mass in B♭ Major ('Schöpfungsmesse') (1801)*, [Hob. XXII:13], New York, Schirmer, 1975

382 —*La vera costanza*, [Hob. XXVIII:8], Vienna, Universal Edition, 1975

383 —*Il mondo della luna*, [Hob. XXVIII:7], Kassel, London, Bärenreiter, 1976

384 —*Stabat Mater*, [Hob. XXbis], London, Faber Music, 1977

385 —*Streichquartette*, [Hob. II:6, III:1–4, 6–8, 10, 12, 19–49, 57–83]. Urtext Ausgabe, (with Reginald Barrett-Ayres), Vienna, Doblinger, 1977–

386 —*Non nobis Domine*, [Hob. XXIIIa:1], Vienna, Munich, Doblinger, 1978

387 —*Notturno No. 2 in F*, [Hob. II:26], Vienna, Munich, Doblinger, 1979

388 —*Notturno No. 3 in C*, [Hob. II:32], Vienna, Munich, Doblinger, 1979

422 —*Der büssende Sünder. Introduzione*, [MH 147], Vienna, Doblinger, 1968

423 —*Rebecca als Braut. Intrada*, [MH 76], Vienna, Doblinger, 1968

MENDELSSOHN, FELIX

424 —Foreword to *Concerto for Violin and Orchestra in E minor, op. 64: a facsimile*, New York, London, Garland Publishing, 1991

MOZART, JOHANN GEORG LEOPOLD

425 —*Sinfonia, G major, for String Orchestra*, London, Eulenburg, 1956, 1957

426 —*Sinfonia in B-Dur für Streicher und Basso Continuo*, Vienna, Doblinger, 1970

427 —*Sinfonia in G-Dur für Streicher und Basso Continuo*, Vienna, Doblinger, 1970

428 —*Cassatio ex G*, Vienna, Doblinger, 1974

MOZART, WOLFGANG AMADEUS

429 —*Missa C-moll*, (K.427 [417a]), London, Eulenburg, 1956; Frankfurt, New York, C.F. Peters, 1956, 1984; Adlis-Zurich, Edition Kunzelmann, 1956, 1984

430 —*Maurerische Trauermusik*, (K.477), Kassel, Bärenreiter, 1956. Separate edition (taken from *W.A. Mozart, Neue Ausgabe Sämtlicher Werke*, Serie IV, Werkgruppe 11, Band 10), Kassel, Bärenreiter, 1978, 1979; Edwin F. Kalmus, 1980, 1990

431 —*W.A. Mozart. Neue Ausgabe Sämtlicher Werke*, Serie IV, Werkgruppe 11, Band 9, *Sinfonien: Sinfonie in Es*, (K.543), *Sinfonie in g*, (K.550) (I. Fassung), *Sinfonie in g*, (K.550) (II. Fassung), *Sinfonie in C*, (K.551), Kassel, Basle, London, Bärenreiter, 1957, 1986 (see nos. 432–4)

432 —*Sinfonie in Es*, (K.543), Kassel, Bärenreiter, 1958, 1988 (see no. 431)

433 —*Sinfonie in g*, (K.550), Kassel, Bärenreiter, 1958. 2nd version with clarinets (taken from *W.A. Mozart, Neue Sämtlicher Werke*, Serie IV, Werkgruppe 11, Band 9), Kassel, Bärenreiter, 1986 (see no. 431)

434 —*W.A. Mozart: Neue Ausgabe Sämtlicher Werke. Kritischer Bericht*, Serie IV, Werkgruppe 11, Band 9, Kassel, Bärenreiter, 1963 (see no. 431)

435 —*Symphony in D*, (K.385), *'Haffner' Symphony*, (edited by doctoral students of the City University of New York under the supervision of H.C. Robbins Landon), London, Faber Music, 1971

436 —*Missa for Archbishop Colloredo*, (K.337). Four-part chorus, New York, Schirmer, 1973

437 —*Credo Mass (Missa in C, K.257)*. Mixed chorus with piano or organ accompaniment, New York, Schirmer, 1974

438 —*Organ Solo Mass (Missa brevis in C, K.259)*. Mixed chorus with piano or organ accompaniment, New York, Schirmer, 1974

439 —*Piccolomini Mass (Missa brevis in C, K.258)*. Mixed chorus with piano or organ accompaniment, New York, Schirmer, 1974

440 —*Kyrie*, (K.322), for four-part chorus, New York, Schirmer, 1977

441 —*Kyrie* (K.323), for four-part chorus, New York, Schirmer, 1977

442 —*Kyrie* (K.341), for four-part chorus, New York, Schirmer, 1977

443 —*Requiem*, (K.626), Leipzig, Breitkopf & Härtel, 1991

ORDOÑEZ, CARLOS D'

444 —*Sinfonia per tre cori*, Vienna, Universal Edition, 1972

PICCINI, NICCOLO

445 —*Concerto in D-Dur für Flöte, Streicher und Basso Continuo*, Vienna, Doblinger, 1981

SALOMON, JOHANN PETER

446 —*Romance D-Dur für Solo-Violine und Streicher*, Vienna, Doblinger, 1970

VANHAL, JOHANN BAPTIST

447 —*Sinfonia G-moll*, Vienna, Doblinger, 1965

VIVALDI, ANTONIO LUCIO

448 —*Magnificat. Ossecensis, per soli, coro ed orchestra*, Vienna, Universal Edition, 1961

REVIEWS OF BOOKS

449   1993 (ii/1), 101: V. Braunbehrens (trans-lated by E.L. Kanes), *Maligned Master: the Real Story of Antonio Salieri*, (London, Scolar Press, 1993)

450   1993 (ii/3), 60: P. Clive, *Mozart and His Circle: a Biographical Dictionary* (London, Dent, 1993)

451   1995 (iii/7), 54: C. Wolff (trans. by M. Whittall), *Mozart's Requiem: Historical and Analytical Studies, Documents, Score* (Oxford, Clarendon Press, 1994)

HAYDN YEARBOOK

452   1962 (i), 234–40: D. Bartha and L. Somfai, *Haydn als Opernkapellmeister* (Budapest, Verlag der ungarischen Akademie der Wissenschaften, 1960)

453   1963/4 (ii), 117–18: A. Weinmann, *Verzeichnis der Musikalien aus dem k.k. Hoftheater-Musik-Verlag* (Vienna, Wiener Urtext Ausgabe, 1962). A. Weinmann, *Kataloge Anton Huberty (Wien) und Christoph Torricella* (Vienna, Wiener Urtext Ausgabe, 1962)

454   1965 (iii), 174: K. Geiringer, *Haydn: a Creative Life in Music* (Garden City, New York, Anchor Books [Doubleday], 1963)

455   1967 (iv), 214–16: L. Somfai, *Joseph Haydn, Sein Leben in zeitgenössischen Bildern, gesammelt, erläutert und mit einer Ikonographie der authentischen Haydn-Bildnisse versehen* (Kassel, Bärenreiter; Budapest, Corvina, 1966)

456   1969 (vi), 217–18: R. Schaal (ed.), *Thematisches Verzeichnis der Sämtlichen Kompositionen von Joseph Haydn, zusammengestellt von Alois Fuchs 1839*, facsimile ed. (Wilhelmshaven, Heinrichs-hafers Verlag, 1968)

457   1969 (vi), 218: B.S. Brook (ed.), *The Breitkopf Thematic Catalogue – the Six Parts and Sixteen Supplements 1762–1787* (New York, Dover Publications, 1966)

458   1970 (vii), 321–3: W. Kirkendale, *Fuge und Fugato in der Kammermusik des Rokoko und der Klassik* (Tutzing, Hans Schneider, 1966)

459   1971 (viii), 300–1: A. Tyson, *Thematic Catalogue of the Works of Muzio Clementi* (Tutzing, Hans Schneider, 1967)

460   1978 (ix), 361–4: J. Haydn, *Thematisch-biblographisches Werkverzeichnis, zusammengestellt von Anthony van Hoboken*, Band II (Tutzing, Hans Schneider, 1969)

461   1978 (ix), 364–6: H. Unverricht, *Geschichte des Streichtrios* (Tutzing, Hans Schneider, 1969)

462   1980 (xi), 209–10: J.P. Larsen, *Three Haydn Catalogues*, 2nd facsimile ed. with a survey of Haydn's œuvre (New York, Pendragon Press, 1979)

463   1980 (xi), 211–12: A.P. Brown, *Carlo d'Ordoñez, 1734–1786: a Thematic Catalogue* (Detroit, Information Co-ordinators, 1978)

464   1980 (xi), 212–13: R. Benton, *Ignace Pleyel: a Thematic Catalogue of His Compositions* (New York, Pendragon Press, 1977)

465   1980 (xi), 218–19: I. Leux-Henschen (ed.), *Joseph Martin Kraus in seinen Briefen* (Stockholm, Reimers, 1978)

466   1981 (xii), 192: B. Brevan, *Les Changements de la Vie Musicale Parisienne de 1774 à 1799* (Paris, Presses Universitaires de France, 1980)

467   1981 (xii), 192–3: R.N. Freeman, *Franz Schneider (1737–1812): a Thematic Catalogue of His Works* (New York, Pendragon Press, 1979)

468   1981 (xii), 197: H. Scholz-Michelitsch, *Georg Christoph Wagenseil, Hofkomponist und Hofklaviermeister der Kaiserin Maria Theresia* (Vienna, Wilhelm Braumüller Universitäts-Verlagsbuchhandlung, 1980)

469   1981 (xii), 198: *Symposium Gottfried Bessel (1672–1749), Diplomat in Kurmainz – Abt von Göttweig, Wissenschaftler und Kunstmäzen* (Mainz, Gesellschaft für Mittelrheinische Kirchen-geschichte, 1979)

470   1983 (xiv), 227–8: U. Tank, *Studien zur Esterházyschen Hofmusik von etwa 1620 bis 1790* (Regensburg, Gustav Bosse, 1981)

471   1983 (xiv), 228–9: K. Geiringer, in collaboration with I. Geiringer, *Haydn: a Creative Life in Music*, 3rd rev. and enlarged ed. (Los Angeles, London, Berkeley, University of California Press, 1982)

472   1983 (xiv), 229–230: S. Sadie, *The New Grove Mozart* (London, Macmillan, 1982)

473   1984 (xv), 232: C. Hogwood and R. Luckett (eds.), *Music in Eighteenth-Century England* (Cambridge, Cambridge University Press, 1983)

474   1985 (xvi), 275: A. Ziffer, *Kleinmeister zur Zeit der Wiener Klassik* (Tutzing, Hans Schneider, 1984)

THE MUSICAL TIMES

475   1989 (cxxx), 411–12: A. Steptoe, *The Mozart–Da Ponte Operas* (Oxford, Oxford University Press, 1988)

DIE MUSIKFORSCHUNG

476   1969 (xxii), 390: M.A. Vos, *The Liturgical Choral Works of Johann Christian Bach* (Ph.D. diss. Musicology, Washington University, St Louis, MO, 1969)

477   1969 (xxii), 390: W. Witzenmann, 'Autographs of Marco Marrazoli in the Biblioteca Vaticana. Part I', in *Analecta Musicologica*, vii (1969), 38–86

SOUNDINGS

478   1983/4 (xi), 72–4: A. Tyson (ed.), *Beethoven Studies 3* (Cambridge, Cambridge University Press, 1982)

THE TIMES LITERARY SUPPLEMENT

479   27 April 1984, 474: G. Pestelli (trans. by E. Cross), *The Age of Mozart and Beethoven* (Cambridge, Cambridge University Press, 1984)

480   15 March 1985, 291: A. Hyatt King, *A Mozart Legacy: Aspects of the British Library Collections* (London, British Library, 1984)

481   6 December 1985, 1398: A.M. Hanson, *Musical Life in Biedermeier Vienna* (Cambridge Studies in Music) (Cambridge, Cambridge University Press, 1985)

REVIEWS OF MUSIC

HAYDN YEARBOOK

482   1962 (i), 215–18: J. Haydn, *List und Liebe (La vera costanza), Komische Oper in zwei Akten.* Deutsche Bearbeitung by G. Schwalbe and W. Zimmer (Vienna, Universal Edition, [1961])

483   1962 (i), 224–7: J. Haydn, *Barytontrios Nr. 49–72. Joseph Haydn Werke*, Reihe XIV, Band 3, ed. H. Unverricht (Munich, Henle, 1958). J. Haydn, *Barytontrios Nr. 73–96. Joseph Haydn Werke*, Reihe XIV, Band 4, ed. H. Unverricht (Munich, Henle, 1958)

484   1962 (i), 232–3: J. Haydn, *Symphony, F sharp minor (No. 45, 'Farewell Symphony')*, Facsimile of the original Haydn manuscript, with a foreword by L. Somfai (Budapest, Hungarian Academy of Sciences, 1959)

485   1962 (i), 232–3: J. Haydn, *Messe B-dur ('Schöpfungs Messe')*. Facsimile (Munich, Henle, 1957)

486   1963/4 (ii), 95–7: J. Haydn, *Lo Speziale. Joseph Haydn Werke*, Reihe XXV, Band 3, ed. H. Wirth (Munich, Henle, 1959)

487   1965 (iii), 172: J.M. Kraus, *Sinfonie C-moll*, ed. R. Engländer (Stockholm, Almqvist & Wiksell, 1960)

488   1968 (iv), 207–9: J. Haydn, *L'infedeltà delusa. Joseph Haydn Werke*, Reihe XXV, Band 5, ed. D. Bartha and J. Vécsey (Munich, Henle, 1964). J. Haydn, *L'incontro improvviso. Joseph Haydn Werke*, Reihe XXV, Band 6, ed. H. Wirth (Munich, Henle, 1962–3)

489   1969 (vi), 210–12: J. Haydn, *Sinfonien 1773–4. Joseph Haydn Werke*, Reihe I, Band 7, ed. W. Stockmeier (Munich, Henle, 1966). J. Haydn, *Messe Nr. 12 (Harmoniemesse). Joseph Haydn Werke*, Reihe XXIII, Band 5, ed. F. Lippmann (Munich, Henle, 1966)

490   1969 (vi), 212–13: J. Haydn, *Il ritorno di Tobia, Oratorio. Joseph Haydn Werke*, Reihe XXVIII, Band 1 and 2, ed. E.F. Schmid (Munich, Henle, 1963)

491   1969 (vi), 213–14: J. Haydn, *Armida, Dramma Eroico. Joseph Haydn Werke*, Reihe XXV, Band 12, ed. W. Pfannkuch (Munich, Henle, 1965)

[REVIEWS OF MUSIC: Haydn Yearbook –
continued]

492   1971 (viii), 314–15: J. Haydn, *Madrigal 'The
Storm' 1792 für gemischten Chor und Orchester*, ed. F.
Szekeres (Vienna, Munich, Doblinger, 1969)

493   1971 (viii), 315: G. Werner, *Symphonia da
chiesa*, ed. I. Sulyok (Vienna, Doblinger, 1969)

494   1975 (ix), 369–70: J. Haydn, *Barytontrios
Nr. 97–126. Joseph Haydn Werke*, Reihe XIV, Band
5, ed. M. Härting and H. Walter (Munich,
Henle, 1968)

495   1975 (ix), 370–71: J. Haydn, *Cantata
Applausus. Joseph Haydn Werke*, Reihe XXVII,
Band 2, ed. H. Wiens in association with I.
Becker-Glauch (Munich, Henle, 1969)

496   1975 (ix), 371–2: J. Haydn, *Werke mit
Baryton. Joseph Haydn Werke*, Reihe XIII, ed. S.
Gerlach (Munich, Henle, 1969)

497   1975 (ix), 373–5: J. Haydn, *Konzerte für
Violine und Orchester. Joseph Haydn Werke*, Reihe III,
Band 1, ed. H. Lohmann and G. Thomas
(Munich, Henle, 1969)

498   1975 (ix), 381: J. Haydn, *String Quartet in
G*, Op. 77, no. 1 [Hob. III:81]; *String Quartet in
F*, Op. 77, no. 2 [Hob. III:82]. Facsimile of the
original manuscript with commentaries by L.
Somfai (Budapest, Editio Musica, 1972)

499   1980 (xi), 220–21: J. Haydn, *Symphony No.
7 'Le Midi'*, facsimile ed. of the original manuscript
with commentaries by L. Somfai (Budapest,
Editio Musica, 1972)

500   1981 (xii), 201–2: J. Haydn, *Baryton Trios
Nos. 1–24. Joseph Haydn Werke*, Reihe XIV, Band
1, ed. J. Braun and S. Gerlach (Munich, Henle,
1980)

501   1982 (1983) (xiii), 244–9: C. d'Ordoñez,
*String Quartets Op. 1. Recent Researches in the Music
of the Classical Era*, Vol. X, ed. A.P. Brown
(Madison, A-R Editions, 1980). C. d'Ordoñez,
Seven Symphonies. The Symphony 1720–1840, Series
B, vol. IV, ed. A.P. Brown with P.M. Alexander
(New York, London, Garland, 1979). G.
Brunetti, *Nine Symphonies. The Symphony
1720–1840*, Series A, vol. V, ed. N. Jenkins (New
York, London, Garland, 1979)

502   1984   (xv),   233–9:   *The   Symphony
1720–1840*, ed. in chief B.S. Brook (New York,

London, Garland): G.C. Wagenseil, *Fifteen
Symphonies*, ed. J. Kucaba, Series B, vol. III,
(1981). *Austrian Cloister Symphonists*: J.G.
Zechner, *Two Symphonies*; F.J. Aumann, *One
Symphony*; M. Paradeiser; *Three Symphonies*, ed.
R.N. Freeman with M. Meckna, Series B, vol.
VI, (1982). *Salzburg Part 2*: J.E. Eberlin, *Three
Symphonies*, ed. M.M. Schneider-Cuvay; A.C.
Adlgasser, *Four Symphonies*, ed. W. Rainer; J.M.
Haydn, *Five Symphonies*, ed. C. Sherman, Series
B, vol. VIII, (1982). F.L. Gassmann, *Seven
Symphonies*, ed. G.R. Hill; J.K. Vanhal, *Five
Symphonies*, ed. P. Bryan, Series B, vol. X, (1981).
*Seven Symphonies from the Court of Oettingen-
Wallerstein 1773–1795*: J. Fiala, *One Symphony*; A.
Rosetti, *Three Symphonies*; J. Reicha, *One
Symphony*; P. Weinberger, *One Symphony*; F.I. von
Beeke, *One Symphony*, ed. S.E. Murray, Series C,
vol. VI, (1981): C.P.E. Bach, *Six Symphonies*, ed.
C.C. Gallagher and E.E. Helm, Series C, vol.
VIII, (1982). *The Symphony in Sweden Part 1*: J.H.
Roman, *Six Symphonies*, ed. I. Bengtsson; J.M.
Kraus, *Six Symphonies*, ed. B.H. van Boer, Series
F, vol. II, (1982)

503   1993 (xviii), 267–8: J. Haydn, *Sinfonien
1761–1763. Joseph Haydn Werke*, Reihe I, Band 3,
ed. J. Braun and S. Gerlach (Munich, Henle,
1990)

504   1993 (xviii), 268: J. Haydn, *Streichtrios, I.
Joseph Haydn Werke*, Reihe XI, Band 1, ed. B.C.
McIntyre and B.S. Brook (Munich, Henle, 1986)

NOTES

505   1975 (xxxii/1), 124–5: G. Gazzaniga, *Don
Giovanni o sia Il convitato di pietro*, ed. S. Kunze
(Kassel, Bärenreiter, 1974)

506   1975 (xxxii/2), 377–8: J. Haydn, *Orlando
Paladino. Joseph Haydn Werke*, Reihe XXV/II/1,2,
ed. K. Geiringer (Munich, Henle, 1972)

507   1977 (xxxiii/3), 675–8: J.B. Krumpholtz,
Sonata No. 1 from *Four Sonatas for the Harp*, Op.13,
ed. A.L. Lawson (Ross, California, Harp
Publications, 1974). J.B. Krumpholtz, *Sonata No.
1* from *Two Sonatas for the Harp in the Form of Scenes
of Different Character*, ed. A.L. Lawson, (Ross,
California, Harp Publications, 1974). J.B.
Cramer, *Air with Variations or 'Rousseau's Dream'*,
arranged for harp by J.B. Chatterton, ed. A.L.
Lawson (Ross, California, Harp Publications,

1974). R.N.C. Bochsa, *Grande Sonate for the Harp*, ed. A.L. Lawson (Ross, California, Harp Publications, 1974). J.B. Cardon, *Sonata No. 3* from *Four Sonatas for the Harp, Op. 7*, ed. A.L. Lawson (Ross, California, Harp Publications, 1974). N.B. Challoner, *Sonata No. 1* from *Three Sonatas for the Harp, Op. 2*, ed. A.L. Lawson (Ross, California, Harp Publications, 1974). L. van Beethoven, *First, Second and Third Symphonies*. Facsimile of the full scores by Cianchettini and Sperati (London, 1809), introduction by F. Freedman (Detroit, Information Co-ordinators, 1975). F. Danzi, *Konzert Nr. 2 für Flöte und Orchester, D-moll, Op. 31*, ed. D.H. Förster (Zurich, Eulenburg, 1974). F.X. Brixi, *Concerto, fa maggiore, per organo principale*, ed. J. Racek and J. Reinberger (Zurich, Eulenburg, 1973). T.A. Erskine, *Symphony in E♭ major*, ed. D. Johnson (London, Oxford University Press, 1974). J. Triebensee, *Variations sur un Thème de Haydn (Symphonie No. 94)*, ed. A. Myslik (Basle, Kneusslin, 1973)

508   1980 (xxxvi/4), 973: W.A. Mozart, *Sinfonia in C, K551*, ed. K. Köhler. *Documenta Musicologica*, Reihe II: Handschriften-Faksimiles 8, (Kassel, Bärenreiter, 1978)

509   1980 (xxxvi/4), 974: T. Linley, *Anthem: Let God Arise*, ed. G. Beechey. *Recent Researches in the Music of the Classical Era*, 7, (Madison, A-R Editions, 1977)

510   1981 (xxxvii/3), 672–3: W.A. Mozart, *Die Zauberflöte, K.V. 620. Documenta Musicologica*, Reihe II: Handschriften-Faksimiles 7, (Kassel, Bärenreiter, 1979)

511   1983 (xxxix/3), 686–8: A. Vivaldi, *L'Estro Armonico, Op. 3*, ed. G.F. Malipiero (Milan, Ricordi, 1965). A. Vivaldi, *La Stravaganza, Op. 4*, ed. A. Ephrikian (Milan, Ricordi, 1965). A. Vivaldi, *Il Cimento dell'armonia e dell'inventione, Op. 8*, ed. G.F. Malipiero (Milan, Ricordi, 1950). A. Vivaldi, *La Cetra, Op. 9*, ed. G.F. Malipiero (Milan, Ricordi, 1980). G.B. Sammartini, *Sonate a tre stromenti. Six Notturnos for String Trio, Op. 7*, ed. B. Churgin (Chapel Hill, University of North Carolina Press, 1981). W.A. Mozart, *Konzerte für Flöte, für Oboe und für Fagott. Neue Ausgabe sämtlicher Werke*, V/14/3, ed. F. Giegling (Kassel, Bärenreiter, 1981)

512   1987 (xliv/1), 141–2: W.A. Mozart, *Messe C-moll, KV427 (417a): Faksimile der Autographen* (Kassel, Bärenreiter, 1983)

513   1987 (xliv/1), 151–3: J.C. Bach, *Adriano in Siria: Opera Seria in Three Acts, J.C. Bach, Collected Works 5*, ed. E. Warburton (New York, Garland, 1985). J.C. Bach, *Music for Vespers, II: Three Psalm Settings for Soloists, Choir, and Orchestra from Eighteenth Century Manuscript Sources. J.C. Bach, Collected Works 23*, ed. E. Warburton (New York, Garland, 1985). J.C. Bach, *Symphonies Concertantes, I: Eight Symphonies Concertantes. J.C. Bach, Collected Works 30*, ed. R. Maunder (New York, Garland, 1985). J.C. Bach, *Symphonies, I: Twelve Early Symphonic Works from Eighteenth Century Printed Sources. J.C. Bach, Collected Works 26*, ed. E. Warburton (New York, Garland, 1984)

VIDEOCASSETTES

514   *The Rise and Fall of Wolfgang Amadeus Mozart*, writer and narrator, H.C. Robbins Landon [videorecording, BBC-TV], New York, Time-Life Multimedia, 1970, 1979. 1 video-cassette (U-matic), b. & w., 35 mins.

515   *Maestro, a Musical Journey through Venice*, created by H.C. Robbins Landon; presented by John Julius Norwich; writer and music consul-tant, H.C. Robbins Landon, (Five Centuries of Music in Venice), Great Britain, France, A Robclif production for La SEPT [France] and Channel Four [Great Britain], Princeton, New Jersey, Films for the Humanities and Science, 1990–93, 5 videocassettes (VHS), col., *c.* 60 mins. Pt. I – *Venice and the Gabrielis*, Pt. II – *The World of Claudio Monteverdi*, Pt. III – *Venice and Vivaldi*, Pt. IV – *Verdi and Venetian Theatre*, Pt. V – *20th-Century Music in Venice* (see no. 21)

516   *Joseph Haydn and His Symphonies* (including discussion between H.C. Robbins Landon, Christopher Hogwood and Melvyn Bragg), directed by Chris Hunt; London, New York, Iambic Productions for the Decca Record Company, marketed by Polygram Records, 1991. 1 videocassette (VHS), col., 107 mins. (Academy of Ancient Music, cond., Christopher Hogwood).

Notes on the texts

MALCOLM BOYD: 'The music very good indeed': Scarlatti's *Tolomeo et Alessandro* recovered

1   R. Pagano, *Scarlatti, Alessandro e Domenico: due vite in una* (Milan 1985), pp. 213–14.

2   T.E. Griffin, *The Late Baroque Serenata in Rome and Naples: a Documentary Study with Emphasis on Alessandro Scarlatti* (PhD, University of California, Los Angeles, 1983), pp. 616–17. See also the *Diario di Roma* of Francesco Valesio, where it is reported, under the date 27 January 1711, that 'Cardinal Ottoboni is preparing a new opera, a pastoral, which will be performed in his theatre, and Prince Ruspoli is doing likewise' (F. Valesio, *Diario di Roma*, ed. G. Scano (Milan 1977–9), iv, p. 427).

3   Franco Piperno has suggested that Alessandro Scarlatti's *Il Ciro* (libretto by Cardinal Ottoboni) was intended, but that the performance was, for one reason or another, postponed until the following year. See F. Piperno, 'Crateo, Olinto, Archimede e l'Arcadia: rime per alcuni spettacoli operistici romani (1710–1711)', in *Händel e gli Scarlatti a Roma*, ed. N. Pirrotta and A. Ziino (Florence 1987), pp. 363–5.

4   Anatole de Montaiglon (ed.), *Correspondance des Directeurs de L'Académie de France à Rome*, iv (Paris 1893), p. 55.

5   T.E. Griffin, op. cit., p. 616.

6   G.M. Crescimbeni, *L'Arcadia* (Rome, 1708; 2nd ed., 1711), p. 326.

7   The MS. went on sale in an antiquarian bookshop in Rome in the 1940s. It came into the possession of the musicologist Sebastiano Arturo Luciani (1884–1950) and was last reported in August 1981 as belonging to Arigo Perrone of Milan. A microfilm of this source is in the Kirkpatrick archive in the John Herrick Jackson Music Library, Yale University. See S.A. Luciani, 'Un' opera inedita di Domenico Scarlatti', *Rivista musicale italiana*, xlviii (1946), pp. 433–45; and R. Kirkpatrick, *Domenico Scarlatti* (Princeton 1953; reprinted 1983 with additions and corrections), pp. 52 and 472.

8   *Belton House, Lincolnshire* (The National Trust, 1985; 4th ed., 1991), p. 50.

9   I am most grateful to Jane Clark for bringing this score to my attention. I should like also to express my gratitude to Duncan Bowen, Administrator of Belton House, for allowing me to examine the manuscript and other items in the library there, and to John Fuggles, Libraries Adviser to the National Trust, for the loan of a microfilm of the complete score.

10   I am grateful to Elizabeth Gibson for this observation.

11   For details of Tyrconnel's connections with the Academy, see E. Gibson, *The Royal Academy of Music (1719–1728)* (New York 1989).

12   It cannot have been irrelevant to her choice of this operatic plot that, after the death of her husband King Jan III Sobieski, Maria Casimira had favoured her second son, Alexander, as successor to the Polish throne, and that he had left Poland so as not to stand in the way of his elder brother,

James. In the event none of Maria Casimira's sons became king. See K. Waliszewski, *Marysieńka*, trans. Lady Mary Loyd (London 1898), pp. 266–9.

13   In addition to the sources already mentioned, two further copies of the overture are in the library of the Paris Conservatoire (now housed in the Bibliothèque Nationale): MSS. Rés. 2634 and D.12741(7).

14   Kirkpatrick, *Domenico Scarlatti*, p. 51.

15   Scarlatti's original and forward-looking approach to da capo form in this and other arias is discussed in more detail in M. Boyd, 'Domenico Scarlatti as an Opera Composer', *Early Music* (forthcoming).

16   Similar 'pause' signs are found in the vocal parts of Scarlatti's Mass in D (MS. 389 of the Santuario de Aránzazu, Spain) in contexts where the instrumental parts proceed in unbroken semiquavers.

17   R. Strohm, *Essays on Handel and Italian Opera* (Cambridge 1985), p. 58. It is not absolutely certain, however, that an unaltered copy of the 1711 publication of Antonio de' Rossi served as the model for Handel's *Tolomeo*. Ptolemy's recitative at the end of Act I includes the phrase 'E di Seleuce estinta/Tormi dal cor la rimembranza' (libretto, p. 25), but in both Scarlatti's and Handel's settings 'cor' becomes 'sen'. On the other hand, Handel's text could not have been prepared from the Belton House score, which includes revisions to the text in several places where Handel follows the printed 1711 libretto.

18   The total includes duets but not the final aria, which Scarlatti adapted as a *coro*.

19   Tempo directions in Handel's setting are quoted from F.W. Chrysander's edition, vol. lxxvi of *G.F. Händels Werke: Ausgabe der Deutschen Händelgesellschaft* (Leipzig 1878).

GEOFFREY CHEW: Haydn's Pastorellas: Genre, Dating and Transmission . . .

1   I. Becker-Glauch, 'Wiederaufgefundene Kirchenmusikwerke Joseph Haydns', *Die Musikforschung*, xvii (1964), pp. 413ff.; and 'Haydns *Cantilena pro adventu* in D', *Haydn-Studien*, i (1967), pp. 277ff. I also discussed these works in 'The Christmas Pastorella in Austria, Bohemia and Moravia and its Antecedents' (PhD thesis, 2 vols., University of Manchester, 1968), i, pp. 139ff.

2   I. Becker-Glauch, 'Neue Forschungen zu Haydns Kirchenmusik', *Haydn-Studien*, ii (1970), pp. 167–241. See also I. Becker-Glauch, 'Die Kirchenmusik des jungen Haydn', in V. Schwarz (ed.), *Der junge Haydn: Wandel von Musikauffassung und Musikaufführung in der österreichischen Musik zwischen Barock und Klassik* (Graz, 1972), pp. 74–85.

3   H.C. Robbins Landon, *Haydn: Chronicle and Works. Haydn: The Early Years 1732–1765* London and Bloomington, IN, 1980.

4 Modern editions: O. Biba (ed.), *Josef Haydn: Zwei Pastorellen*, Süddeutsche Weihnachtsmusik, vol. vi (Altötting, 1975); G.A. Chew, 'The Christmas Pastorella', vol. ii (versions from Gröbming, together with the possibly inauthentic pastorella attributed to Haydn 'Der Tag, der ist so freudenreich' (Hob. XXIIId:G2), further discussed below); the Gröbming version of d:G1 is also reproduced in Landon, *Haydn: The Early Years*, pp. 276–9.

5 Details of modern editions below in n. 42.

6 Prague, Muzeum české hudby, XLIX.E.244, from Kuks: *Aria pro Adventu â Soprano Solo Due Violini Organo e Violone Del Sig. Giuseppe Haydn*. See Landon, *Haydn: The Early Years*, p. 513.

7 See J.P. Larsen, *Three Haydn Catalogues: Drei Haydn Kataloge*, 2nd ed. (New York, 1979), plate EK 2.

8 See the discussion in Chew, 'The Christmas Pastorella'.

9 See Chew, 'The Christmas Pastorella, i, pp. 214–21; 'The Austrian pastorella and the *stylus rusticanus*: comic and pastoral elements in Austrian Music, 1750–1800', in D.W. Jones (ed.), *Music in eighteenth-century Austria* (Cambridge, 1996), pp. 133–93.

10 Examples of this procedure may be found in the offertory 'Cum quietum silentium' by Valentin Rathgeber, rather archaic in style for its date (1734): see O. Biba (ed.), Valentin Rathgeber, *Offertorium in Sacra Nocte nativitatis Domini Nostri Jesu Christi [...] op. 14/5* (Altötting, 1977).

11 A number of pastoral symphonies were written in the mid-eighteenth century by L. Hoffmann (in manuscript from the Stadtpfarrkirche St Peter in Vienna and at Göttweig) and others.

12 I use this term in the sense employed by Wilhelm Fischer, 'Zur Entwicklungsgeschichte des Wiener klassischen Stils', *Studien zur Musikwissenschaft* (Beihefte der Denkmäler der Tonkunst in Österreich), iii (1915), pp. 24–84.

13 Jiří Berkovec rightly stresses the importance of this development: J. Berkovec, *České pastorely* (Prague, 1987), pp. 30ff., 199; his linking of the term with the 'duplex' (i.e. double feast) of the post-Tridentine liturgy (p. 199, n. 24) seems doubtful, but he goes on to suggest the hypothesis – based on modern practice, rather than eighteenth-century evidence – that the pairing of pastorellas represented a measure to allow for variable timing at certain points in the liturgy. Such pairs are attested in inventories from Osek [Ossegg], 1720, the Jesuit church at Uherské Hradiště, 1730, and elsewhere.

14 Prague, Muzeum české hudby (Museum of Czech Music).

15 See J.F. Dack, *The Origins and Development of the Esterházy Kapelle in Eisenstadt until 1790* (PhD thesis, University of Liverpool, 1976), I, p. 210.

16 Paul Esterházy, *Harmonia caelestis seu moelodiae per decursum totius anni adhibendae ad usum musicorum*, n.p. [Vienna], 1711; modern edition: F. Bónis, ed. (Kassel, 1972ff.); cf. M. Domokos, 'Paul Esterházy: Harmonia caelestis 1711', *Studia musicologica Academiae Scientiarum Hungaricae*, x (1968), pp. 129–51. Publication of a new edition of the *Harmonia caelestis* is expected.

17 The Jesuits' use of pastorellas, while not unique among the religious orders at this date, is attested both in compositions and in the mention of pastorellas in inventories and archives; see, for example, J. Sehnal, 'Hudba v jesuitském semináři v Uherském Hradišti v roce 1730', *Hudební věda*, iv (1967), pp. 139–47; at Eisenstadt, as noted below, the 1737–8 inventory includes a pastorella by the Jesuit J. Stupan.

18 See Domokos, op. cit., p. 130.

19 The folklorist K.M. Klier attempted to explain the curious name of this piece (also referred to in Marie's lullaby in Berg's *Wozzeck*) by suggesting that it was a corruption of Greek: see K.M. Klier, 'Eia popeia – ein griechisches Lied?', *Das deutsche Volkslied*, xxxvii (1935), pp. 4–7; it might more plausibly be regarded as a corruption of a Czech phrase such as 'Hajej, pospi' ('Hush, go to sleep'): see Chew, 'The Christmas Pastorella', I, p. 66.

20 On this song and its sources, see discussion in Chew, 'The Christmas Pastorella', I, pp. 53–74.

21 A very full account of the *Kindelwiegen* and the *Kirchenlieder* associated with it is given by K. Ameln, '"Resonet in laudibus" – "Joseph, lieber Joseph mein"', *Jahrbuch für Liturgik und Hymnologie*, xv (1970), pp. 52–112; however, Ameln makes no mention of 'Hajej můj andílku' or pastorellas. See also J. Berkovec, 'Dobrou noc ti vinšuju', *Zprávy Bertramky* (1967), pp. 55–9; R. Berliner, *Die Weihnachtskrippe*, (Munich, 1955); L. Berthold, 'Die Kindelwiegenspiele', *Beiträge zur Geschichte der deutschen Sprache und Literatur*, lvi (1932), pp. 208–24; S. Cassel, *Weihnachten: Ursprünge, Bräuche und Aberglauben*, Berlin, [1862]; K.M. Klier, 'Das Kindelwiegen zu Weihnachten', *Das deutsche Volkslied*, xli (1939), pp. 132ff.; and Chew, 'The Christmas Pastorella'.

22 A. Gavin, *The Frauds of Romish Monks and Priests*, London, 1691, pp. 362ff., quoted at some length in M. Germer, 'The Austro-Bohemian Pastorella and Pastoral Mass to c. 1780' (Ph.D thesis, New York University, 1989), pp. 95–7.

23 Cf. Chew, 'The Christmas Pastorella'.

24 The surviving Werner pastorellas are listed in the unpublished MS catalogue by J. Hárich, *Werner Gergely József müveinek tématikus katalógusa* (1932), in Budapest, Országos Széchényi Könyvtár; others are attested in the *Catalogus Über die dermalig Brauchbare Chor oder Kirchen Musicalien*: see J. Hárich, 'Die Inventare der Esterházy-Hofmusikkapelle in Eisenstadt', *Haydn Yearbook*, ix (1975), pp. 22ff., and cf. Ulrich Tank, *Studien zur Esterházyschen Hofmusik von etwa 1620 bis 1790*, Kölner Beiträge zur Musikforschung, ci (Regensburg 1981), pp. 171ff.

25 Chew, 'The Austrian pastorella and the *stylus rusticanus*' (see note 9).

26 On the associations of the chalumeau, see the discussion of a pastorella by J.G. Reinhardt, in my 'The Austrian pastorella and the *stylus rusticanus*'.

27 On the probable theology underlying this sequence, see my paper 'Die Vorgeschichte der mitteleuropäischen Pastorella und des stylus rusticanus im 17. Jahrhundert', in J. Sehnal (ed.), *Musik des 17. Jahrhunderts und Pavel Vejvanovský* (Brno 1994), pp. 79–85.

28 The inventory is in manuscript at the convent; the collection of pastorellas, apart from isolated exceptions, was lent out and subsequently lost earlier this century.

29 Budapest, Országos Széchényi Könyvtár, III/339 (not seen by me). This piece must be identical with the Weihnachtslied 'Gloria in excelsis à 4 [...] Tubis et Tympanis atque Flautino' mentioned in Werner's inventory.

30 Budapest, Országos Széchényi Könyvtár, III/334.

31 Budapest, Országos Széchényi Könyvtár, III/336; modern edition: Z. Falvy (ed.), *Weihnachtslied: Kantate für Soli, Chor, Streichorchester und Orgel von Gregor Werner* (London, Zurich, Budapest, etc.), 1969). In the first chorus the angels are suspected by the shepherds as enemies but announce themselves

as 'gegn euch warhafte Freund'; there the usual 'pastoral' fanfares become 'military' fanfares. There follow an 'Aria Angeli', 'Ich bringe nun Frid von oben der kriegerischen Weld', accompanied by concertante organ and pizzicato strings; an instrumental 'Hirten Marsch' over drone basses; a duet for tenor and bass, 'Hiez stöltz enk grad ins glüd'; and a homophonic final chorus (SATB), 'Ey ey du großer Weld Marschal'. The allusion is to Paul Anton Esterházy's distinguished service as cavalry general and *Feldmarschall* in the Seven Years' War: see the summary of his military career in Tank, *Studien zur Esterházyschen Hofmusik*, p. 25.

32 Budapest, Országos Széchéyi Könyvtár, III/330; modern edition: J.F. Dack, *The Origins and Development of the Esterházy Kapelle*, ii, pp. 34–7.

33 See G. Chew, 'The Night-Watchman's Song Quoted by Haydn and its Implications', *Haydn-Studien*, iii (1974), pp. 106–24.

34 *Pastorella alla Hanacha*: Budapest, Országos Széchényi Könyvtár, III/292; modern edition: J.F. Dack, op. cit., ii. pp. 39–46.

35 O. Biba (ed.), op. cit., bb. 25ff.

36 Stift Kremsmünster, D 7/282; modern editions by R. Ewerhart, *Michael Haydn, Lauft, ihr Hirten, allzugleich: Kantate*, Polyphonia sacra (Cologne 1960), and R.G. Pauly (New York 1968).

37 Cf. note 32, above.

38 I. Becker-Glauch, 'Neue Forschungen' (see note 2 above), p. 196.

39 The discussion of d:G1 in Chew, 'The Christmas Pastorella', takes no account of the Weitra source.

40 See O. Biba (ed.), op. cit., foreword.

41 M. Haydn: see above, n. 36; Holzbauer: Mariazell, Benediktinerpriorat, MS. 73, referred to in the nineteenth-century Wondratsch inventory of the Göttweig music as a *Pastorella Chorus* by Zechner (acquired there in 1760): see F.W. Riedel (ed.), *Der Göttweiger thematische Katalog von 1830*, Studien zur Landes- und Sozialgeschichte der Musik, ii–iii (Munich and Salzburg 1979).

42 Modern editions: Pastorella, as above, note 4; Advent aria 'Ein' Magd, ein' Dienerin', H.C. Robbins Landon (ed.), *Cantilena pro Adventu 'Ein' Magd, ein' Dienerin'* (London, 1957); Advent aria *a 2* 'Mutter Gottes, mir erlaube', J.F. Dack, op. cit., ii, pp. 93–8.

43 This is suggested in the *New Grove* work-list for Haydn, revised in J.P. Larsen and G. Feder, *The New Grove Haydn* (London 1982), p. 125.

44 Cf. U. Tank, 'Die Dokumente der Eszterházy-Archive', *Haydn-Studien*, iv (1980), pp. 129–333: documents 36 (21 Dec. 1761), 65 (24 Dec. 1762), 121 (31 Dec. 1763), 166 (24 Dec. 1764), 244 (24 Dec. 1765), 309 (23 Dec. 1766), 373 (23 Dec. 1767), 431 (23 Dec. 1768), 523 (21 Dec. 1769) and 568 (24 Dec. 1770).

45 Prof. Georg Feder has suggested this to me in a private communication; I am very grateful to him for this and for drawing my attention to the Rorate documents.

46 Landon, *Haydn: The Early Years*, p. 276, suggesting their use at 'the Advent service at Lukavec, for the Castle Chapel', with the tentative date *c*. 1760–61.

47 G.A. Griesinger, *Biographische Notizen über Joseph Haydn* (Leipzig 1810), p. 17.

48 O. Biba, 'Haydns Kirchenmusikdienste für Graf Haugwitz', *Haydn-Studien*, vi (1994), 278–87 (the quoted passage is at p. 287).

49 See D. Bartha (ed.), *Joseph Haydn, Gesammelte Briefe und Aufzeichnungen* (Basel, 1965), pp. 52ff.; quoted in Becker-Glauch, 'Neue Forschungen', p. 177.

50 See Landon, *Haydn; The Early Years*, p. 35.

51 See the account by J. Pommer in *Das deutsche Volkslied*, xiii (1911), pp. 190–93.

52 Otto Biba quotes the date as 1827.

53 Prague, Muzeum české hudby, X.A.44. For the references to 'Kráhiv Druž' see, for example, Hoboken, *Joseph Haydn: Thematisch-bibliographisches Werkverzeichnis* (Mainz 1957–78), ii, p. 172 under Hob XXIIId:3, and index; Landon, *Haydn: Chronicle and Works. Haydn at Eszterháza 1766–1790* (London and Bloomington, IN, 1978), p. 245 and index; O. Biba, *Josef Haydn: Zwei Pastorellen*, foreword. Two pages from this manuscript (the 'Canto Solo besser Alto Solo' and the 'Organo') are reproduced in facsimile in M. Poštolka, *Mladý Joseph Haydn: jeho vývoj ke klasickému slohu* (Prague 1988), pp. 155–6; Poštolka's discussion of this manuscript (pp. 154 and p. 196 n. 389) silently corrects the provenance to Dvůr Králové.

54 Biba, op. cit.; cf. W. Deutsch and G. Hofer (eds.), *Die Volksmusiksammlung der Gesellschaft der Musikfreunde in Wien: Sonnleithner-Sammlung*, Schriften zur Volksmusik, ii (Vienna 1969ff.).

55 Pastorella d:G1: Prague, Muzeum české hudby, XLIX.E.229; Mass: XLIX.E.286. Both manuscripts are inscribed 'Sub Regente Chori Fr. Caecilio Wagner. Pro Choro Frum. Misericordiae Kukusij' or equivalent; they are both in the same upright format and they share the same thickish paper, besides the correspondence of the handwriting. Cäcilius Wagner (1750–84), who may or may not be the copyist in question, worked also as *regens chori* at Vienna and Graz, according to Dlabacz, *Allgemeines historisches Künstler-Lexikon für Böhmen und zum Theil auch für Mähren und Schlesien* (Prague, 1815), iii, col. 317.

56 Landon, *Haydn: The Early Years*, p. 275.

57 See G. Feder, 'Drei Publikationen zur Haydn-Forschung', *Die Musikforschung*, xvii (1964), pp.62–6 (especially p. 66); G. Feder, 'Die Überlieferung und Verbreitung der handschriftlichen Quellen zu Haydns Werken (Erste Folge)', *Haydn-Studien*, I (1965), pp. 3–42 (especially pp. 20–1); English translation of latter in 'Manuscript Sources of Haydn's Works and their Distribution', *Haydn Yearbook*, iv (1968), pp. 102–39.

58 The Brothers of Mercy were a nineteenth-century order. The Hospitallers of St John of God were founded in Spain in 1537 and recognized by Pius V in 1572; by the eighteenth century the order had 300 hospitals in Europe and South America, with brothers cultivating medical and surgical skills. See N. McMahon, *The Story of the Hospitallers of St John of God* (Westminster, MD, 1959).

59 See Haydn's letter of 20 March 1768, concerning a performance of his *Stabat Mater* at the Hospitallers in the Leopoldstadt in Vienna; Landon reproduces it and comments: 'If the second known performance of the *Stabat Mater* took place at the Viennese Convent of the Brothers of Mercy [*sic*], perhaps that institution – or its Eisenstadt branch – had something to do with the first performance in 1767.' (Haydn had previously led the orchestra at the Vienna house.) See Landon, *Haydn at Eszterháza*, p. 144.

60 Dlabacz, *Allgemeines historisches Künstler-Lexikon*. I am especially grateful for the kindness of Markéta Kabelková, of the Muzeum české hudby, who has compiled lists of the entries

in Dlabacz's *Lexikon* by religious order, and who made her list of the Hospitallers available to me.

61   Dlabacz, op. cit., ii, col. 78, s.v. Kneer: 'Diesem würdi-gen Manne verdanke ich alle Nachrichten, die sich auf die Künstler aus seinem Orden beziehen, und durch welche er den Ruhm seiner für die Künste so eingenommenen Ordensbrüder verbreitet hat.'

62   Dlabacz, op. cit., ii, col. 77.

63   Prague, Muzeum české hudby, XLIX.E.230.

64   Kuks version: Prague, Muzeum české hudby, XLIX.E.242; Brno version: Brno, Moravské muzeum, Hudebněhistorické oddělení, A 10563 ('Del Sig. Jos. Heyden'). Modern edition: Chew, 'The Christmas Pastorella', ii; cf. discussion in Chew, I, and in Becker-Glauch, 'Neue Forschungen zu Haydns Kirchenmusik'.

65   The manuscripts in question are Prague, Muzeum české hudby, XLIII.C.300–301, XLIX.E.239–241, 251, 256, 258, 260, 273; all these mss., for both symphonies and offertories as well as the pastorella, are in the same format and apparently by the same hand, and have a characteristic ampersand above the title. The symphonies and offertories, but not the pastorella, are all numbered ('No. 20', etc.) as well: this numbering system, not used for the other Kuks Haydn manuscripts, extends also into works by other composers (e.g. in XLIII.C.296–8, three symphonies by Dittersdorf).

66   'Maria Jungfrau rein': Muzeum české hudby, XLIX.E.244; 'Was meine matte Brust', Muzeum české hudby, XLIX.E.265.

A. PETER BROWN: The Sublime, the Beautiful and the Ornamental . . .

1   See H.C. Robbins Landon, *Haydn: Chronicle and Works: Haydn in England 1791–1795* (London and Bloomington, IN, 1976).

2   C. Burney, *A General History of Music from the Earliest Ages to the Present Period* (1789), ed. By Frank Mercer (London 1935), p. 958.

3   A copy, with an inscription from the author, formed part of Haydn's estate; it is now in the National Szèchènyi Library, Budapest, Ha I.15.

4   For a catalogue of Charles Burney's network see P.A. Scholes, *The Great Dr. Burney: His Life, His Travels, His Works, His Family and His Friends* (London 1948), I, pp. xv–xx. See also K.S. Grant, *Dr. Burney as Critic and Historian of Music* (Ann Arbor, MN 1983). For a recent related study of Burney and Hester Thrale, see V. Rumbold, 'Music Aspires to Letters: Charles Burney, Queeney Thrale and the Streatham Circle', *Music and Letters*, lxxiv (1993), pp. 24–38.

5   C.L.H. Papendiek, *Court and Private Life in the Time of Queen Charlotte: Being the Journals of Mrs. Papendiek, Assistant Keeper of the Wardrobe and Reader to Her Majesty*, ed. by Mrs V.D. Broughton (London 1887), p. 290.

6   G.A. Griesinger, *Biographische Notizen über Joseph Haydn* (Leipzig, 1810), pp. 56–57 as translated by V. Gotwals in *Haydn: Two Contemporary Portraits* (Madison, WI, 1963), p. 33.

7   A recent, if flawed, account of the 'ancient' musical movement in England is W. Weber, *The Rise of the Musical Classics in Eighteenth-Century England: A Study in Canon, Ritual and Ideology* (Oxford, 1992). See the reviews by Pat Rogers in

The Times Literary Supplement, 27 November 1992, pp. 22–3, and A. Peter Brown in *The American Historical Review*, June 1993, pp. 871–2. See also H.M. Schueller, 'The Quarrel of the Ancients and the Moderns', *Music and Letters*, xli (1960), pp. 313–30; P. Lovell, 'Ancient Music in Eighteenth-Century England', *Music and Letters*, lx (1979), pp. 401–15; and G.B. Wright, 'Haydn in London' (Master of Arts Thesis, University of Wisconsin, 1961).

8   J. Hawkins, *A General History of the Science and Practice of Music* (London, 1776); new edition with the author's post-humous notes (London 1875).

9   See 'An Essay by John Marsh, Introduced by C.L. Cudworth', *Music and Letters*, xxxvi (1955), pp. 155–64, which originally appeared in *The Monthly Magazine*, ii/12 (Supplement 1796), pp. 981–5. See also correction to the text in iii/2 (February 1797), p. 125.

10   See letters in *The Monthly Magazine* ii/9 (Oct. 1796), pp. 701–2; ii/11 (Dec. 1796), pp. 847–8; iii/13 (Jan. 1797), pp. 19–20; iii/16 (April 1797), pp. 260–61; iii/18 (June 1797), pp. 425–6; iv/23 (Oct. 1796 [recte 1797]), pp. 269–70.

11   C. Burney, *An Account of the Musical Performances in Westminster Abbey, and the Pantheon on May 26th, 27th, 29th; and June the 3rd, and 5th, 1784 in Commemoration of Handel* (London 1785).

12   See the letter from Charles Burney to Christian Ignatius Labrobe dated as 'April 1800' by R. Lonsdale in *Dr. Charles Burney: A Literary Biography* (Oxford 1965), p. 401.

13   According to an exaggerated account by Giuseppe Carpani, these Handelian encounters 'struck him as if he had been put back to the beginning of his studies and had known nothing up to that moment. He meditated on every note and drew from those msot learned scores the essence of true musical grandeur'. See Carpani, *Le Haydine* (Milan 1812), pp. 162–3.

14   For modern surveys of these topics see S.H. Monk, *The Sublime: A Study of Critical Theories in XVIII-Century England* (New York 1935); W.J. Hipple, *The Beautiful, The Sublime, and The Picturesque in Eighteenth-Century British Aesthetic Theory* (Carbondale, XX, 1957); and T.E.B. Wood, *The Word 'Sublime' and its Context 1650–1760* (The Hague and Paris, 1972). All citations to Burke's *A Philosophical Inquiry into the Origin of our Ideas of the Sublime and Beautiful* are to the modern edition by J.T. Boulton (London 1958). An outstanding modern survey of the musical side is R.B. Larsson, 'The Beautiful, the Sublime, and the Picturesque in Eighteenth-Century Musical Thought in Britain' (PhD. thesis, State University of New York at Buffalo, 1980). See also S. McVeigh, *Concert Life in London from Mozart to Haydn* (Cambridge 1993), pp. 149–66.

15   According to Larsson, 'The Beautiful, the Sublime, the Picturesque . . .' (p. 151), this is reported in Leigh and Sotheby, *A Catalogue of the Miscellaneous Library of the Late Charles Burney* (London 1814).

16   See M. Hörwarthner, 'Joseph Haydns Bibliothek – Versuch einer literarhistorischen Rekonstruktion' in *Joseph Haydn und die Literatur seiner Zeit*, ed. H. Zeman, *Jahrbuch für Österreichische Kulturgeschichte* vi, pp. 157–208.

17   See C.L. Johnson, 'Giant HANDEL and the Musical Sublime', *Eighteenth-Century Studies*, xix (1985–6), 515–33.

18   Burke, *Philosophical Inquiry*, p. 124.

19   Burke, *Philosophical Inquiry*, pp. 82–3.

20   For the forces involved see Burney, *An Account of the Musical Performances . . . in Commemoration of Handel*, pp. 16–21 and the plates between pp. 107 and 113.

21   Burke, *Philosophical Inquiry*, pp. 122–3.

22   Most of these are excerpted in *Music and Aesthetics in the Eighteenth and Early Nineteenth Century*, ed. by P. Le Huray and J. Day (Cambridge 1981), with selections in addition to Burke from de Jaucourt, Sulzer, Michaelis, Kant, Millin, Lichtenthal, Crotch and Schilling. One might add to these the brief comment in John Baillie, *An Essay on the Sublime* (London 1747), pp. 38–9.

23   Dating from Nicholas Temperley, 'Crotch, William' in *New Grove Dictionary of Music*, ed. S. Sadie (London 1980), v, p. 67.

24   W. Crotch, *The Substance of Several Courses of Lectures on Music, Read at the University of Oxford, and in the Metropolis* (London 1831).

25   The dating of the Lectures is based on the letters between Burney and Crotch quoted below (see notes 31, 33, and 34).

26   Joshua Reynolds, *Fifteen Discourses Delivered in the Royal Academy* (London 1906); U. Price, *Essays on the Picturesque, as Compared with the Sublime and the Beautiful and, on the Use of Studying Pictures for the Purpose of Improving Real Landscape* (London 1798); and J. Harris, *Three Treatises*, 2nd ed. (London 1765).

27   See J. Rennert, *William Crotch 1775–1847: Composer, Artist, Teacher* (Lavenham, 1975), pp. 93–6.

28   Crotch, *Lectures*, pp. 30–1, as quoted from U. Price, *Essays on the Picturesque* 3 vols. (London, 1810). I was unable to locate the passage in Price.

29   The movement was printed in a keyboard reduction in the Specimens, I, pp. 10–13.

30   Burney, *History*, ed. F. Mercer, ii. Appendix 1, p. 1033.

31   See Haydn's complaint in the letter of 6 July 1776 containing his autobiography for *Das gelehrte Österreich* given in H.C. Robbins Landon, *Haydn: Chronicle and Works. Haydn at Eszterháza 1766–1790* (London and Bloomington, IN, 1978), pp. 397–9.

32   Burney, *History*, ed. F. Mercer, pp. 1034–6.

33   Op. cit., pp. 1038–9.

34   Crotch, *Lectures*, p. 34. See also the examples in the Specimens of the sublime as given in the Table (p. 53).

35   Crotch, *Lectures*, pp. 142–3.

36   Compiled from the reviews cited in Landon, *Haydn in England*, passim.

37   Burney, *A General History*, ed. F. Mercer, ii, p. 960, and 'Haydn, Joseph' in A. Rees, *The Cyclopaedia; or Universal Dictionary of the Arts Sciences and Literature* (London, 1802–19), xvii, n.p.

Burney tended to use the beautiful and sublime in a rather casual manner and does not maintain the strong distinctions laid out by Burke and later by Crotch (Larrson, 'The Beautiful, the Sublime, and the Picturesque', pp. 151–7, 174–5). When Burney writes of 'movements and passages that are sportive, playful, and even grotesque' ('Haydn, Joseph' in Rees, *Cyclopaedia*), he seems to be clearly referring to the musical equivalent of the picturesque, Crotch's category of the 'ornamental'.

38   Landon, *Haydn in England*, p. 247.

39   Op. cit., pp. 250–1.

40   Op. cit., p. 149.

41   Op. cit., p. 150.

42   Burke, *Inquiry*, p. 83.

43   It is this writer's view that Haydn did not conceive the so-called 'Paris' Symphonies for an orchestra any different from those he had experienced at Eszterháza and in Vienna, whereas in London the circumstances were experienced first-hand and he adjusted to both the larger size of the ensemble and the acoustics, as well as the size of the hall.

44   The parenthesis occurs in the refrain's return from bb. 98–121 and the stretch beginning in b. 122 to the conclusion of the movement.

45   Adagio cantabile is from the Piano Trio version, only Adagio is indicated in the Symphony adaptation.

46   Griesinger, *Biographische Notizen*, p. 114; translated in Gotwals, *Haydn*, p. 61.

47   In Symphony no. 88 the trumpets and timpani do not play in the first movement, first entering in the slow movement (where they normally would be silent), a situation noted by contemporary critics. See Landon, *Haydn at Eszterháza*, pp. 629–30; also *Haydn in England*, p. 339. The *Allgemeine musikalische Zeitung* article referred to by Landon and attributed by him to Zelter is found in vol. I (5 December 1798), cols. 152–5.

48   See A.H. King, 'The Origin of the Title "The Jupiter" Symphony', in *Mozart in Retrospect: Studies in Criticism and Bibliography* (London 1955), p. 264.

49   Friedrich Blume, 'Romantik', in *Die Musik in Geschichte und Gegenwart*, xi, cols. 820–2 (trans. by M.D. Herter Norton as *Classic and Romantic Music* (New York 1970), pp. 157–9. Blume's remarks on the eighteenth-century finale seem oversimplified when he writes that 'While in Haydn and Mozart there is still no finale that does not round off the cycle in a natural and spontaneous manner, serenely reconciling all contrasts, the Romantic composer approaches the finale of his cycle with uncertainty'. After all, it was Mozart who used the phrase 'finis coronat opus' with regard to the end of *Idomeneo*, and some of Haydn's finales move in such a direction. Neither McVeigh, *Concert Life in London*, nor L.A. McLamore, 'Symphonic Conventions in London's Concert Rooms circa 1755–1790' (PhD. thesis, University of California Los Angeles, 1991), address this question.

50   Symphonies nos. 97 and 98 seem, except for the slow movement of no. 98, to be less complex aesthetically and musically, making one wonder if these were not responses to the rivalry with Pleyel during the 1792 season.

51   J.-J. Momigny, *Cours complet d'harmonie et de composition, d'aprés une théorie nouvelle et générale de la musique, basée sur des principes incontestables, puisés dans la nature, d'accord avec tous les bons ouvrages pratiques anciens et modernes* (Paris 1806), ii, pp. 583–606. See also the fine explication of this by M.S. Cole, 'Momigny's Analysis of Haydn's Symphony No. 103', *Music Review*, xxx (1969), pp. 261–84.

52   Momigny's association of the opening with prayer probably derives from the French cathedral practice of accompanying the chant of male voices with a serpent, a timbre perhaps reminiscent of Haydn's orchestration of low strings with bassoons.

53   Burke, *Philosophical Inquiry*, p. 39.

54   Landon, *Haydn in England*, p. 516.

55   See Longinus, *On Sublimity*, trans. by D.A. Russell (Oxford 1965), p. 12. The fact that the authenticity of the quotation of this passage from Genesis was in dispute during the eighteenth century does not affect the argument, since all readers of Longinus considered the passage sublime. The most thorough explication is in H.-J. Horn, 'FIAT LUX: Zum kunsttheoretischen Hintergrund der "Erschaffung" des Lichtes in Haydns Schöpfung', *Haydn Studien* iii (1974), pp. 65–84. See also N.H. Waldvogel, 'The Eighteenth-Century

Aesthetics of the Sublime and the Valuation of the Symphony' (PhD. thesis, Yale University, 1992), pp. 1–76.

56   Crotch, *Lectures*, p. 141. See also H. Irving, 'William Crotch on "The Creation"', *Music and Letters*, lxxv (1994), pp. 548–60.

57   For further development of this idea in music, see A.P. Brown, 'The Creation and The Seasons: Some Allusions, Quotations, and Models from Handel to Mendelssohn,' *Current Musicology* li (1993), pp. 26–58.

58   See also L. Somfai, 'The London Revision of Haydn's Instrumental Style', *Proceedings of the Royal Musical Association*, c (1974), pp. 159–74, and A.P. Brown, 'Critical Years for Haydn's Instrumental Music: 1787–1790', *The Musical Quarterly*, lxii (1976), pp. 374–94.

ALBI ROSENTHAL: The Contract between Joseph Haydn and Frederick Augustus Hyde (1796)

1   H.C. Robbins Landon, *Haydn: the Years of 'The Creation' 1796–1800*, London and Bloomington, IN, 1977, pp. 101f.

2   Shortly after the London auction a rudimentary description of the contract was issued in a leaflet entitled 'The Haydn Contract' under the imprint of 'john wilson & richard macnutt'. Jens Peter Larsen provided a succinct account of its significance in 'A Haydn Contract', *Musical Times*, cxvii (1976), pp. 737f.

3   The words '30th' and 'July' were inserted by Haydn in his own hand.

4   Charles Humphries and Wm C. Smith, *Music Publishing in the British Isles*, 2nd ed., Oxford 1970.

5   *The Catalogue of Printed Music in the British Library*, London 1984, xxx, p. 91

6   Anthony van Hoboken, *Joseph Haydn: Thematisch-bibliographisches Werkverzeichnis*, ii, Mainz 1971, p. 246.

7   Landon, op cit., p. 102.

8   H.C. Robbins Landon, *The Collected Correspondence and London Notebooks of Joseph Haydn*, London 1959, p. 179; Dénes Bartha (ed.), *Joseph Haydn, Gesammelte Briefe und Aufzeichnungen*, Kassel 1965, p. 362 (original German).

9   Landon, op. cit. (note 1), p. 101.

10   Ms. in the National Széchényi Library, formerly in Haydn's possession.

11   Landon, op. cit. (note 1), p. 101.

12   Quoted by Landon, op. cit. (note 1), p. 469, from Edward Olleson, 'Georg August Griesinger's Correspondence with Breitkopf & Härtel', *Haydn Yearbook* iii (1965), p. 10; original German also in Otto Biba (ed.), *'Eben komme ich von Haydn . . .'. Georg August Griesingers Korrespondenz mit Joseph Haydns Verleger Breitkopf & Härtel 1799–1819*, Zürich 1987, pp. 28ff. The quartets referred to by Griesinger are Haydn's op. 76, nos. 1–3 (Hob. III:75–77).

13   Ovid, *Epistolae Ex Ponto*, iii, 4, 79.

CHRISTOPHER HOGWOOD: In praise of arrangements: the 'Symphony Quintetto'

1   S. Wesley, *Lectures* (British Library, Add. 35015, f.225).

2   S. Wesley, *Reminiscences* (British Library, Add. 27593, ff.154, 71v, 153).

3   For keyboard arrangements of Haydn's music see K.G. Fellerer, 'Klavierbearbeitungen Haydnscher Werke im frühen 19. Jahrhundert' in *Festkrift Jens Peter Larsen*, eds. Schiørring, Glahn and Hatting (Copenhagen 1972), pp. 301–16.

4   Published by Mollo (Vienna 1802).

5   Until 1970 these variations were thought to be by the Abbé Josef Gelinek, and even the Hoboken catalogue considered them a sketch for the string quartet setting. F. Eibner, 'Die authentische Klavierfassung von Haydns Variationen über das "Gott erhalte"', *Haydn Yearbook*, vii (1970), pp. 281–306.

6   H.C. Robbins Landon (ed.), *The Collected Correspondence and London Notebooks of Joseph Haydn* (London 1959), p. 41.

7   Now in the Moldenhauer Collection, Library of Congress, Washington, D.C.

8   Landon (ed.), *Collected Correspondence*, p. 117.

9   Landon (ed.), *Collected Correspondence*, p. 123.

10   Symphonies nos. 67, 63, 69, 75, 79, 64, 61, 51, 72, 24, plus Hob.Ia:13 and Ia:C2.

11   A. Searle, 'The Royal Philharmonic Society Scores of Haydn's "London" symphonies', *Haydn Yearbook*, xiv (1984), pp. 173–86.

12   These trios are being republished by Doblinger in the Diletto Musicale series; the editor is Rudolph Führer.

13   For a detailed discussion of Haydn's own arrangement of the Adagio from Symphony no. 102 see F. Krummacher, 'Klaviertrio und sinfonischer Satz' in *Quaestiones in musica. Festschrift für Franz Krautwurst zum 65. Geburtstag*, ed. F. Brusniak and H. Leuchtmann (Tutzing 1989), pp. 325–35.

14   I am grateful to Robin Myers for her help in searching for these entries.

15   Stephen Storace, 'Deux Quintettes et un Sestette pour Deux Violons, Taille, Violoncelle, Flute et Clavecin ou Piano Forte Op. II . . . London [1784]'. The exemplar in the British Library lacks the flute part, but a complete set exists in the Gesellschaft der Musikfreunde, Vienna.

16   Hubert Unverricht notes a later entry for Book 3 in the *Allgemeine musikalische Zeitung* (February 1801) in 'Die Simrock-Drucke von Haydns Londoner Sinfonien', *Studien zur Musikgeschichte des Rheinlandes*, iii (Cologne 1965), p. 248. Simrock's title pages maintained that the piano was necessary only for symphonies nos. 1–6.

17   In particular by Harry Newstone for his provocative new editions of the London symphonies for Edition Eulenburg (1992–).

18   On the collaborative contract between author and performer, and its sorry decline during the nineteenth century, see R.G. Collingwood, *The Principles of Art* (Oxford 1938), pp. 321ff.

19   A new edition of these arrangements, based on the Salomon manuscript and edited by the present writer, is to be published by Oxford University Press.

20   Catalogued as No. 4 of the Rave Items in the Alfred Newman Collection. I am grateful to the librarians, Steve Hanson and Ned Comstock, for permission to reproduce extracts from the MS. and for supplying the photographic material, to David Newman and Heather Jarman for helping to locate the manuscript, and especially to H.C. Robbins Landon, in the first instance, for kindly lending me a microfilm of the entire collection more than fifteen years ago.

21   Arthur Searle has kindly compared the script with that of Ayrton's Commonplace Book (British Library, Add. 60358).

22 See A. Tyson, 'Salomon's Will', *Studien der Musikgeschichte des Rheinlandes*, iii (Cologne 1965), pp. 43–5.

23 It is similar to Heawood no. 1846; see E. Heawood, *Watermarks, mainly of the 17th and 18th centuries* (Hilversum, 1950). See also watermark 145 in A.H. Shorter, *Paper Mills and Paper Makers in England 1495–1800* (Hilversum 1957).

24 No nicknames are given by Salomon.

25 For details of altered passages see Searle, 'The Royal Philharmonic Society Scores', pp. 181ff.

26 Salomon made several deliberate alterations to Haydn's 'Menuet' or 'Minuetto' titles: to no. 95 he added 'Moderato'; in no. 99 he corrected 'Trio' to read 'Alternativo', to no. 100 he added 'Allegretto' to the 'Moderato'; in no. 101 he substituted 'Alternativo' for 'Trio', but in no. 102 he used 'Minuetto 2do'; and in no. 104 he deleted 'Trio' and wrote 'Minuetto 2do' ('Minuetto Alternativo' in the print). Whether these changes are related to scoring, tempo, key or length is hard to determine, but they are clearly not casual.

27 This may have been an English preference, since Simrock's parts all revert to '*fz*'.

28 On variation and 'non-uniformity' in Haydn's quartet autographs, and his corrections in opp. 64 and 71/74, see papers by James Webster and Georg Feder in C. Wolff (ed.), *The String Quartets of Haydn, Mozart, and Beethoven. Studies of the Autograph Manuscripts* (Cambridge, MA, 1980), pp. 62–120.

29 We find this on the title pages of the Cimador arrangements for sextets of Mozart's symphonies made, according to Fétis, because the Haymarket orchestra would not, or could not play Mozart! See under 'Cimador' in F.-J. Fétis, *Biographie Universelle des Musiciens et Biographic Générale de la Musique* (Brussels 1835–44).

30 See H.C. Robbins Landon, *Haydn. Chronicle and Works. Haydn in England 1791–1795* (London and Bloomington, IN 1976), p. 595, and C. Rosen, *The Classical Style* (London 1971), p. 348.

31 Hubert Unverricht suggests that Salomon was responsible for nine of the twelve, without mentioning the remaining three. H. Unverricht, 'Salomon' in S. Sadie (ed), *New Grove Dictionary of Music and Musicians* (London 1980), xvi, pp. 428–9.

32 Letter to Charles Burney (4 May 1791); see R.S. Walker (ed.), *A Selection of Thomas Twining's Letters 1734–1804*, Studies in British History, xxv (Lampeter 1991), I, p. 373.

33 Wesley, *Lectures*, f.229.

DAVID WYN JONES: From Artaria to Longman & Broderip: Mozart's music on sale in London

1 Three days later *The Times* included a shorter announcement, quoted in C. Eisen, *New Mozart Documents. A supplement to O.E. Deutsch's Documentary Biography* (London 1991), p. 154. Haydn seems to have heard of the death by 20 December; in a letter of that date to Maria Anna von Genzinger he expresses the hope that the rumour is untrue. See H.C. Robbins Landon, *The Collected Correspondence and London Notebooks of Joseph Haydn* (London 1959), pp. 122–4.

2 Landon, op. cit., p. 125.

3 C. Burney, 'Mozart' in A. Rees, *The Cyclopaedia; or Universal Dictionary of Arts, Sciences, and Literature* (London 1819), xxiv, n.p.

4 C. Burney, *A General History of Music from the Earliest Ages to the Present Period (1789)*, modern ed. by F. Mercer (New York 1935), ii, pp. 958–60.

5 C. Burney, *A General History*, p. 960.

6 A. Peter Brown, 'The Earliest English Biography of Haydn', *Musical Quarterly*, lix (1973), pp. 339–54. H.C. Robbins Landon, *Haydn. Chronicle and Works: Haydn at Eszterháza 1786–1790* (London and Bloomington, IN, 1978), pp. 595–602. S. McVeigh, 'The Professional Concert and Rival Subscription Series in London, 1783–1793', *RMA Research Chronicle*, xxii (1989), pp. 1–135.

7 C. Eisen, op. cit., pp. 136–54. S. McVeigh, *Concert Life in London from Mozart to Haydn* (Cambridge 1993), pp. 127–8. S. McVeigh, op. cit., pp. 11–12, 33–103. C. Price, 'Italian Opera and Arson in Late Eighteenth-Century London', *Journal of the American Musicological Society*, xlii (1989), pp. 68–71. C. Price, J. Milhous and R.D. Hume, *Italian Opera in Late Eighteenth-Century London. The King's Theatre, Haymarket 1778–1791* (Oxford 1995), pp. 414, 429–32.

8 T. Busby, *Concert Room and Orchestra Anecdotes of Music and Musicians Ancient and Modern* (London 1825), vol, i, pp. 126–7.

9 Advertised in *The Daily Universal Register*, 24 February 1786. Exemplar in British Library, 7896. h. 40. (9).

10 Advertised in *The Times*, 3 July 1788.

11 *The Public Advertiser*, 17 January 1784.

12 W. Sandys and S.A. Foster, *The History of the Violin and other Instruments played on with the Bow from the remotest Times to the Present* (London 1864), pp. 300–12.

13 The advertisement is given in C. Eisen, op. cit., p. 140.

14 A performance of the *Kegelstatt* trio, in advance of publication, was given at the Anacreontic Society on 12 November 1788; an account of the concert is given in *The Times*, 14 November 1788. For performances of concertos and symphonies by Mozart see C. Eisen, op. cit., pp. 140–9 and S. McVeigh, op. cit., pp. 33–103.

15 For a summary of Artaria's attitude to the publication of symphonies see D.W. Jones, 'Why did Mozart compose his last three Symphonies? Some new hypotheses', *Music Review*, li (1990 [1992]), pp. 285–7.

16 See C. Eisen, op. cit., pp. 139, 147, and Ulrich Drüner, 'Bibliographie der zu Mozarts Lebzeiten unternommenen Nachdrucke seiner Werke', *Mozart Jahrbuch* (1993), p. 100.

17 R. Lonsdale, *Dr. Charles Burney. A Literary Biography* (Oxford 1965), pp. 326–30, 336.

18 An advertisement by Longman & Broderip in *The Morning Chronicle*, 5 January 1791, includes a large number of publications by a variety of composers but the latest work by Mozart is the 'op. 15' publication from 1789. A catalogue issued by the firm in 1792 (British Library, Hirsch IV 1110 [4]) has no music by Mozart.

19 S. McVeigh, op. cit., pp. 65–101.

20 The exemplars of the Artaria print in Cu do not have the import label but are bound in a set of parts that belonged to the Anacreontic Society (information kindly supplied by the music librarian, Richard M. Andrewes). For newspaper accounts of performances of these symphonies by the society see C. Eisen, op. cit., pp. 143–4.

21 Information kindly supplied by the music librarian, Martin Thacker.

Anmerkungen

WALTER BRAUNEIS: Die Wiener Freimanrer unter Kaiser Leopold II.: Mozarts Zauberflöte als emblematische Standortbestimmung

1 Ludwig Abafi, *Geschichte der Freimaurerei in Oesterreich-Ungarn*, 5 Bände, Budapest 1890–99; Eugen Lennhoff-Oskar Posner, *Internationales Freimaurer-Lexikon*, Wien 1980 (unveränderter Nachdruck von 1932); Ausstellungskatalog *Zirkel und Winkelmaß – 200 Jahre Große Landesloge der Freimaurer*, Wien 1984; Ausstellungskatalog *250 Jahre Freimaurerei in Österreich*, Schloß Rosenau bei Zwettl 1992; Ausstellungskatalog *Freimaurer – Solange die Welt besteht*, Wien 1992.

2 Budapest, Ungarisches Staatsarchiv / Magyar Orszagos Levéltár (MOL Budapest), Degh-Schriften Bd. 41/1459 (zitiert nach der Dissertation von Eva Huber, 'Sozialstruktur der Wiener Freimaurer 1780–1790', I. Teil, 1. Band, Wien 1991, S. 116).

3 Das rote Templerkreuz ist in der freimaurerischen Emblematik nicht mit dem Rosenkreuz zu verwechseln, unter dem zahlreiche Hochgrade arbeiten und wovon sich deren Gradbezeichnungen ableiten. Siehe: Lennhoff-Posner, *Freimaurer-Lexikon* (Anm. 1), Spalte 1330. Bezeichnenderweise kennt das System des 'Ordens der Gold- und Rosenkreuzer' keinen 'Rosenkreuzergrad' in seinen Ordensstufen.

4 'System der Freymaurer-Loge Wahrheit und Einigkeit zu drey gekrönten Säulen in P+++, Philadelphia 1594 [recte: Prag 1794], beigebunden: 'Gesetzbuch', § xx.

5 HHStA Wien, VA 67, fol. 27r (Sachverhaltsdarstellung von Johann Eubert Boedecker in: 'Beylagen zu den Protocollen des zu Wilhelmsbad gehaltenen General-Convents').

6 Abafi (Anm. 1), Band 5, S. 78.

7 Ein solcher Ritterbruder der ersten Stunde war der Mozart-Gläubiger und Großkaufmann Johann Michael Puchberg. Er war vor 1773 in die Loge 'Zu den drei Adlern' in Wien aufgenommen worden. Die drei Symbolischen Grade hatte er sehr rasch durchlaufen: am 17. Oktober 1773 wurde er in den Schottischen Meistergrad (IV. Grad) erhoben und am 1. März 1776 als Armiger (Knappe) 'ab Iride' in den Inneren Orden der Strikten Observanz aufgenommen. Es war dies die unterste und für einen Nichtadeligen zugleich letzte zugängliche Stufe der V. Grades. In diesem Rang bekleidete er die Ehren-Charge eines 'Commendator der Armigeral-Comthurei Obersiebenbrunn'. Siebenmal wird Puchberg von Mozart in den zwanzig erhaltenen Bettelbriefen als 'Ordensbruder' tituliert.

8 Ludwig Aigner, 'Die neuen Rosenkreuzer', in: *Latomia – Neue Zeitschrift für Freimaurerei*, 23. Jg., No. 8 vom 7. April 1900, S. 59ff., No. 9 vom 21. April 1900, S. 68ff., No. 10 vom 5. Mai 1900, S. 76ff.; Horst Möller, 'Die Bruderschaft der Gold- und Rosenkreuzer. Struktur, Zielsetzung und Wirkung einer anti-aufklärerischen Geheimgesellschaft', in: *Freimaurer und Geheimbünde im 18. Jahrhundert in Mitteleuropa* (hrsg. von Helmut Reinalter), Frankfurt am Main 1989³, S. 199ff.

9 Jacob Katz, 'Der Orden der Asiatischen Brüder', in: Reinalter, *Freimaurer und Geheimbünde* (Anm. 8), S. 240ff.

10 Norbert Schindler, 'Der Geheimbund der Illuminaten: Aufklärung, Geheimnis und Politik', in: Reinalter, *Freimaurer und Geheimbünde* (Anm. 8), S. 284ff.; Manfred Agethen, *Geheimbund und Utopie – Illuminaten, Freimaurer und deutsche Spätaufklärung*, München 1984.

11 *Georg Forster's Briefwechsel mit Samuel Thomas Sömmerring* (hrsg. von Hermann Hettner), Braunschweig 1877, S. 117f.

12 Das Siegel der Großen Landesloge von Österreich ziert ein der rosenkreuzerischen Emblematik entlehnter gekrönter Doppeladler mit Hammer und Winkelmaß in den Klauen als Symbol der Macht nach Osten und Westen. Anstelle des Herzschildes befindet sich ein aus zwei ineinandergeschobenen Dreiecken gebildetes Hexagramm mit dem alten Meisterwort 'Jehova'. Das Siegel der Provinzialloge zeigt auf Dreieckskonsole mit österreichischem Bindenschild den mit eigenem Herzblut seine Jungen nährenden Pelikan, das Hauptsymbol der Rosenkreuzer als Sinnbild des Opfertodes Christi. Flankiert wird das Emblem von einem Hexagramm mit 'Circumsphäre' und einem aus einem bärtigen Männerbildnis und einem weiblichen Profil gebildeten Januskopf als Symbol des männlichen und weiblichen Prinzips in der Natur.

13 Alois Blumauer, 'Gesundheit auf den hoch[würdigen] Großm[eister] von B[or]n', in: *Journal für Freymaurer*, 2. Jg., 3. Viertel 1785, S. 193ff.

14 Zitiert nach: Edith Rosenstrauch-Königsberg, *Freimaurer, Illuminat, Weltbürger – Friedrich Münters Reisen und Briefe in ihren europäischen Bezügen*, Berlin 1984, S. 74.

15 Hermann Beigel, *Verfassung der Provinzial- und Grossloge von Oesterreich-1784*, Wien 1877, S. 22 (§ LXXXVIII).

16 Besprochen in der 'Uebersicht der im Jahr 5784 erschienenen neuen Maurerschriften', in: *Journal für Freymaurer*, 1. Jg., 4. Viertel 1784, S. 221.

17 Ernst Schönmann, 'Das kaiserliche Handbillet', in: *Festschrift "25 Jahre Libertas"*, Wien 1985; siehe auch; Hans-Josef Irmen, *Mozart – als Mitglied geheimer Gesellschaften*, Mechernich 1988, S. 147ff.

18 'Gegenwärtiger Zustand der Freymaurerey im Orient von Wien', in: *Journal für Freymaurer*, 2. Jg., 4. Viertel 1785, S. 200.

19 Zitiert nach: Heinz Schuler, 'Mozart von der Wohltätigkeit – Die Mitglieder der gerechten und vollkommenen St.-Johannis-Freimaurer-Loge 'Zur Wohltätigkeit im Orient von Wien', in: *Mitteilungen der Internationalen Stiftung Mozarteum* 1–4/1988, S. 19.

20 HHStA Wien, VA 65/2, fol. 1–110 ('Gesetzbuch der Provinz Oesterreich' vom 24. Juni 1786; darin: V. Hauptstück, § LXXXVIII).

21 Gerald Fischer-Colbrie, 'Die Baron Eckerschen Geheimorden und das Kaiserliche Handbillet' (in Vorbereitung).

22 MOL Budapest, Degh-Schriften Bd. 89/9: Protokoll

vom 12. August 1788 (zitiert nach E. Huber, Anm. 2, S. 177).

23 Auf die Möglichkeit einer offiziellen Bearbeitung eines über die Symbolischen Grade hinausgehenden Hochgrades nach dem Josephinischen Freimaurerpatent hat erstmals Gerald Fischer-Colbrie hingewiesen. Siehe: 'Zur Gründung der Linzer Freimaurerloge "Zu den sieben Weisen"', in: *Mitteilungen des Oberösterreichischen Landesarchivs* 14 (1984), S. 434f.

24 MOL Budapest, Degh-Schriften Bd. 89/9 (zitiert nach E. Huber, Anm. 2, S. 178).

25 Ritual für eine Schottische Meistererhebung mit gleichzeitiger Aufnahme als Andreasritter, in: HHStA Wien, VA 64, fol. 78^r–88^v (insbesondere fol.82r).

26 MOL Budapest, Degh-Schriften Bd. 89/9 (zitiert nach E. Huber, Anm. 2, S. 177f.).

27 HHStA Wien, VA 65/2, fol. 1–110 ('Gesetzbuch der Provinz Oesterreich' vom 24. Juni 1786; darin: § XIV).

28 Sammlung der Mitgliederlisten habsburgischer Freimaurerlogen aus dem 18. Jahrhundert von Gerald Fischer-Colbrie – Linz/Donau (F-C Linz), P 2/90–91.

29 HHStA Wien, VA 37, fol. 355 (Mitteilung von Franz Xaver Aigner an Kaiser Leopold II. vom 27. Februar 1792); F-C Linz (Anm. 28), P 11/92.

30 HHStA Wien, Zinzendorf-Tagebuch, Eintragung zum 19. Juni 1792. Siehe auch: Gustav Brabée, 'War Kaiser Leopold II. Freimaurer?', in: *Allgemeine österreichische Freimaurer-Zeitung*, Nr. 14 vom 16. Oktober 1875, S. 101ff.

31 F-C Linz (Anm. 28), W 6/90 mit Begleitschreiben.

32 Manfred Schuler, 'Mesmer und die Mozarts', in: *Beiträge zum Internationalen wissenschaftlichen Symposion anläßlich des 250. Geburtstages von Mesmer (Merseburg 1984)*, Stuttgart 1985, S. 218, 223, 224ff.

33 Die Gründungsmodalitäten sind in den Akten des Österreichischen Verwaltungsarchivs (Pergen-Akten, H 24–26) und des Haus-, Hof- und Staatsarchivs (VA 41) gut dokumentiert. Die Ansprache am Stiftungstag erschien 1792 in gedruckter Form: *Rede auf die Konstituzionsfeier der sehr ehrwürdigen Loge zur L[iebe] u[nd] W[ahrheit] im O[rient] von W[ien] gehalten am 24. 2. 5791.* Zur weiteren Geschichte siehe: Huber, 'Sozialstruktur' (Anm. 2), S. 182ff., 191ff.; Aigner, 'Rosenkreuzer' (Anm. 8), S. 78.

34 Günter Mühlpfordt, 'Europarepublik im Duodezformat. Die internationale Geheimgesellschaft "Union" – ein radikalaufklärerischer Bund der Intelligenz (1786–1796)' in: Reinalter, *Freimaurer und Geheimbünde* (Anm. 8), S. 319ff.

35 Georg Kloss, *Annalen der Loge zur Einigkeit, der Englischen Provincial-Loge, so wie der Provincial- und Directorial-Loge des eclectischen Bundes zu Frankfurt am Main. 1742–1811*, Frankfurt am Main 1842 (Reprint 1972), S. 276.

36 Zitiert nach: Alec Mellor, *Logen-Rituale-Hochgrade – Handbuch der Freimaurerei*, o.O. 1985, S. 408f.; siehe auch: HHStA Wien, VA 73, fol. 345ff. (Ritual: 'Le Templier Ordre Militaire sonsten auch Gran Elu').

37 MOL Budapest, Degh-Schriften Bd. 7/31 (zitiert nach E. Huber, Anm. 2, S. 188).

38 Adam Wolf, *Leopold II. und Marie Christine. Ihr Briefwechsel 1781–1792*, Wien 1867, S. 136.

39 Mozarts masonischer Lebensweg in den Symbolischen Graden ist bis auf das genaue Datum seiner Meistererhebung gut dokumentiert. Siehe: Otto Erich Deutsch, *Mozart und die Wiener Logen*, Wien 1932 (Nachdruck mit Ergänzungen von Rudolf Klein, Wien 1990); Philippe A. Autexier, *Mozart et*

Liszt sub Rosa, Poitiers 1984; Harald Strebel, *Der Freimaurer Wolfgang Amadé Mozart*, Stäfa 1991; Ausstellungskatalog *Bruder Wolfgang Amadeus Mozart*, Schloß Rosenau bei Zwettl 1990; H.C. Robbins Landon, *Mozart and the Masons*, London and New York 1991^2; Gerald Fischer-Colbrie, 'Wie sah Mozarts Freimaurerschurz aus?', in: Ausstellungskatalog *Mozart in Linz*, Linz 1991, S. 39ff.

40 Wilgert te Lindert, 'Friedrich Hegrad – Ein Logenbruder Mozarts', in: *Österreichische Musikzeitschrift* 1/1993, S. 3ff. (Erstveröffentlichung der Aufnahmerede für Mozart vom 14. Dezember 1784).

41 *Wiener Musenalmanach für 1786*, Wien 1786, Beilage zwischen S. 46 und 47. Die Melodie wird 1799 in Berlin von F.M. Böheim in seine *Auswahl von Maurer-Gesängen mit Melodien der vorzüglichsten Componisten*, Zweite Abteilung, S. 270f. (Nr. 108) aufgenommen und mit einem neuen Text ('Euch Schönen grüßet unser Lied') unterlegt.

42 Joseph Franz Ratschky, 'Ueber den Bann der Freymaurer', in: *Journal für Freymaurer*, 2. Jg, 3. Viertel 1785, S. 94.

43 Heinz Schuler, *Mozart und die Freimauerei. Daten-Fakten-Biographien*, Wilhelmshaven 1992; Gerald Fischer-Colbrie, 'Die Mitgliederliste der Freimaurerloge "Zur gekrönten Hoffnung" aus Mozarts Sterbejahr aufgefunden', in: *Mitteilungen der Internationalen Stiftung Mozarteum* 3–4/1993, S. 35ff.

44 In der Literatur wurde bisher stets der 18. November 1791 als Uraufführungstag angenommen. Dem amerikanischen Musikwissenschaftler Dexter Edge ist es kürzlich gelungen, das tatsächliche Datum aus einer bisher nicht beachteten Zeitungsnotiz zu ermitteln. Siehe: Cliff Eisen, *New Mozart Documents – A supplement to O.E. Deutsch's documentary biography*, London 1991, S. 71, Nr. 112.

45 In jüngster Zeit wurden mehrere Ergänzungsversuche unternommen: Friedrich Georg Zeileis (1982), Rainer Bischof (1991), Rudolf Klein (1992) und Zdeněk Košler (1993).

46 Den Haag, Archiv des Grootosten der Nederlanden, Handschriften der Klossianischen Bibliothek, Sign. XIII A 11 (zitiert nach E. Huber, Anm. 2, S. 20).

47 Joseph Baurnjöpel, 'Grundlinien eines eifrig arbeitenden Freimaurers in Dreimal Drei, Wien 1793' Transkribiert von Friedrich Gottschalk und herausgegeben unter dem Titel 'Eine Wiener Freimaurerhandschrift aus dem 18. Jahrhundert von Bruder [Joseph] Baurnjöpel'. Mit einem biographischen Abriß von Julius Fischer, Graz 1986, S. 89, 12, 10, 328 (in der Reihenfolge der Zitate).

48 Emil Karl Blümml, 'Ausdeutungen der "Zauberflöte"', in: *Mozart-Jahrbuch 1923*, München 1923, S. 109ff.; Edgar Istel, 'Mozart's "Magic Flute" and Freemasonry', in: *The Musical Quarterly* 13/1927, S. 510ff. (Deutsche Ausgabe: Die Freimaurerei in Mozarts Zauberflöte', Berlin 1928); Amélie André-Gédalge, 'Le Symbolisme de la flûte enchantée', in: *Le Symbolisme*, Février 1928, S. 39ff. (Wiederabdruck: Mars-Avril 1955, S. 271ff.); Alfons Rosenberg, *Die "Zauberflöte" – Geschichte und Deutung von Mozarts Oper*, München 1964 (1972^2); Jacques Chailley, *'La Flûte enchantée' – Opéra maçonnique*, Paris 1968 (1983^2 und 1991^3; Englische Ausgabe: *The Magic Flute – Masonic Opera*, New York 1971, London 1972); ders., 'Die Symbolik in der "Zauberflöte"', in: *Mozart-Jahrbuch 1967*, Salzburg 1968, S. 100ff.; Peter Horwath, 'Symbolism in Die Zauberflöte – Origin and Background of the Symbolism of "Sevenfold", "Mighty", and "All-consuming Sun Disk"', in: *The Opera Quarterly* 3/1991, S. 58ff.;

Wolfgang Kelsch, 'Der Freimaurer Mozart und seine Zauberflöte', in: *Quellenkundliche Arbeit Nr. 27 der Forschungsloge 'Quatuor Coronati'*, Bayreuth 1990, S. 7ff.; Gisa Aurbek, 'Neue Thesen zu Musik und Freimaurerritual in Mozarts Zauberflöte', in: *Internationaler Musikwissenschaftlicher Kongreß zum Mozartjahr 1991 (Baden⁄Wien)*, Band II: Free Papers, Tutzing 1993, S. 451ff.; Ute Jung⁄Kaiser, 'Das Bilderrätsel der "Zauberflöte". Ikonographische Konstanten von der Uraufführung bis heute', in: *Musica* 4/1993, S. 205ff.

49 Zur Ägyptomanie der Mozart⁄Zeit siehe: Wilfried Seipel, 'Goethe, Ägypten und die Zauberflöte', in: Ausstellungskatalog *Die Klangwelt Mozarts*, Wien 1991, S. 159ff.; Jean⁄Marcel Humbert, Die Zauberflöte (Katalogtext zu dem von Nicole Wild verfaßten Beitrag 'Ägypten in der Oper'), in: Ausstellungskatalog *Ägyptomania*, Wien 1994, S. 273ff.

Daß das Ägyptische einen so bestimmenden Faktor im Szenarium der *Zauberflöte* ausmacht, hängt vermutlich auch mit einem bisher nicht beachteten Ereignis zusammen: Im Frühjahr 1791 war Alessandro Conte di Cagliostro alias Giuseppe Balsamo, Begründer von Hochgradlogen nach ägyptischem Ritus sowie einer Adoptionsloge mit Namen 'Isis', von der päpstlichen Inquisition zum Tode verurteilt worden. Das Todesurteil, kurz darauf in eine lebenslange Festungshaft umgewandelt, wurde voller Emotionen diskutiert, die Prozeßführung vereinzelt als einseitig und ungerecht gebrandmarkt. Die *Preßburger Zeitung* brachte 1791 nach dem in der Wiener Stadt⁄ und Landesbibliothek bewahrten Portheim⁄Katalog mehr als dreißig ausführliche Meldungen und Berichte zur Person Cagliostros. In Wien war sogar im engsten Umkreis von Van Swieten eine Verteidigungsschrift für Cagliostro, verfaßt von Ignaz Ferdinand Arnold unter dem Pseudonym Cajetan Tschink (Unparteyische Prüfung des zu Rom erschienenen kurzen Inbegriffes von dem Leben und den Thaten des Josephs Balsamo oder des sogenannten Grafen Cagliostro. Wien 1791), in Druck erschienen (freundlicher Hinweis von Univ. Prof. Dr. Ernst Wangermann, Salzburg). In der 'Theaterbibliothek Emanuel Schikaneders und der Gesellschaft der Kavaliere' hat sich auch das 1791 gedruckte Textbuch zu dem Lustspiel *Cagliostro* von Natale di Roviglio erhalten. Cagliostro und seine ägyptische Hochgradmaurerei waren demnach Mitte 1791 in aller Munde. Auch dies könnte Schikaneder, der an der theatralischen Umsetzung von tagespolitischen Neuigkeiten stets interessiert war, bewogen haben, sich des erfolgreichen Moderomans *Séthos* des Abbé Jean Terrasson zu bedienen und wesentliche Passagen des dort geschilderten ägyptischen Rituals fast wörtlich zu übernehmen.

50 Richard van Dülmen, *Der Geheimbund der Illuminaten, Darstellung⁄Analyse⁄Dokumentation*, Stuttgart⁄Bad Cannstatt 1975, S. 49ff. ('Illuminaten⁄Ordens⁄Directions⁄System'). Neben der illuminatischen Chiffre 'Ägypten' wäre zu erwähnen, daß bei Minervalsammlungen der Illuminaten den in der Mitte der Loge aufgelegten Tapis eine Pyramide zierte. Siehe hiezu: Johann Heinrich Faber, *Der ächte Illuminat*, Edesse (*recte*: Frankfurt) 1788, S. 68, 78.

51 Ritual (Anm. 25). fol. 82r.

52 Auf die Personifikation des 'Flammenden Sterns' in der 'sternenflammenden Königin' hingewiesen hat schon: Paul Nettl, 'Sethos und die freimaurerische Grundlage der "Zauberflöte"', in: *Bericht über die musikwissenschaftliche Tagung der Internationalen Stiftung Mozarteum in Salzburg vom 2. bis 5.*

August 1931, Leipzig 1932, S. 145. Zur emblematischen Bedeutung des 'Flammenden Sterns' in den gradspezifischen Ritualen siehe: HHStA Wien, VA 65/1, fol. 71r ('Der flammende Stern kann seine Beziehung auf das heilige Feuer haben, das beständig in Salomons Tempel brannte. Das Licht der Vernunft müsse gleichfalls beständig alle ihre [d.h. des künftigen Freimaurers] Handlungen erleuchten.') und fol. 83v ('. . . welcher den mittelsten Raum des Tempels erleuchtet, und Recht unter die vornehmsten Zieraten der Loge gerechnet wird'), sowie VA 73, fol. 279v ('Dieser flammende Stern stellet uns die Allerheiligste Gottheit, den großen Jehova, den dreyeinigen Gott, Vatter, Sohn, und heiligen Geist vor.') Weiters siehe: Louis Guillemain de Saint Victor, *Vollständige Sammlung der ganzen Adon⁄Hiramitischen Maurerey, enthaltend die Katechismen der ersten vier Grade, . . .*, Leipzig 1786, S. 71 ('. . . der flammende Stern ist das Symbol der Sonne der Welt.').

53 Baurnjöpel (Anm. 47), S. 25, 329. Als Rangabzeichen wird die Sonnenscheibe im Ritual eines der zahlreichen Schottischen Systeme ausdrücklich genannt: 'Der Meister vom Stuhl, so den Salomon vorstellet, trägt, als der Weiseste, die Sonne an seinem Band und wird Großmächtiger . . . genannt.' Siehe: HHStA Wien, VA 73, fol. 228v ('Grade eines kleinen Architect. oder Schottischer⁄Baumeister⁄Gesell'). Ein solches Sonnen⁄Bijou abgebildet in: Ausstellungskatalog *Freimaurer* . . . (Anm. 1), Kat. Nr. 11/6.

54 Sarastros Arie ist in den Logen zu einem beliebten Gesangsstück bei den Weihehandlungen geworden. Erstmals ist die Hallenarie (mit einer Zusatzstrophe) in F.M. Böheims 'Freimaurer⁄Lieder mit Melodien' (2 Teile, Berlin 1793) unter Nr. 20 nachweisbar.

55 HHStA Wien, VA 65/1. S. 55f. (ehem. fol. 19): 'Wiener Ritual' – Allgemeine Freymaurer Verordnungen (Artikel 3 und 9).

56 F⁄C Linz (Anm. 28), W 4S/86.

57 Irmen, *Mozart . . .* (Anm. 17), S. 22.

58 Ritual (Anm. 25), fol. 83r.

59 Österreichische Nationalbibliothek Wien – Musiksammlung, Sign. 685.928 A.M. (Gieseke⁄Libretto), zwischen S. 48 und 49 (fol. 50r und 50v).

60 Ritual (Anm. 25), fol. 78r.

61 'Von dem maurerischen Adoptionssystem, und die Adoptionslogen in Paris', in: *Journal für Freymaurer*, 2. Jg., 1. Vierteljahr 1785, S. 180ff. Ein Jahr später erscheint in Leipzig ein auf Louis Guillemain de Saint Victor zurückgehendes Ritualbuch der ersten vier Grade 'nebst Anhang über die Adoptionsmaurerey'.

62 Andreas O'Reilly, *Annalen der Loge Wahrheit und Einigkeit zu 3 gekrönten Säulen im Orient von Prag*, Prag o. J. (um 1790), S. 332. Die Chronik ist dem Logenreglement (Anm. 4) beigebunden.

63 HHStA Wien, VA 41, fol. 327v (Bericht des Oberst⁄Burggrafen Heinrich Rottenhan an Kaiser Leopold II. vom 29. Januar 1792).

64 Baurnjöpel (Anm. 47), S. 167ff.

65 Ritual (Anm. 25), fol. 85r.

66 Albrecht Juergens, 'Christliche Ritter in der "Zauberflöte" – Über die Rolle der "Geharnischten" in Mozarts letzter Oper', in: *Literatur in Bayern* (hrsg. vom Institut für Bayerische Literaturgeschichte der Universität München) 18/1989, S. 18ff. In diesem Zusammenhang siehe auch die christliche Deutung der *Zauberflöte* durch: Joseph Hölzl. 'Die Idee der Erlösung in der Zauberflöte' (ungedruckte

Diplomarbeit an der Kath. Theol. Hochschule Linz), Linz 1979.

67 In diesem Zusammenhang blieb bisher Abbé Maximilian Stadlers Hinweis auf Kirnbergers Kompositionslehre nahezu unberücksichtigt. Siehe: Maximilian Stadler, *Nachtrag zur Vertheidigung der Echtheit des Mozart'schen Requiem*, Wien 1827, S. 12f.

68 Mühlpfordt, 'Union' (Anm. 34), S. 337.

69 'Emanuel Schikaneder. Geschildert von seinem Neffen Joseph Carl Schikaneder', in: *Der Gesellschafter oder Blätter für Geist und Herz*, 18. Jg., 71. Blatt vom 3. Mai 1834, S. 359.

70 Gieseke Libretto (Anm. 59), nach S. 106 (fol. 108r).

71 Walther Brauneis, 'Das Frontispiz im Alberti Libretto von 1791 als Schlüssel zu Mozarts "Zauberflöte"', in: *Mitteilungen der Internationalen Stiftung Mozarteum* 3–4/1993, S. 49ff. Zur Emblematik der Pyramide siehe auch: HHStA Wien, VA 73, fol. 287r (Katechismus des Grades eines Vollkommenen Meisters: 'Was bedeutet die Pyramide, welche in ihrer Loge ist? – Das Grabmahl Hyrams in dem Allerheiligsten.'). Auch in den pyramidenförmigen Thronsitzen der Priester Sarastros geht es weniger um den vielzitierten Einfluß der ägyptischen Mysterien als vielmehr um das symbolhafte Bekenntnis zur Nachfolge Hirams. Zu Alberti siehe: Fischer Colbrie (Anm. 43), S. 39.

72 HHStA Wien, VA 67, fol. 19r und 24v ('Ritual des 3ten, oder des Frey Maurer Meister Grades').

73 Zu dieser Frage war 1956 die Behauptung aufgetaucht, Mozart hätte unter dem Decknamen 'Mindarus' dem Illuminatenorden angehört (siehe: Manfred Fr[. . .] I[. . .] O[. . .], 'Mozart als Logenbruder', in: *Mensch und Schicksal* 20/1956, S. 4f.). Von Hans Josef Irmen (Anm. 17) wurde dann 1988 eine Zugehörigkeit Mozarts zum Orden der 'Asiatischen Brüder' zur Diskussion gestellt.

74 *Mozart. Briefe und Aufzeichnungen* (gesammelt und erläutert von Wilhelm A. Bauer und Otto Erich Deutsch), Band IV, Anhang B. Nachträge, Kassel 1963, S. 536f. (Nr. 872a).

75 Ritual (Anm. 25), fol. 78r. Die keineswegs zufällige Differenzierung zwischen Pentagramm und Hexagramm findet sich auch im Deckengemälde des 'Grand Temple' in der Londoner Freemasons' Hall. Hier steht der fünfzackige Stern für die deistisch ausgerichteten Symbolischen Logen, die nach den 1723 festgeschriebenen 'Constitutions' von James Anderson dem Freimaurer religiöse Toleranz garantierten. Dem Pentagramm ist der sechszackige Stern als Emblem der die Symbolischen Grade ausweitenden, theistisch orientierten Erkenntnisstufe des 'Royal Arch' (Grad des Geheiligten königlichen Gewölbes) gegenübergestellt. Dieser IV. Grad oder 'Schottischer Meistergrad', wie er auf dem Kontinent genannt wurde, war als Reaktion katholischer Freimaurerkreise entstanden, die in Andersons 'Alten Pflichten' eine Ent Christianisierung der alten Bauhüttentradition befürchteten. Erst im Unionsvertrag von 1813 wurden dann beide Richtungen unter der Oboedienz der Großloge von England vereinigt.

76 [Carlo Antonio Pilati], *Briefe aus Berlin über verschiedene Paradoxe dieses Zeitalters. An den Verfasser der Briefe aus Wien an einen Freund in Berlin*, ²Berlin Wien 1784 (Gesellschaft der Musikfreunde in Wien – Bibliothek, Sign. 19.765/1).

77 HHStA Wien, VA 64, fol. 80v. ('Hier giebt der schottische O[ber] Meister das Wort, und zwar J[ehova] herunter, und A[donai] kömmt von den Aufsehern an ihn hinauf').

78 Alfred Meißner, *Rococo Bilder*, Gumbinnen 1871, S.

145. Der von Meißner überlieferte Logenname 'Zur Wahrheit und Eintracht' wird bis heute vielfach bei Veröffentlichungen ungeprüft übernommen, obwohl es sich dabei um eine irrtümliche Kontaminierung mit dem Namen der berühmten Wiener Loge 'Zur wahren Eintracht' handelt.

79 Goethe über *Faust* II. Teil zu Eckermann am 29. Januar 1827.

80 Prag, Archiv des Nationalmuseums / Archiv Národní muzeum, Bestand/Fond Latomica, Inv. Nr. 10/49, Karton 17/C/24 (Mitgliederliste vom 5. Juli 1790).

81 Bayerisches Staatsarchiv München, Sign, GR Fasz. 927 Nr. 6/11 (Mitgliederliste vom 5. Juli 1791).

82 Zu Gieseke siehe: Fischer Colbrie, Mitgliederliste (Anm. 43), S. 38f.

83 Caterino Mazzolà war 1780 vom Dresdner Hof für Opern Impresario Antonio Bertoldi als Theaterdichter und, damaliger Praxis entsprechend, als Regisseur verpflichtet worden. Der Dresdner Hof hatte aufgrund der Vereinbarungen im Subventionsvertrag mit Bertoldi neben dem Theatergebäude auch für Orchester und Kapellmeister sowie für den Theaterdichter zu sorgen, während der Impresario für die Opernbetrieb, die Spielplangestaltung und das Engagement der Interpreten verantwortlich war. Mazzolà war demnach ein vom Hof bezahlter Poet, aber nicht der Hofpoet. Als solcher wird zu Mazzolàs Zeiten in den Dresdner Hofkalendern ausdrücklich Giovanni Ambrogio Migliavacca genannt. Siehe auch: Ortrun Landmann, 'Dresden und Mozart – Mozart und Dresden. Eine Quellenbetrachtung', in: *Mozart Jahrbuch 1991* (Bericht über den Internationalen Mozart Kongreß 1991), Teilband 1, Kassel 1992, S. 385ff.

84 Paul Nettl, *Mozart und die königliche Kunst*, Prag 1932, S. 52ff.; Wolfgang Kelsch, 'Osiris, eine Freimaureroper aus dem Jahr 1781 und Mozarts "Zauberflöte"', in: *Jahrbuch der deutschen Forschungsloge "Quatuor Coronati"*, Bd. 28, Bayreuth 1991, S. 17ff.; Max F. Kaufmann, 'Giuseppe Parini und Caterino Mazzolà', in: *Mozart e i suoi contemporanei italiani* (Kongreßbericht Rovereto 1993), Rovereto 1995 (in Druck).

85 Freundlicher Hinweis von Frau Dr. Ortrun Landmann (Sächsische Landesbibliothek Dresden). Siehe auch: Walther Brauneis, 'Wir weihen diesen Ort zum Heiligtum . . .' – Marginalien zur Uraufführung von Mozarts "Kleiner Freimaurer Kantate" und des ihm zugeschriebenen Kettenliedes "Zum Schluss der Loge"', in: *Österreichische Musikzeitschrift* 1/1993, S. 12ff.

86 Adam Wandruszka *Leopold II.*, 2. Band, Wien München 1965, S. 378f.

87 Denis Silagi, *Ungarn und der geheime Mitarbeiterkreis Kaiser Leopolds II.*, München 1960, S. 101ff.

88 Silagi (Anm. 87), S. 105ff., 121ff.

89 Die Gleichsetzung Sarastros mit Ignaz von Born stammt von Moritz Alexander Zille ('Die Zauberflöte', in: *Freimaurer Zeitung*, Leipzig 1865). Siehe auch: Ders., *Die Zauberflöte. Text Erläuterungen für alle Verehrer Mozarts*, Leipzig 1866.

90 Alfons Rosenberg, *W. A. Mozart – Der verborgene Abgrund*, Zürich 1976, S. 59.

91 Joachim Reiber, 'Wanderd erkennen. Das literarische Umfeld der "Zauberflöte"', in: *Wege zu Mozart*, Band 2: *W.A. Mozart in Wien und Prag – Die großen Opern* (hrsg. von Herbert Zeman), Wien 1993, S. 193ff.

92 Riedel war 1780 in die Prager Loge 'Zu den drei gekrönten Sternen' aufgenommen worden. In den

Mitgliederlisten wird er bis 1788 stets nur im Lehrlingsgrad und als in Florenz abwesend geführt; vgl.: Abafi (Anm. 1), Band 3, S. 98; F.C. Linz (Anm. 28), P 3/82–88. Siehe auch: Alfred Körner, 'Andreas Riedel. Ein politisches Schicksal im Zeitalter der Französischen Revolution' (ungedruckte Dissertation), Köln 1969.

93 Leopold Alois Hoffmann, 'Die Einweihung in das Geheimniß der schreklichen Unbekannten', in: *Wiener Zeitschrift*, 1. Jg., 3. Band, 8. Heft 1792, S. 156f.

94 Den Haag, Archiv des Grootosten der Nederlanden, Handschriften der Klossianischen Bibliothek, Sign, 191 D 29 (für die Vermittlung dieses Archivstückes ist Herrn Arch. Dipl. Ing. Ferdinand Zörrer, Wien, zu danken).

95 Tomislav Volek-Ivan Bittner, *[Auf] Mozartschen Spuren in böhmischen und mährischen Archiven*, Prag 1991, S. 11 und Abb. 19.

96 Das vermutlich einzige erhalten gebliebene Libretto der Lemberger Erstaufführung bewahrt die Biblioteca del Conservatorio di Musica 'Benedetto Marcello' in Venedig (Sign.: Stampe ant[iche] tratt[ati] 16). Ein aus diesem Anlaß auch in polnischer Sprache gedrucktes Libretto soll sich in der Bibliothek des Instytut Sztuki P.A.N. in Warschau befinden. Siehe auch: Jolanta Bilińska, 'Die Rezeption von Mozarts Opernschaffen in Polen von 1783–1830', in: *Mozart-Jahrbuch 1992*, Salzburg 1993, S. 13f.; Jerzy Got, *Das österreichische Theater in Lemberg im 18. und 19. Jahrhundert. Aus dem Theaterleben der Vielvölkermonarchie*, Wien 1995, S. 47f. (in Druck).

97 Tomislav Volek, *Mozart a Praha*, Praha 1973, Abb. 5 (nach S. 48).

98 Johann Friedrich Schütze, *Hamburgische Theater-Geschichte*, Hamburg 1794, S. 684ff.

99 Paul Nettl, 'Zur Geschichte der freimaurerischen Deutung der "Zauberflöte"', in: *Das Jahrbuch der Weltfreimaurerei*, Wien 1935, S.75ff. (freundliche Mitteilung von Bruno Nettl, Illinois).

100 Gustav Kuéss-Bernhard Scheichelbauer, *200 Jahre Freimaurerei in Österreich*, Wien 1959, S. 80f.

101 Aigner, 'Rosenkreuzer' (Anm. 8), S. 78.

102 Gustav Brabée, 'Zwei Freimaurer-Audienzen bei Kaiser Franz II. (2. V. u. 8. XII. 5793)', in: *Allgemeine österreichische Freimaurer-Zeitung*, III. Jg., Nr. 4 vom 29. Februar 1876, S. 25ff.

103 Den Haag, Archiv des Grootosten der Nederlanden, Handschriften der Klossianischen Bibliothek, Vierte Sammlung VI 6 (zitiert nach E. Huber, Anm. 2, S. 196).

104 Gustav Brabée, 'Kaiser Franz II., die Wiener Freimaurer, und die Wiener Jakobiner', in: *Allgemeine österreichische Freimaurer-Zeitung*, III. Jg., Nr. 8 vom 30. April 1876, S. 61.

105 Jiří Beránek, *Tajemství Lóží. Svobodné zednárství bez legend a mýtů*, Prag 1994, S. 143 ff.; Prag, Staatliches Zentralarchiv / Státní ústřední archiv, Bestand des Gubernialpräsidiums/Fond Presidium gubernia 1791–1806, Fasz. 12/301, 348: Auflösungserklärung von 1794. Aus Anlaß der letzten Zusammenkunft erschien gleichzeitig in Druck: *Endliches Schicksal des Freymaurer Ordens in einer Schlußrede, gesprochen von Br[uder ...], vormals Redner der Loge zu [...] am Tage ihrer Auflösung*, [Prag] 1794.

106 Österreichisches Verwaltungsarchiv Wien, Pergen-Akte X/A3.

107 MOL Budapest, Degh-Schriften Bd. 7/16: Schreiben von Johann Eubert Boedeker an Franz Xaver Aigner vom 16.

April 1793 (zitiert nach E. Huber, Anm. 2, S. 181).

108 Silagi (Anm. 86), S. 104.

109 Gerald Fischer-Colbrie, 'Eine Linzer Flugschrift von 1794 über die Zauberflöte – Erstaufführungen, Textänderungen, Ausdeutungen', in: *Historisches Jahrbuch der Stadt Linz 1991*, Linz 199, S. 29ff.; Manfred Schuler, 'Die Zauberflöte – ein Mittel politischer Agitation in Mannheim 1794', in: *Mozart und Mannheim (Kongreßbericht Mannheim 1991)*, Frankfurt/Main etc. 1994, S. 197ff. Eine Zusammenstellung weiterer Bearbeitungen des *Zauberflöte*-Sujets bietet: Paul Nettl, 'Deutungen und Forsetzungen der "Zauberflöte"', in: *Wolfgang Amadeus Mozart, Die Zauberflöte – Texte-Materialien-Kommentare (rororo opernbuch)*, Reinbek bei Hamburg 1988, S. 192ff. Zu ergänzen wäre hier die 1818 in Wien enstandene *Travestierte Zauberflöte* von Karl Meisel, vor allem aber der unvollendet gebliebene Versuch einer Fortsetzung unter dem Titel 'Der Zauberflöte Zweiter Teil' von Franz Grillparzer aus dem Jahr 1826. Mit scharfer Ironie wandte sich diese theatralische Satire gegen die Aufhebung der geheimer Umtriebe verdächtigten 'Ludlamshöhle' durch Metternichs Polizei.

110 Kurzzeitig war von Schikaneder auch noch ein dritter Teil zur *Zauberflöte* geplant. Siehe: Leipziger *Allgemeine Musikalische Zeitung*, 6. Jg., Nr. 2 vom 12 Oktober 1803, Spalte 32.

111 Auch das von Franz Jäger (dem Älteren) gestaltete 'Papagenotor' am Theater an der Wien bezieht sich in der Darstellung von Papageno mit drei seiner gefiederten Kinder auf den 'Zweiten Teil' der *Zauberflöte*.

112 Brauneis (Anm. 70), S. 49.

113 *Der Sammler*, Nr. 87 vom 21. Juli 1812, S. 350.

OTTO BIBA: Nachrichten über Joseph Haydn, Michael Haydn und Wolfgang Amadeus Mozart in der Sammlung handschriftlicher Biographien der Gesellschaft der Musikfreunde in Wien

1 Archiv der Gesellschaft der Musikfreunde in Wien, Gesellschaftsakten, 439 ex 1825.

2 Ernst Ludwig Gerber: *Neues historisch-biographisches Lexikon der Tonkünstler*, [. . .], 4 Bände, Leipzig, 1812–14.

3 Ignaz von Mosel (1772–1844).

4 Maximilian Stadler (1748–1833).

5 Archiv der Gesellschaft der Musikfreunde in Wien, Gesellschaftsakten, 486 ex 1826.

6 Ebenda, 531 ex 1826.

7 Signatur 10907/134.

8 Geißler, der sich in der Musikszene seiner Zeit mehrfach und vor allem durch sein historisch-dokumentarisches Interesse verdient gemacht hat, starb 1860 im 74. Lebensjahr in Wien (Bibliothek der Gesellschaft der Musikfreunde in Wien, Partensammlung).

9 Wie Anmerkung 6.

GERDA MRAZ: Musikerportraits in der Sammlung Lavater

1 Vgl. Wilhelm Beetz, *Die Porträtsammlung der Nationalbibliothek in ihrer Entwicklung*, Graz 1935; *Bilder und Bücher. 200 Jahre ehem. Familien-Fideikommiß-Bibliothek des Hauses*

Habsburg-Lothringen. 200 Jahre Porträtsammlung. Österreich 1945 bis 1955, bearb. v. Walter G. Wieser und Wilhelm Zrounek, Ausstellungskatalog, Wien 1985.

2 Es ist nahezu unverständlich, daß sich eine reiche Literatur mit den physiognomischen Schriften befaßt hat und befaßt, ohne die bildlichen Quellen für dieses literarische Schaffen zu kennen. Ein Grund ist sicherlich der private Status der Sammlung, aber auch seit 1918/1921 hat sich nichts daran geändert. Friedrich Otto Pestalozzi hat die Wiener Sammlung einer ersten Betrachtung unterzogen ('Johann Caspar Lavaters Kunstsammlung', Neujahrsblatt der Chorherrenstube 138, Zürich 1916), und im Zuge des wachsenden Interesses an der physiognomischen Aussagekraft sind einzelne Teile in den letzten Jahren für Ausstellungen herangezogen worden, insbesondere im Zusammenhang mit Goethe.

3 Vgl. z.B. *Die Beredsamkeit des Leibes. Zur Körpersprache in der Kunst,* hrsg. v. Ilsebill Barta Fliedl und Christoph Geissmar, Salzburg-Wien 1992, Katalog zur gleichnamigen Ausstellung in der Albertina; Norbert Borrmann, *Kunst und Physiognomik. Menschendeutung und Menschendarstellung im Abendland,* Köln 1954.

4 Edmund Heier, *Studies on Johann Caspar Lavater (1741–1801) in Russia,* Bern 1991.

5 Anna Marie Jaton, *Johann Caspar Lavater. Philosoph – Gottesmann, Schöpfer der Physiognomik. Eine Bildbiographie,* Zürich 1988; Horst Weigelt, *Johann Kaspar Lavater. Leben, Werk und Wirkung,* Göttingen 1991; *Das Antlitz Gottes im Antlitz des Menschen. Zugänge zu Johann Kaspar Lavater,* herausgegeben von Karl Pestalozzi und Horst Weigelt, Göttingen 1994.

6 Über verschiedene Aspekte der neuentdeckten Natur und ihre Bedeutung für die Kunst vgl. *Natur und Kunst,* hrsg. v. Götz Pochat und Brigitte Wagner, Graz 1987 (= Kunsthistorisches Jahrbuch Graz 23).

7 Johann Caspar Lavater, *Physiognomische Fragmente. Zur Beförderung der Menschenkenntnis und Menschenliebe,* Dritter Versuch, Leipzig-Winterthur 1777, S. 195.

8 *Physiognomische Fragmente* 3, S. 197f.

9 Ebenda, S. 199.

10 Johannes Pfenninger (1765–1825) stammte aus einer armen, kinderreichen Bauernfamilie. Schon als 8jähriger zeichnete er leidenschaftlich gern, so daß ihn sein Pate zu einem Ofenmaler brachte. Sein Talent konnte hier natürlich nicht befriedigt werden, aber, da die Familie zu arm war, als daß sie den Knaben zu einem Maler hätte in die Lehre geben können, blieb nur die Hoffnung auf den verständnisvollen Pfarrer Lavater. Pfenninger war inzwischen 13 Jahre alt geworden, als ihn Lavater zu seinem Schwager, dem Miniaturenmaler Schmoll brachte. Dort machte er gute Fortschritte, wurde aber von Schmoll bald für alle möglichen Dienste, nur nicht die Malerei, herangezogen. Dieses Schicksal blieb ihm treu: Er wechselte zu Lavater, für den er vor allem Schreibarbeiten machen mußte, dann zu einem Kupferstecher, für den er zu kolorieren hatte. In diesen Jahren dürfte er Porträtaufträge für Lavater erfüllt haben. 1793 schließlich machte er sich, von Lavater ermuntert, nach Rom auf, ohne ein Wort italienisch zu sprechen. Dort endlich konnte er sechs Jahre von seiner Kunst leben.

11 *Physiognomische Fragmente* 3, S. 202.

12 E. Refardt, *Der Goethe-Kayser,* Zürich 1950 (= 138. Neujahrsblatt der Allgemeinen Musikgesellschaft Zürich).

13 Vgl. *Karikaturen – Karikaturen?,* Zürich 1972 (Ausstellungskatalog).

14 *Physiognomische Fragmente* 3, S. 196.

15 Jaton (Anm. 5), S. 30f.

ROBERT MÜNSTER: Bestände mit mehrstimmigen Musikhandschriften aus Kloster-, Stifts- und Domkirchen in Bayern seit dem 16. Jahrhundert

1 R. Münster, 'Die Katalogisierung von Musikhandschriften in nichtstaatlichem Besitz in Bayern', in: *Musik in Bayern* 16, 1978, S. 15ff.; ders., 'Die Erfassung von Musikhandschriften in Altbayern in Schwaben', in: *Bibliotheksforum Bayern* 9, 1981, S. 183ff.; ders., 'Die Kataloge Bayerischer Musiksammlungen', in: *Bibliotheksforum Bayern* 20, 1992, S. 169ff.; ders., 'Die Erfassung älterer Kirchenmusikalien in Altbayern und Schwaben – Erfahrungen, Ergebnisse, Möglichkeiten für die Praxis', in: *Sinfonia sacra,* Zeitschrift für katholische Kirchenmusik, 3. Jg., H. 1/1995, S. 42ff. – 1977 wurde auch von der Universitätsbibliothek Würzburg eine Erfassung der Musikhandschriften in Franken gestartet. Vgl. Martin Seelkopf, 'Die Erfassung von Musikhandschriften in Franken', in: *Bibliotheksforum Bayern* 9, 1981, S. 192ff. In Franken konnten jedoch keine klösterlichen Bestände festgestellt werden (vgl. Gertraut Haberkamp und Martin Seelkopf, *Die Musikhandschriften katholischer Pfarreien in Franken, Bistum Würzburg,* München 1990, mit ausführlicher Einleitung [KBM 17]). Beginnend mit *KBM* 3 ist auch die Arbeitsgruppe Deutschland des RISM (Répertoire International des Sources Musicales), Arbeitsstelle München, unter Leitung von Dr. Gertraut Haberkamp an der Erfassung von Musikhandschriften in Bayern stark beteiligt.

2 Darstellungen der Musikpflege in den bayerischen Klöstern im Überblick s. R. Münster, 'Die Musik in den bayerischen Klöstern seit dem Mittelalter', in: *Musik in Bayern: I. Bayerische Musikgeschichte,* hrsg. von R. Münster und Hans Schmid, Tutzing 1972, S. 243ff.; ders., 'Die Musikpflege in den bayerischen Benediktinerklöstern zur Barockzeit', in: *Studien und Mitteilungen zur Geschichte des Benediktinerordens* 92, 1981, S. 91ff.

3 Nähere Auskünfte über die erhaltenen Werke einzelner Komponisten können bei der Arbeitsgruppe Deutschland des RISM, Arbeitsstelle München, Bayerische Staatsbibliothek, Postfach 340150, D–80328, München, eingeholt werden.

4 RISM, Einzeldrucke vor 1800, Bd. 1ff., Kassel u.a. 1971ff. Berücksichtigt sind vielfach Drucke über 1803 hinaus.

JIŘÍ SEHNAL: Die adeligen Musikkapellen im 17. und 18. Jahrhundert in Mähren

1 Diarium Monasterii Gradicensis pro anno 1693. Staatsarchiv (weiter nur StA) Brünn, E 55, Sign, II/4, kart. 2.

2 P. Balcárek, 'Zpráva o hudebnících v korespondenci kardinála Dietrichsteina' [Eine Nachricht über Musiker in der Korrespondenz des Kardinals Dietrichstein], in: *Hudební věda* 5, 1968, S. 464–5.

3 StA Brünn, G 140, kart. 442. Für die freundliche Auskunft danke ich Herrn Dr. Pavel Balcárek (Brünn).

4 J. Sehnal, 'La musica alla corte dei vescovi di Olomouc dal sec. XIII alla metà del sec. XVII', in *Quadrivium* XI/1, 1970, S. 159–263.

5 J. Košulič, 'Mikulov a počátky barokní hudby na Moravě' [Nikolsburg und die Anfänge der Barockmusik in Mähren], in *Jižní Morava* 1973, S. 122–34.

6 J. Sehnal, 'La musica ...', S. 163–4.

7 P. Nettl, 'Die Wiener Tanzkomposition in der 2. Hälfte des 17. Jahrhunderts', in: *Studien zur Musikwissenschaft* 8, 1921, S. 45–175; ders., 'Zur Geschichte der Musikkapelle des Fürstbischofs Karl Liechtenstein-Kastelkorn von Olmütz' in: *Zeitschrift für Musikwissenschaft*, 4, 1921/22, S. 458–95.

8 J. Sehnal, 'Pohled do instrumentáře kroměřížské kapely v 17. a 18. století' [Blick ins Instrumentarium der Kremsierer Musikkapelle im 17. und 18. Jh.], in: *Umění a svět* 2–3, 1959, S. 53–91; ders., 'Die Musikkapelle des Olmützer Bischofs Karl Liechtenstein-Castelcorn in Kremsier', in: *Kirchenmusikalisches Jahrbuch* 51, 1967, S. 79–123; ders., *Pavel Vejvanovský a biskupská kapela v Kroměříži*, Kroměříž 1993. Eine deutsche Fassung dieser Arbeit wird vorbereitet.

9 A. Breitenbacher, 'Hudební archiv kolegiátního kostela sv. Mořice v Kroměříži' [Das Musikarchiv der Kollegiatkirche St. Moriz in Kremsier], in: *Časopis vlasteneckého spolku musejního v Olomouci* 40, 1928; Ergänzungen daselbst 42, 1930, und 47, 1935.

10 J. Sehnal–J. Pešková, *Caroli de Liechtenstein-Castelcorno episcopis Olomucensis operum artis musicae collectio Cremsirii reservata*, Praha 1995 (in Vorbereitung).

11 R. Zuber, *Osudy moravské církve v 18. století 1695–1777* [Geschichte der Kirche in Mähren im 18. Jh.] Praha 1987, S. 118.

12 J. Sehnal, 'Počátky opery na Moravě' [Anfänge der Oper in Mähren] in: *Acta Universitatis Palackianae Olomucensis, fac. philos.*, Supplementum 21, Praha 1974, S. 56, 62–3.

13 J. Sehnal, daselbst, S. 63.

14 J. Bombera, 'K významu Liechtenštejnova zpěváckého semináře v Kroměříži' [Zur Bedeutung des Liechtensteinschen Sängerseminars in Kremsier], in: *Hudební věda* 16, 1979, S. 331–9.

15 J. Sehnal, 'Die Harmoniemusik in Mähren von 1750 bis 1840', in: *Kongressberichte Oberschützen/Burgenland 1988, Toblach/Südtirol 1990* (Alta musica, Bd. 14), Tutzing 1992, S. 244.

16 J. Sehnal, 'Das Musikinventar des Olmützer Bischofs Leopold Egk aus dem Jahr 1760 als Quelle vorklassischer Instrumentalmusik', in: *Archiv für Musikwissenschaft* 29, 1972, S. 285–317.

17 J. Sehnal, 'Die Musikkapelle des Olmützer Erzbischofs Anton Theodor Colloredo-Waldsee (1777–1811)', in: *Haydn Yearbook* X, 1978, S. 132–50; ders., 'Hudební kapela Antona Theodora Colloredo-Waldsee (1777–1811) v Kroměříži a v Olomouci' (eine ausführliche tschechische Fassung der vorigen Arbeit), in: *Hudební věda* 13, 1976, S. 291–347.

18 J. Sehnal, 'Die Musikkapelle des Olmützer Bischofs Maximilian Hamilton (1761–1776)', in: *Die Musikforschung* 24, 1971, S. 411–17.

19 J. Sehnal, 'Die Harmoniemusik ...', S. 246–8.

20 S. Gerlach, 'Haydns Orchestermusiker von 1761 bis 1774', in: *Haydn-Studien* 4, 1976, S. 39.

21 S. Anm. 17.

22 J. Sehnal, 'Die Harmoniemusik ...', S. 251–7.

23 J. Sehnal, 'Nové příspěvky k dějinám hudby na Moravě v 17. a 18. století' [Neue Erkenntnisse zur Musikgeschichte

Mährens im 17. und 18. Jh.], in: *Acta musei Moraviae–scien. soc.* 60, 1975, S. 164–5.

24 J. Sehnal, *Hudba v olomoucké katedrále v 17. a 18. století* [Musik in der Olmützer Kathedrale im 17. und 18. Jh.], Brno 1988, S. 164. Von ihm stammte Musik zu dem am 13. April 1770 bei den Minoriten zu St. Jakob in Olmütz aufgeführten Oratorium 'Der vor seinem meineydigen Sohn Absalom zu sterben verlangende David' (Universitätsbibliothek Olmütz, Sign. 600.745). Der Aust ist auf dem Titelblatt als 'der Zeit Capellmeister in Grätz' (Hradec Kralove?) tituliert.

25 Vgl. das Libretto *L'Anagilda* (1737) in O. Biba, 'Zur mährischen Musikgeschichte', in *Österreichische Musikzeitschrift* 1987, S. 152, und Libretti *Arsace* (1738), *Elisa* (1738), *Cleonice e Demetrio* (1740) bei J. Sehnal, 'Počátky opery ...', S. 57–9 (s. Anm. 12).

26 Am 31. Mai 1744 heiratete Umstatt zu St. Jakob in Brünn Franzisca, Tochter eines Tuchhändlers Johann Schräck aus Olmütz. Nach den Taufmatrikeln dieser Kirche wurden hier folgende Kinder getauft: Franciscus Ser. Antonius (4. September 1745) und Elisabetha Johanna (12. November 1747). Vgl. Matrikeln von St. Jakob im Stadtarchiv Brünn.

27 Abteilung für Musikgeschichte des Mährischen Landesmuseums in Brünn, Sign. A 20.194.

28 Dieselbe Quelle wie in Anm. 26.

29 Vgl. Taufen seiner Kinder bei St. Jakob in Brünn: Leopold Joannes Nep. (24. Oktober 1740), Franciscus X. Josephus Leopold (27. November 1741), Katharina und Anna Gabriela Antonia (9. April 1746) und Vinzenz Joseph (23. Februar 1748).

30 Taufmatrikel von St. Jakob in Brünn (10. November 1741).

31 T. Straková, 'Hudba na brtnickém zámku v 17. století' [Musik im Schloß Brtnice im 17. Jh.], in *Acta Musei Moraviae–scien. soc.* 50, 1965, S. 183–202.

32 T. Straková, 'Hudba na brtnickém zamku v 18. století' [Musik im Schloß Brtnice im 18. Jahrhundert] in: *Acta Musei Moraviae–scien. soc.* 51, 1966, S. 231–68.

33 T. Straková, 'Brtnický hudební inventář' [Das Musikinventar aus Brtnice], in: *Acta Musei Moraviae–scien. soc.* 48, 1963, S. 231–68; dies., 'Das Musikalieninventar von Pirnitz (Brtnice)', in *Studia minora fac. philos. Universitatis Brunensis* F9, 14, 1965, S. 279–89.

34 Am 30. September 1642 finden wir ihn mit diesem Titel als Pate in der Taufmatrikel in Bzenec, die im StA Brünn aufbewahrt ist.

35 J. Sehnal, *Hudba ...*, S. 191.

36 StA Brünn, C 2, O 15p, 1–40.

37 B. Indra, 'Zámecká kapela ve Frýdku v 2. polovině 18. století' [Die Schloßkapelle in Frýdek in 2. Hälfte des 18. Jh.], in: *Časopis Slezského muzea*, ser. B, 16, 1967, S. 85–6.

38 H. Kazárová, 'Kdo byl Johann Baptista Danese' [Wer war Johann Baptista Danese], in: *Taneční listy*, 1991, Nr. 1, S. 15–17, Nr. 2, S. 13–15.

39 J. Sehnal, 'Počátky opery ...', S. 59, 65–8.

40 J. Bombera, 'K významu ...', S. 342.

41 A. Breitenbacher, *Hudební archiv z bývalé piaristické koleje v Kroměříži* [Das Musikarchiv des ehemaligen Piaristenkollegiums in Kremsier], Kroměříž 1937.

42 J. Sehnal, 'Das Musikinventar ...', S. 298.

43 J. Sehnal, 'Vztah Františka Xavera Richtera k Holešovu [Bestand doch eine Beziehung F.X. Richters zu Holešov?], in: *Hudební věda* 28, 1991, S. 242–3; Ergänzung dazu, daselbst 29, 1992, S. 79.

44 B. Indra, 'Archivní materiály k starším hudebním dějinám Slezska' [Archivquellen zur älteren Musikgeschichte Schlessiens], in: *Slezský sborník* 56, 1958, S. 115–16.

45 Daselbst, S. 114.

46 K. Ditters von Dittersdorf, *Lebensbeschreibung*, Leipzig 1801; K. Holl, *C. Ditters von Dittersdorf Opern für das wieder-hergestellte Johannisberger Theater*, Heidelberg 1913. R. Zuber, *Karel Ditters z Dittersdorf*, Šumperk 1970, Knihovnička Severní Moravy 11; K. Boženek, 'Hudeoně dramatická centra ve Slezsku v 18. století' [Die musikdramatischen Zentren in Schlesien im 18. Jh.], in: *Časopis Slezského muzea* 20, 1971, S. 141–3; J. Trojan, 'Neznamý spolupracovník Dittersdorfův' [Ein unbekannter Mitarbeiter von Dittersdorf], in *Severní Morava* 34, 1977, S. 47–50; R. Zuber, 'Karel Ditters z Dittersdorfu mezi Jánským Vrchem a Vídní [K. Ditters von D. zwischen Jánský Vrch und Wien], in: *Mimoř. Kulturní zpravodaj Jesenicka* 1980, S. 3–9; ders., 'Příspěvky k životopisu Karla Ditterse z Dittersdorfu' [Beiträge zum Lebenslauf des Karl Ditters von Dittersorf] in: *Mimoř. Kulturní zpravodaj Jesenicka* 1984, S. 3–15; *Carl Ditters von Dittersdorf 1739–1799. Sein Wirken in Österreichisch-Schlesien und seine letzten Jahre in Böhmen*, hrsg. von H. Unverricht in Zusammenarbeit mit P. Koukal und W. Bein, Würzburg 1993; 'Carl Ditters von Dittersdorf, Leben – Umwelt – Werk', hrsg. von H. Unverricht, *Musik des Ostens* 15 (in Vorbereitung).

47 V. Helfert, *Hudební barok na českých zámcích* [Das Musikbarock in den böhmischen Schlössern], Praha 1916, Rozpravy ČA cís. Františka Josefa, tř. 1, č. 55; ders., *Hudba na jaroměřickém zámku* [Musik im Schloß Jaroměřice], Praha 1924, Rozpravy ČAVU, tř. 1, č. 69.

48 A. Plichta, 'Johann Sebastian Bach und Johann Adam Graf von Questenberg', in: *Bach-Jahrbuch* 1981, S. 23–8.

49 Nach der Ansicht Frau Mag. Dagmar Neumann (Wien) kam die erste Aufführung dieser Oper erst im Jahr 1737 zustande.

50 H. Kazárová, 'Kdo byl . . .'. Vgl. Anm. 38.

51 H. Kazárová, 'Šlechtická divadla a tanec' [Die Theater des Adels und der Tanz], in: *Taneční listy* 1993, Nr. 5, S. 14–16, Nr. 6, S. 14–15.

52 Neben der in Anm. 47 zitierten Literatur sind noch fol-gende Arbeiten zu erwähnen: O. Veselý, 'Rod Míčů' [Der Stammbaum Míča], in *Hudební věda* 5, 1968, S. 264–95; Sammelband *O životě a umění* [Über das Leben und Kunst in Jaroměřice], red. von A. Plichta, Brno 1974, mit der Studie von T. Straková, 'Jaroměřice nad Rokytnou a jejich význam v hudebním vývoji Moravy' [Jaroměřice nad Rokytnou und ihre Bedeutung für die Musikentwicklung in Mähren], S. 393–404; A. Plichta, 'Hudba a hudebníci v Jaroměřicích po smrti Jana Adama z Questenberka 1752–1790' [Musik und Musiker in Jaroměřice nad Rokytnou nach dem Tod des J. A. Questenberg], in: *Hudební věda* 23, 1986, S. 166–74; J. Dvořáková, 'Hudební život v Jaroměřicích nad Rokytnou v 18. století a František Václav Míča' [Das Musikleben in Jaroměřice nad Rokytnou im 18. Jh. und F.V. Míča], in: *Opus musicum* 26, 1994, S. 129–41.

53 F.V. Míča, Sinfonia in Re – Partitura, vyd. J. Racek, Praha 1946; T. Straková – J. Chovanec, 'Sonátová forma a míčovský problém [Die Sonatenform und das Problem der Autorschaft Míčas], in: *Musikologie* 2, 1949, S. 209–14; J. Trojan, 'Sinfonia in Re – otázka v tónech' [Sinfonia in Re – eine Frage in Tönen], in: *Opus musicum* 9, 1977, S. 111–13.

54 B. Indra, 'Archivní materiály . . .', S. 116–17.

55 K. Vetterl, 'Bohumír Rieger a jeho doba' [Bohumír

Rieger und seine Zeit], in: *Časopis Matice moravské* 53, 1929, S. 45–6.

56 Abteilung für Musikgeschichte des Mährischen Landesmuseums in Brünn, Sign. A 13.268.

57 StA Brünn, E 81, kart. 164.

58 Er heiratete am 2. März 1734 bei St. Jakob in Brünn Františka Chmelníčková aus Náměšť. Vgl. die Traumatrikel dieser Kirche im StA Brünn.

59 K. Vetterl, 'Bohumir Rieger . . .' S. 45–86, 435–500; J. Racek, 'Oratorien und Kantaten von G. Fr. Händel auf dem mährischen Schloße von Náměšť', in: *Opera Univ. Purkynianae Brunensis, Fac. philos.* F3, 8, 1959, S. 46–67; J. Sehnal, 'Gluck im Repertoire des Schloßtheaters des Grafen Haugwitz in Náměšt nad Oslavou', in: *Kongreßbericht Gluck in Wien*, hrsg. von G. Croll und M. Woitas, Kassel 1989, S. 171–7.

60 J. Sehnal, 'Z kulturněhistorické minulosti zámku Nová Horka u Studénky' [Aus der kulturhistorischen Vergangenheit des Schlosses Nová Horka bei Studénka], in: *Vlastivědný věstník moravský* 37, 1985, S. 171–8.

61 Diarium anni 1722 in StA Brünn, E 55, II/13, den 22. November 1722.

62 J. Sehnal, 'Nové poznatky k dějinám hudby na Moravě v 17. a 18. století' (Neue Erkenntnisse zur Musikgeschichte Mährens im 17. und 18. Jh.), in: *Acta Musei Moraviae – scien. soc.* 60, 1975, S. 165–70.

63 StA Brünn, E 55, II/18, den 4. Mai 1727.

64 StA Olmütz, MKO, kart. 702.

65 M. Zemek, 'Posloupnost prelátů a kanovníků olo-moucké kapituly od počátku až po nynější dobu' [Die Aufeinanderfolge der Prälaten und Domherren des Olmützer Kapitels vom Anfang bis zu unserer Zeit], Teil 1658–1944, Olomouc 1945, Maschinenschrift im StA Olmütz.

66 Ch. d'Elvert, 'Der Althansche Christus-Orden – der christliche Vertheidigungsbund', in: *Notizenblatt der historischen Sektion der k.k. Mährisch-Schlesischen Gesellschaft zu Beförderung des Ackerbaues, der Natur und Landeskunde* 1883, S. 12–13.

67 C. Abbate, *Regulae contrapuncti . . . In Castro Vallis B.M. de Oslavan 1629*. (Facsimile nach dem einzig erhaltenen Exemplar in der Musikbibliothek Peters in Leipzig), Leipzig, Zentralantiquariat 1977.

68 E. Bohn, *Die musikalischen Handschriften des 16. und 17. Jahrhundert in der Stadtbibliothek zu Breslau*, Breslau 1890, S. 179. Vgl. auch E. Trolda, 'Česká církevní hudba v období generál-basovém' [Tschechische Kirchenmusik in dem Generalbaßzeitalter], in: *Cyril* 61, 1935, S. 3.

69 Von diesem Druck erhielt sich nur eine Stimme in der Österreichischen Nationalbibliothek in Wien. Vgl. RISM, Recueils imprimés 16.–17. siècles, 1628³; unter den Autoren sind G.F. Anerio, S. Bernardi, A. Cometta, N. Corradini, Galiazzi, R. Giovanelli, R. Lasso, F. Milleville, F. Pio und Sabbatini vertreten. Für das Aufmerksammachen auf diesen Druck danke ich Herrn Prof. Dr. Ernst Hintermaier (Salzburg).

70 O. Urban, 'Sbírka hudebnin z hradu Sádku u Třebíče' [Eine Musikaliensammlung aus der Burg Sádek bei Třebíč], in: *Vlastivědný zpravodaj Třebíč 1964*, Nr. 2, S. 6–9; ders., 'Hudební sbírka Františka Kajetána Chorynského z hradu Sádku u Tebíče' [Die Musikaliensammlung des F.K. Chorynský aus der Burg Sádek bei Třebíč], in: *Studie Muzea Kroměřížska* 1991, S. 36–40.

71 V. Gregor, 'Zámecká kapela ve Slezských Rudolticích v 2. polovině 18. století [Die Schloßkapelle in Slezské Rudoltice in der 2. Hälfte des 18. Jh.] in: *Slezský sborník* 54, 1956,

ANMERKUNGEN

S. 402–6; B. Indra, 'Archivní materiály . . .', S. 117–18; K. Boženek, 'Hudebně dramatická . . .', S. 137–8; J. Svátek, 'Hudba a divadlo na zámcích Slezské Rudoltice a Velké Hoštice' [Musik und Theater auf den Schlössern Slezské Rudoltice und Velké Hoštice], in Studia Muzea Kroměřížska 1991, S. 48–50; P. Koukal, 'The first known opera performance at the count Hodic's Castle in Slezské Rudoltice', in: Die Musik der Deutschen im Osten und ihre Wechselwirkung mit den Nachbarn, Bonn 1994, S. 399–402.

72 E. Klimešová, 'Strážnice', in: Opus musicum 1, 1969, S. 178–9; T. Straková – J. Sehnal – S. Přibáňova, Průvoade po archívních fondech Ústavu dějin hudby Moravského musea v Brně [Führer durch die Archivsammlungen des Instituts für Musikgeschichte des Mährischen Museums in Brünn], Brno 1971, S. 87–9.

73 J. Sehnal, 'Ze života hudebníků Kroměřížské biskupské kapely v 17. století' [Aus dem Leben der Musiker der bischöflichen Kapelle in Kremsier im 17. Jh.], in: Hudobnovedné štúdie 7, 1966, S. 131.

74 P. Koukal, 'Dvě poznámky k hudebnímu dění na zámku v Telči' [Zwei Bemerkungen zum Musikleben im Schloß Telč], in: Studie Muzea Kroměřížska 1991, S. 46–7.

75 J. Sehnal, Pavel Vejvanovský..., S. 40, 62.

76 StA Brünn, E 55, II/5, den 21. August 1695.

77 J. Racek, 'Inventář hudebnin tovačovského zámku z konce 17. století' [Das Musikalieninventar des Schlosses Tovačov vom Ende des 17. Jh.], in: Musikologie 1, 1938, S. 45–68.

78 J. Sehnal, Hudba..., S. 180.

79 H. Stekl, 'Harmoniemusik und "türkische Banda" des Fürstenhauses Liechtenstein', in: Haydn Yearbook x, 1978, S. 166.

80 StA Brünn, Traumatrikeln aus Podivín.

81 StA Brünn, E 81, kart. 164.

82 J. Sehnal, 'Zwei Meisterwerke österreichischer Orgelbauer in Feldsberg (Valtice, CSFR)', in: Österreichisches Orgelforum, 1992/1, S. 303–7.

83 B. Indra, 'Archivní materiály . . .', S. 115; ders., 'Šlechtická kapela ve Velkých Hošticích v druhé polovině 18. století [Die adelige Kapelle in Velké Hoštice in der zweiten Hälfte des 18. Jh.] in: Slezský sborník 53, 1955, S. 122–4; V. Gregor, 'Zámecká kapela . . .', S. 405–6; ders. 'K šlechtické kapele a divadlu ve Velkých Hošticích v 2. polovině 18. století' [Zu der adeligen Kapelle und zum Theater in Velké Hoštice in der 2. Hälfte des 18. Jh.], in: Slezský sborník 56, 1958, S. 559–60; K. Boženek, 'Hudebně dramtická . . .', S. 138–41; J. Sehnal, Hudba . . . , S. 50–2; J. Svátek, 'Hudba . . .', S. 48–50.

84 J. Sehnal, Pavel Vejvanovský, S. 40.

85 F. Czerny, 'Schloß Ullersdorf, in: Unsere Heimat 12, 1932, S. 107.

86 Die Bludover Musikalien sind in der Universitätsbibliothek Olmütz aufbewahrt. Es handelt sich um die Opern Phaeton (Paris 1683) und Amadis (Paris 1684). Die handschriftlichen Stimmen sind mit Bemerkung 'Musée de la Grotte de Versailles' versehen. Vgl. J. Sehnal, 'Vývoj figuralní hudby na chrámovém kůru ve Velkých Losinách' [Die Figuralmusik auf dem Kirchenchor in Velké Losiny], in: Acta Musei Moraviae – scien. soc. 53/54, 1968–1969, S. 30–31.

87 Der spätere Choralist der Olmützer Kathedrale Franz Wilhelm Marshofer stand im Jahr 1738 als Klavierlehrer im Dienst einer Gräfin zu Žerotín in Brünn, die ihn im Jahr 1744 nach Wien mitnahm und ihm Lehrstunden bei G. Chr. Wagenseil bezahlte. Sehnal, Hudba..., S. 178–9.

88 B.J. Dlabač, Allgemeines historisches Künstler-Lexikon für Böhmen..., 3. Bd., Prag 1815, S. 110.

89 Dieser Musiker hat mit dem bekannten F.A. Rösler/Rosetti nichts gemein.

90 P. Janská, 'Hudební kultura na zámku ve Vranově nad Dyjí v 17. a 18. století [Die Musikkultur im Schloß Vranov nad Dyjí im 17. und 18. Jh.], in: Jižní Morava 1988, S. 39–53.

91 A. Plichta, in O životě..., S. 70; vgl. Anm. 52.

269

Index of Composers / Komponistenregister

NB: Die allererste Note wird nur anfangs gespielt um dem Volck den Ton zu geben.

poco Adagio.